A HANDBOOK
on
THE BOOK OF DANIEL

The Handbooks in the **UBS Handbook Series** are detailed commentaries providing valuable exegetical, historical, cultural, and linguistic information on the books of the Bible. They are prepared primarily to assist practicing Bible translators as they carry out the important task of putting God's Word into the many languages spoken in the world today. The text is discussed verse by verse and is accompanied by running text in at least one modern English translation.

Over the years church leaders and Bible readers have found the UBS Handbooks to be useful for their own study of the Scriptures. Many of the issues Bible translators must address when trying to communicate the Bible's message to modern readers are the ones Bible students must address when approaching the Bible text as part of their own private study and devotions.

The Handbooks will continue to be prepared primarily for translators, but we are confident that they will be useful to a wider audience, helping all who use them to gain a better understanding of the Bible message.

Helps for Translators

A HANDBOOK ON

The Book of Daniel

by René Péter-Contesse
and John Ellington

UBS Handbook Series

United Bible Societies
New York

Books in the series of **Helps for Translators** may be ordered from a national Bible Society or from either of the following centers:

United Bible Societies
European Production Fund
D-70520 Stuttgart 80
Postfach 81 03 40
Germany

United Bible Societies
1865 Broadway
New York, NY 10023
U.S.A.

L.C. Cataloging-in-Publication Data:

Péter-Contesse, René
    [Manuel du traducteur pour le livre du Daniel. English]
    A handbook on the Book of Daniel / by René Péter-Contesse and John Ellington.
        p. cm. — (UBS handbook series) (Helps for translators)
    Includes bibliographical references and index.
    ISBN 0-8267-0126-4
    1. Bible. O.T. Daniel—Translating. 2. Bible. O.T. Daniel—Criticism, interpretation, etc. I. Ellington, John. II. Title. III. Series. IV. Series: Helps for translators.
    BS1555.2.P46513 1994
    224'.506—dc20   93-33287
                                              CIP

ABS-1/94-500-BB-1-105036

Contents

CONTENTS

Preface

This Handbook, like others in the series, concentrates on exegetical information important for translators, and it attempts to indicate possible solutions for translational problems related to language or culture. The authors do not consciously attempt to provide help that other theologians and scholars may seek but which is not directly related to the translation task. Such information is normally sought elsewhere. However, many church leaders and interested Bible readers have found these Handbooks useful and informative, and we hope that this volume will be no exception.

The format of *A Handbook on The Book of Daniel* follows the general pattern of earlier volumes in the series. The Revised Standard Version (RSV) and Today's English Version (TEV) texts are presented in parallel columns, first in larger segments that will make possible an overview of each section of discourse, and then in bold print, normally verse by verse, followed by detailed comments and discussion. RSV serves as the base upon which the discussion takes place, and quotations from the verse under discussion are printed in **boldface**. Quotations from other verses of RSV and from other versions are printed between quotation marks and in normal typeface. TEV serves as a primary model of how a translation may take shape; however, many other versions are provided as well, especially where they offer models that may be more satisfactory than those of TEV.

A limited Bibliography is included for the benefit of those interested in further study. The Glossary explains technical terms according to their usage in this volume. The translator may find it useful to read through the Glossary in order to become aware of the specialized way in which certain terms are used. An Index gives the location by page number of some of the important words and subjects discussed in the Handbook, especially where the Handbook provides the translator with help in rendering these concepts into the receptor language.

The editor of the UBS Handbook Series continues to seek comments from translators and others who use these books, so that future volumes may benefit and may better serve the needs of the readers.

Abbreviations Used in This Volume

General Abbreviations, Bible Texts, Versions, and Other Works Cited
(For details see Bibliography.)

AB	Anchor Bible	NCV	New Century Version
A.D.	*Anno Domini* (in the year[s] of our Lord)	NASB	New American Standard Bible
AT	An American Translation	NEB	New English Bible
B.C.	Before Christ	NEB/REB	Agreement, NEB and its revision, REB
CTAT	*Critique textuelle de l'Ancien Testament*	NIV	New International Version
FRCL	*La Bible en français courant* (French common language version)	NJB	New Jerusalem Bible
		NJV	*TANAKH*: New Jewish Version
GECL	*Die Gute Nachricht* (German common language version)	NRSV	New Revised Standard Version
HOTTP	Preliminary and Interim Report on the Hebrew Old Testament Text Project	NVSR	*La nouvelle version Second revisée*
		REB	Revised English Bible
HOTTP/ CTAT	Agreement, HOTTP and CTAT	RSV	Revised Standard Version
KJV	King James Version	RSV/NRSV	Agreement, RSV and its revision, NRSV
LB	The Living Bible	TEV	Today's English Version
Mft	Moffatt	TOB	*Traduction œcuménique de la Bible*
NAB	New American Bible		

Books of the Bible

Gen	Genesis	Isa	Isaiah
Exo	Exodus	Jer	Jeremiah
Lev	Leviticus	Ezek	Ezekiel
Num	Numbers	Dan	Daniel
Deut	Deuteronomy	Hos	Hosea
Josh	Joshua	Hab	Habakkuk
1,2 Sam	1,2 Samuel	Zeph	Zephaniah
1,2 Kgs	1,2 Kings	Hag	Haggai
1,2 Chr	1,2 Chronicles	Zech	Zechariah
Neh	Nehemiah	Mal	Malachi
Est	Esther	Matt	Matthew
Psa	Psalm(s)	1,2 Cor	1,2 Corinthians
Pro	Proverbs	1,2 Thes	1,2 Thessalonians
Song	Song of Songs (Song of Solomon)	Heb	Hebrews
		Rev	Revelation

Translating Daniel

The Book of Daniel is very much like the New Testament book, the Revelation to John, both in its style and in its type of literature. The primary aim of each of these two books is to strengthen faith and to encourage believers in all times, regardless of what trials and persecutions they may face. They are the writings of a kind of nonviolent resistance movement.

Contents of the Book of Daniel

The Book of Daniel is divided into two main parts that are almost equal in length. But these two parts are of two slightly different genres (that is, different literary types, or kinds of writing).

The first part (chapters 1–6) contains six *stories* about Daniel that are more or less independent of each other. They focus on Daniel and his three companions, who were young Jews that had been deported to Babylon at the end of the seventh century B.C. These stories show the kinds of pressures, threats, and punishments inflicted on the Jews by their oppressors.

The second part of the book (chapters 7–12) tells about several *visions* that God gave to Daniel. Daniel is directly forbidden to publish these visions until the appointed time. The visions reveal to Daniel the history of the Jewish people, who were successively placed under the domination of several foreign nations. But at last God gives them freedom, establishes his kingdom and fully manifests his own authority.

These are the basic themes of Daniel, and the following outline gives more details of the structure of the book:

Regarding the additional material written in Greek and included in some versions of Daniel, see the discussion under **The text of Daniel** below.

The questions of date and authorship

Traditionally, most Jewish and Christian scholars in the past believed that the Book of Daniel was written in the sixth century B.C. either by Daniel or by an unknown writer who was a contemporary of the main character of the book and who may have worked from documents provided by Daniel himself (see 7.1). Parts of the book are written in the first person (see 9.2 and 10.2, for example), which seems to suggest that it was written by Daniel himself. In either case this means that we are dealing with a prophet who predicted future events in rather specific detail and several centuries before they actually happened.

On the other hand, the majority of scholars today feel that the book was written much later. These writers see a number of historical problems in the book, including (1) the dating of the siege of Jerusalem, (2) the fact that Belshazzar was never fully the King of Babylon, and (3) the references to Darius the Mede, who presumably did not come to power until 522 B.C. After weighing all the evidence, Louis Hartman, for example, concludes that "the arguments for a date shortly before the death of Antiochus IV Epiphanes in 164 are overwhelming" (*The Jerome Biblical Commentary*, page 448). This would mean that an anonymous author presented past events in the form of prediction. However, Joyce Baldwin surveys much the same evidence and reaches a very different conclusion. She states that, although "scholarly opinion is divided . . . , a late sixth- or early fifth-century date of writing for the whole best suits the evidence" (Baldwin, pages 45-46).

Still other scholars adopt a position much less rigid than either of those outlined above. They see the possibility that the final form of the Book of Daniel may have been the result of an anonymous editor working at the time of Antiochus Epiphanes, but using material originally produced by Daniel or some other sixth-century writer, or by Daniel and the other writer. According to one version of this theory, the stories in chapters 1–6 may have been written at an earlier period and circulated independently before being reworked and inserted in a later second-century document. In this case Daniel would have been a real, historical figure who was a well-known hero. The later editor would have then attributed the visions of the second half of the book to him.

The technique of using the name of a well-known figure of the past for literary purposes should not be thought of as forgery or dishonesty. It was rather a literary technique commonly used in ancient times, especially in periods of persecution, when it would have been impossible to have communicated the message in direct and clear terms.

Fortunately, however, Bible translators are not required to solve the problem of authorship once and for all. And there are few places in the Book of Daniel where questions of authorship or date of writing actually affect the translation. So translators must simply translate this book in such a way as to allow their readers to find comfort in the knowledge that God is sovereign and active, even when surrounding events seem to indicate otherwise.

The text of Daniel and the ancient versions

By comparison with other biblical books, the text of Daniel has been preserved in a relatively satisfactory state. It presents very few serious textual difficulties. And the problems that do exist can be dealt with in the course of this Handbook.

One very unusual feature of this book is the fact that it has been transmitted to us partially in Hebrew and partially in another language, Aramaic, which is closely related to Hebrew. The beginning and end of the book are in Hebrew, but in the middle of the fourth verse of chapter 2 it switches abruptly to Aramaic at the point in the story where the magicians of the king of Babylon begin to speak. The remainder of this chapter, as well as chapters 3 through 7, are written in Aramaic. Then, beginning at 8.1, the remainder of the book is again in Hebrew.

It is difficult to explain this unusual fact. Perhaps the entire book was originally written in Aramaic, and then parts of it were later translated into Hebrew. But if this were the case, readers may wonder why. Or possibly the opposite happened: it may have been written first in Hebrew and then partially translated into Aramaic. Or perhaps the writer intentionally wrote part of the book in one language and part in the other. But if this were the case, once again readers may wonder why. In any case, it is impossible to give a final answer to these questions.

The text in Hebrew and Aramaic was translated into Greek at the end of the second century B.C. in the collection of Jewish Greek Scriptures that is now called the Septuagint. During the first half of the first century of the Christian era, this Greek version was judged to be too free and was therefore revised by a Jewish scholar named Theodotion. The revision he made now bears his name. These two Greek translations as well as the Syriac and Latin versions sometimes offer readings that are different from those of the Hebrew-Aramaic text, and sometimes they help readers to understand the meaning more clearly. Translators may therefore occasionally be led to adopt a text attested in one or more of the ancient versions rather than to follow the Hebrew-Aramaic original.

A complete listing of textual problems dealt with in the *Preliminary and Interim Report of the Hebrew Old Testament Text Project* (HOTTP) is given in the Appendix to this Handbook, page 337. This list also shows whether certain modern English versions have adopted the same reading as the one recommended by HOTTP.

We should also mention here an additional problem posed by the Greek versions of Daniel: they contain two rather lengthy additions that are not found in the original. These passages are not generally found in modern Protestant Bibles, but they have been adopted as a part of Scripture in the Catholic tradition. The two passages in question are:

(1) the liturgical texts inserted in chapter 3, "The Prayer of Azariah" (3.24-45 in the alternate numbering system) and "The Song of the Three Young Men" (3.46-90); and

(2) three stories that have no direct connection with the book except that Daniel plays an important role. They are the story of Susanna, in which

Daniel is still a child (added as chapter 13), as well as the stories of "Bel" (14.1-22) and "The Dragon" (14.23-42).

The translation problems involved in these supplementary sections are not dealt with in this manual.

The following table may be a helpful reference tool for translators as they work through the Book of Daniel. It shows in parallel columns the places where different verse numbering systems are used in this book.

RSV/TEV	Hebrew	Vulgate	Septuagint	Theodotion
3.24-30	3.24-30	3.91-97	3.91-97	3.91-97
4.1-3	3.31-33	3.98-100	omitted	4.1-3
omitted	omitted	3.24-25	3.24,25	3.24,25
omitted	omitted	3.26-45	3.26-45	3.26-45
omitted	omitted	3.46-51	3.46-51	3.46-51
omitted	omitted	3.52-90	3.52-90	3.52-90
4.4-37	4.1-34	4.1-34	4.4-37	4.4-37
5.13b-15	5.13b-15	5.13b-15	omitted	5.13b-15
5.18-22	5.18-22	5.18-22	omitted	5.18-22
5.24-25	5.24-25	5.24-25	omitted	5.24-25
5.31	6.1	5.31	6.1	6.1
6.1-28	6.2-29	6.1-28	6.2-29	6.2-29

It will be noted that all the verse numbering problems in Daniel occur in the first half of the book.

Style and language

The first six chapters of the Book of Daniel are written in narrative style and do not introduce any serious problems for the translator. Only the passage found in 4.10-14 provides a difficult challenge, because the writing involves two levels of language: the narrative and the symbolic (see the commentary).

On the other hand, chapters 7–12 are filled with difficulties because of the literary genre peculiar to these chapters. Stylistically speaking, a vision is not a narration or a description. The writer is intentionally imprecise or vague to a certain extent in order to convey ideas that he cannot state in direct, clear language because of the difficult circumstances under which he is living. So the translator is faced with the question of the degree to which it is permissible or desirable to make explicit any information that is not stated directly but would have been understood by readers of the original.

In such a case as this, should the intention of the author be respected to such an extent that the translation is unclear and the modern reader is confused? Or should needs of the modern reader be focused on at the expense of the literary work itself? Somehow a balance needs to be maintained. There will be certain information that is implicit in the original that will need to be made explicit in the translation because of the difference between the structure of the original and the language of translation. But there will be cases where it will be wiser to retain indirect ways of speaking of certain matters. However, it will sometimes be difficult to decide between the needs of the reader and faithfulness to the literary style of the original.

The message of Daniel

Whoever the author or authors, and regardless of when the book may have been written, there is one thing that seems to be widely acknowledged today: the stories and visions of the Book of Daniel are applied in the first place to a historical period that is thought to be that of Antiochus IV Epiphanes, who was the Seleucid king in the second quarter of the second century B.C. This is clearly suggested in certain texts (see, for example, 8.15-27), even if opinion is divided with regard to other texts.

Furthermore, it is undeniable that Christian tradition has seen in the various affirmations of the book a foreshadowing or announcement of the coming of Jesus Christ, the Messiah sent by God (see 7.13-14; 11.31; 12.11 in connection with Matt 24.15 and Mark 13.14). Finally, the affirmations of the book concerning the end of time (especially chapter 12) have furnished the occasion to certain well-meaning believers to discern in their time the "true" fulfillment of the predictions of Daniel and to determine in a very precise way the date of the end of the world. But in each case the cherished predictions have so far been contradicted by actual events.

Nevertheless, to admit that the story of Daniel may be applied to such a historical event, whether ancient or recent, does not have to mean that it concerns only that event. The "eleventh horn" of 7.8 is not *only* Antiochus Epiphanes; it is not *only*, as certain people think, the "Wicked One" about which the Apostle Paul speaks in 2 Thes 2.1-10; it is not *only* the Emperor Nero, or Napoleon, or Adolf Hitler, or any of the other persecutors of the Jews or of Christians down through the past twenty centuries. This "eleventh horn" was first of all Antiochus Epiphanes, but with good reason believers of every century have been able *also* to recognize other cruel tyrants oppressing those who remain faithful to the true God. These same believers have drawn from the Book of Daniel the strength and courage to confront the trials that they faced with calmness and confidence.

The title of the book

In the original Hebrew-Aramaic text as well as in the ancient versions, this book simply bears the name of the main character, Daniel. The meaning of this name is "God is my judge." This is probably to be understood in the positive sense as "God is the one who upholds my rights" rather than negatively "God is the one who judges (condemns) me." In most cases translators are advised not to try to translate the meaning of the proper name "Daniel" but to transcribe it in their own language. The meaning of the name may be explained in the introduction to the book or in a footnote.

In some cases it will be possible to use a title like "The Book of Daniel." But more often the relationship between "book" and "Daniel" should be made clear. The title will then read "The book about (or concerning) the prophet Daniel" rather than "the book written by Daniel." However, a more descriptive title may also be considered. Some possible models are "Daniel's faithfulness to the living God," or "The faith and obedience of Daniel," or "Daniel, an example of loyalty to the true God."

Part One:

The Story of Daniel and His Friends

Daniel 1.1–6.28

As indicated in the introductory section of the Handbook, the Book of Daniel is divided into two main sections. Translators may wish to show this by using two levels of headings as in Today's English Version (TEV). The main section from the beginning of the book to the end of chapter six may be entitled **The story (or stories) of Daniel and his friends.** It is probably better to include the friends along with Daniel rather than saying simply "Daniel and the Kings of Babylon" (as in New American Bible [NAB]).

Daniel and His Friends

The young men at Nebuchadnezzar's court: 1.1-21

REVISED STANDARD VERSION

TODAY'S ENGLISH VERSION
THE STORY OF DANIEL AND HIS FRIENDS
(1.1–6.28)

The Young Men at Nebuchadnezzar's Court

1 In the third year of the reign of Jehoiakim king of Judah, Nebuchadnezzar king of Babylon came to Jerusalem and besieged it. 2 And the Lord gave Jehoiakim king of Judah into his hand, with some of the vessels of the house of God; and he brought them to the land of Shinar, to the house of his god, and placed the vessels in the treasury of his god. 3 Then the king commanded Ashpenaz, his chief eunuch, to bring some of the people of Israel, both of the royal family and of the nobility, 4 youths without blemish, handsome and skilful in all wisdom, endowed with knowledge, understanding learning, and competent to serve in the king's palace, and to teach them the letters and language of the Chaldeans. 5 The king assigned them a daily

1 In the third year that Jehoiakim was king of Judah, King Nebuchadnezzar of Babylonia attacked Jerusalem and surrounded the city. 2 The Lord let him capture King Jehoiakim and seize some of the Temple treasures. He took some prisoners back with him to the temple of his gods in Babylon, and put the captured treasures in the temple storerooms. 3 The king ordered Ashpenaz, his chief official, to select from among the Israelite exiles some young men of the royal family and of the noble families. 4 They had to be handsome, intelligent, well-trained, quick to learn, and free from physical defects, so that they would be qualified to serve in the royal court. Ashpenaz was to teach them to read and write the Babylonian language. 5 The king also gave

8

portion of the rich food which the king ate, and of the wine which he drank. They were to be educated for three years, and at the end of that time they were to stand before the king. 6 Among these were Daniel, Hananiah, Mishael, and Azariah of the tribe of Judah. 7 And the chief of the eunuchs gave them names: Daniel he called Belteshazzar, Hananiah he called Shadrach, Mishael he called Meshach, and Azariah he called Abednego.

8 But Daniel resolved that he would not defile himself with the king's rich food, or with the wine which he drank; therefore he asked the chief of the eunuchs to allow him not to defile himself. 9 And God gave Daniel favor and compassion in the sight of the chief of the eunuchs; 10 and the chief of the eunuchs said to Daniel, "I fear lest my lord the king, who appointed your food and your drink, should see that you were in poorer condition than the youths who are of your own age. So you would endanger my head with the king." 11 Then Daniel said to the steward whom the chief of the eunuchs had appointed over Daniel, Hananiah, Mishael, and Azariah; 12 "Test your servants for ten days; let us be given vegetables to eat and water to drink. 13 Then let our appearance and the appearance of the youths who eat the king's rich food be observed by you, and according to what you see deal with your servants." 14 So he hearkened to them in this matter, and tested them for ten days. 15 At the end of ten days it was seen that they were better in appearance and fatter in flesh than all the youths who ate the king's rich food. 16 So the steward took away their rich food and the wine they were to drink, and gave them vegetables.

17 As for these four youths, God gave them learning and skill in all letters and wisdom; and Daniel had understanding in all visions and dreams. 18 At the end of the time, when the king had commanded that they should be brought in, the chief of the eunuchs brought them in before Nebuchadnezzar. 19 And the king spoke with them, and among them all none was found like Daniel, Hananiah, Mishael, and Azariah; therefore they stood before the king. 20 And in every matter of wisdom and understanding concerning which the king inquired of them, he found them ten times better than all the magicians and enchanters that were in all his kingdom. 21 And Daniel continued until the first year of King Cyrus.

orders that every day they were to be given the same food and wine as the members of the royal court. After three years of this training they were to appear before the king. 6 Among those chosen were Daniel, Hananiah, Mishael, and Azariah, all of whom were from the tribe of Judah. 7 The chief official gave them new names: Belteshazzar, Shadrach, Meshach, and Abednego.

8 Daniel made up his mind not to let himself become ritually unclean by eating the food and drinking the wine of the royal court, so he asked Ashpenaz to help him, 9 and God made Ashpenaz sympathetic to Daniel. 10 Ashpenaz, however, was afraid of the king, so he said to Daniel, "The king has decided what you are to eat and drink, and if you don't look as fit as the other young men, he may kill me."

11 So Daniel went to the guard whom Ashpenaz had placed in charge of him and his three friends. 12 "Test us for ten days," he said. "Give us vegetables to eat and water to drink. 13 Then compare us with the young men who are eating the food of the royal court, and base your decision on how we look."

14 He agreed to let them try it for ten days. 15 When the time was up, they looked healthier and stronger than all those who had been eating the royal food. 16 So from then on the guard let them continue to eat vegetables instead of what the king provided.

17 God gave the four young men knowledge and skill in literature and philosophy. In addition, he gave Daniel skill in interpreting visions and dreams.

18 At the end of the three years set by the king, Ashpenaz took all the young men to Nebuchadnezzar. 19 The king talked with them all, and Daniel, Hananiah, Mishael, and Azariah impressed him more than any of the others. So they became members of the king's court. 20 No matter what question the king asked or what problem he raised, these four knew ten times more than any fortuneteller or magician in his whole kingdom. 21 Daniel remained at the royal court until Cyrus, the emperor of Persia, conquered Babylonia.

TEV Section Heading: The Young Men at Nebuchadnezzar's Court.

As in the main title above, it is advisable to avoid naming only Daniel. And it may be better to be more precise than TEV by saying "Young Jews in the court of the king of Babylon" or something similar. New Revised Standard Version (NRSV) has "Four Young Israelites at the Babylonian Court."

If only one level of headings is being used, it will be better to say "Daniel and his friends in the court of the king" instead of saying simply "The young men . . . ."

1.1   RSV   TEV

In the third year of the reign of Jehoiakim king of Judah, Nebuchadnezzar king of Babylon came to Jerusalem and besieged it.

In the third year that Jehoiakim was king of Judah, King Nebuchadnezzar of Babylonia attacked Jerusalem and surrounded the city.

In the third year: there has been a great deal written about the apparent conflict between this statement and Jeremiah, where the text speaks of "the fourth year" (Jer 25.1; 46.2). This difference has been accounted for by some writers by the fact that the year when the king began to reign was counted differently in Babylonia and in Israel. In any case the text of Daniel says "in the third year," and this is what must be translated.

Jehoiakim: on the reign of King Jehoiakim, see 2 Kgs 23.36–24.6 as well as 2 Chr 36.5-7. In those languages where there is no distinction between the /k/ and /ch/ sounds, special care must be taken in the transliteration of this proper name, so that there is a clear distinction between Jehoiakim and his son Jehoiachin (2 Kgs 24.6).

King: in certain languages there is no exact equivalent for the word "king," since this kind of hierarchy, or classification of levels of people in society, does not exist in the culture of the receptor language. So it may be necessary to use the word for "chief" or resort to an expression meaning "big boss," "the one who commands," or something similar. One language in the Asia-Pacific Region has to say "older brother with uplifted name." In some languages it will be more natural to place the title before the name, and in others it will sound better after the name. Translators should ask themselves which sounds better, "King Jehoiakim of Judah," or "Jehoiakim, king of Judah," or possibly "the king of Judah, Jehoiakim." The same kind of order should probably also be used with King Nebuchadnezzar in the expressions that follow.

Nebuchadnezzar: this name appears thirty-two times in the Book of Daniel, all of them in the first five chapters. Some older Catholic versions of the Bible use a different spelling based on the ancient Greek and Latin versions of the Old Testament, but most modern English versions are agreed on the above spelling. This form therefore is the one that should be the basis of transliteration into other languages.

Babylon: In the Bible **Babylon** may mean "Babylon" or "Babylonia" in modern terms. That is, it may refer to the capital city or to the whole region. The king resided in the capital but was ruler over the entire country. For this reason TEV uses the term "Babylonia." Some languages may prefer to say "the country of Babylon."

Came to Jerusalem and besieged it: the first of these two verbs is very common and is usually translated "come," "come in," or "go," "go in." In some languages the choice between "come" and "go" depends on the supposed position of the writer. Given the context, it may be better to select a more precise word or phrase as in TEV. However, translators should be careful not to choose a verb that may contradict the next one (as the choice in TEV seems to do). New Jerusalem Bible (NJB) may be a good model, with "marched on Jerusalem." The second verb, **besieged**, involves placing soldiers on all sides of a city in order to cut off all supplies of arms and food. In this way the inhabitants of the city would eventually be required to surrender to the surrounding forces.

Also, in some languages it will be much more natural to supply the information that King Nebuchadnezzar was accompanied by his army, since it may sound absurd to say that one person was able to surround or lay siege to an entire city. An additional model for this verse may be "During the third year that King Jehoiakim was ruling over Judah, King Nebuchadnezzar of Babylonia marched with his army to the city of Jerusalem and surrounded it in order to make the inhabitants give up."

1.2	RSV	TEV
	And the Lord gave Jehoiakim king of Judah into his hand, with some of the vessels of the house of God; and he brought them to the land of Shinar to the house of his god, and placed the vessels in the treasury of his god.	The Lord let him capture King Jehoiakim and seize some of the Temple treasures. He took some prisoners back with him to the temple of his gods in Babylon, and put the captured treasures in the temple storerooms.

Lord: the word used here is the Hebrew *'adonai* and has the basic meaning of "master." It is often used of God but may also be used of human beings. The same Hebrew root is used in verse 10 of this chapter as a title to show respect for an earthly king. With the exception of the prayer of Daniel in chapter 9, this word is not used elsewhere in the book.

Jehoiakim king of Judah: since this same expression is used in the previous verse, it may be considered awkward in some languages to repeat it again so soon in the translation. TEV uses the abbreviated form "King Jehoiakim" and does not repeat the name of the land over which he ruled. In other languages it may be adequate to say simply "Jehoiakim" without the title. It is, however, not advisable to use the title without the proper name, since two kings were mentioned in verse 1 above.

Gave . . . into his hand: the word **hand** in a context such as this symbolizes power or authority. So the meaning is simply that the Lord allowed Nebuchadnezzar to capture Jehoiakim and his forces and to exercise authority over them (compare 2 Chr 36.5-7). New English Bible (NEB) may serve as a possible model, since it translates "delivered . . . into his power." Revised English Bible (REB) maintains the use of the word "hand" by using the English idiom "handed King Jehoiakim over to him . . . ," while NRSV reads "let . . . fall into his power." Historians indicate that Jehoiakim was defeated by Nebuchadnezzar. But Jehoiachin (Jehoiakim's son), together with his queen, his ministers, and his servants, went out of the city and surrendered to Nebuchadnezzar, who captured them and the treasures (compare 2 Kgs 24.1-17). Zedekiah was then crowned king. Ten years later the Babylonian army laid siege to the city and eventually captured it. 2 Kgs 25.9 indicates that it was not just the Temple but also the rest of the city that was burned.

With some of the vessels: this means that Nebuchadnezzar was also allowed to have power over the possessions of his enemy. The word **vessels** is a very general term in Hebrew but is used here to refer to certain containers made of gold and silver from which people could drink. They were customarily used in the ritual of the Temple and were therefore considered sacred. The word occurs twice in this verse and may be translated "sacred containers" or "objects used in worship." In languages where there is no general word for "containers," it may be necessary to use something like "cups and bowls."

House of God: this refers to the Temple of the true God that was built by King Solomon in Jerusalem. In view of the context, this should probably be translated explicitly as "the Temple," or as "the House of the True God" in those languages where there is no special word for Temple.

He brought them . . . : the Hebrew text at the end of this verse is unclear. The plural pronoun **them** actually refers back to "Jehoiakim"—a singular noun. But the plural pronoun seems to refer to the captured prisoners from the nobility rather than to the objects taken from the Temple. This is why TEV says "took some prisoners back . . . ." NAB, however, follows the ancient versions in making the pronoun refer to the treasures that were captured. Several English versions remain ambiguous. In New Jewish Version (NJV), NJB, and NRSV, "them" seems to refer both to the king (plus the captured prisoners) and the Temple treasures.

Shinar: at the time the Book of Daniel was written, this was simply another name for the country of Babylonia (of which Babylon was the capital city), and it should therefore be translated as "Babylonia" (compare Gen 11.2). Unless this is done, it is possible that the reader is likely to understand that the prisoners and the sacred objects were taken to some place other than Babylonia.

The house of his god: this expression stands in contrast to the reference to the Temple above. The word rendered **god** may be translated just as well as a plural, "gods." And, in fact, this is what is done in *Traduction œcuménique de la Bible* (TOB) as well as in TEV. In some languages it is impossible to pluralize the word for God and very difficult to use it for anything other than the true God. For this reason some translators may find it necessary to render this expression "the place where he worshiped" or "the house of his religion."

While this expression is a part of the Hebrew text, it is omitted by one ancient version and therefore eliminated in a number of modern translations including NAB, NJB, and NRSV. Translators are nevertheless advised to include it in their rendering.

The treasury of his god: this may be translated "his temple treasury," "holy treasury," or "the place where sacred treasures are hidden (or kept)."

1.3   RSV   TEV

Then the king commanded Ashpenaz, his chief eunuch, to bring some of the people of Israel, both of the royal family and of the nobility,	**The king ordered Ashpenaz, his chief official, to select from among the Israelite exiles some young men of the royal family and of the noble families.**

Then: this word translates the common Hebrew conjunction to mark additional information, often translated "and," and it does not necessarily emphasize the immediate sequence of events as the RSV rendering may seem to indicate. It has been left untranslated in TEV, NJB, and REB. Anchor Bible (AB) renders it "later."

The king: since two different kings have been mentioned in the previous verses, it may be better in some languages to make it clear that in this case the reference is to King Nebuchadnezzar. In other languages it may be possible to say something like "that king . . . ," which would clearly refer back to the last mentioned king, Nebuchadnezzar.

Eunuch: this term originally designated a castrated male person who was entrusted with the care of women's quarters in the royal household. However, it eventually came to be used to refer to any trusted official of the king, without reference to the sexuality of the person. Here the focus is clearly on the level of responsibility of the man named Ashpenaz and not on his physical status or that of those officials for whom he was given oversight. It is therefore much better to translate "his chief officer" (NJV), "his palace master" (NRSV), "the commander of his overseers," or "the head of his trusted officers."

To bring: this verb is taken by TEV to mean "select," but it may also be understood in the sense of "bring into his (royal) presence."

Some of the people of Israel: that is, some of the people who had been captured and deported to Babylonia, as described in the previous verse. Instead of "people" (the Hebrew literally says "sons of Israel"), TEV anticipates the following verse and gives the information found there, translating "young men." This may also be a good idea in other languages.

Of the royal family and of the nobility: in some languages the closest natural equivalent may be something like "from the family of the headman and from the families of the respected elders," or "from the tribe of the chief and from the clans of the chief's advisors."

RSV	TEV
youths without blemish, handsome and skilful in all wisdom, endowed with knowledge, understanding learning, and competent to serve in the king's palace, and to teach them the letters and language of the Chaldeans.	They had to be handsome, intelligent, well-trained, quick to learn, and free from physical defects, so that they would be qualified to serve in the royal court. Ashpenaz was to teach them to read and write the Babylonian language.

The text of RSV continues the thought of the previous verse without a break. But TEV and some other modern versions start a new sentence at the beginning of this verse, adding the words "They must be . . . ." Technically, what follows is the direct object of the verb in verse 3.

Youths: according to the word used here, these young men were adolescents of at least fifteen years of age. The NJB rendering "boys" may be misleading. The translation should not give the impression that they were little boys before the age of puberty. REB, with a new sentence at this point, begins "They were to be young men . . . ."

The writer then goes on to list the physical and intellectual qualities required of the young men who were to be chosen.

Without blemish: the word translated **blemish** involves any physical deformity or defect. It is very similar to the word used in Leviticus to describe those men who were to be excluded from the priestly service (Lev 21.17-23) and the animals not allowed as sacrifices (Lev 22.17-25). To be without blemish means much more than just to be "healthy" (Living Bible [LB]). Rather it is to be translated "without any physical defect" (New International Version [NIV]), "bodily without fault" (NEB), or "physically perfect." Note that this element has been transposed to the end of the list of desired qualities in the TEV rendering because it seems more natural there, but it has not been omitted.

Handsome: this involves physical attractiveness, which may vary from culture to culture. However, if possible a very general term should be chosen. In some languages it may be more natural to change the order of the various elements in this list, using the words that are more common before the more technical ones.

Skilful in all wisdom, endowed with knowledge, understanding, learning: in many languages it will be very difficult to find separate terms for **wisdom**, **knowledge**, **understanding**, and **learning**. And in fact the list is probably not intended to give clearly distinct intellectual qualities. However, because the writer is fond of using lists, it may be important to try to find expressions indicating: (1) the inborn quality of common sense; (2) the aptitude or the ability to learn new things; and (3) breadth of knowledge. One possible restructuring of these elements might be "They had to be handsome and free from physical defects. They also had to be intelligent, well trained, and quick to learn."

Competent to serve in the king's palace: this is not merely another quality added to the above list, but rather it seems to be more of a summary and result of all the different qualities mentioned. For this reason several modern versions (French common language translation [FRCL] and NAB as well as TEV) add something like "in order that they might be qualified to serve . . . ." In languages where there is no special word for **palace**, translators sometimes have to resort to an expression like "the king's big house." But it will be noted that the context here already has the qualifying word showing that it is the residence of the king.

TEV again begins a new sentence following the detailed description of the kind of young men that were to be sought. This new sentence focuses on the duty of Ashpenaz to train these men. In other languages it may be better to begin such a sentence "Ashpenaz was expected to teach them . . ." or "The king charged Ashpenaz to see that they learned . . . ."

Letters and language: the first of these two words is one that is ordinarily used of a written document (inscription, letter or book). The RSV rendering is ambiguous, since the English word "letters" may be understood as either a complete written message or the individual symbols of the alphabet used in writing. Here it is better to understand it as "writings" (REB) or "literature" (NRSV). Once again, it may be more natural in some languages to reverse the order of these two elements. In some languages the idea of literature may be unfamiliar, but there will probably be some way of talking about "written things," and this may be the nearest equivalent available.

Of the Chaldeans: this is a transliteration of the Hebrew word that denotes first of all the inhabitants of "Chaldea" or Babylonia. The Greek translation, in fact, reads "of the Babylonians." TEV and NIV have chosen to use the more commonly known name "Babylonia." This is especially advisable, since the name of the city of Babylon is mentioned in verse 1 above. A different meaning of the same term will be seen in 2.2 and the verses that follow.

1.5 RSV	TEV
The king assigned them a daily portion of the rich food which the king ate, and of the wine which he drank. They were to be educated for three years, and at the end of that time they were to stand before the king.	The king also gave orders that every day they were to be given the same food and wine as the members of the royal court. After three years of this training they were to appear before the king.

The **king** referred to here is still Nebuchadnezzar. Since he is said to have given orders in verse 3 above, it may be more natural to add the word "also" to the verb in this verse (as in TEV). The pronoun **them** refers to the young men who had been chosen according to the standards outlined in verse 4.

A daily portion of the rich food which the king ate: the Hebrew expression does not mean that the amount of food given to the king would be diminished in order to feed the young men. Rather these youths would be served the same kind of food as that which was served to members of the royal household. Since the use of the word **portion** may give the wrong impression, this should probably be translated something like "the king commanded that his servants give them the same kind of food that they gave to the king and his family every day." The adjective **rich** used to describe the food here is unnecessary, since it does not reflect anything in the original text, and it would probably be understood that the royal meals would be of good quality.

The wine which he drank: as in the case of the food, this indicates the same kind of wine that the king and other members of the royal court drank. The word for **wine** here indicates a fermented drink made from the juice of grapes. It was considered a luxurious and sometimes dangerous drink (see Prov 23.29-35). But here the emphasis is on the fact that it was fit for a king. In areas where grapes and wine are unknown, it may be necessary to borrow the term from a major world language. In such cases it will be essential to provide a glossary explanation.

In many languages it will be advisable to put the food and drink elements together in a more natural way. REB says "a daily allowance of food and wine from the royal table," while NRSV has "a daily portion of the royal rations of food and wine."

They were to be educated . . . : the passive form in this verse will have to be made active in many languages. In such cases the subject of the verb "educate," "train," or "teach" should probably be rather general: "teachers should train them . . . ." The King James Version [KJV] rendering of the verb as "nourish" is not correct.

They were to stand before the king: the Hebrew expression "to stand before someone" usually means "to be or to enter in service to someone" (compare Deut 10.8), and this should be made clear in the translation. Consider, for example, "they would enter royal service" (NJB), "they were to enter the king's service" (NJV, NAB, and NIV), or "the young men would become counselors to the king."

1.6   RSV   TEV

Among these were Daniel, Hana-   Among those chosen were Daniel,
niah, Mishael, and Azariah of the   Hananiah, Mishael, and Azariah, all
tribe of Judah.   of whom were from the tribe of
                                    Judah.

Among these: that is, among those who were selected for training. This may be translated in some languages ". . . in the group of those who had been chosen," and in some cases it may be more natural at the end of the sentence rather than at the beginning.

Of the tribe of Judah: literally "children of Judah" as in KJV, but the Hebrew expression "children of . . ." or "sons of . . ." does not indicate only a relationship of children to their own father. It can also express the idea of membership in a group. Here it indicates "members of the tribe of Judah," as the RSV rendering shows. Compare the frequent expression "sons (or children) of Israel," meaning "Israelites" or "people of Israel," and also "sons of the prophets," meaning "members of the group of prophets," in 1 Kgs 20.35, for example.

A possible restructuring of this verse may read "Four men from the tribe of Judah were in the group of those who were chosen. Their names were Daniel, Hananiah, Mishael, and Azariah." Or, as REB has it, "Among them were certain Jews: Daniel . . . ."

1.7 RSV TEV

And the chief of the eunuchs gave them names: Daniel he called Belteshazzar, Hananiah he called Shadrach, Mishael he called Meshach, and Azariah he called Abednego.

The chief official gave them new names: Belteshazzar, Shadrach, Meshach, and Abednego.

The chief of the eunuchs: see verse 3 above.

Gave them names: a literal translation of this phrase sounds strange in English. Normally names are given to persons or things that do not have any. If they already have names, then we more naturally say "renamed them," "gave them new names," "added more names to them," or "gave them different names." This explains the renderings of TEV and REB. It is possible also to say "gave them Babylonian names" (as in the German common language version [GECL]). To give a new name to someone was a way of showing that the person giving the name had authority over the other person. It may be possible in some cases to state this explicitly in order to avoid misunderstanding. For example, we may say "To show that they were under his authority, the chief officer gave them new names: . . . ."

Belteshazzar: this name that was given to Daniel should be carefully distinguished from the name of the king "Belshazzar" in chapter 5. The two names are different in the original languages but were transcribed in the same way in the Greek versions of Daniel. For purposes of instruction it will be wise to distinguish these two names, both in the way they are spelled and in the way they are pronounced. This will make it possible for Bible students to avoid confusing the two different persons.

He called . . . : note that this expression is repeated four times in RSV. This does not reflect the Hebrew original and is probably unnecessary in most other languages. The original does, however, clearly show which new name corresponds to which old name. This may be lost in some languages if TEV is followed too closely.

But Daniel resolved that he would not defile himself with the king's rich food, or with the wine which he drank; therefore he asked the chief of the eunuchs to allow him not to defile himself.	Daniel made up his mind not to let himself become ritually unclean by eating the food and drinking the wine of the royal court, so he asked Ashpenaz to help him,

But: the transition word used in RSV usually indicates rather strong contrast in English. However, it may be better left untranslated in other languages. In fact it is omitted by many English versions, including TEV and REB. NEB begins this verse with "Now . . . ," while Moffatt (Mft) has "however."

Resolved: literally "put (set) in his heart." For the Jews the heart was the seat of the will and intelligence of a person, rather than of the emotions and feelings. One commonly-used English idiom that reflects the meaning of the Hebrew expression is "made up his mind" (TEV). Some other verbs that may be used to express the same idea are "intended," "determined," "resolved," or "purposed."

While the text speaks only of Daniel's resolve, verse 12 shows that his friends were also determined not to be made unclean by eating the king's food. In some languages it may be necessary to include them here in this verse.

Defile himself: this expression carries the idea of making someone ritually unclean or unworthy of being in God's presence. This may be the result of physical uncleanness or perhaps some activity or event. In ancient times meat usually came from animals offered in sacrifice to a deity. Ordinary secular slaughtering of animals was rarely practiced. So for Daniel, a good Jew, to eat the meat of an animal that had been offered in sacrifice to Babylonian gods would constitute a serious offense against his God and would therefore make him impure or ritually unclean. It was the same with regard to the wine, since a small amount of it would have been poured out as a libation, or drink offering, to the Babylonian gods. Several English versions use the verb "contaminate" to convey this idea. NJB has "incur pollution." Even if the food was not ritually unclean for a Jew, to eat and drink the royal fare would be like a pledge of loyalty to the king instead of remaining loyal to and dependent on God.

Rich food: see verse 5.

Therefore: the word connecting the two parts of this verse is important. It is because Daniel determined in his heart not to become contaminated (in the first part of the verse) that he took the step of making the request of the chief official (later in the verse). For this reason many versions use words like "so . . ." (TEV, An American Translation [AT], NAB, Mft) or "therefore . . . ." While "and" (NIV) is an accurate literal rendering, in English it is weak and does not fully show the logical relationship between the two parts of the verse.

The chief of the eunuchs: see verses 3 and 7. In order to avoid repeating this title several times, it may be advisable in some languages to replace it with the proper name, Ashpenaz, as TEV does in this verse.

To allow him not to defile himself: that is, not to make him eat the food and drink the wine. Another way of making this clearer may be to say "requested that he not be forced to eat the food and drink the wine that would make him ritually unclean" or "begged him to be protected from the corruption that would come to him from eating and drinking the king's food."

1.9	RSV	TEV

And God gave Daniel favor and compassion in the sight of the chief of the eunuchs;	and God made Ashpenaz sympathetic to Daniel.

Gave . . . favor and compassion: the first of the two nouns here indicates "goodness," "kindness," or "grace." The second noun has the meaning of "pity" or "compassion" in some contexts, but here the meaning seems to be more like "goodwill" or "sympathy." However, the expression should probably be taken as a whole. The two words are frequently combined in the Psalms and elsewhere in the Old Testament. TEV translates the whole expression "made Ashpenaz sympathetic to Daniel."

In the sight of: the emphasis here, of course, is not on any kind of physical sight, but rather "in relation to . . . ." However, in many languages the expression "in the eyes of . . ." may be used in this figurative sense. In some languages it will be appropriate to use a causative verb or construction. For example, "God caused the chief official to look on Daniel with kindness and compassion" (compare REB).

The chief of the eunuchs: see verses 3, 7, and 8. Here again it is possible to use the proper name Ashpenaz rather than the longer and more difficult title, if this is more natural in the receptor language.

1.10	RSV	TEV

and the chief of the eunuchs said to Daniel, "I fear lest my lord the king, who appointed your food and your drink, should see that you were in poorer condition than the youths who are of your own age. So you would endanger my head with the king."	Ashpenaz, however, was afraid of the king, so he said to Daniel, "The king has decided what you are to eat and drink, and if you don't look as fit as the other young men, he may kill me."

And: the transition word at the beginning of this verse should probably be stronger than the simple conjunction found in RSV. TEV has "however," and NIV translates the same word as "but." NAB has "nevertheless." It is important to show contrast between the fact that Ashpenaz was sympathetic toward

Daniel, and at the same time that he was afraid of what the king might do to him.

The chief of the eunuchs: see verses 3, 7, and 8. Here this expression can be shortened to "the official" (NIV), or the proper name Ashpenaz may be used, depending on which is more natural in the receptor language.

Lest: this is a somewhat archaic usage in English and can easily be left untranslated, especially if the verse is restructured. Mft provides a good model for such rewording: "My lord the king has ordered your meat and drink, and I am afraid of his noticing . . . ." This establishes the events in the order in which they occurred and will probably be more easily understood in many languages.

My lord: this is the same word that is used in verse 2 above to refer to God, but here it clearly refers to the king and is used as a kind of title in order to show respect. In some versions this has been rendered by another respectful title that is more natural in the language of translation. FRCL, for example, has the equivalent of "his majesty." TEV has chosen simply to leave it out altogether.

See that you were in poorer condition: the emphasis here is on the physical condition of the young men that would result from their diet. In some languages it may be necessary to say simply "see that you are thinner than the others" or "notice that your bodies are not as good (or strong) as those of the others."

Endanger my head with the king: the most important thing about this expression is that it shows that the chief official was afraid of losing his life if he did as Daniel suggested. In many versions the more literal image of a person having his head cut off is in focus, but NJV, for example, simply says "you will put my life in jeopardy with the king." Some other possibilities are "the king would have my head cut off," "I would lose my life," or "the king would take my life."

1.11   RSV   TEV

Then Daniel said to the steward whom the chief of the eunuchs had appointed over Daniel, Hananiah, Mishael, and Azariah;

So Daniel went to the guard whom Ashpenaz had placed in charge of him and his three friends.

Then: again the Hebrew text has the very common conjunction that may be translated in a variety of ways according to the context. While most versions give the idea of a sequence of events by using **Then** as in RSV, it is translated "But" in AB and Mft. TEV has "So," and NJV leaves it out altogether. It is probably best to translate "Then," giving the idea that what follows is next in a sequence of events. Having failed to get Ashpenaz to agree to his proposal, Daniel goes to a lesser official.

Steward: the word used here is somewhat doubtful, but it is probably related to an Akkadian word that means "overseer." Most modern English versions translate it "guard" (TEV, NIV, NJB, NJV, and NRSV). REB has "the attendant." But it will be possible in some languages to say simply "the person in charge of the young men." KJV has what looks like a proper name here, "Melzar," but this is an erroneous translation, since the word has the definite article before it both here and in verse 16. It is important that the translation make it clear that this is not the same person as the chief official named Ashpenaz.

The chief of the eunuchs: see verses 3, 7, and 8 above. Here the proper name Ashpenaz is used by TEV in place of the descriptive title.

Over Daniel . . . : the second mention of Daniel in this verse may be considered unnatural in some languages. Instead of mentioning all four names again in this verse, it may be better to follow the TEV model and say something like "over him and his three friends" or "over the four young men."

1.12	RSV	TEV

"Test your servants for ten days; let us be given vegetables to eat and water to drink.	"Test us for ten days," he said. "Give us vegetables to eat and water to drink."

Test: the force of the imperative is softened in Hebrew by the addition of a particle, so that the resulting form is not a command but more of a polite request. This particle is used especially when an inferior is speaking to a superior person. In order to avoid giving the impression that Daniel and his friends gave an order to the guard, it may be well to insert the word "please" (see NRSV) or something similar (as in NIV, NJB, NAB, and AB). Mft attempts to convey the same idea with "I pray you."

Your servants: Daniel and his companions refer to themselves indirectly as "your servants" in order to acknowledge their subordination to the guard. This is a common way of showing respect in Hebrew, but for the sake of clarity in most languages, it is usually required that a word-for-word rendering be avoided here. Otherwise the reader may understand that the guard is being asked to put some others to the test rather than Daniel and those with him. This would, of course, misrepresent the meaning of the text. The most natural rendering will probably be the pronoun meaning "us." In those languages having inclusive and exclusive forms of the first person plural pronouns, the "us" in this verse, as well as "our" in verse 13, will clearly be exclusive, since the hearer is not included.

For ten days: this is a relatively short time, but a period of ten days for spiritual testing is a common theme in this type of literature (compare Rev 2.10).

Let us be given: even in languages where passive forms exist, this may not be the most natural way of saying what Daniel and his companions intended. In most cases the more direct wording, "give us . . ." (TEV, NEB/REB, NIV, NAB), will be best. But in some languages it is possible to say "Let us have . . ." (Mft) "Let them give us . . ." (KJV) or "Please give us . . . ." This should not be understood as a request for permission, but a polite appeal for a particular type of food that would not normally have been given.

Vegetables: this may be a very difficult concept to translate in some languages. The Hebrew word so translated comes from a very similar word that means "sowing" or "a thing sown" and is closely related to the word for "seed." It may be necessary to say something like "plants" or "planted things." The whole point of the request is to avoid having to eat meat and drink wine. For this reason it will be important in many languages to add the word "only," as in NJB or FRCL: "let them give us only vegetables to eat and water to drink."

The relationship of the two verb phrases in this verse may be made clearer in some languages by using a structure similar to that of AB's rendering: "Please test us, your servants, for ten days by giving us only vegetables to eat and water to drink," or simply "Please test us for ten days . . . ."

1.13   RSV   TEV

Then let our appearance and the appearance of the youths who eat the king's rich food be observed by you, and according to what you see deal with your servants."

Then compare us with the young men who are eating the food of the royal court, and base your decision on how we look."

Then: that is, after the trial period of ten days. If necessary this may be made explicit in the translation.

Appearance: the external appearance or physical condition was to be the basis for the comparison between the two groups: "compare our looks" (NJB and NEB).

Let . . . be observed by you: the Hebrew original is more literally "let them [indefinite] compare before you our appearance." The passive construction of RSV should probably be made active in most languages by saying something like "you observe . . ." or "you watch . . . ." TEV simplifies the structure of the verse by using the verb "compare," which suggests observing the two different groups of young men. This may be a good model for some languages to follow. In other languages it may be necessary to say something like "Examine us and examine the other young men who have been eating the king's food, in order to see who looks better. Then you can decide what to do with us."

Rich food: see verses 5 and 8.

Deal with . . . according to what you see: this may be understood to mean "do with your servants as you see fit" (NJV). But most understand it to mean "treat us on the basis of what you see . . . ."

Toward your servants: as in verse 12 above, this simply means "toward us" and should undoubtedly be translated that way in most languages.

1.14   RSV   TEV

**So he hearkened to them in this   He agreed to let them try it for
matter, and tested them for ten   ten days.
days.**

    So: the choice of a transition word here will probably be determined by considerations in the translator's language. In many cases it will be unnecessary to have one at this point.
    He: the pronoun here refers to the guard, and some versions have seen fit to express this more explicitly. NJB, for example, has "the man . . . ," and NEB translates "the guard."
    Hearkened to them in this matter: NRSV says "so he agreed to this proposal," that is, he approved of their proposition. Another way of saying the same thing may be "decided to do what they asked" or ". . . agreed to this plan" (NJV).
    Tested them for ten days: see verse 12. While RSV and TEV, following the Hebrew, have only the pronoun **them**, it may be necessary in some languages to replace the pronoun with a complete noun phrase like "Daniel and his friends" or "the four young men."

1.15   RSV   TEV

**At the end of ten days it was seen   When the time was up, they looked
that they were better in appearance   healthier and stronger than all those
and fatter in flesh than all the   who had been eating the royal food.
youths who ate the king's rich food.**

    At the end of ten days: since the precise duration of the test has already been mentioned twice (see verses 12 and 14), it may be more natural in some cases to say simply "At the end of the time agreed on," "After the period of testing was completed," or "When they had finished the experiment." But if it is not unnatural, translators may repeat the time period.
    It was seen: this passive expression may be rendered actively by saying "he (the guard) saw . . . ," making the guard the subject of the verb "to see." Or instead of **it was seen that they were better in appearance**, it may be more natural to say "they looked better . . . ." This is, in fact, what most English versions do at this point.
    Fatter in flesh: in ancient Jewish culture stoutness or plumpness was considered a positive thing. In certain modern cultures, especially in the West, where people have more than enough to eat, this is considered negative. Translators should be careful to translate in such a way that the readers do not think of this as negative. In some cases it may even be necessary to say something more general, like "better nourished" (NEB and NIV), "better fed" (NAB), "in superior health," or "in better physical condition." The text stresses

that Daniel and his friends were in better condition that all the others, who ate the king's royal diet. This emphasis should be included in the translation.

The king's rich food: see verse 5. Here again it is important to avoid giving the impression that the king was deprived of his own food in order that it might be given to the young men. NEB has "the food assigned them by the king."

1.16   RSV   TEV

So the steward took away their rich food and the wine they were to drink, and gave them vegetables.

So from then on the guard let them continue to eat vegetables instead of what the king provided.

So: as a result of what he saw, the guard acted. The transition word is therefore important. In some cases it will be possible to begin this verse with "That is why . . ." (FRCL), "Because of this," or "Therefore . . . ," but most English versions have "So . . . ."

The steward: see comments on verse 11.

Took away: in this context the verb used emphasizes the fact that the food was withdrawn, or put aside, in order to be replaced by something else. The form of the verb in English may seem to convey the idea that this was something that happened only once. However, the Hebrew verb shows that it was a regular occurrence. This is brought out in TEV by the addition of the expression "from then on . . . ," making it clear that this became a regular habit. In some languages this can be communicated by using the habitual form of the verb. Or it may be handled by the use of other verbs, as in "continued to take away . . ." (NAB) or "kept on removing . . ." (NJV).

And gave them vegetables: as in the earlier reference, it may be clearer to add "only." On the word for **vegetables**, see the discussion under verse 12.

1.17   RSV   TEV

As for these four youths, God gave them learning and skill in all letters and wisdom; and Daniel had understanding in all visions and dreams.

God gave the four young men knowledge and skill in literature and philosophy. In addition, he gave Daniel skill in interpreting visions and dreams.

The form of this verse is awkward in RSV, since it follows the basic structure of the Hebrew, beginning with the phrase that is essentially the object of the verb that comes later in the sentence. It is surprising how many modern English versions retain this structure (NIV, NEB, NAB, NJB). In many languages it will be more natural to begin with the subject, God, and the verb "to give," then followed by the object of the verb. However, there may be cases where the structure of RSV will be perfectly natural.

As for these four youths . . . them: as indicated above, this structure may be awkward and should probably be changed in the translation.

Learning and skill in all letters and wisdom: compare verse 4 above. The first quality mentioned is a more general term, while the second is in two parts and involves ability in the area of literature and philosophy. Thus the word translated **skill** in RSV goes with both **letters** and **wisdom**. NAB, Mft, and AB speak of "literature and science." REB speaks of "knowledge, understanding of books, and learning of every kind."

And: the conjunction here should probably be expanded to make it clear that, in addition to the gifts received by Daniel along with his three companions, God also gave him another ability that was not shared by the others. Instead of a simple "and" it may be better to say "God added to Daniel the ability to . . ." or "in addition to what he received from God along with his friends, Daniel also acquired . . . ."

Understanding in all visions and dreams: or "was able to understand every kind of vision and dream," or "had power to interpret any kind of dream or vision." The distinction between a dream and a vision is difficult in some languages. The term "vision" is used more than thirty times in the Book of Daniel and usually indicates the special revelation of events that would take place in the future. A vision is usually thought of as being distinguished from a dream, in that the person involved is fully awake when it takes place, while in a dream he is in a state of sleep. But this distinction is not always maintained in the Old Testament writings. In some languages translators may have to say "dreams and special revelations," using the more commonly known term first in the sentence.

1.18	RSV	TEV

At the end of the time, when the king had commanded that they should be brought in, the chief of the eunuchs brought them in before Nebuchadnezzar.	At the end of the three years set by the king, Ashpenaz took all the young men to Nebuchadnezzar.

At the end of the time: the translation should make it clear that this refers not to the period of ten days mentioned in verses 12, 14, and 15, but rather to the period of three years fixed by King Nebuchadnezzar in verse 5. So it may be advisable to make this clear, as is done in TEV.

That they should be brought in: the third person plural pronoun, **they**, is at best ambiguous. It may refer to the four young men on whom the story has focused from verse 6 to this point; or it may refer to all the young men selected earlier in the story (verses 3-5). But here it refers to the whole group, as is made clear in verse 19. For this reason some translators may want to follow the TEV model in saying "all the young men."

The chief of the eunuchs: see verses 3, 7, 8, 9.

Brought them in: TEV avoids the repetition of this phrase, and this may be advisable in many other languages.

Before Nebuchadnezzar: if the name of the king is mentioned at the beginning of the verse with regard to the time period, then it will probably be a bit strange to use it again here. In that case translators are advised to say simply "the king."

1.19	RSV	TEV

And the king spoke with them, and among them all none was found like Daniel, Hananiah, Mishael, and Azariah; therefore they stood before the king.	The king talked with them all, and Daniel, Hananiah, Mishael, and Azariah impressed him more than any of the others. So they became members of the king's court.

Spoke with them: here again the pronoun refers to all the candidates. So it may be better to say "with them all." The king interviewed the young men to determine who had profited most from the period of training. The context indicates that this was a conversation in which the king both talked and listened to the responses of the young men. The verb chosen in the translator's language should be one that clearly indicates a two-way conversation. Both Mft and NJB have "conversed with," and AB translates "interviewed . . . ."

None was found like: the basis of comparison was undoubtedly their competence to serve in the royal court. In some cases it may be wise to make this explicit, using something like "none of the other young men were as able as" or "none of the rest of the group were equal in wisdom."

Therefore: this shows the relationship between the two statements in this verse. It was because of their competence that they entered into the service of the king. The word that joins the two statements should make this clear in the translation.

They stood before the king: as indicated in the comments on verse 5, this expression refers to active service to the king and not just a one-time presentation or availability in case of need. In some languages we can say "became members of the king's court" (NJB as well as TEV) or "became his (the king's) personal attendants" (Mft). In some languages it may be more natural to say something like "the king chose them to serve him . . . ."

1.20	RSV	TEV

And in every matter of wisdom and understanding concerning which the king inquired of them, he found them ten times better than all the magicians and enchanters that were in all his kingdom.	No matter what the question the king asked or what problem he raised, these four knew ten times more than any fortuneteller or magician in his whole kingdom.

Daniel and his associates are compared, not only with the other young men who received the same training as they did (verse 19), but also with professional advisors to the king who were already at work in Babylonia.

Ten times better: in the areas of **wisdom and understanding** (see verse 4), which cannot normally be measured in figures, the number **ten** takes on a symbolic value. So **ten times better** means something like "infinitely better." But if in the receptor language the number ten does not convey this idea, then the translator may consider saying something like "very much better," "infinitely better," or "better without measure." All English versions, however, seem to retain the formal equivalent using the number ten. It may also be necessary to state in what respect these young men were better than the magicians and enchanters: they were superior to the others with respect to wisdom and understanding. So it may be good to say "ten times wiser," depending on the structure of the verse as a whole.

Magicians and enchanters: the first of these two terms (in Hebrew *chartom*) gives the idea of someone who specializes in predicting the unknown and performing magical or religious feats. The second (*'ashaf* in Hebrew) gives more the idea of someone having a mystical power to deflect from another person any harmful events that may have been revealed to him in a dream. For further discussion of this type of word, see 2.2 below.

1.21 RSV	TEV
And Daniel continued until the first year of King Cyrus.	**Daniel remained at the royal court until Cyrus, the emperor of Persia, conquered Babylonia.**

Some Hebrew manuscripts of this verse have "continued there," that is, in the court of the king, and this is probably what is meant even without the explicit addition. This will probably need to be made clear in the translation as has been done in most modern English versions.

Continued: the verb used here is actually the ordinary verb "to be" in Hebrew. In a number of languages it will be impossible to translate this literally, since it will have no meaning at all; or it may be understood to mean "continued to live" (this, in fact, is how Mft has understood it). The meaning, however, seems to be that he continued in the service of the king. The immediate context (verses 19-20) clearly favors this interpretation. AT has "retained his position."

Until the first year of King Cyrus: some commentators think that the mention of the first year of King Cyrus—that is, the first year of his rule over a conquered Babylonia—refers to the texts in 2 Chr 36.22-23 and Ezra 1.1-3, and supposes that Daniel took advantage of the circumstances to return to Israel in 538 B.C. But since that would contradict 10.1 (the third year of the reign of Cyrus), these commentators are forced to conclude that chapters 1 and 10 come from two different traditions regarding Daniel. However, the preposition **until** does not necessarily mean that Daniel could not have continued further beyond the time mentioned, although this is strongly implied. Since Cyrus was king of Persia for some time before conquering Babylonia, TEV has included that information in the text. But in view of the uncertainties at this point, it may be better to translate simply "Daniel continued to serve the king until the time when Cyrus became king" or "Daniel remained in his job in the royal court until King Cyrus took over."

Nebuchadnezzar's First Dream

Daniel 2.1-49

The king dreams about a great statue: 2.1-13

RSV

1 In the second year of the reign of Nebuchadnezzar, Nebuchadnezzar had dreams; and his spirit was troubled, and his sleep left him. 2 Then the king commanded that the magicians, the enchanters, the sorcerers, and the Chaldeans be summoned, to tell the king his dreams. So they came in and stood before the king. 3 And the king said to them, "I had a dream, and my spirit is troubled to know the dream." 4 Then the Chaldeans said to the king, "O king, live for ever! Tell your servants the dream, and we will show the interpretation." 5 The king answered the Chaldeans, "The word from me is sure: if you do not make known to me the dream and its interpretation, you shall be torn limb from limb, and your houses shall be laid in ruins. 6 But if you show the dream and its interpretation, you shall receive from me gifts and rewards and great honor. Therefore show me the dream and its interpretation." 7 They answered a second time, "Let the king tell his servants the dream, and we will show its interpretation." 8 The king answered, "I know with certainty that you are trying to gain time, because you see that the word from me is sure 9 that if you do not make the dream known to me, there is but one sentence for you. You have agreed to speak lying and corrupt words before me till the times change. Therefore tell me the dream, and I shall know that you can show me its interpretation." 10 The Chaldeans answered the king, "There is not a man on earth who can meet the king's demand; for no great and powerful king has asked such a thing of any magician or enchanter or Chaldean. 11 The thing that the king asks is difficult, and none can show it to the king except the gods, whose dwelling is not with flesh."

TEV

Nebuchadnezzar's Dream

1 In the second year that Nebuchadnezzar was king, he had a dream. It worried him so much that he couldn't sleep, 2 so he sent for his fortunetellers, magicians, sorcerers, and wizards to come and explain the dream to him. When they came and stood before the king, 3 he said to them, "I'm worried about a dream I've had. I want to know what it means." 4 They answered the king in Aramaic, "May Your Majesty live forever! Tell us your dream, and we will explain it to you." 5 The king said to them, "I have made up my mind that you must tell me the dream and then tell me what it means. If you can't, I'll have you torn limb from limb and make your houses a pile of ruins. 6 But if you can tell me both the dream and its meaning, I will reward you with gifts and great honor. Now then, tell me what the dream was and what it means." 7 They answered the king again, "If Your Majesty will only tell us what the dream was, we will explain it." 8 At that, the king exclaimed, "Just as I thought! You are trying to gain time, because you see that I have made up my mind 9 to give all of you the same punishment if you don't tell me the dream. You have agreed among yourselves to go on telling me lies because you hope that in time things will change. Tell me what the dream was, and then I will know that you can also tell me what it means." 10 The advisers replied, "There is no one on the face of the earth who can tell Your Majesty what you want to know. No king, not even the greatest and most powerful, has ever made such a demand of his fortunetellers, magicians, and wizards. 11 What Your Majesty is asking for is so difficult that no one can do

12 Because of this the king was angry and very furious, and commanded that all the wise men of Babylon be destroyed. 13 So the decree went forth that the wise men were to be slain, and they sought Daniel and his companions, to slay them.

it for you except the gods, and they do not live among human beings."

12 At that, the king flew into a rage and ordered the execution of all the royal advisers in Babylon. 13 So the order was issued for all of them to be killed, including Daniel and his friends.

TEV Section Heading: Nebuchadnezzar's Dream

Since King Nebuchadnezzar had a second dream as described in chapter 4, it may be advisable to give a more precise section heading such as "Nebuchadnezzar's first dream." Or translators may choose to give more details about the dream and say "Nebuchadnezzar dreams about a statue" or "Nebuchadnezzar has a troublesome dream." REB focuses on a different aspect of the story, using the title "Daniel's wisdom."

This chapter bears a remarkable resemblance to Genesis 41, where Joseph becomes the interpreter of the strange dream of the King of Egypt. Much of the vocabulary is similar, and it may be helpful for translators to compare their renderings of these two stories.

2.1   RSV   TEV

In the second year of the reign of Nebuchadnezzar, Nebuchadnezzar had dreams; and his spirit was troubled, and his sleep left him.

In the second year that Nebuchadnezzar was king, he had a dream. It worried him so much that he couldn't sleep,

In the second year: it has been suggested by some scholars that this should read "In the twelfth year . . . ," because the second year seems to be inconsistent with the information given in 1.5 and 1.18, and it does not seem to allow for the three-years training period. There is, however, no manuscript evidence for this, and so translators are advised to translate the text as it stands.

Of the reign of Nebuchadnezzar: the long, complicated name of the king is mentioned twice in succession in RSV, as in the Hebrew text, but it will very likely be more natural to change one or the other into a pronoun in other languages. Translators may say "In the second year of his reign, Nebuchadnezzar . . ." or "In the second year of Nebuchadnezzar's reign, he . . . ."

Had dreams: literally "dreamed dreams"—the noun and the verb have the same root. While the Hebrew is plural in form, the meaning is probably singular. The focus of the passage is on one particular dream that caused difficulty. Hence the singular is used in TEV, NAB, and NJV. NJB, on the other hand, highlights the plural by translating "had a series of dreams." But it is probably better to use the singular form in most languages.

His spirit troubled him and his sleep left him: the word for spirit is more naturally rendered "mind" in English (see TEV, NIV, and NEB, for example). And the expression his sleep left him is translated by NJV "he was overcome by sleep," following one understanding of the traditional Hebrew text. But the meaning of the text is unclear, and most English versions adopt the interpretation "sleep fled from him." However, this is not the usual way of expressing this idea in English. Rather, people would more naturally say "he couldn't sleep" (TEV) or "he was losing sleep."

The relationship between these two clauses is also worthy of attention. They are not two independent facts or separate results of the dream but are very closely related, with the last clause stating the result of the clause before it. For this reason translators may consider the rendering of NEB as a possible model to follow: "his mind was so troubled that he could not sleep." REB restructures further, with ". . . was troubled by dreams he had, so much so that he could not sleep."

2.2	RSV	TEV
	Then the king commanded that the magicians, the enchanters, the sorcerers, and the Chaldeans be summoned, to tell the king his dreams. So they came in and stood before the king.	so he sent for his fortunetellers, magicians, sorcerers, and wizards to come and explain the dream to him. When they came and stood before the king,

Then: the transition is a probably to be understood as a logical one rather than being just a reference to the passing of time. NRSV and AB use "so," as does TEV.

Commanded . . . be summoned: there is no way of knowing precisely who the king commanded to call the people listed in this verse, and in a sense it is not important. But in some languages it will be grammatically impossible to make such a statement without specifying someone, even if a very indefinite term must be used. The whole verse may have to be restructured, beginning something like "Then the king ordered someone to call . . . ."

Magicians, enchanters, and **sorcerers**: the first two of these terms are introduced in 1.20. The third term (*mekashef* in Hebrew) is very similar to the one translated **enchanters** here and in 1.20. This is another example of the writer's fondness for lists, but these words are not used so much as technical terms but more as various alternative words for "sorcerers" or "fortune tellers."

Chaldeans: the fourth word in this list is a proper name originally designating the inhabitants of Chaldea, that is to say, the Babylonians in general (see 1.4). But since these people had a reputation for mastery of divination and the occult, the word became a common noun meaning "specialists in the occult." Here and in verses 4, 5, and 10 this term is translated "diviners" (Mft), "wizards" (TEV), and "astrologues" (NIV). One commentator sums up the situation in these words: "Since the term 'Chaldeans' can occur in the midst of the other terms (4.7; 5.7, 11) as well as at their end (2.2, 10), it is evident that in this context it does not have its original ethnic meaning. In this chapter this is probably the case when the term occurs alone, as summing up all the other synonyms (2.4-5, 10)." (AB, page 138).

In some languages the four terms used here may have to be reduced to two or three, due to a lack of terms having this meaning. Translators should try to think of all the kinds of people that may be called on in their culture to explain the meanings of dreams. And in those languages where it is impossible to come up with separate terms for the different words used in the text here, it is possible to resort to a more general formulation by expressing the idea of "all the specialists in divination and magic," or possibly "wise men in matters of dreams." But given the habit of the writer to use lists, it may be better to retain this characteristic style where possible.

To tell the king his dreams: most English versions are ambiguous at this point, but it may be necessary in some languages to decide which is true in order to translate the passage. AB (page 144) explains as follows: "That he demands his soothsayers to tell him the dream itself should not be taken to mean that he had forgotten it; rather, he uses this as a test in order to have assurance that they can give him a reliable interpretation of it (verse 9)." Other interpreters feel that the king may have forgotten the dream, and that this is the first sign of his mental problems detailed in chapter 4. However, if translators are forced to choose between these two interpretations, it is more likely that the king remembers the dream, and that he is deliberately not telling the experts its contents.

Stood before the king: the text has precisely the same words as in 1.5 and 1.19, where the meaning is more generally "to serve in the royal court." Here, however, the context seems to require a more literal understanding of standing ready or being available to do what the king ordered on this occasion.

Note that TEV makes this last sentence into a subordinate clause introducing verse 3: "When they . . . ." This may be a good model for certain other languages to follow.

2.3	RSV	TEV
	And the king said to them, "I had a dream, and my spirit is troubled to know the dream."	he said to them, "I'm worried about a dream I've had. I want to know what it means."

The king said: since the previous verse refers to the king by his title three times (RSV), it may be more natural in some languages to use a pronoun in place of the noun at the beginning of this verse: "he said . . . ." But in others it will be perfectly natural to repeat the title here.

I had a dream: literally "I dreamed a dream" (compare verse 1 above). In some languages people may say "I saw a dream" or "I slept a dream." Whatever is natural should be used in the translation.

My spirit is troubled: see comments on "his spirit troubled him" in verse 1 above.

To know the dream: as in the previous verse, this may mean either "to know what the dream was" (because he had forgotten it) or "to know what the dream meant" (because he did not understand it). Most likely the latter is the intended meaning of the writer.

In some languages it may be necessary to make clear the relationship between **my spirit is troubled** and **to know the dream**. Some possible models are "I had a dream that will allow my spirit no rest until I know what it means" (NAB), "my mind is troubled by a wish to understand it" (NJB), or "I want to know what the dream means because my mind is very upset."

2.4 RSV	TEV
Then the Chaldeans said to the king,ᵃ "O king, live for ever! Tell your servants the dream, and we will show the interpretation."	**They answered the king in Aramaic,ᵃ "May Your Majesty live forever! Tell us your dream, and we will explain it to you."**
ᵃ Heb adds *in Aramaic,* indicating that the text from this point to the end of chapter 7 is in Aramaic	ᵃ *From here to the end of chapter 7, the language used is Aramaic, not Hebrew.*

Chaldeans: compare verse 2. The translation should not give the impression that only one category of specialists mentioned in verse 2 came to speak to the king. Those addressing the king are actually spokesmen for the entire group. In some languages it may be possible, as in TEV and GECL, to translate this by using the third person plural pronoun.

The words "in Aramaic" (TEV) are found only in a footnote in RSV, although they are included in parentheses in the text of NRSV. They are also omitted by GECL and placed in the left margin by NJB, because they are considered an editorial note added to the text. It is, in fact, at this point that the text of Daniel changes from Hebrew to Aramaic and continues thus to the end of chapter 7. However, it is also possible that these words were a part of the original text, because this is the beginning of a quotation from Aramaic-speaking people. Probably it is better to retain this in the translation, as has been done in NIV, NJV, and many others, as well as in TEV. But in those translations where footnotes are being used, it may be advisable to explain the problem in more detail.

O king, live forever: the use of the vocative form **O king . . .** was the usual respectful way of addressing royalty in the Semitic languages, but this often sounds quite unnatural in translation. It is used more than twenty times in the next five chapters, and an effort should be made to find a natural equivalent in other languages. In English the most natural equivalent is probably "your majesty," as in TEV (and in most cases also in NEB and NJB). But the receptor language may have a very different form of address to begin talking to a chief, a president, or some other very important person. Naturalness in the language should determine the form here; but it is likely that a literal rendering of "your majesty" will sound awkward.

The words **live forever** are used to express the desire that the king will have a long life. While it is unnecessary to give a word-for-word translation, it is probably advisable to maintain the theme of "life" in whatever form is used. In English the most natural wording may be "Long live the king!" as in NEB/REB. In other languages translators may something like "may the king remain (or continue)!" or "may the chief never die!"

Tell your servants the dream: the specialists are not asking that the king tell his dream to someone else (as his household servants, for example) but to them. Referring to themselves in the third person as **servants** is a way of showing respect and acknowledging their subordination to the king, as with Daniel and his companions in 1.12. But it is a mistake in most languages to translate this literally. It is usually much more natural to say simply "tell us your dream," or perhaps retaining something of the form, "we are your servants. So tell us your dream . . . ." In those languages distinguishing between inclusive and exclusive forms of the first person plural pronoun, the exclusive form should be used here.

These experts could not believe that the king was really demanding that they tell him the content of the dream. They understood him to be asking only for the interpretation. But the king's response makes it clear that he was asking for both the content and the meaning.

Show the interpretation: the verb here translated **show** occurs at least eight times in this chapter and is used as a sort of technical term for revealing the unknown. NRSV actually translates it using the English verb "reveal." While the object of this verb is most often the word for "interpretation" as in this case, in verse 6 both "the dream and its interpretation" are objects. And in verse 28 the object is the word "mystery." In some languages it will be more natural to use an expression like "cause to see the meaning . . . ."

2.5　　　　　　RSV　　　　　　　　　　　　　　　　TEV

The king answered the Chaldeans, "The word from me is sure: if you do not make known to me the dream and its interpretation, you shall be torn limb from limb, and your houses shall be laid in ruins.	The king said to them, "I have made up my mind that you must tell me the dream and then tell me what it means. If you can't, I'll have you torn limb from limb and make your houses a pile of ruins.

The king answered the Chaldeans: literally "answered and said to the Chaldeans . . . ." Aramaic, like Hebrew, often uses two verbs where many other languages use only one. Even RSV reduces the two verbs to one in this context, but compare KJV. Also, in many languages it may be smoother to leave **the Chaldeans** implicit and say simply "the king answered . . . ," as in REB.

The word from me is sure: this phrase, repeated in verse 8 below, gives the idea of a firm decision or decree. The notion of this strong resolution has been communicated in other English versions as "This is what I have decided: . . ." (NAB), "I hereby decree: . . ." (NJV), "This is my declared intention" (NEB), "This is my firm decision" (REB), and "What I say, I mean" (Mft).

The dream and its interpretation: some other ways of phrasing this may be "what I dreamed and what it means" or "the story and meaning of my dream."

You shall be torn limb from limb: or "you will be cut into pieces." This expression describes a form of torture that was fairly common in ancient times. Because it is a passive expression, it will have to be reworded in many languages. Some may use a causative form: "I will cause someone to mutilate you." Others may use an expression like "I will order them (indefinite) to cut you to pieces."

Your houses shall be laid in ruins: this passive form will also have to be made active in many languages. According to some scholars the Aramaic word corresponding to **ruins** is derived from a verb meaning "to destroy." But others think that it comes from a root evoking the idea of ugliness, horror, or garbage. This is why NJB has ". . . turned into dunghills." NJV, however, translates "your houses will be confiscated" but acknowledges in a footnote that the meaning is uncertain. It is probably best to understand it in terms of the total destruction of their homes.

2.6	RSV	TEV
	But if you show the dream and its interpretation, you shall receive from me gifts and rewards and great honor. Therefore show me the dream and its interpretation."	But if you can tell me both the dream and its meaning, I will reward you with gifts and great honor. Now then, tell me what the dream was and what it means."

But: the conjunction used should introduce the contrast between what will happen to the experts if they fail to fulfill the king's request, as compared to what will happen if they are successful. In some languages it may be preferable to say something like "If, on the other hand . . ." (NJB).

Show the dream and its interpretation: the original text does not state the indirect object of the verb **show**, but the pronoun "me" is unquestionably meant and has been supplied in a number of modern versions. It should probably be added in other languages if it is not clearly understood. It will be noted that these words are repeated at the end of this verse. Given the importance of this formula, it may be a good idea to retain the form at that point unless it would be unnatural to do so.

You shall receive from me: this is a rather awkward way of saying simply "I will give you . . . ." Naturalness in the receptor language should determine how this is translated.

Gifts and rewards: the use of these two terms side by side is a way of expressing a superlative idea in Aramaic. For this reason, in some languages it will be possible to render the idea by using a single noun or a noun accompanied by an adjective: "wonderful gifts" or "special presents." Or we may choose to modify the verb as in NEB: "you will be richly rewarded" (NEB).

Great honor: what is involved here is probably some honorary titles or actual political responsibilities accompanied by material gifts (compare 5.7).

2.7 RSV	TEV
They answered a second time, "Let the king tell his servants the dream, and we will show its interpretation."	They answered the king again, "If Your Majesty will only tell us what the dream was, we will explain it."

Answered a second time: literally "answered again and saying." This is essentially a repetition of their request in verse 4. The text does not provide the object of the verb **answered**, but in those languages where one is required, it is clearly the king.

Let the king tell his servants . . . : again the indirect reference to the king (rather than saying "you") and to themselves as **his servants** (instead of simply "us") are ways of showing respect and were very natural in ancient times. But the use of the pronouns is recommended in most languages today.

Show its interpretation: that is, "show you what it means."

2.8-9 RSV	TEV
8 The king answered, "I know with certainty that you are trying to gain time, because you see that the word from me is sure 9 that if you do not make the dream known to me, there is but one sentence for you. You have agreed to speak lying and corrupt words before me till the times change. Therefore tell me the dream, and I shall know that you can show me its interpretation."	8 At that, the king exclaimed, "Just as I thought! You are trying to gain time, because you see that I have made up my mind 9 to give all of you the same punishment if you don't tell me the dream. You have agreed among yourselves to go on telling me lies because you hope that in time things will change. Tell me what the dream was, and then I will know that you can also tell me what it means."

Answered: literally "answered saying . . . ." In some languages the context may require a word that gives a stronger expression of emotion. NJB has "retorted," REB "rejoined"; TEV says "exclaimed," while FRCL renders the verb "cried out."

I know with certainty: given the emotive impact of this passage, the RSV rendering sounds somewhat stilted and weak. Some other versions have said "It is clear to me" (NJV and REB), "I see quite plainly" (Mft), and "Just as I thought!" (TEV).

You are trying to gain time: literally "you are buying time," that is, "you are looking for a way to have some more time" or "you are trying to delay the punishment." NAB has "you are bargaining for time."

The word from me is sure: see verse 5.

There is but one sentence for you: these words indicate that the same sentence, or verdict, will be applied to all of those involved. Other ways of saying this are "you will all receive the same punishment," or "they (indefinite) will punish every one of you in the same way," or "the same penalty will be given to all of you," or "the same judgment will be pronounced on all of you," or "I will have you all punished in the same way."

You have agreed to speak lying and corrupt words: this gives a part of the reason for the judgment that would be passed and may therefore require a restructuring of the verse in some languages. It is important that the verb form used indicates a continuing process rather than a single event. This is why TEV has "to go on telling me lies . . . ." Some other possible renderings of these words may be "you conspired to continue deceiving me . . ." or "you plotted to keep on tricking me with lies . . . ."

Till the times change: it is obvious that it is not a change in time that was hoped for as much as a change in the attitude of the king that would come with the passage of time. If necessary it is possible to say "until I change my mind" or something similar. Other versions have rendered this as "in the hope that with time things may alter" (NEB/REB), "hoping the situation will change" (NIV), "till the crisis is past" (NAB).

Therefore tell me . . . : or "So I want you to tell me . . . ," or "I demand that you reveal to me what the dream was, so that I can be assured that you are able to tell me what it means."

2.10 RSV	TEV
The Chaldeans answered the king, "There is not a man on earth who can meet the king's demand; for no great and powerful king has asked such a thing of any magician or enchanter or Chaldean.	The advisers replied, "There is no one on the face of the earth who can tell Your Majesty what you want to know. No king, not even the greatest and most powerful, has ever made such a demand of his fortunetellers, magicians, and wizards.

Chaldeans: see verses 2, 4, and 5.

Not a man on earth: the experts in the occult were convinced that there was no person in the world that could do what the king was asking. The use of the word **man** is not intended to refer only to males. For this reason many versions say "no one" or "no person." This response, however, does seem to suggest that there may be celestial beings that would be able to do so (compare verse 11 below), and so the sense may be "no human being."

Meet the king's demand: literally "tell the king's matter." The English idiom of RSV may be more naturally rendered "do what the king asks" (NIV and the New Century Version [NCV]). Again the king is referred to indirectly in keeping with proper court behavior. But in most languages this will come out differently: "what you are asking, sir" or "what your majesty commands." The most natural equivalent should be sought in the receptor language rather than simply repeating the form of either RSV or TEV.

No great and powerful king has asked such a thing: the idea here is that no king, regardless of how powerful and great he may be, has ever made such an impossible request. Compare the TEV rendering above. Apparently, in the minds of these "wise men," only a very powerful king could make such a request.

Magician or enchanter or Chaldean: here the text has only three of the four terms found in verse 2. The word for "sorcerer" should therefore be omitted here. Of course, if they were combined in verse 2, there will be no way to make this distinction here.

2.11	RSV	TEV

The thing that the king asks is difficult, and none can show it to the king except the gods, whose dwelling is not with flesh."	What Your Majesty is asking for is so difficult that no one can do it for you except the gods, and they do not live among human beings."

The king: twice again in this verse Nebuchadnezzar is referred to by the words "the king," although he is being addressed directly. As usual, it will probably be more natural to use the second person singular pronouns: "Sir, what you ask is difficult, and no one can show it to you . . . ."

Difficult, and none can show it . . . : the conjunction "and" may be misleading. What this really means is that the request of the king was so difficult to fulfill that no one could do it. Compare AB's rendering: "so difficult that no one but divine beings can reveal it." In some languages it may be more common to say "it is not possible for anyone to reveal it . . ." or "no one could ever declare it . . . ."

Except the gods: the power of celestial beings that was hinted at in the previous verse is stated directly here. Instead of **gods**, some translators may prefer "divine beings," "spirits," or "heavenly creatures." And in some cases we may have to resort to "creatures that are appealed to as God."

Whose dwelling is not with flesh: here the word **flesh**, as often in Scripture, is used to refer to human beings and emphasizes their frailty and weakness. This is brought out in Mft's rendering "mortal men." Because of the remoteness of the gods, human beings are not able to consult with them and know their secrets. It will probably be important in some cases to translate the idea of **not with** as "very distant from." Compare REB: "who dwell remote from mortals."

2.12   RSV   TEV

Because of this the king was   At that, the king flew into a
angry and very furious, and com-   rage and ordered the execution of
manded that all the wise men of   all the royal advisers in Babylon.
Babylon be destroyed.

Many versions, including both RSV and TEV, begin a new paragraph here.
However, others (NAB, NJB, NEB/REB) make the paragraph break at verse 14,
while NJV makes it at verse 13. Given the close relationship between the anger
of the king and the statement of his advisers that provoked it, it may be better
not to make a break at this point unless translators are following the principle
of beginning a new paragraph after every direct quotation.

Because of this: that is, because of the statement quoted in the previous
verse. Most English versions have "At this . . ." or "At that . . . ." But NIV has
"This made the king so angry . . . ." Other languages may prefer "Because of
what they said . . ." or "As soon as they finished saying that . . . ."

Angry and very furious: the Aramaic puts together two terms that mean
almost the same thing to express a single idea (compare verse 6, "gifts and
rewards"). The idea here is that of extreme anger. It has been rendered
"became violently angry" (NAB), "flew into a violent rage" (NJV), and "lost his
temper" (NEB).

And commanded: the relationship between the king's violent anger and
his order is less clear in RSV. Clearly it was because of his anger that he issued
the decree. This may be made clearer in some languages by saying something
like "became so angry that he commanded . . . ."

All the wise men of Babylon: the more general Aramaic word for **wise
men** here is intended to include all four of the terms given in verse 2
(magicians, sorcerers, enchanters, and Chaldeans).

Be destroyed: instead of the verb "destroy," this context may require
"execute" or simply "kill." And in languages where the passive form is
unnatural or nonexistent, translators may need to say "ordered the death of
. . ." or "commanded that they (indefinite) slaughter . . . ." In verse 14 it
becomes clear that it was "the king's guard" that was to carry out this order.

2.13   RSV   TEV

So the decree went forth that the   So the order was issued for all of
wise men were to be slain, and they   them to be killed, including Daniel
sought Daniel and his companions,   and his friends.
to slay them.

So . . . and: the structure of this verse has been changed in some English
versions to begin with "When the decree was issued . . ." (NAB) or "On
publication of the decree . . ." (NJV).

The decree went forth: in some languages wording like that of RSV is unnatural. It may even give the impression that the decree had a will of its own. The idea, of course, is that the decree was published, which probably means that it was read out in public; but the agent who makes this happen will have to be expressed in many cases. Translators may consider "when the king made known his will . . . ," "when they (indefinite) announced the decision of the king . . . ," or "when messengers announced the king's decree . . . ."

The wise men: again this refers to all the experts mentioned earlier (verses 2 and 10). This should be made clear, as in TEV "all of them."

Be slain: it is quite likely that what is planned here is the gathering and mass execution in public of the all the **wise men** of the kingdom in a spectacular fashion. It is possible to understand the text as meaning "were being put to death." This would indicate that the executions had already begun, but this is less probable. Once again the passive may have to be rendered as active: "that they should die" or "that the executioners should kill them."

They sought: this is an indefinite form that gives a passive idea: "Daniel and his friends were sought." But it may be possible to say "some men went out and found Daniel and his friends" or ". . . went to get . . . ." REB has "a search was made . . . ."

God shows Daniel the meaning of the dream: 2.14-23

RSV	TEV
	God Shows Daniel What the Dream Means

RSV:

14 Then Daniel replied with prudence and discretion to Arioch, the captain of the king's guard, who had gone out to slay the wise men of Babylon; 15 he said to Arioch, the king's captain, "Why is the decree of the king so severe?" Then Arioch made the matter known to Daniel. 16 And Daniel went in and besought the king to appoint him a time, that he might show to the king the interpretation.

17 Then Daniel went to his house and made the matter known to Hananiah, Mishael, and Azariah, his companions, 18 and told them to seek mercy of the God of heaven concerning this mystery, so that Daniel and his companions might not perish with the rest of the wise men of Babylon. 19 Then the mystery was revealed to Daniel in a vision of the night. Then Daniel blessed the God of heaven.
20 Daniel said:

"Blessed be the name of God for ever
    and ever,
  to whom belong wisdom and
    might.
21 He changes times and seasons;
  he removes kings and sets up

TEV:

14 Then Daniel went to Arioch, commander of the king's bodyguard, who had been ordered to carry out the execution. Choosing his words carefully, 15 he asked Arioch why the king had issued such a harsh order. So Arioch told Daniel what had happened.

16 Daniel went at once and obtained royal permission for more time, so that he could tell the king what the dream meant. 17 Then Daniel went home and told his friends Hananiah, Mishael, and Azariah what had happened. 18 He told them to pray to the God of heaven for mercy and to ask him to explain the mystery to them so that they would not be killed along with the other advisers in Babylon. 19 Then that same night the mystery was revealed to Daniel in a vision, and he praised the God of heaven:
20   "God is wise and powerful!
      Praise him forever and ever.
21   He controls the times and the seasons;
      he makes and unmakes kings;
      it is he who gives wisdom and understanding.

kings;
he gives wisdom to the wise
and knowledge to those who have
understanding;
22 he reveals deep and mysterious
things;
he knows what is in the darkness,
and the light dwells with him.
23 To thee, O God of my fathers,
I give thanks and praise,
for thou hast given me wisdom and
strength,
and hast now made known to me
what we asked of thee,
for thou hast made known to us
the king's matter."

22 He reveals things that are deep and
secret;
he knows what is hidden in darkness,
and he himself is surrounded by
light.
23 I praise you and honor you, God of my
ancestors.
You have given me wisdom and
strength;
you have answered my prayer
and shown us what to tell the
king."

TEV Section Heading: God shows Daniel what the dream means

Some other ways of expressing this heading are "God reveals the meaning of the king's dream (to Daniel)" or "Daniel learns the meaning of the king's dream."

2.14	RSV	TEV

Then Daniel replied with prudence and discretion to Arioch, the captain of the king's guard, who had gone out to slay the wise men of Babylon;

Then Daniel went to Arioch, commander of the king's body-guard, who had been ordered to carry out the execution. Choosing his words carefully,

The structure of this verse should probably be changed in many languages to a more logical order. As it stands the RSV text of verses 14 and 15 has **Daniel replied . . .** at the beginning of verse 14, but the content of what he said occurs in verse 15 after certain other material that is not directly a part of the actual quotation. Furthermore, the use of the verb **replied** in RSV is curious, since it is not clear what Daniel is replying to. REB restructures the whole verse as follows: "As Arioch, captain of the royal bodyguard, set out to execute the wise men of Babylon, Daniel made a discreet and tactful approach to him."

With prudence and discretion: as in verses 6 and 12, the joining of two nouns of similar meaning may be a means of expressing what might otherwise be stated as an adjective plus a noun. NAB has "prudently took counsel . . . ." Other versions, however, prefer to preserve two nouns in translation, giving the idea of "wisdom and tact." NJB has "with shrewd and cautious words." Note that this element is shifted to the end of the verse in TEV in order to introduce the quotation in the following verse.

Captain of the king's guard: Arioch was apparently the chief of that group of soldiers who were given the responsibility of protecting the king from danger. This was a very high position in the royal court. This expression is the

Aramaic equivalent of the Hebrew term for "bodyguard" or "guard" found several times in 2 Kgs 25.8-20. Since this bit of information may require rather a lot of words, it may be a good idea in some languages to place it in parentheses. Translators may consider something like "Now, this man was the chief of the warriors chosen to protect the king." In many countries today there is a well-known equivalent for this group in the form of special police or a presidential bodyguard. Note AB "chief of the royal police."

Who had gone out to slay . . . : the verb tense in RSV may be misleading. What is important here is to indicate that Arioch "was on his way to kill the Babylonian sages" (NJB) or "setting out to execute the wise men . . . ." (NEB).

2.15	RSV	TEV

he said to Arioch, the king's captain, "Why is the decree of the king so severe?" Then Arioch made the matter known to Daniel.	he asked Arioch why the king had issued such a harsh order. So Arioch told Daniel what had happened.

Said: literally "answered saying." In many languages it may be better to use the verb "asked," since a question follows.

The king's captain: the meaning is the same as "the captain of the king's guard" in the previous verse, and this may therefore be considered redundant in some languages.

Why . . . ? The original uses direct discourse here, but in some languages indirect discourse may be preferred in this context (see TEV). Translators must use whichever model is best suited to their own language.

So severe: or "so brutal," "so harsh," "so cruel." If direct discourse is being used, the question may be rephrased: "What is the reason for such a harsh order from the king."

Made the matter known to Daniel: there are probably a number of different ways of expressing the idea here; for example, "told Daniel what it was all about," or "explained the whole affair," or simply "explained everything" (NEB).

2.16	RSV	TEV

And Daniel went in and besought the king to appoint him a time, that he might show to the king the interpretation.	Daniel went at once and obtained royal permission for more time, so that he could tell the king what the dream meant.

And: instead of the common conjunction found in the Aramaic here, it may be better in this context to highlight the urgency of the situation by translating "at once" as in TEV, or "Immediately" (FRCL) or "So . . ." (NEB and NJV).

Besought the king to appoint him a time: RSV may be understood in the sense that Daniel asked for an appointment, during which time he would talk with the king in more detail. However, the meaning is almost certainly that he asked for a postponement of the accomplishment of the king's order. NJB says that he asked "for a stay of execution."

2.17 RSV	TEV
Then Daniel went to his house and made the matter known to Hananiah, Mishael, and Azariah, his companions,	Then Daniel went home and told his friends Hananiah, Mishael, and Azariah what had happened.

Then . . . and . . . : it will be more natural in some languages to change the first part of this verse into a subordinate clause, saying something like "When Daniel got home . . . ," or "After Daniel arrived at home . . . ," or "Having gone back home, Daniel . . . ."

Made the matter known: this is the same expression as in verse 15, where Arioch explains the situation to Daniel. In this case Daniel passes the information on to his friends.

2.18 RSV	TEV
and told them to seek mercy of the God of heaven concerning this mystery, so that Daniel and his companions might not perish with the rest of the wise men of Babylon.	He told them to pray to the God of heaven for mercy and to ask him to explain the mystery to them so that they would not be killed along with the other advisers in Babylon.

In RSV the sentence begun in the previous verse continues in this verse. But it will probably be better in most languages to start a new sentence here, as some modern English versions do. The sentence can probably begin "They were to ask God . . . ," or "He urged them to pray . . . ," or something similar.

The God of heaven: this same expression is found four more times in this chapter (verses 19, 28, 37 and 44). This was a common way of referring to the LORD during a certain period in the life of the Jewish people. But because of its similarity to a pagan expression, it was later rejected. Compare also "King of heaven" in 4.37 and "Lord of heaven" in 5.23.

This mystery: the word for **mystery**, which appears again in verses 19, 27-30, 47, and in 4.9 [Aramaic 4.6], is a loan word from Persian. Here the mystery involved is the meaning of the king's dream. In some languages it will be important to state this by saying "the mystery of the king's dream" or "the secret meaning of what the king dreamed." Some interpreters have stated that **this mystery** refers to the situation of Daniel, and his friends who were threatened with death, but this is hardly convincing.

Daniel and his companions: in this context it will probably be more natural in many languages to use the pronoun "they" or "them" (depending on the structure of the sentence) instead of the more lengthy noun phrase, since this is an indirect quotation of what Daniel said to his three companions. In some cases, however, it may be more natural to transform it into a direct quote.

That . . . might not perish: literally "that they (indefinite) might not execute (Daniel and his friends)." For some languages the more literal version may provide a better model than either RSV or TEV.

With the rest of the wise men: the way the original is worded, it is uncertain whether or not the executions had already begun. If it is impossible to leave this question open in the translation, then it is probably better to consider that the execution had not yet begun (see verse 13). Also, the original wording does not indicate that Daniel and his friends selfishly sought to escape alone from the punishment that would be inflicted on the others. They were attempting to insure the survival of all the wise men of Babylon, as verse 24 confirms.

2.19	RSV	TEV
	Then the mystery was revealed to Daniel in a vision of the night. Then Daniel blessed the God of heaven.	Then that same night the mystery was revealed to Daniel in a vision, and he praised the God of heaven:

The mystery was revealed: on the word for **mystery**, see the verse above. Also, the passive form **was revealed** will have to be made active in some cases. Since the context clearly shows that it was God who revealed the meaning of the dream, it will be possible to translate "Then God revealed (or uncovered, or made known) the mystery to Daniel . . . ."

A vision of the night: some translations give the impression that this was a mere dream (see FRCL), but the Aramaic word is different from the one for "dream" in verses 4 and 5. Most modern English versions retain the word **vision** and so apparently maintain the distinction between a simple dream and a special revelation from God. In this context the words **of the night** seem to mean "that very night." TEV makes this clear with "that same night."

Blessed: the Aramaic verb so translated may be used either of a superior to an inferior or of an inferior towards his superior. But the meaning is quite different in these two cases. When God or a superior person "blesses" someone, the meaning is that he "does good to," "grants his favor to," or "confers benefit on" the person. But if a person of lesser status is said in Aramaic or Hebrew to "bless" a king or to "bless" God, the meaning is rather to "honor," "give praise to," or "acknowledge the greatness of" the superior person. In this case Daniel is said to have **blessed the God of heaven**. So the meaning is clearly "praised" (NIV as well as TEV). In certain languages it may be necessary to resort to an expression like "say good things about the God of heaven" or "tell how good the God of heaven is."

2.20   RSV   TEV

Daniel said: **"God is wise and powerful!**
  "Blessed be the name of God   **Praise him forever and**
     for ever and ever,   **ever.**
  to whom belong wisdom
     and might.

Verses 20-23 constitute the first of four brief passages that may be classified as hymns of praise. The others are found at 4.3; 4.34-35; and 6.26-27. Since these are in a rather special, poetic type of language in the original, they should be rendered as poetry insofar as this is possible and natural in the translation. TEV and many other modern versions set these verses off in poetic format to highlight their special character. The same devices used in translating the Psalms and other poetic passages should also be applied to these passages.

The poem in this chapter begins with the pronouncement of a "blessing" on God (compare Psa 113.2 and Job 1.21). The sense of the poem is the acknowledgment of God's greatness or the giving of praise and honor to him. Note that the two elements of this verse have been reordered in TEV, giving the reason for the praise before actually offering praises. This should be considered in the receptor language before deciding which is most natural. Note also that TEV omits the words **Daniel said** at the beginning of this verse because they are redundant.

Blessed be: On the verb "to bless," see the comments in the previous verse. Here the verb is used in a passive form that will have to be made active in other languages. In many cases it will be natural to say something like "Praise be to . . . ," or we may be forced to say "Let people praise . . ." or "Let us thank . . . ."

The name of God: the use of expressions like **the name of God** for God himself is a common Semitic style that keeps a certain distance between the human and the divine. This was done out of a sense of respectful submission to God. But the expression actually means simply "God" and should probably be translated this way in most languages. If there are special means of showing respect for God in the receptor language, they should be considered in this context.

For ever and ever: literally "from eternity to eternity." REB and NRSV render this "from age to age." Another possible translation might be "Let people never cease praising God . . . ," incorporating the idea of **for ever and ever** in the verb phrase "let people never cease . . . ."

To whom belong wisdom and might: the order of this phrase may well be reversed in some languages, making **wisdom and might** the subject of the verb "own" or "possess," as in "wisdom and might are owned by God . . . ," or "wisdom and power belong to him (God)." But it may be better to restructure the whole statement by saying something like "God is the possessor of wisdom and power. Praise him (his name) eternally." This is essentially the same as the TEV solution which is even simpler from the point of view of structure.

In verses 20-22 Daniel speaks of God in the third person singular ("he" and "him"), while in verse 23 he addresses God directly in the second person singular, "you" ("thee" and "thou" in the archaic English of the KJV, and preserved by RSV when God is addressed). If this grammatical change of person is not clumsy in the language, it may be retained. However, in most cases it is probably better to put everything in the second person (as in GECL) or in the third person. In most English versions the pronoun shift seems to present no particular problem.

2.21   RSV   TEV

RSV	TEV
He changes times and sea- sons; he removes kings and sets up kings; he gives wisdom to the wise and knowledge to those who have understand- ing;	**He controls the times and the seasons; he makes and unmakes kings; it is he who gives wisdom and understanding.**

He: see the above comment on the pronouns referring to God.

Changes times and seasons: the verb used here expresses somewhat indirectly the idea that God has authority over time and history. This is in contrast with the Babylonian idea of history, which seemed to indicate that the gods could do nothing to modify its course.

The two nouns in Hebrew have a rather general meaning, and it is probably unnecessary to try to make a careful distinction between them. GECL translates the two by a single term in German. FRCL translates "time and history," but this is not to be understood as separate and precise renderings. Rather the two are to be taken together. Most English versions translate simply "times and seasons," but Mft has "epochs and eras." Note the similar expression in Gen 1.14.

Removes . . . sets up: in many languages it will be more natural to reverse the order of these two verbs. In some cases there are special words for the installation (enthronement) of a king and for his removal (dethronement). Or translators may also consider saying "he gives authority (power) to kings, and he takes their power (authority) away."

Gives wisdom to the wise and knowledge to those who have understanding: in some languages these two parallel statements would be nonsense, because the wise already have wisdom and those who have understanding would also have knowledge. It will be much more logical to say "He is the one who makes a person wise, and it is he who gave understanding to those who have it" or something similar. TEV does not say who receives the wisdom and understanding, but it is probably better to make this clear in many languages.

Some possible models for this statement are "If people have wisdom and understanding, it comes from God," "It is God who gives people wisdom and understanding," or "God is the one who makes people wise and lets them understand matters."

2.22

RSV	TEV
he reveals deep and mysterious things; he knows what is in the darkness, and the light dwells with him.	He reveals things that are deep and secret; he knows what is hidden in darkness, and he himself is surrounded by light.

Deep and mysterious things: most commentators see this as a reference to the fact that God enabled Daniel to understand the secret of Nebuchadnezzar's dream. The two nouns used together here do not refer to two separate and distinct ideas but simply serve to reinforce each other. The idea of "depth" is often used in the figurative sense of something profound or difficult to comprehend (as in Job 12.22) and is not to be taken literally. Other languages may use a very different kind of figure, such as "high" or "heavy," to express the idea of something difficult to understand. The second word used here is not the same as "mystery" in verse 18 but rather has the idea of "hidden things." However, the meaning is not really very different.

Darkness . . . light: the reference to **darkness** is merely a continuation of the same thought as above. Even those things that are in the darkest places are not unnoticed by God. The contrast between darkness and light is a common theme throughout Scripture. The Aramaic expression translated by RSV as **the light dwells with him** may be understood to mean that God is surrounded by light (TEV; compare Exo 24.17 and Psa 104.2) or that he is the source of light (compare Isa 60.19). In either case this affirmation should be seen in the context of the previous line. God knows what is in the darkness, because he is inseparable from the light (compare Psa 139.12).

2.23

RSV	TEV
To thee, O God of my fathers, I give thanks and praise, for thou hast given me wisdom and strength, and hast now made known to me what we asked of thee, for thou hast made known to us the king's matter."	I praise you and honor you, God of my ancestors. You have given me wisdom and strength; you have answered my prayer and shown us what to tell the king."

Thee . . . thou: at this point Daniel shifts from indirect to direct address and is now speaking more intimately to God. See the comments at the end of verse 20 with regard to the pronouns referring to God in Daniel's prayer.

O God of my fathers: the use of the vocative **O** will be unnecessary in many languages. And the word translated **fathers** in RSV really refers to the entire line of preceding generations. For this reason it should probably be translated "ancestors" (as in TEV, FRCL, NRSV, and others). In those languages where the expression "the God of my ancestors" might imply that Daniel did not share the same God, some adjustment must be made, possibly "O my God and the God of my ancestors" or something similar.

Give thanks and praise: here the two verbs reinforce each other, but the first carries the particular sense of expressing gratitude, and it is good to bring this out in the translation.

For: this shows the reason for the praise and thanks offered. In other languages it may be translated "because."

Me . . . me . . . we . . . us: it is important to maintain the distinction between the singular (referring only to Daniel) and plural pronouns (referring to Daniel and his three companions but excluding the hearer). This corresponds precisely to the story as it is told in the earlier verses. All four men prayed (verse 18), but the revelation was given to Daniel (verse 19). Yet, at the end of Daniel's recorded prayer, it becomes clear that at least some degree of revelation came to the other men as well. Nevertheless it would be a mistake to follow TEV by translating "my prayer" instead of "our prayer" at this point.

The king's matter: this may have to be filled out in certain languages. It refers, of course, to the whole problem of Nebuchadnezzar's dream and the inability of his advisors to provide the interpretation. However, translators should be careful not to say too much at this point. NEB has "what the king is concerned to know," while REB says "you have given us the answer for the king." NJB speaks of "the king's problem."

Daniel explains the dream: 2.24-45

RSV	TEV
	Daniel Tells the King the Dream and Explains It
24 Therefore Daniel went in to Arioch, whom the king had appointed to destroy the wise men of Babylon; he went and said thus to him, "Do not destroy the wise men of Babylon; bring me in before the king, and I will show the king the interpretation."	24 So Daniel went to Arioch, whom the king had commanded to execute the royal advisers. He said to him, "Don't put them to death. Take me to the king, and I will tell him what his dream means."
25 Then Arioch brought in Daniel before the king in haste, and said thus to him: "I have found among the exiles from Judah a man who can make known to the king the interpretation." 26 The king said to Daniel, whose name was Belteshazzar, "Are you able to make known to me the dream that I have seen and its interpretation?" 27 Daniel an-	25 At once Arioch took Daniel into King Nebuchadnezzar's presence and told the king, "I have found one of the Jewish exiles who can tell Your Majesty the meaning of your dream." 26 The king said to Daniel (who was also called Belteshazzar), "Can you tell me what I dreamed and what it means?" 27 Daniel replied, "Your Majesty, there is no wizard, magician, fortuneteller, or astrol-

swered the king, "No wise men, enchanters, magicians, or astrologers can show to the king the mystery which the king has asked, 28 but there is a God in heaven who reveals mysteries, and he has made known to King Nebuchadnezzar what will be in the latter days. Your dream and the visions of your head as you lay in bed are these: 29 To you, O king, as you lay in bed came thoughts of what would be hereafter, and he who reveals mysteries made known to you what is to be. 30 But as for me, not because of any wisdom that I have more than all the living has this mystery been revealed to me, but in order that the interpretation may be made known to the king, and that you may know the thoughts of your mind. 31 "You saw, O king, and behold, a great image. This image, mighty and of exceeding brightness, stood before you, and its appearance was frightening. 32 The head of this image was of fine gold, its breast and arms of silver, its belly and thighs of bronze, 33 its legs of iron, its feet partly of iron and partly of clay. 34 As you looked, a stone was cut out by no human hand, and it smote the image on its feet of iron and clay, and broke them in pieces; 35 then the iron, the clay, the bronze, the silver, and the gold, all together were broken in pieces, and became like the chaff of the summer threshing floors; and the wind carried them away, so that not a trace of them could be found. But the stone that struck the image became a great mountain and filled the whole earth. 36 "This was the dream; now we will tell the king its interpretation. 37 You, O king, the king of kings, to whom the God of heaven has given the kingdom, the power, and the might, and the glory, 38 and into whose hand he has given, wherever they dwell, the sons of men, the beasts of the field, and the birds of the air, making you rule over them all—you are the head of gold. 39 After you shall arise another kingdom inferior to you, and yet a third kingdom of bronze, which shall rule over all the earth. 40 And there shall be a fourth kingdom, strong as iron, because iron breaks to pieces and shatters all things; and like iron which crushes, it shall break and crush all these. 41 And as you saw the feet and toes partly of potter's clay and partly of iron, it shall be a divided kingdom; but some of the firmness of iron shall be in it, just as you saw iron mixed with the miry clay. 42 And as the toes of the feet were partly iron and partly clay, so the kingdom shall be partly strong and

oger who can tell you that. 28 But there is a God in heaven, who reveals mysteries. He has informed Your Majesty what will happen in the future. Now I will tell you the dream, the vision you had while you were asleep.

29 "While Your Majesty was sleeping, you dreamed about the future; and God, who reveals mysteries, showed you what is going to happen. 30 Now, this mystery was revealed to me, not because I am wiser than anyone else, but so that Your Majesty may learn the meaning of your dream and understand the thoughts that have come to you.

31 "Your Majesty, in your vision you saw standing before you a giant statue, bright and shining, and terrifying to look at. 32 Its head was made of the finest gold; its chest and arms were made of silver; its waist and hips of bronze, 33 its legs of iron, and its feet partly of iron and partly of clay. 34 While you were looking at it, a great stone broke loose from a cliff without anyone touching it, struck the iron and clay feet of the statue, and shattered them. 35 At once the iron, clay, bronze, silver, and gold crumbled and became like the dust on a threshing place in summer. The wind carried it all away, leaving not a trace. But the stone grew to be a mountain that covered the whole earth.

36 "This was the dream. Now I will tell Your Majesty what it means. 37 Your Majesty, you are the greatest of all kings. The God of heaven has made you emperor and given you power, might, and honor. 38 He has made you ruler of all the inhabited earth and ruler over all the animals and birds. You are the head of gold. 39 After you there will be another empire, not as great as yours, and after that a third, an empire of bronze, which will rule the whole earth. 40 And then there will be a fourth empire, as strong as iron, which shatters and breaks everything. And just as iron shatters everything, it will shatter and crush all the earlier empires. 41 You also saw that the feet and the toes were partly clay and partly iron. This means that it will be a divided empire. It will have something of the strength of iron, because there was iron mixed with the clay. 42 The toes—partly iron and partly clay—mean that part of the empire will be strong and part of it weak. 43 You also saw that the iron was mixed with the clay. This means that the rulers of that empire will try to unite their families by intermarriage, but they will not be able to, any more than iron can mix with clay. 44 At the time of those

partly brittle. 43 As you saw the iron mixed with miry clay, so they will mix with one another in marriage, but they will not hold together, just as iron does not mix with clay. 44 And in the days of those kings the God of heaven will set up a kingdom which shall never be destroyed, nor shall its sovereignty be left to another people. It shall break in pieces all these kingdoms and bring them to an end, and it shall stand for ever; 45 just as you saw that a stone was cut from a mountain by no human hand, and that it broke in pieces the iron, the bronze, the clay, the silver, and the gold. A great God has made known to the king what shall be hereafter. The dream is certain, and its interpretation sure."

rulers the God of heaven will establish a kingdom that will never end. It will never be conquered, but will completely destroy all those empires and then last forever. 45 You saw how a stone broke loose from a cliff without anyone touching it and how it struck the statue made of iron, bronze, clay, silver, and gold. The great God is telling Your Majesty what will happen in the future. I have told you exactly what you dreamed, and have given you its true meaning."

TEV Section Heading: Daniel tells the king the dream and explains it.

Another possible way to sum up the content of this section may be to say "Daniel does what the king wants" or "Daniel describes and explains the dream."

2.24	RSV	TEV

Therefore Daniel went in to Arioch, whom the king had appointed to destroy the wise men of Babylon; he went and said thus to him, "Do not destroy the wise men of Babylon; bring me in before the king, and I will show the king the interpretation."

So Daniel went to Arioch, whom the king had commanded to execute the royal advisers. He said to him, "Don't put them to death. Take me to the king, and I will tell him what his dream means."

Therefore: literally "Because of all that." The majority of the English versions simply translate "So . . ." or "Therefore . . . ." But AB begins this verse with "Accordingly . . . ." In translation it will be important to use whatever transition word naturally fits this context, showing a logical relationship of cause and effect.

Went in . . . went: the use of these two verbs that are very similar in meaning may be considered redundant, and the two can easily be reduced to one without changing the meaning of the text. In fact some ancient Greek manuscripts omit "went in," and this is followed by NEB and certain other modern versions.

Whom the king had appointed . . .: some translations (GECL, for example) do not give this information here in this verse, since it is given in verses 12-14 above. But because this is the beginning of a new section, and also because of the distance from the previous section, it is probably not harmful to state it once again in this context.

Do not destroy . . . : compare verse 12, where the original command to destroy the wise men of Babylon was given.

The entire direct quotation in this verse may be better rendered indirectly in some languages. The translation will then read something like "He (Daniel) asked Arioch not to kill the wise men . . . , but to take him to the king so that he could give the interpretation of the dream."

Bring me in before the king: if this is a part of a direct quotation, there will be various ways of making it sound natural, depending on the usage of the translator's language. Some may say, for example, "take me into the presence of the king," or "allow me to speak to the king," or "permit me to see the king."

I will show the king the interpretation: instead of the verb **show** it will be much better in most languages to find a verb that is more appropriate to the context, such as "tell," "explain," "reveal" or "interpret." And instead of **the king** it may be better in some cases to use the object pronoun "him."

2.25	RSV	TEV
	Then Arioch brought in Daniel before the king in haste, and said thus to him: "I have found among the exiles from Judah a man who can make known to the king the interpretation."	At once Arioch took Daniel into King Nebuchadnezzar's presence and told the king, "I have found one of the Jewish exiles who can tell Your Majesty the meaning of your dream."

Then Arioch brought in Daniel . . . in haste: the words used here carry the idea of an action performed eagerly and in a hurry. Some versions use words like "immediately," "quickly" (NAB), or "at once" (TEV and NIV). AB begins this verse "Rushing excitedly . . . ." NJB translates "lost no time . . . ." NEB, on the other hand, takes it to mean "in great trepidation," but this interpretation is not recommended.

Among the exiles from Judah: literally "among the sons of the removed of Judah." Some other ways of saying this may be "among those brought here from Judah" or "among the Jewish exiles" (REB). Translators should also be careful of the structure of this verse. It is possible that this secondary information about Daniel will have to be made a separate sentence and placed after the main message to the king. It may be possible to say, for example, "I have found someone who can interpret your dream. He is one of those Jewish exiles."

To the king: within the direct quotation it will be more natural in most cases to use the pronoun in place of the noun, "to you."

The interpretation: we know, of course, that the interpretation is of the troublesome dream that is at the center of the whole story. But in some languages it may be desirable to state this clearly.

2.26   RSV   TEV

The king said to Daniel, whose name was Belteshazzar, "Are you able to make known to me the dream that I have seen and its interpretation?"	The king said to Daniel (who was also called Belteshazzar), "Can you tell me what I dreamed and what it means?"

Said: literally "answering said." See verse 5. Since what follows is a question in this case, it may be advisable to follow the model of REB and use the verb "asked . . . ."

Whose name was Belteshazzar: see 1.7. Since this is a second name, the translation may well add a word like "also" (compare TEV and NIV). Another possibility is to follow the GECL model by saying something like "whose Babylonian name was Belteshazzar." Or in some cases translators may prefer to say "whose other name was Belteshazzar."

Are you able . . . ? The king's question is not simply a request for information. It is more likely an expression of serious doubt. For this reason it has been suggested that a good translation may add the word "really" (compare NJV and FRCL), which better expresses this element of doubt. NJV has "Can you really make known . . . ?"

The dream that I have seen and its interpretation: instead of using the nouns **dream** and **interpretation**, it will be better in some languages to change these into verbal expressions, as in TEV. But it is important to maintain the two distinct ideas of (a) the content of the dream and (b) its significance.

2.27   RSV   TEV

Daniel answered the king, "No wise men, enchanters, magicians, or astrologers can show to the king the mystery which the king has asked,	Daniel replied, "Your Majesty, there is no wizard, magician, fortuneteller, or astrologer who can tell you that.

Answered: literally "answered saying" as in verse 5 and other verses.

Wise men, enchanters, magicians, or astrologers: compare verse 2, where the list is slightly different. The first word in this list is the same as **wise men** in verse 12. The fourth is not used previously in Daniel; however, it does occur again in 4.7; 5.7, 11.

The king: here again Daniel refers to Nebuchadnezzar in the third person (as in verse 10 above), and this is in keeping with what is natural in Aramaic. But translators should make sure that their rendering of this expression is natural in their language. This will probably mean using the second person singular pronoun "you."

2.28 RSV TEV

but there is a God in heaven who reveals mysteries, and he has made known to King Nebuchadnezzar what will be in the latter days. Your dream and the visions of your head as you lay in bed are these:	But there is a God in heaven, who reveals mysteries. He has informed Your Majesty what will happen in the future. Now I will tell you the dream, the vision you had while you were asleep.

There is a God in heaven: this is the same as the expression used in verse 18 except for the addition of the preposition **in** here. It clearly refers to the true God in both cases. But in some languages a literal rendering of these words will probably not be understood in this way. Translators should insure that the reference is to the true God in their language. Some versions invert the order to say "But there is in heaven a God . . ." (REB).

He has made known . . . : the verb form used here may give the wrong impression that God has already made the meaning of the dream known to Nebuchadnezzar. But this is clearly not the case. While it was already known to Daniel, the king was still unaware of its meaning. For this reason the verb in at least two English versions is in the present tense: "he discloses" (Mft) and "he makes known" (AT). FRCL likewise adopts the present tense. In some languages a near future tense may be more appropriate: "he is about to make known . . . ," or a benefactive verb form such as "he has made known to me for you (or your majesty) . . . ." Or, restructuring more radically but maintaining the past tense, translators may want to consider "the purpose of the dream was to inform Your Majesty of what will happen . . . ."

To King Nebuchadnezzar: once again Daniel refers to the king indirectly, even though he is speaking to him. The polite indirect reference in this case includes the proper name, but in many languages this will be replaced by the pronoun "you" in order to make it sound more natural.

In the latter days: the Aramaic words used here correspond to the common Hebrew expression (Hos 3.5; Isa 2.2; Dan 10.14) and are normally taken as a reference to the end time. So it has been translated "at the end of this age" (NEB/REB) or "in the final days" (NJB). Other versions, however, use less precise terminology. Compare "in the future" (TEV) and "in days to come" (NAB and NIV).

Your dream and the visions of your head as you lay in bed: the use of the two terms **dream** and **visions** does not indicate two separate and distinct revelations. Rather these two terms together are a way of describing the one revelation that the king received. The second expression is in apposition with the first. With slight alterations the three elements **visions**, **head**, and **bed** are repeated in 4.5, 10, 13 (Aramaic 4.2, 7, 10); 7.1, 15.

2.29 RSV	TEV
To you, O king, as you lay in bed came thoughts of what would be hereafter, and he who reveals mysteries made known to you what is to be.	"While Your Majesty was sleeping, you dreamed about the future; and God, who reveals mysteries, showed you what is going to happen.

Note that this verse has been restructured by TEV, so that instead of **To you . . . came thoughts**, the form is more logical and natural in English: "you dreamed . . . ." In fact, placing the pronoun at the beginning seems to emphasize the contrast between the king as the receiver of the form of the revelation and Daniel as the receiver of its meaning. But translators should consider what is the most natural way of expressing this contrast in their own language without blindly following some other version. Some versions have "As for you" here and "as for me" at the beginning of the following verse. (Compare also NAB and AB: "To you . . . To me . . . .")

O king: once again the Semitic formula for indicating respect will probably have to be translated differently in many languages. Compare "Your Majesty" in TEV and NJB. See also 2.4.

What would be hereafter: while this expression is somewhat weaker than "what will be in the latter days" (in verse 28), it refers to essentially the same thing and may have to be translated the same way in some languages.

He who reveals mysteries: compare verses 18, 22, and 28. If necessary for the sake of clarity, translators may say "God, who reveals mysteries."

Made known to you what is to be: AT has "makes known . . ." (see the comments on the verb form in the previous verse).

2.30 RSV	TEV
But as for me, not because of any wisdom that I have more than all the living has this mystery been revealed to me, but in order that the interpretation may be made known to the king, and that you may know the thoughts of your mind.	Now, this mystery was revealed to me, not because I am wiser than anyone else, but so that Your Majesty may learn the meaning of your dream and understand the thoughts that have come to you.

The structure of this verse may have to be radically altered in some languages. The verse contains three main elements:

     (1) the central affirmation of God's revelation;

     (2) a denial of any special powers in Daniel himself; and

     (3) a statement of the purpose of the revelation.

In RSV, as in Aramaic, the order is 2-1-3, but in many other versions sensitive to the language of translation, the order is 1-2-3 or 1-3-2. Translators should be careful to see to it that the most natural structure possible is adopted.

The conjunction translated as **But** in RSV may possibly be left untranslated; but it is very probable that there is a rather strong contrast intended between the king and Daniel, indicated by the structure of the Aramaic, which has the pronoun "you" standing in a prominent position in verse 29, and "I" in a prominent position in this verse. See comments on the previous verse.

As for me: this is an attempt to reflect the fact that the pronoun **me** is given a prominent position in the text. In some languages this may be handled by beginning the sentence "It was to me that God revealed . . ."; but in others this would be an artificially contrived structure. If this is the case, it will be better to put the object in its proper place after the verb.

That the interpretation may be made known: this passive formulation will have to be made active in many languages. It should also be noted that there is a subtle difference in meaning between this expression and the one that follows (**that you may know the thoughts of your mind**). Here the focus is on the more objective explanation of the dream while the following expression involves the king's subjective reaction to it.

The king: "Your Majesty" in TEV. Again the formula for respect used when speaking to royalty should probably be translated by the pronoun "you" in many languages.

The thoughts of your mind: literally "the thoughts of your heart." In Semitic thought the heart is often seen as the seat of intelligence rather than of emotion (see comments on "resolved" in 1.8). This is why most English versions use the word "mind" rather than translating literally "heart."

2.31	RSV	TEV
	"You saw, O king, and behold, a great image. This image, mighty and of exceeding brightness, stood before you, and its appearance was frightening.	"Your Majesty, in your vision you saw standing before you a giant statue, bright and shining, and terrifying to look at.

You saw: this verb is repeated throughout the explanation of the dream (verses 34, 41, 43, and 45) and is a feature of the literary technique of the writer. Unless it is clumsy in the receptor language, the repetition should be retained.

O king: see verse 29.

And behold: the Aramaic interjection translated by these words in RSV is omitted by most modern English versions. Some translators attempt to capture the effect of this element by the use of an exclamation mark at the end of the sentence (see Mft, for example). It is probably better left untranslated in most languages, unless there is a natural way of expressing such an element of surprise and amazement at something that is seen.

Image: the English word may be misleading, since it can refer to any sort of likeness, whether in two dimensions (drawings, photographs) or in three dimensions. Here the likeness is in three dimensions, and the term is better translated "statue" as in the majority of English versions (including NRSV).

There is no hint in the text that the statue was an idol; so words having this meaning should be avoided. In some languages there are different words for statues carved of wood and those made of ceramic material or metal. Since this statue was made mostly of a variety of metals but partially of ceramic material, it will probably be better to use the term that refers to metal objects, if such a distinction is required by the language.

The description of the statue emphasizes two main characteristics at the same time. It is both magnificent and terrifying. The terms **great** and **mighty** and **of exceeding brightness** stress the magnificence of the statue. But the word **frightening** indicates that it also caused great fear. The text also indicates that the giant statue was standing in front of the king. The word **mighty** may be misunderstood as referring to physical strength, but the term used here clearly refers to size.

2.32-33 RSV TEV

RSV	TEV
32 The head of this image was of fine gold, its breast and arms of silver, its belly and thighs of bronze, 33 its legs of iron, its feet partly of iron and partly of clay.	32 Its head was made of the finest gold; its chest and arms were made of silver; its waist and hips of bronze, 33 its legs of iron, and its feet partly of iron and partly of clay.

These two verses consist mainly of the names of body parts and of different kinds of metals. The names of the body parts usually present few problems except for the distinction between **thighs**, **legs**, and **feet**. In some languages a single word normally includes all three of these. In order to distinguish them it may be necessary to say something like "upper leg," "lower leg," and "the bottom (or end) of the leg."

Fine gold: in those cultures where the refining of metals is well known, there will be special terms for the purest form of gold. If such concepts are known it will be appropriate to use that terminology in this case.

The words for the various metals may be impossible to translate in some languages without recourse to borrowing foreign words for **gold**, **silver**, **bronze**, and **iron**. Or in some cases it may be necessary to attempt to show the differences by reference to the relative value or strength of the different metals. In that case **gold** can be "the most precious metal"; **silver** can be "another very precious metal," **bronze** "a less precious metal," and **iron** "an ordinary metal." In verse 40 it becomes clear that the strength of iron is as important as its value. So it may be wise to translate **iron** here as "a very strong metal." The word translated **bronze** may possibly mean "copper" (see NEB note, "*Or* copper"), so translators should not be unduly worried if they have to translate it that way.

Clay: the Aramaic term used here probably indicates ceramic material or baked earth rather than clay, which would seem to refer only to the raw

material used to make ceramic objects. If a language distinguishes between raw clay and baked clay, the latter should be used in translation here. NAB translates "tile," NIV "baked clay," and AB has "terra cotta."

Some commentators describe the combination of iron and clay as ceramic decoration on a basic metal structure, but others think it was a ceramic object covered with metal plates. In fact we do not know how the iron and ceramic material were thought of as being joined. And the translator should try to avoid giving such details. It was, in fact, only what was seen in a dream— which does not lend itself to the logical analysis of material reality.

2.34	RSV	TEV
	As you looked, a stone was cut out by no human hand, and it smote the image on its feet of iron and clay, and broke them in pieces;	While you were looking at it, a great stone broke loose from a cliff without anyone touching it, struck the iron and clay feet of the statue, and shattered them.

As you looked: that is, while he was looking at the statue. In some languages it may be wise to add this information. NIV has "While you were watching . . . ."

A stone: some manuscript evidence adds ". . . from a mountain." (See NAB, NEB/REB, and AT; TEV has "from a cliff.") This information certainly belongs in the larger context (compare verse 45). But in this verse it is probably a scribal addition based on the later verse. It is, however, found in the ancient Greek version. If the receptor language requires this for the sake of clarity, then it may be inserted here. In those languages that have the same term for a small stone and a large rock or boulder, the term used here should be modified in such a way as to indicate that it was very large, more like a boulder.

Was cut out: this passive form must be made active in many languages. It may be rendered "separate" or "become detached." NJB has "broke away," although this may suggest something accidental. The problem is that there is no apparent human cause, but the context implies that there was divine involvement.

By no human hand: here the writer suggests the intervention of God without actually stating it. Other languages may have to say "with no human assistance" or "without the help of any person." See also verse 45.

Broke them in pieces: this expression, which is repeated several times in the Aramaic section of Daniel, may be rendered "shattered," "splintered," or "fragmented."

2.35 RSV	TEV
then the iron, the clay, the bronze, the silver, and the gold, all together were broken in pieces, and became like the chaff of the summer threshing floors; and the wind carried them away, so that not a trace of them could be found. But the stone that struck the image became a great mountain and filled the whole earth.	At once the iron, clay, bronze, silver, and gold crumbled and became like the dust on a threshing place in summer. The wind carried it all away, leaving not a trace. But the stone grew to be a mountain that covered the whole earth.

Here the order of the materials of which the statue was made is modified. It is, in fact, the reverse of what is given in verses 32 and 33, so that the reader now has the impression of looking from bottom to top rather than from top to bottom. Perhaps this is to give a picture of the statue crumbling from the point where it was first struck, "its feet."

All together: literally "as one." Some versions translate "all at once" (NAB) in the sense of "at the same time" (NIV). Most have just "all."

Like the chaff of the summer threshing floors: this image presents numerous difficulties to the translator. In the areas of the world where the seasons of the year do not correspond to those of temperate climates, **summer** may have to be translated something like "after the harvest." Or in some cases it may even have to be left out. The **threshing floor** is the place where people fan the grain in order to get rid of the waste materials that cannot be eaten. The word translated **chaff** is used figuratively and emphasizes the fineness of the pieces into which the statue was broken. In some cases it may be necessary to do away with this figure altogether and say something like "were crushed into a very fine powder."

Not a trace of them could be found: the passive here can be adjusted to say "so that no one could find a trace of them" or "until no trace of them remained." Possibly the TEV model will be helpful in some languages: "leaving not a trace."

But: the Aramaic has only the common conjunction that may be translated "and" or "but." In this context it is probably better to retain **But**, since there seems to be an indication that what follows is unexpected.

Became: NJB provides a better model for some languages, with "grew into . . ." (as in NEB/REB).

Filled the whole earth: the use of the verb "fill" is perhaps not the most precise in this context, since it may give the idea of filling a container. Some other models are "covered the whole earth" (TEV) or "occupying the whole world."

2.36 RSV TEV

"This was the dream; now we will tell the king its interpretation.

"This was the dream. Now I will tell Your Majesty what it means.

This . . . : the demonstrative pronoun refers to all that Daniel has said in verses 31-35. In some languages it may be preferable to say "What I have said up to this point is the actual dream" or "Now I have finished telling you the content of your dream." NEB has "That was the dream," and Mft reads "Such was the dream."

We: the use of the first person plural at this point is surprising. Four different explanations have been proposed:

   a) that this is a royal "we" or plural of majesty; but this hardly suits the context of Daniel before the king;
   b) that "we" refers to Daniel and his three friends; but it is quite likely that the three friends were not present during this conversation with Nebuchadnezzar;
   c) that "we" refers to Daniel and God; but this does not fit the style of Daniel who would have been more likely to say, "God (through me) will give the interpretation";
   d) that "we" is a kind of plural of modesty, a way of showing the humility of the speaker; this allows the speaker to avoid the use of "I," which may be understood as pretentious or a kind of boasting.

While it is impossible to be certain, the last of these four explanations seems most likely. In some languages it may be possible to avoid either pronoun by using an impersonal turn of phrase (for example, a passive in those languages that use such forms naturally). Others may want to consider showing Daniel's dependence on divine help by saying "with the help of God I will tell you . . . ." If the pronoun "we" is used, it should be exclusive of the hearer in those languages that make such distinctions.

The king: this is yet another indirect reference that is probably better translated as a second person singular pronoun (see verse 7).

2.37 RSV TEV

You, O king, the king of kings, to whom the God of heaven has given the kingdom, the power, and the might, and the glory,

Your Majesty, you are the greatest of all kings. The God of heaven has made you emperor and given you power, might, and honor.

O king: or "Your Majesty." See verses 4, 29, and 31.

The king of kings: this is a Semitic equivalent of the superlative in English. (Compare, for example, "Song of Songs," meaning "The most beautiful of all songs," or "the Holy of Holies" for "the Holiest Place of All.") An equivalent expression may be "the supreme chief" or "the greatest of all kings" (FRCL as well as TEV).

The God of heaven: see verse 18.

Has given the kingdom: the kingship of Nebuchadnezzar comes from God and not from the divine nature that he claims (see chapter 3). Another way of saying this is "God . . . has made you king" or ". . . has permitted you to rule." It will be noted that TEV uses the word "emperor" here and "empire" in verses 39-43. But it then reverts to "kingdom" in verse 44. Translators should be aware that the same term is used in all these cases in Aramaic.

The power, the might: these two terms mean practically the same thing, and it is legitimate, when all else fails, to translate them as a single word (as GECL has done). If we attempt to reflect the slight difference between them, the first seems to evoke more the idea of physical strength while the second has to do more with moral strength.

Glory: this is the same word that is translated "honor" in verse 6.

2.38	RSV	TEV

RSV	TEV
and into whose hand he has given, wherever they dwell, the sons of men, the beasts of the field, and the birds of the air, making you rule over them all—you are the head of gold.	He has made you ruler of all the inhabited earth and ruler over all the animals and birds. You are the head of gold.

While this verse is a continuation of the sentence started in the previous verse, it is probably better to begin a new sentence here, as in TEV.

Hand: as seen in 1.2, this word carries the idea of power or authority. According to Daniel, God had made Nebuchadnezzar the ruler of the known world. A literal translation of **hand** will therefore be unlikely to convey the meaning in many languages. Mft translates "into your power."

Wherever they dwell: this expression emphasizes the all-inclusive scope of the king's rule. Such a statement may fit more naturally at the end of the list that follows, rather than here at the beginning.

The sons of men: this Semitic expression refers to all of humanity, since the words "sons of . . ." merely indicate membership in a group (see 1.6). It is not limited either to the younger generation or to the male sex, as the word "sons" may suggest.

Beasts of the field: this refers to all the animals living on the earth, especially those wild animals that are not yet submissive to human domination as the domestic animals are. In certain languages the choice of the noun for **beasts** will make the words **of the field** unnecessary. REB translates simply "wild animals."

Birds of the air: this includes all birds. The words **of the air** will probably be unnecessary in most languages, since this is a Semiticism. The Greek version adds "and the fish of the sea," which often follows "the birds of the air" in Scripture. But no version consulted adopts this reading.

The above list is intended to express the idea of the universal domination of the king over all creation and not merely over certain categories of beings. Translators are advised to avoid giving the impression of any restriction and should probably retain the three categories (human beings, animals, and birds).

Making you rule over them all: this should not suggest that the king is forced to rule against his will. In some languages it will be better to say "allowing you to rule over them all" or "giving you the right to rule . . . ."

You are the head of gold: this corresponds to the first part of the dream in verse 32. To be clearly understood, it may be wise to reword this in some languages, saying "you are like the head of gold in the dream" or "that head of gold represents (or symbolizes, or stands for) you."

2.39 RSV TEV

After you shall arise another kingdom inferior to you, and yet a third kingdom of bronze, which shall rule over all the earth.	After you there will be another empire, not as great as yours, and after that a third, an empire of bronze, which will rule the whole earth.

After you: in some languages it may be necessary to say "After you are gone" or "When you are no longer ruling."

Inferior to you: that is, inferior to your kingdom. Another way of saying this is "another ruler who is not as great [or strong] as you" or "another kingdom that is more limited (less powerful) than yours."

Another kingdom . . . and yet a third kingdom: the style used in this verse leaves out certain elements and may have to be filled in a bit. While the text does not actually say so, it is clear that the second kingdom is symbolized by the silver part of the statue, which is inferior to the gold part. And the **kingdom of bronze** is unquestionably inferior to the second kingdom, as bronze is inferior to silver. So this may have to be stated in some cases.

All the earth is probably an exaggeration, but in the context of this type of vision, it may be translated literally in many languages. It may represent all the people of the earth that were known to the writer of this book.

2.40 RSV TEV

And there shall be a fourth kingdom, strong as iron, because iron breaks to pieces and shatters all things; and like iron which crushes, it shall break and crush all these.	And then there will be a fourth empire, as strong as iron, which shatters and breaks everything. And just as iron shatters everything, it will shatter and crush all the earlier empires.

The word for **iron** occurs three times in this verse, making the RSV rendering heavy. In many languages it will make for smoother reading to reduce this to one or two at the most.

The three verbs that describe the action of iron mean more or less the same (**breaks, shatters,** and **crushes**). It is not necessary for the translator to try to find an exact equivalent for each one of them, since it is the overall effect, rather than the slight differences of meaning, that is important. Furthermore, the parenthetical phrase **and like iron which crushes** is not found in several ancient versions. If it proves difficult to find three similar verbs in the language, it will be sufficient to use two. But if one wishes to retain the style of the ancient text, it is probably unwise to reduce the three to one (although this is done by GECL).

All these: most probably this means "all the earlier kingdoms" (NJB; compare also TEV) or "all the kingdoms that went before it." NEB follows a different assumption about the original text, with "the whole earth," but this is reversed by REB and is not recommended.

2.41   RSV   TEV

And as you saw the feet and toes partly of potter's clay and partly of iron, it shall be a divided kingdom; but some of the firmness of iron shall be in it, just as you saw iron mixed with the miry clay.	You also saw that the feet and the toes were partly clay and partly iron. This means that it will be a divided empire. It will have something of the strength of iron, because there was iron mixed with the clay.

Commentators often feel that verses 41-44 are cluttered with needless repetition. In these four verses **toes**, which were not mentioned earlier, complicate the figure of speech. Also some kind of clay is mentioned seven times. But it is difficult to see any particular significance in the various terms used, and many languages will not have the resources to make such distinctions.

As you saw the feet and toes partly of potter's clay and partly of iron: all this forms a single subordinate clause in Aramaic. For stylistic reasons it may be better in some languages to break it into two shorter units and make a separate sentence of it. For example, "As you have noticed, the feet and toes of the statue are made partly of ceramic and partly of iron."

The word for **clay** or "baked clay" (NIV) is qualified in the original by "of potter." Depending on the word chosen for **clay**, it may be possible to leave this out. On the translation of the idea of **clay**, see verse 33. But a different word is used here. The RSV **miry clay** at the end of the verse seems to focus on the watery character of clay that has not yet been baked or fired, and this is not at all the intent of the writer. It is probably best not to try to distinguish between what the RSV calls **potter's clay** and **miry clay**.

And toes: these words are omitted by some modern versions (NJB) because they are not in some ancient Aramaic texts. However, HOTTP recommends that translators follow the longer text that includes these words. In some languages, however, it may be awkward and unnecessarily redundant to mention the toes, since they would be clearly understood as being included in the word **feet**. If this is the case, the words **and toes** may be left out—for translation reasons rather than for textual reasons.

It shall be . . . : although it is not stated in the text at this point, this is still a part of the explanation of the dream. For this reason TEV adds "This means that . . ." (compare also NAB). This is probably a good model for most other languages to follow.

A divided kingdom: another way of saying this is "will not be united" or "will lack unity." As the end of the verse demonstrates, it is not a question of a separation into several parts but of internal tension. Just as clay and iron do not mix well, so this kingdom will lack cohesion and unity.

2.42	RSV	TEV

And as the toes of the feet were partly iron and partly clay, so the kingdom shall be partly strong and partly brittle.

The toes—partly iron and partly clay—mean that part of the empire will be strong and part of it weak.

The toes of the feet: depending on the kind of word used for **toes**, the reference to **feet** may be omitted as redundant. But in some languages the same word is used for "toes" and "fingers," and in such cases, the words **of the feet** may be important.

The kingdom: in some cases it may be clearer to say "this kingdom" or "the fourth kingdom," since other kingdoms have been mentioned in this context.

Brittle: the word used here clearly stands in opposition to **strong**. In English the word **brittle** is usually reserved for physical objects and rarely applied to abstract ideas such as **kingdom**. But this context calls for a word that can be used for both abstract ideas and physical objects. In some languages the best alternative here may be simply the negation of the previous word, "not strong." Some other possible models are "fragile" (NAB) and "weak" (TEV).

2.43	RSV	TEV

As you saw the iron mixed with miry clay, so they will mix with one another in marriage,[b] but they will not hold together, just as iron does not mix with clay.

You also saw that the iron was mixed with the clay. This means that the rulers of that empire will try to unite their families by intermarriage, but they will not be able to, any more than iron can mix with clay.

[b] Aramaic *by the seed of men*

In this verse, as in verse 41, it may be well to remind the reader that this is a part of the interpretation, by saying something like "This means . . . ," following the TEV model.

Miry clay: the idea here is "baked clay of the earth." While some versions have "muddy clay" (AT and Mft), others translate "clay tile" (NJB), "common clay" (NEB and NJV), or simply "clay" (TEV, NRSV, and REB). The emphasis here seems to be on the ordinariness and weakness of the material used. See the comments on verse 41 above.

They: the third person plural pronoun most likely here refers to the kings or rulers of the empire. This is probably a reference to the intermarriage of the Ptolemies and the Seleucids in 194 B.C. However, NEB and NIV seem to take it more generally as referring to "men" or "people."

Mix with one another in marriage: literally "will mix themselves with the seed of men" (compare KJV). This is a kind of veiled reference to attempts at political alliances by intermarriage between ruling families. In order to avoid misunderstanding it will probably be necessary to follow one of the following models of translation: "try to unite their kingdoms through marriage," "join together by marriage between opposing families," "seal their alliances by intermarriage" (NAB), or "shall intermarry in that kingdom" (Mft).

But they will not hold together: other ways of saying this are "but these alliances will not be stable," "their coming together will not last," or "but they shall not stay united" (NAB). Stated in another way without using negative forms, this may be "but they will fall apart."

2.44   RSV   TEV

And in the days of those kings the God of heaven will set up a kingdom which shall never be destroyed, nor shall its sovereignty be left to another people. It shall break in pieces all these kingdoms and bring them to an end, and it shall stand for ever;	At the time of those rulers the God of heaven will establish a kingdom that will never end. It will never be conquered, but will completely destroy all those empires and then last forever.

In the days of those kings: AB recommends "in the days of those regimes" rather than ". . . of those kings." But there is very little real difference in meaning in this context. What the writer is probably referring to would be the kings of the last-mentioned kingdoms, those compared to iron and clay.

The God of heaven: see verse 18.

A kingdom: while this does refer to the kingdom of God, translators are not advised to render this "his kingdom" (as GECL has done). This would be too direct and would detract from the deliberately puzzling character of the text. The description of this kingdom should be enough to show that it is fundamentally different from the ones before it.

Which shall never be destroyed: this passive construction may be rendered actively, as in TEV "will never end," or "shall remain forever." In other languages it may be better to say "no power will be strong enough to destroy it."

Nor shall its sovereignty be left to another people: this is another passive that will have to be rendered actively in many languages. Some may say "and no other people will be able to take away its authority" or "no other people will have the strength to dominate it."

Break in pieces: maintaining the image of the stone and the statue, this figure focuses on their total destruction, while **bring them to an end** emphasizes the end of the other kingdoms.

Stand for ever: this emphasizes the permanence of the new kingdom. In some languages it will be necessary to say "endure for all time" or "continue always" or "never end." On the idea of **for ever**, compare verses 4 and 20 earlier in this chapter.

2.45	RSV	TEV

RSV	TEV
just as you saw that a stone was cut from a mountain by no human hand, and that it broke in pieces the iron, the bronze, the clay, the silver, and the gold. A great God has made known to the king what shall be hereafter. The dream is certain, and its interpretation sure."	You saw how a stone broke loose from a cliff without anyone touching it and how it struck the statue made of iron, bronze, clay, silver, and gold. The great God is telling Your Majesty what will happen in the future. I have told you exactly what you dreamed, and have given you its true meaning."

Just as you saw . . . : in many languages it will be clearer to start this verse with something like "That is the meaning of the stone you saw . . ." (NAB) or "This is the meaning of the vision of the rock . . ." (NIV).

A stone was cut from a mountain . . . : see verse 34.

The iron, the bronze, the clay, the silver, and the gold: here again the order of the elements has been changed. But this time the order seems to be random. Some Greek versions have the same order here as in verses 32-33, but this is probably due to a deliberate correction of the original text. The modified order should probably be retained, unless the translator's language has strong reasons for requiring something different. Compare verse 35.

A great God: the RSV rendering reflects the Aramaic original in that there is no definite article here. However, the context ("the God of heaven" in verse 44) justifies the use of the definite article, which almost all other English versions adopt. In some languages, however, there are no definite articles, and translators may say "God, who is great . . . ."

To the king: that is, "to you" or "to your majesty." See verse 7.

The dream is certain and its interpretation is sure: the theme of the content and the meaning of the dream is maintained here. AB renders these words "this is certainly the dream and its interpretation is trustworthy." Another way of saying this in some languages may be "This is exactly what you dreamed, and you can be sure that this (what I have told you) is its meaning." The emphasis is on the absolute certainty of both the form and the meaning of the king's dream.

The king rewards Daniel: 2.46-49

RSV	TEV
	The King Rewards Daniel
46 Then King Nebuchadnezzar fell upon his face, and did homage to Daniel, and commanded that an offering and incense be offered up to him. 47 The king said to Daniel, "Truly, your God is God of gods and Lord of kings, and a revealer of mysteries, for you have been able to reveal this mystery." 48 Then the king gave Daniel high honors and many great gifts, and made him ruler over the whole province of Babylon, and chief prefect over all the wise men of Babylon. 49 Daniel made request of the king, and he appointed Shadrach, Meshach, and Abednego over the affairs of the province of Babylon; but Daniel remained at the king's court.	46 Then King Nebuchadnezzar bowed to the ground and gave orders for sacrifices and offerings to be made to Daniel. 47 The king said, "Your God is the greatest of all gods, the Lord over kings, and the one who reveals mysteries. I know this because you have been able to explain this mystery." 48 Then he gave Daniel a high position, presented him with many splendid gifts, put him in charge of the province of Babylon, and made him the head of all the royal advisers. 49 At Daniel's request the king put Shadrach, Meshach, and Abednego in charge of the affairs of the province of Babylon; Daniel, however, remained at the royal court.

TEV Section Heading: The king rewards Daniel.

Many translations take verses 46-49 as the conclusion of the section that begins in verse 24, and therefore they do not have a section heading at this point. And those that do put a heading here seem to focus on slightly different aspects of the content of the section. While TEV speaks of Daniel alone, NRSV broadens the theme to include his companions: "Daniel and His Friends Promoted." NJB, on the other hand, focuses on "The king's profession of faith" rather than his subsequent action in rewarding the young men.

2.46   RSV   TEV

Then King Nebuchadnezzar fell upon his face, and did homage to Daniel, and commanded that an offering and incense be offered up to him.

Then King Nebuchadnezzar bowed to the ground and gave orders for sacrifices and offerings to be made to Daniel.

Fell upon his face: as in Hebrew, the Aramaic verb "fall" in this context does not indicate an involuntary movement as it does in many languages. Rather it is used of a conscious and deliberate action from a higher to a lower position in order to show submission. For this reason the verb in this phrase is often rendered "bowed down" or "prostrated himself," or something similar.

Did homage to Daniel: or "praised Daniel," or "gave honor to Daniel." NRSV translates "worshiped Daniel." The Aramaic word carries the idea of the humble status of one who bows before a superior to show his submission and obedience. When used with the previous verb ("fall down"), it is not a simple alternative for the physical gesture of bowing down, but adds to it the idea of "doing homage" to a person. Translators are advised to retain the two different verbs whenever possible, with the first focusing on the physical act and the second on the attitude of the person. In certain cases it is possible to use an idiomatic expression. For example, in certain areas there is the practice of taking a bit of earth in the hand and rubbing it on the body after bowing down in order to show submission.

Commanded that an offering and incense be offered up to him: the text speaks of "offerings" in the plural. But the Aramaic word used here does not necessarily mean the sacrifice of an animal. It is also used of a cereal offering (compare Lev 2.2). But it certainly involves things that were eaten, in contrast with **incense**, which was a kind of perfume or sweet-smelling element.

To him: that is, "to Daniel," as indicated in TEV. If the pronoun is retained, translators should make certain that it is understood to refer to Daniel and not to the king himself.

2.47	RSV	TEV
	The king said to Daniel, "Truly, your God is God of gods and Lord of kings, and a revealer of mysteries, for you have been able to reveal this mystery."	The king said, "Your God is the greatest of all gods, the Lord over kings, and the one who reveals mysteries. I know this because you have been able to explain this mystery."

This verse is a brief doxology uttered by none other than a non-Jewish monarch. As such it is said to constitute the climax of the whole story. Translators should consider how climaxes are usually marked in their language and consider using such devices at this point.

Said to Daniel: literally "answered Daniel saying . . . ."

Your God: in some languages it is unacceptable to use the possessive form with the word for God. So it may be wiser to say "the God you worship."

God of gods: as in verse 37 ("King of kings"), this kind of expression is the equivalent to the superlative in English. For this reason some versions have translated "the greatest of all gods," as in TEV. Translators should use whatever form is ordinarily used to express the superlative idea in their language.

Lord of kings: this means that the God worshiped by Daniel is ruler over all earthly kings as well as the greatest of divine beings.

A revealer of mysteries: see verses 28 and 29. The same Aramaic words appear in the last clause of this verse.

For: this transition word indicates the relationship between what the king said previously (about the greatness of God) and what follows. It is because Daniel was able to reveal the meaning of his dream that Nebuchadnezzar became convinced of the greatness of God. So this may be stated directly in the translation if it is not clear otherwise. We may say, as in TEV, "I know this because . . . ," or "that is why you were able . . ." (NAB).

2.48   RSV   TEV

Then the king gave Daniel high honors and many great gifts, and made him ruler over the whole province of Babylon, and chief prefect over all the wise men of Babylon.	Then he gave Daniel a high position, presented him with many splendid gifts, put him in charge of the province of Babylon, and made him the head of all the royal advisers.

Gave Daniel high honors: literally "made Daniel great." But the Aramaic verb denotes a position of honor rather than of political power. The question of political power is dealt with later in the verse.

Many great gifts: the use of the two adjectives suggests respectively the quantity and the quality of the presents given.

Made him ruler over the whole province of Babylon: literally "caused him to rule . . . ." While the original has only one verb here, it is applied to two distinct positions. Daniel is firstly made ruler over the province of Babylon, and he is also made **chief prefect**, or superintendent, over the entire group of royal advisors. The term used here should fit the term that occurs in 3.2; see comments there.

2.49   RSV   TEV

Daniel made request of the king, and he appointed Shadrach, Meshach, and Abednego over the affairs of the province of Babylon; but Daniel remained at the king's court.	At Daniel's request the king put Shadrach, Meshach, and Abednego in charge of the affairs of the province of Babylon; Daniel, however, remained at the royal court.

Daniel made request of the king: in other languages it will probably be necessary to make the relationship between the first two propositions much clearer. What Daniel requested was in fact what the king did. In some cases translators may wish to say "Daniel asked the king for something, and the king granted his request . . . ." REB, like TEV, makes the first part of this verse a subordinate clause: "At Daniel's request . . . ."

He appointed: it should be made clear that the pronoun here refers to King Nebuchadnezzar and not Daniel.

Over the affairs of the province of Babylon: since Daniel himself was made ruler over this province, the translation should make it clear that his three friends were given high administrative positions under him. If care is not taken, it is possible to give the wrong impression that they replaced him. This is especially true in light of the fact that the last sentence of this chapter states that Daniel **remained at the king's court**. While he remained at the king's court, he was, in fact, still the ruler of the province of Babylon. The expression **at the king's court** is literally "at the king's door." This emphasizes the readiness of the court counselor to advise the king at any moment.

Daniel's Three Friends Get into Trouble

Daniel 3.1-30

Daniel, the central personality of this book, does not figure in chapter 3 at all. The only connection with Daniel is that his three friends, Shadrach, Meshach, and Abednego, are the main characters here. The fact that Daniel is not mentioned is taken by some writers as an indication that this story originally existed independently. Others have supposed that Daniel simply was not in Babylon when the events reported here took place. Whichever the case may be, this should not affect the translation of the text in hand.

Nebuchadnezzar commands everyone to worship a golden statue: 3.1-7

RSV

TEV

Nebuchadnezzar Commands Everyone to Worship a Gold Statue

1 King Nebuchadnezzar made an image of gold, whose height was sixty cubits and its breadth six cubits. He set it up on the plain of Dura, in the province of Babylon. 2 Then King Nebuchadnezzar sent to assemble the satraps, the prefects, and the governors, the counselors, the treasurers, the justices, the magistrates, and all the officials of the provinces to come to the dedication of the image which King Nebuchadnezzar had set up. 3 Then the satraps, the prefects, and the governors, the counselors, the treasurers, the justices, the magistrates, and all the officials of the provinces, were assembled for the dedication of the image that King Nebuchadnezzar had set up; and they stood before the image that Nebuchadnezzar had set up. 4 And the herald proclaimed aloud, "You are commanded, O peoples, nations, and languages, 5 that when you hear the sound of the horn, pipe, lyre, trigon, harp, bagpipe, and every kind of music, you are to fall down and worship the golden image that King Nebuchadnezzar has set up; 6 and whoever does not fall down and worship shall immediately be cast into a burning fiery furnace." 7 Therefore,

1 King Nebuchadnezzar had a gold statue made, ninety feet high and nine feet wide, and he had it set up in the plain of Dura in the province of Babylon. 2 Then the king gave orders for all his officials to come together—the princes, governors, lieutenant governors, commissioners, treasurers, judges, magistrates, and all the other officials of the provinces. They were to attend the dedication of the statue which King Nebuchadnezzar had set up. 3 When all these officials gathered for the dedication and stood in front of the statue, 4 a herald announced in a loud voice, "People of all nations, races, and languages! 5 You will hear the sound of the playing of oboes, lyres, zithers, and harps; and then all the other instruments will join in. As soon as the music starts, you are to bow down and worship the gold statue that King Nebuchadnezzar has set up. 6 Anyone who does not bow down and worship will immediately be thrown into a blazing furnace." 7 And so, as soon as they heard the sound of the instruments, the people of all the nations, races, and languages bowed down and wor-

as soon as all the peoples heard the sound of the horn, pipe, lyre, trigon, harp, bagpipe, and every kind of music, all the peoples, nations, and languages fell down and worshiped the golden image which King Nebuchadnezzar had set up. shiped the gold statue which King Nebuchadnezzar had set up.

TEV **Section Heading: Nebuchadnezzar commands everyone to worship a gold statue**

Other possible models as a heading for this section are "The order to worship the golden statue" (FRCL) or "The king sets up a statue to be worshiped." REB focuses on the result of not obeying the command to worship the golden image, "The fiery furnace," but this is a heading for the whole chapter, whereas many versions have a new section heading that is similar later in the chapter.

3.1	RSV	TEV
	King Nebuchadnezzar made an image of gold, whose height was sixty cubits and its breadth six cubits. He set it up on the plain of Dura, in the province of Babylon.	King Nebuchadnezzar had a gold statue made, ninety feet high and nine feet wide, and he had it set up in the plain of Dura in the province of Babylon.

Although two important ancient Greek versions of the Old Testament begin this chapter with the date "in the eighteenth year of Nebuchadnezzar . . ." (compare Jer 52.29), no major English version has adopted this reading, and it is not recommended to translators.

King Nebuchadnezzar: the Aramaic text has the proper name first and then the title (as in KJV), but it may be more natural to reverse this order in other languages. Translators should follow whichever order is most natural; they should ask themselves whether they are more likely to say "President X" or "X, the president" in ordinary speech.

Made . . . set up: while these are good literal translations of the words found in the original, this does not mean that the king himself actually did the work of making the statue and setting it up. Therefore it may be better in many languages to use a causative form of the verbs, "caused to be made" and "caused to set up." Or some other means of expressing these ideas may be more natural, such as "ordered that (a statue) be made" and "commanded that it be set up . . . ." TEV uses the forms "had . . . made" and "had . . . set up."

Image of gold: the word **gold** is found also in 2.32 as well as in a dozen other places in Daniel. According to some commentators, the proportions of the **image** or statue suggest that it was probably a sort of symbolic column rather than an exact representation of a human or divine figure, and that perhaps some carving on the column pictured the features of person, whether human or divine. But others feel that it must have had the shape of human features. The church fathers thought it may have been an image of a king who was considered a god, and several modern commentators think it may have been a representation of a Babylonian god; but the information given in verses 12, 14, and 18 does not really make it possible to decide one way or another. If the language has a word for symbolic representation rather than exact likeness, then this word should probably be used in translation rather than the other.

Whose height was sixty cubits and its breadth six cubits: the American edition of TEV translates these dimensions as "ninety feet high and nine feet wide," but the British edition uses the metric system and attempts to be precise, with "twenty-seven meters high and three meters wide." FRCL and GECL, on the other hand, have rounded the numbers to "thirty meters high and three meters wide." If the metric system is used, this seems to be more in keeping with the round numbers of the original. In other languages it will probably be best to use whatever system of measurement is used in speaking of the dimensions of a tree, a house, or some other large structure. For instance, width may be stated in paces and height may possibly be stated in terms of the height of a person. For example, translators may say "taller than fifteen people and about three paces wide." But in many cultures the metric system has become a part of the language and can be used here.

On the plain of Dura: the location of this plain is uncertain. The word **plain** in itself presents a translation problem in certain languages. It is a rather large and relatively flat area sometimes referred to as a plateau in English. It is sometimes used in contrast with hilly country. One commentary takes it to mean "valley." In some languages it may also be necessary to make a decision about the words **of Dura**. The entire expression may have to be translated "the plain called Dura" or possibly "the plain near a town called Dura." Although we cannot be certain, the former is more likely to be the case.

3.2   RSV   TEV

Then King Nebuchadnezzar sent to assemble the satraps, the prefects, and the governors, the counselors, the treasurers, the justices, the magistrates, and all the officials of the provinces to come to the dedication of the image which King Nebuchadnezzar had set up.

Then the king gave orders for all his officials to come together—the princes, governors, lieutenant governors, commissioners, treasurers, judges, magistrates, and all the other officials of the provinces. They were to attend the dedication of the statue which King Nebuchadnezzar had set up.

Sent to assemble: NEB supplies the missing piece of information: "sent out a summons to assemble." Another possibility is "sent messengers out to order . . . to come together." In some languages it will be simpler and more natural to say "called together," or there may be a special word for "summoned."

As has already been noted, the writer of this book is especially fond of lists. The list of officials found here is repeated word for word in verse 3, but at the end of the chapter (verse 27), it is limited to the first three officials, with the addition of a fourth group called "the king's counselors." In this verse the fact that the conjunction **and** is used only before the third term seems to set apart the first two kinds of officials as being of higher rank than the others. The translation should therefore probably be worded in such a way as to separate out the two main groups or categories. This can be done by naming the first two kinds of officials and then saying something like "there were also . . ." or "he also called . . . ," and then listing the others.

The satraps, the prefects, and the governors: while the exact meaning of the terms is debatable, it seems that these three are given in descending order of importance. The **satraps** were in charge of the main divisions of the empire; the **prefects** were high officials responsible directly to the satraps; and the **governors** were heads of the subdivisions within the main divisions. Translators should think of the very highest officials under the president himself and use the terms for these officials in the order of their influence or political importance.

Counselors . . . treasurers . . . justices . . . magistrates: the meaning of these four terms for the lesser officials is less certain. If it is impossible to find four different terms, the number can be reduced. However, if it can be avoided, it is probably not advisable to adopt the solution of GECL, where the entire list is summed up in one term; this would remove an element that is characteristic of the Book of Daniel. In the second group of officials, translators may consider the local equivalents for "elders," "keepers of the treasury (or money)," "judges," "subchiefs," and "police officers."

And all the officials: this phrase is not to be seen as an eighth category, but rather it serves as a summary of what goes before. Instead of the conjunction **and**, some have proposed something like "in short, all the officials . . . ," or "that is to say . . . ," or "that means . . . ."

Dedication: this word comes from a root that means "begin" or "initiate." The actual word is the same as used in the English name for the present day Jewish Festival of Dedication, or "Hanukkah," which celebrates the reestablishment of Temple worship after the reign of Antiochus Epiphanes. In addition to the occurrences here and in the following verse, it also appears in the Aramaic portion of Ezra (6.16, 17), and the corresponding Hebrew term is found eight times (in Num 7.84; Neh 12.27; 2 Chr 7.9, for example). It is mentioned in the New Testament in John 10.22. In some languages it may be best translated "the celebration to begin the worship (of the image)."

3.3	RSV	TEV

Then the satraps, the prefects, and the governors, the counselors, the treasurers, the justices, the magistrates, and all the officials of the provinces, were assembled for the dedication of the image that King	When all these officials gathered for the dedication and stood in front of the statue,

Nebuchadnezzar had set up; and they stood before the image that Nebuchadnezzar had set up.

In addition to repeating word for word the list of government officials just given in the previous verse, this verse contains other repetitions that make it rather heavy in English. The name of the king and the expression **the image that (he) had set up** also appear twice here. Note that TEV avoids this repetition and makes the whole verse into a dependent clause introducing verse 4. Another possible model taking this verse as a separate sentence may be "So all these officials gathered together in front of the statue that the king had made" or "Therefore all the officials assembled and took their places before the statue for the inauguration ceremony" (FRCL).

3.4 RSV	TEV
And the herald proclaimed aloud, "You are commanded, O peoples, nations, and languages,	**a herald announced in a loud voice, "People of all nations, races, and languages!**

The herald: the function of this person was to speak in a loud voice on behalf of the king. In many languages it may have to be translated "a spokesman" or "a messenger for the king." But some languages have a more technical term for the person who makes announcements for the chief. FRCL translates "the master of ceremonies." There is no definite article in the original, so it will be misleading to give the impression that a particular person is in view. Several recent translations have simply "a herald" (TEV, AB, NJB, REB).

You are commanded: this passive construction may be rendered actively as "The king has commanded (is commanding)," or it may possibly be left to be understood by using imperative verb forms for the actions required of those present. Another possibility is to say at the beginning or end of this verse something like "Listen to the king's command."

O peoples . . . : the position of this vocative form in the sentence may have to be changed in some languages. Translators should consider which is the most natural order in their language.

Peoples, nations, and languages: here again we have another list. In this case the exaggerated language serves to show that the king wanted the worship of his statue to be universal. In some cases the three terms may have to be translated "people who come from all countries and who speak all languages."

3.5   RSV   TEV

that when you hear the sound of the horn, pipe, lyre, trigon, harp, bag-pipe, and every kind of music, you are to fall down and worship the golden image that King Nebuchad-nezzar has set up;

You will hear the sound of the trum-pets, followed by the playing of oboes, lyres, zithers, and harps; and then all the other instruments will join in. As soon as the music starts, you are to bow down and worship the gold statue that King Nebuchad-nezzar has set up.

Here again the writer shows his fascination with lists by giving six different words for musical instruments. This list is repeated exactly in verse 7 (according to some ancient manuscripts) and again in verses 10 and 15. Once the list has been established here, it may be repeated in the same way in these other verses. But if the fourfold repetition is unnatural, a more summary statement may be used in the later verses. In many languages where such instruments are not well known, this poses serious translation problems. If it proves impossible to have the same number of instruments as in the biblical text, the number may be reduced (in some manuscripts there are only five names here); however, given the importance of lists in Daniel, it is not recommended that they be replaced by a simple summary statement as, for example, "when the band strikes up . . ." (LB).

Translators who have access to recent issues of *The Bible Translator* may find considerable help in under-standing the various types of musi-cal instruments in the Bible by con-sulting the articles written by Ivor H. Jones (January 1986, pages 101-116 and January 1987, pages 129-143).

Horn: this is the same word as is used for the horn of an animal (as in 7.7, for example). The animal horn was actually made into a kind of trumpet-type musical instrument that was held to the mouth and blown to create a sound. While this instrument was originally made from the horn of an animal, it later came to be made of wood or metal as well.

TRUMPETS AND RAMS' HORNS

Pipe: this was also an instrument held to the mouth and blown to produce pleasant sounds. It is usually translated "flute" (KJV, NIV, NAB, New American Standard Bible [NASB]), but TEV renders it "oboes." Others refer to it as a "clarinet."

75

A PIPE, OR FLUTE

Lyre: this stringed instrument was considered the noblest instrument of all and was used in secular merrymaking. It could have as few as three strings or as many as twelve. The term used is probably a borrowing from Greek and is probably related to our modern word "guitar." It could be played with the fingers or with a thin piece of ivory or metal.

Trigon: based on the form of the name, scholars have suggested that this was a triangular musical instrument, probably with four strings. Perhaps the closest approximation in many cultures may be the "hand piano" or "thumb piano," although this is not technically a stringed instrument.

Harp: this was also a stringed instrument with a large resonator. It probably had ten strings.

Bagpipe: many scholars are convinced that this is not actually the name of a particular instrument, but rather that it referred to the playing together of all the individual instruments mentioned before (so TEV, "and then all the other instruments will join in"). The term probably derived from the Greek meaning "accompanying sound." NEB follows this interpretation, using the general term "music" here. However, one commentator suggests that this may be the name of a sort of drum (AB page 157); NRSV translates the term in this way.

SOME EXAMPLES OF HARP, TRIGON, AND LYRE

The following comparative table shows how these terms have been translated in various modern English versions, and indicates the range of possibilities in translation:

RSV	TEV	NJV	NAB	NEB	NJB
horn	trumpets	horn	trumpet	horn	horn
pipe	oboes	pipe	flute	pipe	pipe
lyre	lyres	zither	lyre	zither	lyre
trigon	zithers	lyre	harp	triangle	zither
harp	harps	psaltery	psaltery	dulcimer	harp
bagpipe	0	bagpipe	bagpipe	...music	bagpipe

And every kind of music: this is probably a summary statement corresponding to "and all the officials" in the list of officials in verse 2 above. It should be translated in such a way as to sum up the list that it follows. It should be noted, however, that NEB translates "singing of every kind," since it takes the word usually translated "bagpipe" in a more general sense.

Fall down: the Aramaic verb used here has a great many applications and is found in a wide variety of contexts. But in this context it clearly involves a voluntary act of bowing low or lying face down in order to show reverence and respect. This idea should be made clear in the translation.

3.6	RSV	TEV

RSV	TEV
and whoever does not fall down and worship shall immediately be cast into a burning fiery furnace."	Anyone who does not bow down and worship will immediately be thrown into a blazing furnace."

Fall down: see verse 5.

Worship: this verb may require an object in many languages. If so, the object in the context is clearly the statue that King Nebuchadnezzar had erected. It should be noted that this is the same verb translated "did homage" in 2.46 and it occurs ten times elsewhere in this chapter (see verses 5, 10, 11, 12, 14, 15, 18, and 28).

Be cast: the passive verb form will almost certainly have to be rendered actively in some languages as "they (indefinite) will cast . . . ," or "someone will throw . . . ," or something similar.

A burning fiery furnace: literally "into the inside of a furnace of burning fire." This was probably a kind of box or room with an opening in the side (see verse 25) and another in the top (verses 21-23). Note that in verse 26 the furnace is said to have a "door" or rather some kind of opening. This indicates that it had the shape of a room or enclosure. Since furnaces are unknown in some cultures, this may be a difficult idea to translate. Some possibilities are "a room filled with very hot fire" or "a small house where things are burned up completely." Other similar terms that people may be familiar with are "oven," "kiln," and "incinerator."

Other possible models for the verse as a whole are "If any person refuses to worship the statue, then they (indefinite) will throw that person into a flaming furnace" or "My men will at once throw you into a hot fire room (or house) if you do not bow down and worship the statue."

3.7 RSV	TEV
Therefore, as soon as all the peoples heard the sound of the horn, pipe, lyre, trigon, harp, bagpipe, and every kind of music, all the peoples, nations, and languages fell down and worshiped the golden image which King Nebuchadnezzar had set up.	And so, as soon as they heard the sound of the instruments, the people of all the nations, races, and languages bowed down and worshiped the gold statue which King Nebuchadnezzar had set up.

The horn, pipe, lyre, trigon, harp, bagpipe: see verse 5. But note that the "bagpipe" of verse 5 is not included in this list in some versions (NIV, NJV, and NRSV) and is not recommended by *Critique textuelle de l'Ancien Testament* (CTAT). It is, however, found in a few Aramaic manuscripts, so there is some justification for including it here. TEV summarizes the list with "the sound of the instruments," and this translation makes the difference between manuscripts irrelevant.

Peoples, nations, and languages: see verse 4.

Fell down: see verse 5.

The three friends are accused of disobedience: 3.8-18

RSV	TEV
	Daniel's Three Friends Are Accused of Disobedience
8 Therefore at that time certain Chaldeans came forward and maliciously accused the Jews. 9 They said to King Nebuchadnezzar, "O king, live for ever! 10 You, O king, have made a decree, that every man who hears the sound of the horn, pipe, lyre, trigon, harp, bagpipe, and every kind of music, shall fall down and worship the golden image; 11 and whoever does not fall down and worship shall be cast into a burning fiery furnace. 12 There are certain Jews whom you have appointed over the affairs of the province of Babylon: Shadrach, Meshach, and Abednego. These men, O king, pay no heed to you; they do not serve your gods or worship the golden image which you have set up." 13 Then Nebuchadnezzar in furious rage commanded that Shadrach, Meshach, and Abednego be brought. Then they brought these men before the king. 14 Nebuchadnezzar said to them, "Is it true, O Shadrach, Meshach, and Abednego, that you do not serve my gods or worship the golden image which I have set up? 15 Now if you are ready when you hear the	8 It was then that some Babylonians took the opportunity to denounce the Jews. 9 They said to King Nebuchadnezzar, "May Your Majesty live forever! 10 Your Majesty has issued an order that as soon as the music starts, everyone is to bow down and worship the gold statue, 11 and that anyone who does not bow down and worship it is to be thrown into a blazing furnace. 12 There are some Jews whom you put in charge of the province of Babylon—Shadrach, Meshach, and Abednego— who are disobeying Your Majesty's orders. They do not worship your god or bow down to the statue you set up." 13 At that, the king flew into a rage and ordered the three men to be brought before him. 14 He said to them, "Shadrach, Meshach, and Abednego, is it true that you refuse to worship my god and to bow down to the gold statue I have set up? 15 Now then, as soon as you hear the sound of the trumpets, oboes, lyres, zithers, harps, and all the other instruments, bow down and worship the statue. If you do not, you will immediately be

sound of the horn, pipe, lyre, trigon, harp, bagpipe, and every kind of music, to fall down and worship the image which I have made, well and good; but if you do not worship, you shall immediately be cast into a burning fiery furnace; and who is the god that will deliver you out of my hands?"

16 Shadrach, Meshach, and Abednego answered the king, "O Nebuchadnezzar, we have no need to answer you in this matter. 17 If it be so, our God whom we serve is able to deliver us from the burning fiery furnace; and he will deliver us out of your hand, O king. 18 But if not, be it known to you, O king, that we will not serve your gods or worship the golden image which you have set up."

thrown into a blazing furnace. Do you think there is any god who can save you?"

16 Shadrach, Meshach, and Abednego answered, "Your Majesty, we will not try to defend ourselves. 17 If the God whom we serve is able to save us from the blazing furnace and from your power, then he will. 18 But even if he doesn't, Your Majesty may be sure that we will not worship your god, and we will not bow down to the gold statue that you have set up."

TEV Section Heading: Daniel's three friends are accused of disobedience

Given the fact that Daniel is not mentioned anywhere in this chapter, and that there is a certain focus on the Jews in general, it may be better not to use his name in the section heading. Translators may consider some other possible section headings such as "Enemies of the Jews denounce the young men" or "The condemnation of the Jewish young men."

3.8	RSV	TEV
	Therefore at that time certain Chaldeans came forward and maliciously accused the Jews.	It was then that some Babylonians took the opportunity to denounce the Jews.

Therefore: literally "For all of this." The transition required in other languages may possibly be translated "Soon afterwards," or even "Taking advantage of this situation." NJV has "Seizing the occasion" (compare also REB), but others begin the verse with an expression relating more to time, "At that point" (NAB) or "At this time" (NIV).

Certain Chaldeans: see comments on 1.4 and 2.2. It has been suggested that the word **Chaldeans** may have its derived meaning of "fortune tellers" here (as in 2.2), and it is translated this way in NIV and Mft. On the other hand many commentators feel that the term is used in its pure geographic sense in this context. In this case it is better translated "Babylonians" as in TEV.

Came forward: in some languages it is possible to say simply "appeared," but in other cases it may be necessary to state before whom these accusers appeared: "appeared before the king" (as clearly seen in the following verse).

Maliciously accused: literally "ate (or chewed up) the pieces of." This idiomatic expression seems to carry the idea of spiteful slander as well as accusation, as the RSV rendering shows.

3.9   RSV   TEV

They said to King Nebuchadnezzar,   **They said to King Nebuchadnezzar,**
"O king, live for ever!   **"May Your Majesty live forever!**

They said: literally "They spoke and said . . ." (see comments on "answered and said" in 2.5).

O king, live for ever: accepted custom of the time required that any address to the king began with this formula. It is identical with that discussed under 2.4.

3.10   RSV   TEV

You, O king, have made a decree,   **Your Majesty has issued an order**
that every man who hears the sound   **that as soon as the music starts,**
of the horn, pipe, lyre, trigon, harp, **everyone is to bow down and wor-**
bagpipe, and every kind of music,   **ship the gold statue,**
shall fall down and worship the
golden image;

You: the pronoun here is emphatic and seems to underline the fact that the accused have gone against the orders of the king himself. If possible, this emphasis should be retained in the translation.

O king: see 2.4.

Made a decree: or, probably better, "sent out (to his subjects) a decree." On the word **decree** compare 2.13.

In some languages it may be more natural to change from indirect to direct speech and say something like "You . . . issued the following order: 'Every person . . .'" (as is done in FRCL).

Horn, pipe, lyre, trigon, harp, bagpipe: see verses 5 and 7. The third repetition of this list may be too much for some languages, and it may be advisable to summarize at this point, as in TEV "as soon as the music starts."

Fall down: see verse 5.

3.11   RSV   TEV

and whoever does not fall down and   **and that anyone who does not bow**
worship shall be cast into a burning **down and worship it is to be thrown**
fiery furnace.   **into a blazing furnace.**

This is a continuation of the recitation of the royal decree and is almost exactly the same as verse 6, with the exception that the Aramaic adverb for "immediately" has been dropped here. If the option of direct discourse was chosen in the previous verse, it should continue until the end of this verse.

3.12 RSV TEV

There are certain Jews whom you have appointed over the affairs of the province of Babylon: Shadrach, Meshach, and Abednego. These men, O king, pay no heed to you; they do not serve your gods or worship the golden image which you have set up."

There are some Jews whom you put in charge of the province of Baby-lon—Shadrach, Meshach, and Abed-nego—who are disobeying Your Majesty's orders. They do not wor-ship your god or bow down to the statue you set up."

In some languages it may be appropriate to introduce this verse with a conjunction marking contrast, since there is a contrast in the text between the command of the king in the previous verse and the disobedience of the Jewish young men described here. Some versions begin this verse with "Now . . ." (NJB, AT, and Mft), and NIV has "But . . . ."

Whom you have appointed over . . . Babylon: see 2.49.

O king: while this vocative occurs in the middle of the verse, it may have to be shifted forward in some languages for the sake of naturalness, if indeed the vocative form is used at all. FRCL, for example, begins the verse with "Your Majesty . . . ." This helps also to show that the quotation of the king's command (verses 10 and 11) is finished, and that the words that follow are addressed to the king once again.

Pay no heed to you: the present tense in RSV, and the TEV rendering "are disobeying . . . ," seem to convey the idea of repeated or habitual disobedience, but the Aramaic verb places the event clearly in the past. It is therefore probably better to translate "have disobeyed you," "paid no respect to," "have disregarded . . ." (REB), or "have ignored . . ." (NJB).

Serve: this word has the same meaning as "worship" in this context and should not be translated in such a way as to focus on the idea of physical work.

Your gods: the Aramaic text presents an ambiguous tradition at this point. On the one hand, the written text has the plural for **gods** and seems to make a general statement (we know that there were many gods in the Babylonian religion). But according to the traditional reading of the synagogue, as marked in the margin of the text, the reader was instructed to read a singular, "your god," at this point. This would then be a direct reference to the god represented by the statue and thus be parallel to **worship the golden image**, which follows. TEV, NJV, and NAB (as well as GECL) adopt the singular, but most other English versions (as well as FRCL) maintain the plural. While both of these options are legitimate, translators are advised to follow the traditional reading of the synagogue, with the singular, and to explain the other reading (plural) in a textual note, if this is considered necessary.

3.13 RSV	TEV
Then Nebuchadnezzar in furious rage commanded that Shadrach, Meshach, and Abednego be brought. Then they brought these men before the king.	At that, the king flew into a rage and ordered the three men to be brought before him.

Then: there may be better ways in some languages to mark the transition between the king's hearing the news about disobedience and his subsequent anger. Some possible models are "As soon as he heard that . . ." or "Immediately . . . ."

Furious rage: this translates two nouns in Aramaic, but the two actually describe a single violent reaction on the part of the king. What is important in translation is to reflect the intensity of Nebuchadnezzar's response. In some cases translators may have to say simply "he was very, very angry."

Be brought: this verb in RSV presents two common translation problems: firstly, it is a passive form and will have to be rendered actively in many languages; and secondly, it does not state where the young men were to be brought. It may be clearer to say something like "that they (indefinite) go and get . . . and bring them to the king" or "that the king's men seize . . . and make them appear before the king."

TEV does not say that the king's command to bring the Jewish youths to him was actually carried out. However, it is probably better in most languages to include this, with something like "Therefore these men appeared before the king," or "So they (indefinite) brought them into the king's presence," or in this context simply "So this was done."

3.14 RSV	TEV
Nebuchadnezzar said to them, "Is it true, O Shadrach, Meshach, and Abednego, that you do not serve my gods or worship the golden image which I have set up?	He said to them, "Shadrach, Meshach, and Abednego, is it true that you refuse to worship my god and to bow down to the gold statue I have set up?

Nebuchadnezzar said . . .: the text says literally "Nebuchadnezzar answered and said . . ." (see discussion at 2.5). But translators may want to avoid the repetition of the proper name by using the pronoun "he" (as in TEV) or the noun "the king" (as in FRCL). The verb that follows may be rendered "asked" or "interrogated them," since the following words are in the form of a question. However, it should be noted that there is no indication in the text that the king gave them a chance to answer this question.

Is it true: the corresponding Aramaic word is found nowhere else in the Old Testament. It is derived from a root that has the idea of solidness or firmness, and it is so rendered in many ancient versions. This meaning has further been confirmed by the discovery of an Aramaic inscription where it is also used. This has led some scholars to think that the best translation of the word may be "Is it deliberate?" (*La nouvelle version Segond revisée* [NVSR], and similarly Lacocque, page 62). But most versions and commentators take it to mean "Is it a fact?" or **Is it true?** (RSV, TEV).

My gods: see verse 12. Here the text does not have the double tradition mentioned in the comment on verse 12. This can, in fact, support the choice of the plural in the previous case and in verse 18. However, it is also possible that, while formally a plural, the word may be understood as having a singular meaning.

3.15	RSV	TEV

Now if you are ready when you hear the sound of the horn, pipe, lyre, trigon, harp, bagpipe, and every kind of music, to fall down and worship the image which I have made, well and good; but if you do not worship, you shall immediately be cast into a burning fiery furnace; and who is the god that will deliver you out of my hands?"	Now then, as soon as you hear the sound of the trumpets, oboes, lyres, zithers, harps, and all the other instruments, bow down and worship the statue. If you do not, you will immediately be thrown into a blazing furnace. Do you think there is any god who can save you?"

The first sentence of this verse in Aramaic is incomplete. Many English versions complete the sense with words similar to **well and good**, as in RSV, or some other phrase meaning "it will be all right for you," or perhaps even "you will not be punished." But these are not a part of the original. Two important commentaries in English provide another way of handling this problem. The translation in AB has "I hope that now, when you hear . . . , you will fall down and worship the image I have made." And Lacocque (page 62) suggests that it be put in the form of a question: "Are you now ready, at the moment you hear . . . , to prostrate yourselves and worship the statue I have made?" A similar solution has been adopted by FRCL, but breaking the long discourse down into two separate sentences, the second of which is a question: "You will again hear the trumpet . . . music. Are you now ready to bow down to worship the statue that I made?"

Horn, pipe, lyre, trigon, harp, bagpipe: see verses 5 and 7.

If you do not worship: in many languages "the statue," or the pronoun "it" referring to the statue, will have to be added after the verb **worship**. But in other cases this may be translated more meaningfully as "if you refuse, ..." Or it may be possible to combine these two suggestions, as in NJB: "if you refuse to worship it . . . ."

You shall . . . be cast: again the passive verb form will have to be translated actively in many languages. See verse 6 above.

Burning fiery furnace: see also verse 6.

Who is the god that will deliver you: a rhetorical question such as this has the same value as a negative affirmation meaning "there is no god that is able to save you." It may be translated this way in languages where the rhetorical question may be misunderstood or is felt to be unnatural in this context. Mft frames the rhetorical question in a different way that may be a good model for some languages: "Where is the god that can save you from my power?"

Out of my hands: a literal translation may be misleading in some cases. NEB/REB, NJV, NJB, and others have "from my power," which accurately translates the meaning of the phrase.

3.16 RSV	TEV
Shadrach, Meshach, and Abednego answered the king, "O Nebuchadnezzar, we have no need to answer you in this matter.	Shadrach, Meshach, and Abednego answered, "Your Majesty, we will not try to defend ourselves.

Shadrach, Meshach, and Abednego: depending on the system for referring to participants in the language of translation, it may be possible to render these proper names by a simple pronoun, "They."

O Nebuchadnezzar: English translations are almost equally divided between those that follow RSV by including the proper name within the quotation, and those that have something like "answered King Nebuchadnezzar . . ." outside the quotation. The problem is essentially one of punctuation. The markings in the traditional Aramaic text yield a rendering like that of RSV. But this is unlikely, since to address the king by his name without using the title would show disrespect by failing to observe proper court formalities, and there is no reason to believe that the young men would have forgotten their manners in this case. Nowhere else in the Book of Daniel is the king addressed only by his name; yet there are many cases where the usual convention of using the title is observed (see 2.4, 29, 31, 37). It is probably best not to follow RSV on this point but to use the more respectful formulas found elsewhere in the Book of Daniel.

We have no need to answer you: this should not be understood as an impertinent remark on the part of the three young men. They were simply stating a fact. NRSV translates "we have no need to present a defense to you in this matter." Some other ways of saying this are "we don't want to try to justify ourselves" (FRCL), "There is no need for us to defend ourselves before you in this matter" (NAB), or "there is no need for further consideration of this matter." For those languages distinguishing we-inclusive and we-exclusive pronouns, the exclusive forms should be used throughout this passage.

3.17-18   RSV   TEV

17 If it be so, our God whom we serve is able to deliver us from the burning fiery furnace; and he will deliver us out of your hand, O king.[c] 18 But if not, be it known to you, O king, that we will not serve your gods or worship the golden image which you have set up."

[c] Or *Behold, our God . . . king. Or If our God is able to deliver us, he will deliver us from the burning fiery furnace and out of your hand, O king.*

17 If the God whom we serve is able to save us from the blazing furnace and from your power, then he will.[b] 18 But even if he doesn't, Your Majesty may be sure that we will not worship your god, and we will not bow down to the gold statue that you have set up."

[b] If the God . . . will; *or* If it is true that we refuse to worship your god or bow down to the gold statue you set up, the God whom we serve is able to save us from the blazing furnace and from your power—and he will.

Verses 17 and 18 may be understood and translated in two radically different ways. The first takes the **If it be so** as meaning "If we are thrown into the fire" or "If the king's sentence is carried out" and pictures the three young men as being perfectly confident that God will be able to deliver them. This understanding is clearly brought out in the NIV rendering of these verses as well as in FRCL. The second possibility, reflected in TEV, NAB, NRSV, and NJB, indicates some doubt on the part of the young men as to whether God will be willing or capable of saving them from the fire. Against this view, the idea that God may not be able to save those who are faithful to him would, according to some writers, be quite surprising in a book like Daniel. For this reason some translators and commentators prefer the first interpretation. On the other hand, it is a fact that Jewish people were sometimes put to death and not saved from their oppressors. Also the words **But if not** at the beginning of verse 18 would make no sense as the contrary of the "if" clause in verse 17. The majority of modern English commentaries therefore tend toward this second interpretation. It is quite possible, as one commentator points out, that the young men "do not doubt the power of their God to deliver them from the king's furnace, but they have no right to presume that he will do so" (Baldwin, page 104). We may therefore translate "if he will not . . ." or "if he does not . . ." rather than "if he can not . . . ."

A third possibility, slightly different from the second, focuses on the existence or nonexistence of a God capable of saving, and yields the meaning "If there is a god who is able to save us from the blazing furnace, it is our God whom we serve . . ." (NEB/REB). There is also considerable linguistic evidence in favor of this interpretation. But the second interpretation is probably best. (Towner, pages 51-52.)

Serve: see verses 12 and 14.

Gods: TEV has "god" in the singular. See verse 12.

The three friends are sentenced to die: 3.19-25

RSV

TEV

Daniel's Three Friends Are Sentenced to Death

19 Then Nebuchadnezzar was full of fury, and the expression of his face was changed against Shadrach, Meshach, and Abednego. He ordered the furnace heated seven times more than it was wont to be heated. 20 And he ordered certain mighty men of his army to bind Shadrach, Meshach, and Abednego, and to cast them into the burning fiery furnace. 21 Then these men were bound in their mantles, their tunics, their hats, and their other garments, and they were cast into the burning fiery furnace. 22 Because the king's order was strict and the furnace very hot, the flame of the fire slew those men who took up Shadrach, Meshach, and Abednego. 23 And these three men, Shadrach, Meshach, and Abednego, fell bound into the burning fiery furnace.

24 Then King Nebuchadnezzar was astonished and rose up in haste. He said to his counselors, "Did we not cast three men bound into the fire?" They answered the king, "True, O king." 25 He answered, "But I see four men loose, walking in the midst of the fire, and they are not hurt; and the appearance of the fourth is like a son of the gods."

19 Then Nebuchadnezzar lost his temper, and his face turned red with anger at Shadrach, Meshach, and Abednego. So he ordered the furnace to be heated seven times hotter than usual. 20 And he commanded the strongest men in his army to tie the three men up and throw them into the blazing furnace. 21 So they tied them up, fully dressed—shirts, robes, caps, and all—and threw them into the blazing furnace. 22 Now because the king had given strict orders for the furnace to be made extremely hot, the flames burned up the guards who took the men to the furnace. 23 Then Shadrach, Meshach, and Abednego, still tied up, fell into the heart of the blazing fire.

24 Suddenly Nebuchadnezzar leaped to his feet in amazement. He asked his officials, "Didn't we tie up three men and throw them into the blazing furnace?"

They answered, "Yes, we did, Your Majesty."

25 "Then why do I see four men walking around in the fire?" he asked. "They are not tied up, and they show no sign of being hurt—and the fourth one looks like an angel."

TEV Section Heading: Daniel's three friends are sentenced to death

The TEV heading seems to cover only a part of the content of verses 19-25, which deal, not only with the pronouncing of the sentence, but also with the actual execution of the sentence and the amazing results. If translators wish to avoid the name of Daniel in the section headings of this chapter, then perhaps some will prefer to say something like "The young men are thrown into the fire" or "The king puts the young men in the blazing fire."

It is interesting to note that, while RSV has only a paragraph break at this point, NRSV starts a completely new section here with the section heading "The Fiery Furnace."

3.19

RSV

TEV

Then Nebuchadnezzar was full of fury, and the expression of his face was changed against Shadrach, Meshach and Abednego. He ordered the furnace heated seven times more than it was wont to be heated.

Then Nebuchadnezzar lost his temper, and his face turned red with anger at Shadrach, Meshach, and Abednego. So he ordered the furnace to be heated seven times hotter than usual.

Was full of fury: most languages have rather vivid ways of describing a person who becomes uncontrollably angry, and just such an expression is required here. Some English models in addition to RSV and TEV above, are "was furious" (NIV) or "flew into a rage" (NEB).

The expression on his face changed: the RSV rendering at this point is rather too mild. The idea is that the extreme anger that is described by **full of fury** became visible on his face. Mft has "his face was distorted with rage." It may be better in some languages to take these two expressions and combine them in a single phrase that captures the vividness of the original, as in NAB: "Nebuchadnezzar's face became livid with utter rage . . . ."

While there is no transition word in RSV (reflecting the original), idiomatic English seems to require something like "So" in TEV. This may also be the case in a number of other languages.

He ordered . . . .: literally "He answered and said"; but in this context the verb "to say" has the force of a command. In many languages it will be necessary to say who it was that the king commanded to carry out his orders. So it will be necessary to say "commanded his servants" or "ordered his men."

Heated . . . be heated: these passive forms in English will have to be made active in many languages; but if the translators have already added "his men" or "his servants," then the whole phrase can be rendered "he commanded the men to heat the furnace . . . more than they normally heated it."

Furnace: see verse 6. In this context it may be more natural in some languages to say that "he commanded his men to make the *fire* burn . . . hotter," particularly if an expression including the term "fire" is used as the equivalent for **furnace**. Even where some term for **furnace** can be found and used, it may be that the more natural way of expressing this idea will be to say that "he commanded that the fire be increased . . ." or something similar.

Seven times more than it was wont to be heated: the repetition of the verb "to heat" may be unnatural in some languages, and if so it can be omitted as in TEV. The number **seven** is more figurative than literal, since there was no thermometer to measure the heat precisely. However, it may be acceptable in many languages to translate it literally here.

3.20	RSV	TEV
	And he ordered certain mighty men of his army to bind Shadrach, Meshach, and Abednego, and to cast them into the burning fiery furnace.	And he commanded the strongest men in his army to tie the three men up and throw them into the blazing furnace.

He ordered: as in the previous verse, this is literally "he said," but the context seems to require a stronger term.

Certain mighty men of his army: the idea here is simply that of "his best troops" or "his most capable fighters," who would have also been the strongest. Mft has "some powerful soldiers."

Bind: that is, "tie up." In some languages it may be necessary to use a fuller expression and say something like "tie the hands and feet of . . . ."

Into the burning fiery furnace: see comments at verse 6. There may be languages in which the repetition of the adjectives at this point will be awkward and should be omitted.

3.21	RSV	TEV

Then these men were bound in their mantles,[d] their tunics,[d] their hats, and their other garments, and they were cast into the burning fiery furnace.

So they tied them up, fully dressed—shirts, robes, caps, and all—and threw them into the blazing furnace.

[d] The meaning of the Aramaic word is uncertain

Then: the transition word here may indicate the next in a sequence of events or focus on the result of the king's command. FRCL makes it more vivid by using "Immediately."

Were bound: this passive form must be made active in many languages, using "they" as the subject (referring back to the powerful soldiers in the previous verse) or using the full noun phrase again.

Once again the writer gives a list; this time it has to do with the articles of clothing worn by the three men being thrown into the blazing furnace. The first of the three words is repeated in verse 27, but the complete list does not reappear. The table below comparing various English versions clearly indicates that the precise meaning of these articles of clothing is uncertain. What is important is to use words indicating that the men were fully clothed, and that their dress included inner garments, outer garments, and something worn on the head.

RSV	TEV	NJB	NEB	NIV	NAB	NJV
mantles	shirts	cloaks	trousers	robes	coats	shirts
tunics	robes	trousers	shirts	trousers	hats	trousers
hats	caps	headgear	hats	turbans	shoes	hats

The translation of the third term in this list in some versions is perhaps misleading. The words **hats** or "caps" are generally used in English to refer to something more modern than the contemporaries of Daniel would have worn. Terms like "turbans" (NIV) or "headdresses" (REB) are more appropriate, since they clearly refer to something less modern. But this kind of distinction may be difficult to reflect in some languages which have only one term that refers to anything worn on the head.

The fourth term in Aramaic is usually translated something like **their other garments** and is probably intended to make clear to the reader that the young men wore all their clothing. In some cases it may be well to translate this "that is, all their clothes."

Into the burning fiery furnace: see verse 20.

3.22 RSV	TEV
Because the king's order was strict and the furnace very hot, the flame of the fire slew those men who took up Shadrach, Meshach, and Abednego.	Now because the king had given strict orders for the furnace to be made extremely hot, the flames burned up the guards who took the men to the furnace.

Strict: the same word is translated "severe" in 2.15. In this context it indicates that the king's order was firm and uncompromising. Many versions (NIV, NAB, NRSV, and NJV) translate the word "urgent." In some languages it may be necessary to say "the king's command was strong." Another possibility is "the king was very angry when he have his command" (NCV).

The flame of the fire: such an expression as this will be seen as redundant in some languages and should be translated simply as "flames" or "fire," but not both.

Slew: in some cases a more general word such as "kill" will be preferred, but in others the context will require "burned up" or some other expression related to death by fire.

Since this verse begins with a kind of explanation of why the guards were burned up in the fire, it may be more natural to change the order of clauses in some languages. Another way of wording this may be something like "The guards who took the young men to the furnace were burned to death because the king had given very strict orders that the furnace be made extremely hot." Or it may be advisable to divide the verse into two sentences, as follows: "Following the strict orders of the king, the furnace had been made as hot as possible. Therefore even the soldiers who had been ordered to throw Shadrach, Meshach, and Abednego into the fire were burned up."

3.23 RSV	TEV
And these three men, Shadrach, Meshach, and Abednego, fell bound into the burning fiery furnace.	Then Shadrach, Meshach, and Abednego, still tied up, fell into the heart of the blazing fire.

And: it will probably be better in many languages to use something other than the simple connector **And** here. NRSV, NAB, NJV, AT, and Mft translate "But," since what follows is somewhat contrary to the reader's expectations that they would also be consumed immediately by the fire. TEV, however, prefers a time transition, "Then."

These three men: the use of this expression as well as the names of the young men may be too much repetition for some languages. In those cases it will be quite adequate to use either the names or this expression, but not both.

Fell: the verb used here should not be one that is used for an accidental fall, but rather one that clearly indicates that the men were very intentionally dropped into the fire by other people. The use of this verb (compare 2.46) confirms the way in which the condemned men were thrown into the furnace, that is, from the top.

Bound: this emphasizes that the three young men were still tied up.

Following the end of verse 23, the Greek versions of Daniel include sixty-six verses not found in the Aramaic text. These verses include the passages commonly referred to as "The Song (or Prayer) of Azariah" and "The Song of the Three Young Men." They can be found in the text of NJB or NAB and in some editions of NRSV. Comments on these verses may eventually be included in a Handbook on the Deuterocanonical portions of the Old Testament. But they will not be dealt with in this volume.

3.24   RSV   TEV

Then King Nebuchadnezzar was astonished and rose up in haste. He said to his counselors, "Did we not cast three men bound into the fire?" They answered the king, "True, O king."

Suddenly Nebuchadnezzar leaped to his feet in amazement. He asked his officials, "Didn't we tie up three men and throw them into the blazing furnace?"

They answered, "Yes, we did, Your Majesty."

Then: the choice of a transition word here will depend somewhat on the way the rest of the verse is rendered. But the context seems to require something stronger than a simple time connection. The account is made more vivid in TEV by the use of "Suddenly," and this marks an abrupt change in the rhythm of the narrative.

Was astonished and rose up in haste: these two phrases joined by the conjunction **and** are very closely related and should perhaps be translated by a single phrase in some languages. It is because of the king's astonishment that he got to his feet quickly. Some possible models are "was so amazed that he jumped up" or "sprang to his feet in amazement" (NJB).

Counselors: the corresponding Aramaic term refers to important people in the royal court, highly placed government officials, or personal advisors to the king. It seems to carry the meaning of "companions (friends) of the king." It will be noted that royal advisors were sometimes referred to as "friends" of the king (see 2 Sam 16.16). REB renders the term here as "courtiers." The term is of Persian origin and does not correspond exactly to any of those listed in

3.2-3. It occurs only in the Book of Daniel (3.27; 4.36; and 6.7, as well as here). It is probably best to translate it "advisers" (NJB and NIV) or "companions" (NJV).

Said: since this verb introduces a question, it may be better to render it "asked."

Did we not cast three men bound into the fire? Neither the king nor his advisors personally took part in the binding and throwing of the three condemned men into the fire. In English and some other languages, the first person plural pronoun **we** can be used generally in a context like this; but if its use presents problems for the translator, this should be restructured in such a way as to avoid misunderstanding. If passive forms are possible, we may consider "How many men did we have tied up and thrown into the fire? Wasn't it three?" Or it is possible to use the indefinite "they," or something like "my servants" in the following: "How many men did my servants tie up and throw into the fire? Wasn't it three?"

True, O king: some other ways of saying this are "That is correct, Your Majesty," "It was indeed three men, sir," or "Sir, what you say is absolutely right."

3.25	RSV	TEV

RSV	TEV
He answered, "But I see four men loose, walking in the midst of the fire, and they are not hurt; and the appearance of the fourth is like a son of the gods."	"Then why do I see four men walking around in the fire?" he asked. "They are not tied up, and they show no sign of being hurt— and the fourth one looks like an angel."[c]

[c] angel; *or* a son of the gods; *or* a son of God.

He answered: the verb used here does not indicate answering a question since no question was asked by the counselors. It merely indicates a continuation of the conversation. It may be better to translate "He continued" or "He went on" (NJB).

But: this marks a very strong contrast, since there are now four men instead of the original three, and they are free instead of being tied up as they had been when thrown into the fire. TEV renders this as another question, "Then why . . . ?"

Loose: in contrast with "bound" in verses 21, 23, and 24.

They are not hurt: literally "there is no wound (injury) on them." Another way of wording this is "their bodies are not burned at all," or translators may want to use a word for injury resulting from fire, if such exists in their language: "no burn-marks can be seen on their bodies."

A son of the gods: on expressions containing "son of . . ." or "sons of . . . ," see comments on 2.25. In Jewish writings the expression "sons of God" (see, for example, Job 1.6) refers to members of the divine court meeting around the LORD. This, of course, makes us think immediately of angels. In the mouth of the Babylonian king, the words "a son of the gods" indicates that the fourth person in the fire resembled one of the gods of the Babylonians. However, the two Aramaic terms translated **appearance** and **like** indicate clearly that it was only a matter of resemblance. In verse 28 below it becomes clear that the person is actually an angel. This is why some versions (TEV and Mft) actually translate "an angel" in this verse. Others have "one of the gods" (AT), or "a god" (NRSV and NEB/REB), or "a divine being" (NJV, FRCL, and AB). It is probably best not to translate literally the words "child of . . ." or "son of . . . ," since this merely indicates membership in the group of divine beings. Compare Gen 6.2; Job 1.6; 38.7; 1 Kgs 22.19; and Psa 148.2.

The three friends are released and promoted: 3.26-30

RSV

TEV

The Three Men Are Released and Promoted

26 Then Nebuchadnezzar came near to the door of the burning fiery furnace and said, "Shadrach, Meshach, and Abednego, servants of the Most High God, come forth, and come here!" Then Shadrach, Meshach, and Abednego came out from the fire. 27 And the satraps, the prefects, the governors, and the king's counselors gathered together and saw that the fire had not had any power over the bodies of those men; the hair of their heads was not singed, their mantles were not harmed, and no smell of fire had come upon them. 28 Nebuchadnezzar said, "Blessed be the God of Shadrach, Meshach, and Abednego, who has sent his angel and delivered his servants, who trusted in him, and set at nought the king's command, and yielded up their bodies rather than serve and worship any god except their own God. 29 Therefore I make a decree: Any people, nation, or language that speaks anything against the God of Shadrach, Meshach, and Abednego shall be torn limb from limb, and their houses laid in ruins; for there is no other god who is able to deliver in this way." 30 Then the king promoted Shadrach, Meshach, and Abednego in the province of Babylon.

26 So Nebuchadnezzar went up to the door of the blazing furnace and called out, "Shadrach! Meshach! Abednego! Servants of the Supreme God! Come out!" And they came out at once. 27 All the princes, governors, lieutenant governors, and other officials of the king gathered to look at the three men, who had not been harmed by the fire. Their hair was not singed, their clothes were not burned, and there was no smell of smoke on them. 28 The king said, "Praise the God of Shadrach, Meshach, and Abednego! He sent his angel and rescued these men who serve and trust him. They disobeyed my orders and risked their lives rather than bow down and worship any god except their own. 29 "And now I command that if anyone of any nation, race, or language speaks disrespectfully of the God of Shadrach, Meshach, and Abednego, he is to be torn limb from limb, and his house is to be made a pile of ruins. There is no other god who can rescue like this." 30 And the king promoted Shadrach, Meshach, and Abednego to higher positions in the province of Babylon.

TEV Section Heading: The three men are released and promoted

The passive verb forms in the TEV section heading will make it a difficult model for some languages. However, it will be relatively simple to make Nebuchadnezzar the subject of active verbs: "The king releases and promotes the three men" or "Nebuchadnezzar honors the three friends."

3.26 RSV TEV

Then Nebuchadnezzar came near to the door of the burning fiery furnace and said, "Shadrach, Meshach, and Abednego, servants of the Most High God, come forth, and come here!" Then Shadrach, Meshach, and Abednego came out from the fire.

So Nebuchadnezzar went up to the door of the blazing furnace and called out, "Shadrach! Meshach! Abednego! Servants of the Supreme God! Come out!" And they came out at once.

Door: if this word is taken in its more restricted sense, it may be misleading. According to some interpreters this was an opening at the top of the furnace or oven, but others see it as an opening in the side. NAB and AB have "opening," while NJB and AT translate "the mouth" of the furnace. A side opening would certainly make it easier for the men on the inside to **come forth**.

Said: the context seems to require more than a bland, literal rendering of this verb. Something like "shouted" or "yelled" is probably called for in many languages.

Shadrach, Meshach, and Abednego: the three names are cited twice in this verse. It is probably best to translate them in the first occurrence, since they are vocatives. However, when the narrative resumes, many translators will probably want to change to the pronoun "they" as in TEV, or to say something like "all three of them" (FRCL).

The Most High God: although this title is used in the Psalms, elsewhere it is found only on the lips of non-Jews (Gen 14.18; Num 24.16 and Isa 14.14) as a name for the God of Israel. It expresses the greatness of this God without necessarily stressing that he is greater than all other gods. For this reason some object to the rendering "the Supreme God" in TEV.

Come forth and come here: these two imperatives are not to be thought of as separate and distinct commands. Rather they have the combined force of the idiomatic English "come out here," urging the men to leave the place where they were in order to come to the place where the king was. Naturalness in the translator's language should be the determining factor as to whether one or two imperatives are used in translation.

Then: note that TEV adds "at once" at the end of the sentence in order to make the narrative more vivid. This can be justified on the grounds that the transition word at the beginning of the sentence may carry this sense.

3.27 RSV TEV

And the satraps, the prefects, the governors, and the king's counselors gathered together and saw that

All the princes, governors, lieutenant governors, and other officials of the king gathered to look at the

the fire had not had any power over the bodies of those men; the hair of their heads was not singed, their mantles[d] were not harmed, and no smell of fire had come upon them.	three men, who had not been harmed by the fire. Their hair was not singed, their clothes were not burned, and there was no smell of smoke on them.

[d] The meaning of the Aramaic word is uncertain

Satraps, prefects, governors . . . : see verse 2.

Counselors: see verse 24.

Gathered together: the verb used here should not give the impression of an official or formal gathering. It was rather a very informal coming together as a result of general curiosity. TEV makes clear the purpose of their gathering: "to look at the three men."

That the fire had not had any power over the bodies . . . : that is, "that their bodies were not harmed by the fire." This is spelled out in greater detail in the remainder of the verse, with particular reference to their hair and their clothing, since these would be the first things the fire would be expected to consume.

No smell of fire: this combination may sound absurd in some languages. It is much more natural in English to say "no smell of smoke" as in TEV. In some cases it may be more natural to say "not even the smell of fire (or smoke)" or "none of them smelled like smoke [fire]." Possibly what is meant is that there was no smell of human flesh being burned.

3.28 RSV	TEV
Nebuchadnezzar said, "Blessed be the God of Shadrach, Meshach, and Abednego, who has sent his angel and delivered his servants, who trusted in him, and set at nought the king's command, and yielded up their bodies rather than serve and worship any god except their own God.	The king said, "Praise the God of Shadrach, Meshach, and Abednego! He sent his angel and rescued these men who serve and trust him. They disobeyed my orders and risked their lives rather than bow down and worship any god except their own.

Nebuchadnezzar: the proper noun may be replaced by a pronoun or by the title "king," if this will be more natural. See 2.5 and 3.14.

Blessed be: the verb "bless" is often difficult to translate, especially when it is used of a human blessing God. In such cases the Aramaic verb (as well as the corresponding Hebrew) has as its primary component the idea of "praise" or "give thanks to." And in some languages it will be necessary to avoid the passive and name the subject of the verb: "I praise God," "I magnify the name of God," or "Let us praise God." See comments on 2.19-20.

The God of Shadrach, Meshach, and Abednego: that is, the God that Shadrach, Meshach, and Abednego worship. Translators should be careful not to give the impression that someone owns God or that God belonged exclusively to the three persons mentioned or was worshiped only by them.

His angel: compare verse 25. The Aramaic term may indicate a messenger or envoy. The translator may wish to use an expression like "heavenly messenger" or "divine messenger," to emphasize the supernatural character of the person sent.

Delivered: grammatically the subject of this verb may be either God or the angel he sent. Since the result will be essentially the same in either case, this is not an extremely important question. However, most languages will force the translator to decide one way or the other. In such cases it is probably better to make it clear that God is the subject of the verb.

Who trusted in him: this refers to the three persons named, Shadrach, Meshach, and Abednego. King Nebuchadnezzar also calls them **his servants**, meaning God's servants.

Set at nought the king's command: since it is the king who is speaking, it will be unnatural in certain languages for him to refer to himself as "the king." The clear meaning is that they "disobeyed the royal command" (NEB/REB) or, more directly, "disobeyed my orders" (TEV).

Yielded up their bodies: in many languages it may be necessary to indicate an indirect object, if the verb **yielded up** is maintained: "They yielded their bodies to punishment" or "They gave their bodies over to their torturers." The ancient Greek version, the Septuagint, actually supplies such an indirect object, and REB follows this, translating "yield themselves to the fire." Or there may be other meaningful ways of rendering this idea; for example, "willingly surrendered" or, more colloquially, "put their lives on the line."

Rather than serve . . . . : some translators may prefer to say "in order not to have to serve . . . ." For **serve** and **worship** see these verbs used together in verses 12, 14, and 18.

3.29 RSV	TEV
Therefore I make a decree: Any people, nation, or language that speaks anything against the God of Shadrach, Meshach, and Abednego shall be torn limb from limb, and their houses laid in ruins; for there is no other god who is able to deliver in this way."	"And now I command that if anyone of any nation, race, or language speaks disrespectfully of the God of Shadrach, Meshach, and Abednego, he is to be torn limb from limb, and his house is to be made a pile of ruins. There is no other god who can rescue like this."

There is no paragraph break in RSV or most other versions at this point, but TEV begins a new paragraph here. However, the flow of the narrative may require that the speech of the king not be divided at this point.

Therefore: another way of showing the transition may be to say "Consequently." FRCL has "This is why . . . ," and NJV begins the verse with "I hereby give an order . . . ."

Make a decree: the verb used here gives the idea of a public proclamation from the highest authority. In some situations it may be advisable to say something like "as king I command that . . ."

In Aramaic the rest of the verse is probably indirect discourse, but in many languages it may be desirable to shift to direct discourse and present the actual text of the decree within quotation marks. It must be noted, however, that this will mean a quotation within another quotation, and this presents serious problems in some languages. Translators must simply resort to the most natural form in their own language, whether indirect or direct discourse.

People, nation, or language: these are the same words as found in the list in verse 4; only the form is slightly different. As in the previous case the idea of universality is what is important. But the focus is on any individual who may show disrespect for the God of these young men. A possible model for restructuring this verse is GECL: "This is why I communicate the following order to all peoples (nations and languages) (of my kingdom): If anyone speaks . . . ."

Speaks anything against: the Aramaic word carries the idea of negligence or lack of respect. Some other possible wordings are "speaks disrespectfully of" (NJB) or "says a word against" (Mft). Several English translations (NRSV, NEB/REB, NAB, and NJV) use the rather strong verb "blaspheme" or the noun "blasphemy" to convey the idea of this verb.

The God of Shadrach, Meshach, and Abednego: see comments on this expression in verse 28.

Shall be torn limb from limb: this is essentially the same expression as in 2.5, but in the third person singular form here. The fact that it is a passive will require adjustment in some languages. If it has to be made active, translators may consider having the king say something like "my men will cut him to pieces," or "my servants will dismember him."

Houses laid in ruins: this verb will also have to be made active in those languages where the passive form is unnatural or nonexistent. As above, we may say "my men will demolish their houses" or "my servants will totally destroy their houses."

For: this shows the relationship between the statement that follows and the decree itself. It is because there is no other god capable of such a dramatic deliverance that the decree has been issued. While it may be possible simply to present this as a separate statement at the end of the decree as in TEV, it is probably better to show the relationship more clearly. Some possible transition words are "because" (AB and KJV) or "the reason is that . . . ."

No other god: the Aramaic word in this context is a common noun, so it would be a mistake to spell the word **god** with a capital letter as in KJV. Further, the whole phrase may have to be reworded in some languages, since it is inconceivable that there would be another god. In those cases translators may have to say something like "there is no other power."

Deliver: see the use of the term in verses 15, 17, and 28.

3.30   RSV   TEV

Then the king promoted Shadrach,   **And the king promoted Shad-**
Meshach, and Abednego in the   **rach, Meshach, and Abednego to**
province of Babylon.   **higher positions in the province of**
                                             Babylon.

Then: some other ways of making the transition to this verse are "After that" or "As a result of this." NJV has "Thereupon."

Promoted: literally, "caused to prosper." This expression may be understood in two rather different ways: it may be understood as a promotion in rank with respect to their previous situation (2.49), or being reinstated to their previous positions. Translators are advised to give the first interpretation in the text and, if necessary, explain the second in a footnote. A literal rendering, "caused . . . to prosper" (NASB), is not advised, since most versions adopt the idea of promotion. TEV fills out the meaning by adding "to higher positions." In other languages translators may have to say "gave them more important jobs than before," "confided in them to a greater extent," or "entrusted them with greater responsibilities than previously."

The province of Babylon: see 2.49.

Translators using certain versions will note that there is a difference of numbering following this verse. Those verses numbered 1 through 3 of chapter 4 in most English versions are numbered as verses 31-33 of this chapter in translations following the numbering of the text in Aramaic. Whichever numbering system is followed, it is important to note that the next passage belongs with the narrative that follows, not with the story of 3.1-30.

Nebuchadnezzar's Second Dream

Daniel 4.1-37

Verses 1-3 in this chapter are found at the end of chapter 3 in NAB and NJB. These two versions follow the numbering system in the Aramaic text, and so there is a difference of three verses when compared with other English versions. The content of verse 4 in RSV and TEV will thus be found in verse 1 in these two versions. This difference continues throughout the chapter. This Handbook will indicate the alternate numbering system within square brackets.

The organization of this chapter may be outlined as follows:

1-3	Introduction to the dream—including a hymn of praise
4-18	The report of the dream by Nebuchadnezzar (first person)
19-27	Daniel's interpretation (third person)
28-33	The fulfillment of the dream (third person)
34-37	King Nebuchadnezzar's restoration and praise (first person)

This chapter presents special difficulties for the translator because of the embedded quotations it contains. Nebuchadnezzar's account of the dream is in itself a quotation, and it contains the quotation from the watchful angel in verses 14b-17. Then, in the section dealing with the interpretation of the dream, Daniel quotes Nebuchadnezzar, who in turn was quoting the angel (verse 23b). Translators should be aware of these dangers and attempt to make clear at all times who is speaking.

The king dreams of a great tree: 4.1-18 [3.31–4.15]

RSV

1 King Nebuchadnezzar to all peoples, nations, and languages, that dwell in all the earth: Peace be multiplied to you! 2 It has seemed good to me to show the signs and wonders that the Most High God has wrought toward me.
3   How great are his signs,
       how mighty his wonders!
    His kingdom is an everlasting king-
       dom,

TEV

Nebuchadnezzar's Second Dream

1 King Nebuchadnezzar sent the following message to the people of all nations, races, and languages in the world:
    "Greetings! 2 Listen to my account of the wonders and miracles which the Supreme God has shown me.
3   "How great are the wonders God
        shows us!
     How powerful are the miracles he
        performs!

and his dominion is from generation to generation.

4 I, Nebuchadnezzar, was at ease in my house and prospering in my palace. 5 I had a dream which made me afraid; as I lay in bed the fancies and the visions of my head alarmed me. 6 Therefore I made a decree that all the wise men of Babylon should be brought before me, that they might make known to me the interpretation of the dream. 7 Then the magicians, the enchanters, the Chaldeans, and the astrologers came in; and I told them the dream, but they could not make known to me its interpretation. 8 At last Daniel came in before me—he who was named Belteshazzar after the name of my god, and in whom is the spirit of the holy gods—and I told him the dream, saying, 9 "O Belteshazzar, chief of the magicians, because I know that the spirit of the holy gods is in you and that no mystery is difficult for you, here is the dream which I saw; tell me its interpretation. 10 The visions of my head as I lay in bed were these: I saw, and behold, a tree in the midst of the earth; and its height was great. 11 The tree grew and became strong, and its top reached to heaven, and it was visible to the end of the whole earth. 12 Its leaves were fair and its fruit abundant, and in it was food for all. The beasts of the field found shade under it, and the birds of the air dwelt in its branches, and all flesh was fed from it.

13 "I saw in the visions of my head as I lay in bed, and behold, a watcher, a holy one, came down from heaven. 14 He cried aloud and said thus, 'Hew down the tree and cut off its branches, strip off its leaves and scatter its fruit; let the beasts flee from under it and the birds from its branches. 15 But leave the stump of its roots in the earth, bound with a band of iron and bronze, amid the tender grass of the field. Let him be wet with the dew of heaven; let his lot be with the beasts in the grass of the earth; 16 let his mind be changed from a man's, and let a beast's mind be given to him; and let seven times pass over him. 17 The sentence is by the decree of the watchers, the decision by the word of the holy ones, to the end that the living may know that the Most High rules the kingdom of men, and gives it to whom he will, and sets over it the lowliest of men.' 18 This dream I, King Nebuchadnezzar, saw. And you, O Belteshazzar, declare the interpretation, because all the wise men of my kingdom are not able to make

God is king forever; he will rule for all time.

4 "I was living comfortably in my palace, enjoying great prosperity. 5 But I had a frightening dream and saw terrifying visions while I was asleep. 6 I ordered all the royal advisers in Babylon to be brought to me so that they could tell me what the dream meant. 7 Then all the fortunetellers, magicians, wizards, and astrologers were brought in, and I told them my dream, but they could not explain it to me. 8 Then Daniel came in. (He is also called Belteshazzar, after the name of my god.) The spirit of the holy gods is in him, so I told him what I had dreamed. I said to him: 9 Belteshazzar, chief of the fortunetellers, I know that the spirit of the holy gods is in you and that you understand all mysteries. This is my dream. Tell me what it means.

10 "While I was asleep, I had a vision of a huge tree in the middle of the earth. 11 It grew bigger and bigger until it reached the sky and could be seen by everyone in the world. 12 Its leaves were beautiful, and it was loaded down with fruit—enough for the whole world to eat. Wild animals rested in its shade, birds built nests in its branches, and every kind of living being ate its fruit.

13 "While I was thinking about the vision, I saw coming down from heaven an angel, alert and watchful. 14 He proclaimed in a loud voice, 'Cut the tree down and chop off its branches; strip off its leaves and scatter its fruit. Drive the animals from under it and the birds out of its branches. 15 But leave the stump in the ground with a band of iron and bronze around it. Leave it there in the field with the grass.

" 'Now let the dew fall on this man, and let him live with the animals and the plants. 16 For seven years he will not have a human mind, but the mind of an animal. 17 This is the decision of the alert and watchful angels. So then, let all people everywhere know that the Supreme God has power over human kingdoms and that he can give them to anyone he chooses—even to the least important of men.'

18 "This is the dream I had," said King Nebuchadnezzar. "Now, Belteshazzar, tell me what it means. None of my royal advisers could tell me, but you can, because the spirit of the holy gods is in you."

known to me the interpretation, but you are able, for the spirit of the holy gods is in you."

TEV Section Heading: Nebuchadnezzar's Second Dream

Some other possible models for this section heading are "King Nebuchadnezzar has another dream" or "Nebuchadnezzar dreams about a great tree." The first dream of Nebuchadnezzar is, of course, described in 2.1-13. REB gives the following title to this chapter: "Nebuchadnezzar's madness."

If translators are following the outline of this book as given in the introductory section of this handbook, a subheading may be introduced here for verses 1-18: "The king dreams of a great tree."

4.1[e]   RSV   TEV
[3.31]

King Nebuchadnezzar to all peoples, nations, and languages, that dwell in all the earth: Peace be multiplied to you!

King Nebuchadnezzar sent the following message to the people of all nations, races, and languages in the world:
"Greetings!

[e] Ch 3.31 in Aramaic

This chapter begins in the style of a royal proclamation, in which the name of the king is cited first and is followed by a description of the persons the proclamation is addressed to. In many languages it may be more natural to change the order or to add the information that what follows (verse 1b-18) is indeed a proclamation from the king. TEV does this by saying "sent the following message . . . ." In other languages the translator may begin with "This is a proclamation (or, an announcement) from Nebuchadnezzar, the king . . ." or "What follows is an order from King Nebuchadnezzar . . . ."

Peoples, nations, and languages: as in 3.4, 7, 29, this list is intended to cover all political, ethnic, and linguistic groupings, in order to show that the whole world is included. The words **in all the earth** may be an exaggeration, but it is true that Nebuchadnezzar reigned over most of the world he and his contemporaries knew about.

Peace be multiplied to you: the formula using the word **peace** is similar to what is usually found in ancient letters and decrees. The TEV rendering "Greetings" seems a bit weak and perhaps a bit too modern. There may be a wide variety of ways of wishing people prosperity in other languages, but here the well-wishing is especially emphasized by the use of the word **be multiplied**. Some possible English models are: NEB "May all prosperity be yours!" REB "May your prosperity increase!" NIV "May you prosper greatly!" NJB "May you prosper more and more"; NJV "May your well-being abound"; NRSV "May you have abundant prosperity!" and FRCL "I wish you perfect peace!"

4.2   RSV   TEV
[3.32]

It has seemed good to me to show the signs and wonders that the Most High God has wrought toward me.

Listen to my account of the wonders and miracles which the Supreme God has shown me.

It has seemed good to me: or "It pleases me." Mft perhaps captures the flavor a bit better with "It is my royal pleasure . . . ." Another way of saying this in some languages may be "I thought it would be a good idea to describe . . . ." Note that NRSV has modified the word order by placing this part at the end of the verse: ". . . I am pleased to recount."

Signs and wonders: although two different Aramaic words are used here, there was probably no thought of two separate and distinct kinds of happenings. The two terms may be adequately translated as "wonderful miracles" (AB) or "miraculous signs." In many languages it is not unnatural to use two different terms to speak of a single kind of event. An additional reason for translating by two distinct terms is the fact that the same two terms are used again in the poetic setting of the following verse as seemingly separate items. The corresponding Hebrew phrase containing two words can be found in Exo 7.3; Deut 4.34; 6.22; and Isa 8.18 ("signs and portents"). And a similar pair of words is found frequently in the New Testament (Mark 13.22 and John 4.48, for example).

Most High God: see 3.26.

Has wrought toward me: the English of RSV is archaic and the TEV rendering "has shown me" may be subject to misunderstanding. The verb here seems to speak of things actually done and not just shown to Nebuchadnezzar. AB renders this expression "has performed in my regard," which is quite similar to NIV "has performed for me." NRSV gives a revision of RSV: "has worked for me."

4.3   RSV   TEV
[3.33]

**How great are his signs,
  how mighty his wonders!
His kingdom is an everlasting
  kingdom,
and his dominion is from
  generation to generation.**

**"How great are the wonders
  God shows us!
How powerful are the miracles he performs!
God is king forever; he will
  rule for all time.**

The words of this verse are set off as poetic in TEV, and they do, in fact, constitute poetry. (See the comments at the beginning of 2.20-23.) The first two lines are clearly parallel:

great	=	mighty
signs	=	wonders

On **signs** and **wonders** see verse 2 above. TEV makes it clear that God's wonders are directed toward human beings: "shows us." This kind of clarification may be a good idea in a number of other languages. But again the verb "show" may be too weak.

The third and fourth lines of the poem are also parallel:

kingdom	=	dominion
everlasting	=	from generation to generation

Note that TEV also renders two of the pronouns by the noun "God." This may also be desirable in a number of other languages.

Dominion: this term is used to indicate authority or power to rule over or impose one's will on others. It occurs frequently in the book of Daniel. NIV speaks of "authority to rule" in other contexts (7.6) although it uses the same word as RSV in this verse.

From generation to generation: this may not always be the most natural way to express the permanence of God's rule. Since two different expressions are called for by the parallel structure, translators may consider the use of a negation such as "his rule will never end" for the second of the pair. REB has "through all generations."

4.4   RSV   TEV
[4.1]

I, Nebuchadnezzar, was at ease in my house and prospering in my palace.	**"I was living comfortably in my palace, enjoying great prosperity.**

This is numbered as verse 1 in NJB and NAB, following the Aramaic text. But most English versions follow the numbering system of RSV and TEV.

I, Nebuchadnezzar: in some languages it will be quite natural for a person to repeat his own name following the first person singular pronoun. In others this will be awkward and should be omitted. Still others may say "I, the king . . ." in such a context.

At ease in my house and prospering in my palace: once again this is an example of parallelism. The meaning of the two phrases is simply "doing extremely well" or "getting along just fine." Another way of saying this may be "everything was going very well for me . . . ." The translator must be careful to avoid suggesting that **my house** and **my palace** refer to two different buildings. They are just different ways of talking about the king's residence. In some languages the only way to avoid confusion may be to reduce the parallel construction to a single statement. On the translation of **palace**, see 1.4.

The form of the verbs conveying the ideas "be content" and "prosper" should not communicate the idea that this was the king's situation at a particular time, but rather that it was true continually over a period of time. In some languages the habitual form of the verb will adequately transmit this meaning. REB translates the whole parallel structure as follows: ". . . was living contentedly at home in the luxury of my palace."

4.5 RSV	TEV
[4.2]	
I had a dream which made me afraid; as I lay in bed the fancies and the visions of my head alarmed me.	**But I had a frightening dream and saw terrifying visions while I was asleep.**

Although there is no conjunction in RSV or in the Aramaic, there is a clear need in most languages for a transition word that shows a contrast with what has just been stated. This is why TEV begins with "But," as does REB. Another way to begin this verse is "And then . . ." (Knox) or "Then one night . . . ." In some languages a shift verb form may also be appropriate here.

This verse is yet another example of parallelism ("a dream" = "the fancies and the visions"; "made me afraid" = "alarmed me"). One way of avoiding giving the impression that two different events are in view is to introduce the second part of the parallel structure with something like "in fact . . ." or "indeed . . ." or "that is to say . . . ."

4.6 RSV	TEV
[4.3]	
Therefore I made a decree that all the wise men of Babylon should be brought before me, that they might make known to me the interpretation of the dream.	**I ordered all the royal advisers in Babylon to be brought to me so that they could tell me what the dream meant.**

Therefore: this RSV rendering represents the common conjunction that has a wide variety of meanings and is frequently left untranslated in many languages. In this context it is certainly not as strong as the RSV rendering may suggest.

I made a decree: literally "from me is issued a decree . . . ." This is the same expression as in 3.29. But the passive formulation is not recommended in most languages.

Wise men: see 2.12.

That they might make known: while the plural pronoun **they** is used here, this should not be understood to mean that the king expected a separate explanation from each of the wise men. So in languages where the more literal rendering is likely to be misunderstood, it may be better to translate "so that someone (one of them) might tell me . . . ."

4.7 RSV	TEV
[4.4]	
Then the magicians, the enchanters, the Chaldeans, and the astrologers came in; and I told them the dream, but they could not make known to me its interpretation.	Then all the fortunetellers, magicians, wizards, and astrologers were brought in, and I told them my dream, but they could not explain it to me.

Magicians, . . . astrologers: on this list, see the same terms in 2.2; **astrologers** occurs in 2.27. And note especially that the term **Chaldeans** is not to be understood in its purely geographical sense.

They: similar to the previous verse, it may be better to translate this as "none of them" or something similar.

Could not make known to me: literally "did not make known to me . . . ." But the focus is clearly on their inability to provide the interpretation rather than on any unwillingness on their part. REB has "but they were unable to interpret it for me."

4.8 RSV	TEV
[4.5]	
At last Daniel came in before me— he who was named Belteshazzar after the name of my god, and in whom is the spirit of the holy gods[g]—and I told him the dream, saying,	Then Daniel came in. (He is also called Belteshazzar, after the name of my god.) The spirit of the holy gods[d] is in him, so I told him what I had dreamed. I said to him:
	[d] gods; or God.

[g] Or *Spirit of the holy God*

At last: the exact meaning of the corresponding Aramaic expression is uncertain. The main word in the expression is derived from a root meaning "after," "next," or "another." Many versions take it to mean **At last** (as in RSV and NRSV) or "Finally" (NIV, NJV, NAB, REB). Others render it "A little later" (FRCL), which is similar to TEV "Then . . . ." NEB follows the meaning "yet another." It is probably best to adopt a rendering that approximates the meaning "finally" or "at last."

Before me: it will be noted that TEV takes this information as included in "came in."

He who was named Belteshazzar: see 1.7, where this new name was given. The name and its explanation are rightly taken as parenthetical information in TEV and certain other versions. If parentheses are not used in the language of translation, then some other device should be found to indicate that this explanation of Daniel's other name is aside from the main story line.

After the name of my god: one of the principal Babylonian deities was called "Bel" (see Isa 46.1), which is another name for Marduk. The relationship between the name of the deity and Daniel's other name is not strictly one of derivatiòn from the actual words, but of resemblance in spelling. The name actually comes from *Balatsu-usur,* meaning "may he protect his life."

And in whom is the spirit of the holy gods: the punctuation of RSV indicates that this is a part of the parenthetical thought of the king. Similar punctuation is used in NIV. But in other versions where parentheses are used (TEV, Mft), this phrase is not so marked. In most languages it will probably be better to make this a new sentence outside any parentheses. Some possible ways of wording it are "The spirit of the holy gods is in him," "He is moved by the spirit of the holy gods," or "This man is endowed with the spirit of the holy gods." The plural noun **gods** may legitimately be translated as a singular as in one ancient version of this book, but in the mouth of the non-Jewish monarch, the plural is probably better.

In some languages it will be considered redundant and unnecessary to use the adjective **holy** with the word for **gods**, since it would be unimaginable to think of an unholy god. But unless the use of the adjective is unnatural, it should be retained for emphasis.

The word **holy** itself presents serious problems for translators. Even if it is omitted for contextual reasons here and in the following verse, it cannot be avoided in other passages. The adjective often refers to something belonging to God or completely separated from the ordinary things of life, and only rarely focuses on moral purity. In this context one possible translation is "the gods [God] who are completely separate from human beings" or ". . . who are entirely different from us."

4.9 RSV	TEV
[4.6]	
"O Belteshazzar, chief of the magicians, because I know that the spirit of the holy^g gods is in you and that no mystery is difficult for you, here is^h the dream which I saw; tell me its interpretation.	Belteshazzar, chief of the fortune-tellers, I know that the spirit of the holy gods^d is in you and that you understand all mysteries. This is^e my dream. Tell me what it means.
^g Or *Spirit of the holy God* ^h Cn: Aramaic *visions of*	^d gods; *or* God. ^e *Probable text* This is; *Aramaic* Visions of.

O Belteshazzar: in many languages there is no form for the vocative that would be the equivalent of **O**. In such cases it should of course be omitted. Other languages will have different kinds of words to call the attention of a person addressed.

Chief of the magicians: compare 2.48, where Daniel is called "chief prefect over all the wise men." The word used here is the Aramaic equivalent of the first Hebrew word in the list in 2.2. There is, however, no contradiction between the two titles. This one does not mean that Daniel is chief of only one category of wise men. Detached from the list, this word takes on a more general meaning. If necessary in order to avoid a contradiction, the translator is allowed to use the same term as the one for "wise men" in 2.48.

Because . . . : beginning with this conjunction, the structure of RSV is a bit awkward. In many languages it will be preferable to break it down into two sentences, beginning the second with "Therefore." For example, "I know that the spirit of the holy gods is in you and that there is nothing that you do not understand. Therefore I am telling you my dream . . . ." Or it may be possible to turn the wording around to say "I am telling you my dream because I know that the spirit of the holy gods is in you and that you understand all mysteries."

The spirit of the holy gods: see comments on verse 8 above.

No mystery is difficult for you: this negative construction may be expressed positively as in TEV, if this will be more natural.

The last part of this verse is literally "The visions of my dream that I saw, and its interpretation, tell me." It is grammatically possible to understand this wording in two different ways:

(a) "Tell me the dream that I had and its interpretation" (compare KJV, NASB). This seems unlikely, since the king himself goes on to disclose the content of the dream, beginning with the following verse.

(b) "(Here is) the dream that I had; tell me its interpretation." This assumes that the reader is meant to understand a demonstrative ("this is") at the beginning of the sentence. This is the solution generally adopted in modern versions and recommended to translators.

Here is the dream: while the majority of modern English versions have something like this or "listen to the dream . . ." (compare REB, AB), these words are not found in the original text. For this reason they are omitted by NAB and NJV. But a slight change in the text gives the meaning of RSV instead of "visions of (my dream)."

4.10 [4.7] RSV	TEV
The visions of my head as I lay in bed were these: I saw, and behold, a tree in the midst of the earth; and its height was great.	**"While I was asleep, I had a vision of a huge tree in the middle of the earth.**

It will be noted that certain modern versions set out verses 10 through 17 in poetic format (NRSV, REB, and NJB); but this is not recommended in most languages.

The visions of my head: compare verse 5 and 2.28.

As I lay in my bed: a literal rendering of this expression may give the false impression that the king was actually awake. But this was clearly not the case, and the reader should understand that this was a dream. For this reason several modern versions say "While I was asleep" (TEV, GECL).

And behold: the Aramaic interjection used here (as in 2.31) is found only in the description of a vision. In addition to this occurrence it is also found in verse 13, and in 7.2, 5, 7, 8 (two times), and 13. Its Hebrew counterpart occurs in 8.3, 5, 15, 19; 9.18; 10.5, 10, 16; 11.2; 12.5. It is used to enliven the narrative and heighten the excitement of the reader. There may or may not be an equivalent in other languages. In many cases it is best to omit it altogether. Translators should be careful not to force the usage of a particle that is not really natural in the language in such a context.

A tree in the midst of the earth: the exact geographical location of the tree is unimportant. What is significant is that it is the center of attention for the whole world. The tree is a common biblical symbol for life and power. Ezekiel, for example, speaks of a tall tree being brought low and of a low tree being raised up (Ezek 17.22-24).

And its height was great: this separate sentence may easily be translated by a single adjective in many languages. But the focus seems to be more on the height of the tree than on its overall size.

4.11   RSV   TEV
[4.8]

The tree grew and became strong, and its top reached to heaven, and it was visible to the end of the whole earth.	It grew bigger and bigger until it reached the sky and could be seen by everyone in the world.

Grew and became strong: the two verbs in Aramaic indicate clearly a change in the state of the tree. While it was already said to be very tall in the previous verse, some languages may require something like "grew still taller and more powerful" (similar to FRCL).

Its top reached to heaven: literally "its height touched the skies." The word translated **top** here is the same as the one for "height" in verse 10. The word translated **heaven** in RSV is not intended to speak of the dwelling place of God but refers to the sky. However, in some languages there is only one word for the two ideas. In this context it may be possible in some cases to translate ". . . reached to the clouds."

It was visible: the passive formulation in this case may be legitimately translated "they (indefinite) could see it" or "people could see it."

To the end of the whole earth: according to some primitive notions, the earth was thought of as an immense flat disk. It would therefore be possible to see the top of the tree from any point in the world. But it must be kept in mind that this is a figure of speech and its literal validity is not in focus. The whole phrase may be rendered "people could see it from everywhere in the world" or "they could observe the tree from all over the earth."

4.12   RSV   TEV
[4.9]

Its leaves were fair and its fruit abundant, and in it was food for all.	Its leaves were beautiful, and it was loaded down with fruit—enough for

The beasts of the field found shade under it, and the birds of the air dwelt in its branches, and all flesh was fed from it.	the whole world to eat. Wild animals rested in its shade, birds built nests in its branches, and every kind of living being ate its fruit.

This verse constitutes an example of double parallelism within six lines. The structure may be outlined according to the following scheme, in which "=" marks items that are parallel to each other:

$$A = B \qquad\qquad D = E$$
$$+ \qquad\qquad = \qquad\qquad +$$
$$C \qquad\qquad\qquad\qquad F$$

The translator may conserve this structure if it is natural in the receptor language. Or it may be possible to simplify it, as in GECL,

$$([A = B] \qquad\qquad = \qquad\qquad [D = E])$$

and then combine lines C and F into a single element at the end of the verse; thus GECL has "It carried thick leaves and abundant fruit. In its shadow rested the animals; birds nested in its branches; and everything that lived received its nourishment from it [the tree]." Another possible model is the following: "It had beautiful leaves and much fruit on it. Animals rested under it and birds nested on its branches. It provided enough food for everyone on earth to eat."

In it was food for all: it may be very inappropriate to use the preposition **in** to describe the relationship between the tree and its fruit. NCV has "On the tree was food for everyone." Another way of saying this is "it provided enough food for all."

The beasts of the field . . . birds of the air: in many languages the words **of the field** and **of the air** are redundant and may be omitted. Compare 2.38.

Dwelt: while the Aramaic word is general, the context with birds as subject makes it more appropriate in some languages to say "built their nests" as in TEV or "found shelter" (REB). NRSV has "nested in its branches."

All flesh: the expression is used to refer to every kind of living creature, whether animal or human.

Was fed from it: once again the passive form will have to be translated actively in many languages. It is possible to say something like "every creature got what it needed to eat from it" or "every living being ate from it."

4.13   RSV   TEV
[4.10]

"I saw In the visions of my head as I lay in bed, and behold, a watcher, a holy one, came down from heaven.	"While I was thinking about the vision, I saw coming down from heaven an angel, alert and watchful.

The Aramaic text of the beginning of this verse is almost identical with the beginning of verse 10. It is possible to translate "While I was still lying in (my) bed" or "While I was still sleeping . . . ." The TEV rendering may give the impression that the king had woken up and was pondering the meaning of the first part of the vision when the second came. But it is more likely that he was still sleeping when the dream continued. This interlude is taken as nonpoetic in those versions that set the rest of this section off in poetic format.

And behold: see verse 10 as well as 2.31.

A watcher, a holy one: literally "(a being) watchful and holy." In the Book of Daniel these two adjectives are used to describe a heavenly being that never sleeps and is always in the presence of the holy God. This is almost invariably taken by scholars as reference to an angel, although some consider these a special class of angels. Translators should take care that a literal translation of these terms does not give the impression that two different beings are intended. In order to avoid this difficulty, some modern versions have simply rendered the whole expression as "an angel who is vigilant" or "a holy watcher" (NRSV). Since angels are considered divine beings, some translators are content to leave the idea of their holiness as included in the term "angel" itself. But this would definitely not be the case if the NIV "messenger" is used as a model.

Heaven: while this is the same word as used for "sky" in verse 11, the present context makes it proper to translate **heaven** in this case if the receptor language distinguishes between "sky" and "heaven."

4.14 RSV	TEV
[4.11]	
He cried aloud and said thus, 'Hew down the tree and cut off its branches, strip off its leaves and scatter its fruit; let the beasts flee from under it and the birds from its branches.	He proclaimed in a loud voice, 'Cut the tree down and chop off its branches; strip off its leaves and scatter its fruit. Drive the animals from under it and the birds out of its branches.

He cried aloud: or "announced with force." The same expression is used at the beginning of 3.4.

And said thus: this may easily be omitted as redundant in a number of languages.

Hew down . . . cut off . . . strip off . . . scatter: this series of imperative verb forms may seem to be addressed to the king as he observed the dream. But verse 17 seems to indicate that the angel is speaking to his own companions. In order to avoid confusion, the audience addressed by the angel's statement may have to be made clearer by introducing these imperatives with "He shouted to his companions . . . ."

Let the beasts flee: this means more than simply allowing the animals to run away. They are to be driven out by chopping down the tree. In some languages a causative verb form will be appropriate here: "Cause the animals to run away . . . ." And it may be better to reverse the order of the last two verb phrases or to show their relationship more clearly. Most English versions, including TEV, make it sound as if the animals were still standing around and the birds still in the branches after the tree had been cut down. This is, of course, contrary to what we know of nature. It will be possible in certain languages to say "Drive the animals and birds away from the tree by cutting it down. Yes, cut it down and chop off the branches. Strip off the leaves and take away its fruit."

Under it . . . out of its branches: compare verse 12.

4.15
[4.12]

RSV	TEV
But leave the stump of its roots in the earth, bound with a band of iron and bronze, amid the tender grass of the field. Let him be wet with the dew of heaven; let his lot be with the beasts in the grass of the earth;	But leave the stump in the ground with a band of iron and bronze around it. Leave it there in the field with the grass. " 'Now let the dew fall on this man, and let him live with the animals and the plants.

In this verse we pass almost imperceptibly from a symbolic vision of the fate of the tree (representing the king) to a more realistic description of the fate of the king himself. In Aramaic, where the noun for "tree" is masculine, the transition from "it" and "its" to "him" and "his" is not evident. It has been suggested that if possible the translator should respect this scheme and avoid an abrupt change in the middle of the verse like that in TEV, which begins a new paragraph and translates the pronoun as "this man." And in languages that do not have different pronouns to refer to trees (or tree trunks) on the one hand and to human beings on the other hand, this will be possible; however, in those languages where the pronouns must be different, it may be necessary to follow the TEV model and make a clear break. Note that REB also uses a blank line to indicate this break.

But: the strong contrastive conjunction at the beginning of this verse is important, since it introduces a shift from destruction to preservation. Some other possibilities are "nevertheless" (KJV) or "yet" (NASB).

The stump of its roots: the tree was to be cut down close to the ground so that a stump with its roots still in the earth would remain.

Bound: a literal translation of this verb may give the impression that the metal bands were present before the tree was cut down. The intent of the writer, however, is that those who cut down the tree should also bind it. For this reason it will be better in some languages to use another imperative form of the verb here: "bind it . . ." or "encircle it . . . ."

With a band of iron and bronze: literally "in binding of iron and bronze." The word translated **band** is not necessarily singular in meaning, so translators should not present the idea of a single band made of two kinds of metal. The image is rather a picture of two or more bands made of iron and bronze encircling the stump. The idea of "binding" may be adequately translated "fetters" (NJV), "hoops" (NJB), or "chains" (FRCL). And **bronze** may also possibly be translated "brass."

The grass of the field: the words **of the field** here and **of the earth** toward the end of the verse may be omitted as redundant in many languages.

Let him be wet: as indicated above, the pronoun **him** is translated "this man" in TEV, referring to King Nebuchadnezzar, and a new paragraph is begun. Translators will have to consider whether this model should be reproduced in their languages. NIV also begins a new paragraph at this point.

The dew of heaven: the words **of heaven** may be considered superfluous in many languages. This is simply another common usage in Aramaic and Hebrew, similar to "the birds of the air" or "the grass of the field" in this context.

Let his lot be with the beasts in the grass of the earth: **his lot** in English means "his fate" or "his destiny." It is possible to understand this fate as a condemnation to live **in the grass** or on the ground "among the plants" (NIV) like the animals. Or it may be a condemnation to obtain his food from the herbs of the land. Both RSV and TEV clearly follow the first interpretation. The NJV rendering, "and share the earth's verdure with the beasts," is more ambiguous. NAB comes down clearly on the other side: "(Let) his lot be to eat, among the beasts, the grass of the earth." This interpretation, also adopted by FRCL and a number of other versions, seems to be supported by the context, since the following verse indicates that his mind will be that of an animal.

4.16 RSV TEV
[4.13]

let his mind be changed from a man's, and let a beast's mind be given to him; and let seven times pass over him.	For seven years he will not have a human mind, but the mind of an animal.

Let his mind be changed: literally the text speaks of the "heart" being changed (compare KJV). But the "heart" here is to be understood as the seat of the intelligence. Therefore the translation **mind** is justified in English. In other languages, however, it may be perfectly acceptable to retain "heart" in this context, or to use some other organ thought of as being the seat of intelligence. This, of course, is not to be understood as a "heart transplant" or a "brain transplant" in which the king literally receives the organ of an animal. Rather, he will act as if he is being driven by the mind of an animal.

Let seven times pass over him: the oldest and most common interpretation of the **seven times** is that seven years is intended. The use of the word for "time" as "year" is peculiar to Daniel (compare 4.23, 25, 32; 7.25; 12.7), but it is well established. So it is probably best in most languages to translate "years" here. Note also that TEV has restructured this verse and placed the time element at the beginning of the sentence.

4.17
[4.14]

RSV	TEV
The sentence is by the decree of the watchers, the decision by the word of the holy ones, to the end that the living may know that the Most High rules the kingdom of men, and gives it to whom he will, and sets over it the lowliest of men.'	This is the decision of the alert and watchful angels. So then, let all people everywhere know that the Supreme God has power over human kingdoms and that he can give them to anyone he chooses—even to the least important ones.'

The parallelism at the beginning of this verse should be translated in such a way as to avoid making the reader think of two different events. The word **sentence** corresponds to **decision**; and **the watchers** obviously has the same meaning as **the holy ones**. For this reason TEV has combined the two.

By the decree . . . by the word: it is important that the translation avoid giving the impression that the angels are capable of making decisions themselves. They are, in fact, only messengers or bearers of the decision made by God. For this reason FRCL translates "transmitted by . . . ."

Watchers . . . holy ones: see verse 13.

To the end that . . . : this shows the purpose of the decision communicated by the angels. The TEV rendering "So then" at the beginning of a new sentence may seem weak if translated literally into some languages. "In this way" or "As a result" may be better.

The living: that is, all persons who are alive, wherever they may be.

The Most High: the Aramaic word used here occurs sometimes along with the name of God (as in 3.26; 4.2; 5.18, 21). But here and in a number of other cases it occurs alone, that is, unaccompanied by the word for "God" (4.24, 25, 32, 34; 7.18, 22, 25, 27). The corresponding Hebrew expression is often used in the Psalms in parallel with other terms for God. In some languages it is possible to say "the Most High One," and this will be understood as referring to God, but in other languages it will be indispensable to add the word for God, even when it is not actually present in the text. It should be noted that this expression is also used in the New Testament to refer to God. It is a favorite of Luke (1.32, 35, 76; 6.35; Acts 7.48, for example).

Rules: literally "is powerful over."

The kingdom of men: although singular in form, the word for **kingdom** has a collective meaning and should probably be translated as a plural in most languages (as in "human kingdoms," TEV). Also, the two occurrences of the pronoun **it** which follow refer to **kingdom** and should be made plural.

Gives: the verb used here carries a sense of "being able to" that is probably better rendered "can give," as in TEV, NAB, FRCL, and GECL.

The lowliest of men: the Aramaic term has the sense of positive humility, rather than a negative sense that may possibly communicate the idea of "the scum of the earth." It is therefore perhaps better to translate something like "the most humble person" or "the meekest of all people."

4.18   RSV   TEV
[4.15]

This dream I, King Nebuchadnezzar, saw. And you, O Belteshazzar, declare the interpretation, because all the wise men of my kingdom are not able to make known to me the interpretation, but you are able, for the spirit of the holy gods[i] is in you."

"This is the dream I had," said King Nebuchadnezzar. "Now, Belteshazzar, tell me what it means. None of my royal advisers could tell me, but you can, because the spirit of the holy gods[f] is in you."

[f] gods; *or* God.

[i] Or *Spirit of the holy God*

While there is no paragraph break in RSV, several other modern versions make one here, including TEV, REB, and NRSV. This is probably because this verse constitutes a sort of summary and conclusion of what the king had to say to Daniel. In some languages it may be wise to mark this by introducing this verse with a phrase like "Then King Nebuchadnezzar added (concluded) . . . ." If this is done, it will probably be more natural not to have the name of Nebuchadnezzar included in the direct quotation.

The word translated **declare** at the beginning of this verse is the ordinary verb meaning "say" or "tell." Therefore translators should not look for special vocabulary to render this verb.

All the wise men . . . are not able . . . : the negative marker is moved from the verb to the subject in TEV for the sake of naturalness. This may be a good model to follow in some cases. Also, it may be more natural to say "were not able" instead of **are not able**.

The interpretation: the repetition of this word may make the translation heavy in some languages. This can be avoided by using an expression of similar meaning, such as "what it means," or by omitting it in the second case, as in TEV.

The spirit of the holy gods: see verses 8 and 9.

Daniel explains the second dream: 4.19-33 [4.16-30]

                    RSV   TEV
                                                   Daniel Explains the Dream

19 Then Daniel, whose name was Belteshazzar, was dismayed for a moment, and his thoughts alarmed him. The king said, "Belteshazzar, let not the dream or the interpretation alarm you." Belteshazzar answered, "My lord, may the dream be for those who hate you and its interpretation for your enemies! 20 The tree you saw, which grew and became strong, so that its top reached to heaven, and it was visible to the end of the whole earth; 21 whose leaves were fair and its fruit abundant, and in which was food for all; under

19 At this, Daniel, who is also called Belteshazzar, was so alarmed that he could not say anything. The king said to him, "Belteshazzar, don't let the dream and its message alarm you."

Belteshazzar replied, "Your Majesty, I wish that the dream and its explanation applied to your enemies and not to you. 20 The tree, so tall that it reached the sky, could be seen by everyone in the world. 21 Its leaves were beautiful, and it had enough fruit on it to feed the whole world. Wild animals rested which beasts of the field found shade, and in whose branches the birds of the air dwelt— 22 it is you, O king, who have grown and become strong. Your greatness has grown and reaches to heaven, and your dominion to the ends of the earth. 23 And whereas the king saw a watcher, a holy one, coming down from heaven and saying, 'Hew down the tree and destroy it, but leave the stump of its roots in the earth, bound with a band of iron and bronze, in the tender grass of the field; and let him be wet with the dew of heaven; and let his lot be with the beasts of the field, till seven times pass over him'; 24 this is the interpretation, O king: It is a decree of the Most High, which has come upon my lord the king, 25 that you shall be driven from among men, and your dwelling shall be with the beasts of the field; you shall be made to eat grass like an ox, and you shall be wet with the dew of heaven, and seven times shall pass over you, till you know that the Most High rules the kingdom of men, and gives it to whom he will. 26 And as it was commanded to leave the stump of the roots of the tree, your kingdom shall be sure for you from the time that you know that Heaven rules. 27 Therefore, O king, let my counsel be acceptable to you; break off your sins by practicing righteousness, and your iniquities by showing mercy to the oppressed, that there may perhaps be a lengthening of your tranquillity."

28 All this came upon King Nebuchadnezzar. 29 At the end of twelve months he was walking on the roof of the royal palace of Babylon, 30 and the king said, "Is not this great Babylon, which I have built by my mighty power as a royal residence and for the glory of my majesty?" 31 While the words were still in the king's mouth, there fell a voice from heaven, "O King Nebuchadnezzar, to you it is spoken: The kingdom has departed from you, 32 and you shall be driven from among men, and your dwelling shall be with the beasts of the field; and you shall be made to eat grass like an ox; and seven times shall pass over you, until you have learned that the Most High rules the kingdom of men and gives it to whom he will." 33 Immediately the word was fulfilled upon Nebuchadnezzar. He was driven from among men, and ate grass like an ox, and his body was wet with the dew of heaven till his hair grew as long as eagles' feathers, and his nails were like birds' claws.

under it, and birds made their nests in its branches.

22 "Your Majesty, you are the tree, tall and strong. You have grown so great that you reach the sky, and your power extends over the whole world. 23 While Your Majesty was watching, an angel came down from heaven and said, 'Cut the tree down and destroy it, but leave the stump in the ground. Wrap a band of iron and bronze around it, and leave it there in the field with the grass. Let the dew fall on this man, and let him live there with the animals for seven years.'

24 "This, then, is what it means, Your Majesty, and this is what the Supreme God has declared will happen to you. 25 You will be driven away from human society and will live with wild animals. For seven years you will eat grass like an ox and sleep in the open air, where the dew will fall on you. Then you will admit that the Supreme God controls all human kingdoms and that he can give them to anyone he chooses. 26 The angel ordered the stump to be left in the ground. This means that you will become king again when you acknowledge that God rules all the world. 27 So then, Your Majesty, follow my advice. Stop sinning, do what is right, and be merciful to the poor. Then you will continue to be prosperous."

28 All this did happen to King Nebuchadnezzar. 29 Only twelve months later, while he was walking around on the roof of his royal palace in Babylon, 30 he said, "Look how great Babylon is! I built it as my capital city to display my power and might, my glory and majesty."

31 Before the words were out of his mouth, a voice spoke from heaven, "King Nebuchadnezzar, listen to what I say! Your royal power is now taken away from you. 32 You will be driven away from human society, live with wild animals, and eat grass like an ox for seven years. Then you will acknowledge that the Supreme God has power over human kingdoms and that he can give them to anyone he chooses."

33 The words came true immediately. Nebuchadnezzar was driven out of human society and ate grass like an ox. The dew fell on his body, and his hair grew as long as eagle feathers and his nails as long as bird claws.

TEV **Section Heading: Daniel explains the dream**
While the story continues, it is a good idea to divide such a long stretch of discourse into different sections. What follows is the explanation of the dream, which Daniel gives to King Nebuchadnezzar. Some other model headings are "Daniel interprets the second dream" (NRSV), "The king hears Daniel's explanation," or "The meaning of the dream is revealed to Nebuchadnezzar."

4.19	RSV	TEV
[4.16]		

RSV: Then Daniel, whose name was Belteshazzar, was dismayed for a moment, and his thoughts alarmed him. The king said, "Belteshazzar, let not the dream or the interpretation alarm you." Belteshazzar answered, "My lord, may the dream be for those who hate you and its interpretation for your enemies!

TEV: At this, Daniel, who is also called Belteshazzar, was so alarmed that he could not say anything. The king said to him, "Belteshazzar, don't let the dream and its message alarm you."

Belteshazzar replied, "Your Majesty, I wish that the dream and its explanation applied to your enemies and not to you.

Whose name was Belteshazzar: this information, repeated from verse 8, may possibly be omitted in some languages if the repetition is considered unnatural.

Dismayed . . . alarmed . . . : these two verbs are similar in meaning and may be translated by one verb in many languages. A single verb is, in fact, used in Nebuchadnezzar's response to the situation.

For a moment: NRSV revises this to "for a while," while NIV has "for a time." The term indicates a relatively short period of time, but not necessarily a matter of mere seconds. It has been omitted altogether by TEV, but this is not advised.

The king said: literally "answered and said" (see 2.5). Instead of this, GECL has the first person pronoun, "and I said to him . . . ." This is based on the idea that the entire chapter is the king's own narration (see 4.1). But given the distance from the introduction and the intervening section heading, it is appropriate to maintain the third person singular of the original.

My lord: translators should use whatever title is appropriate for them when addressing a king or an important chief (compare 1.10).

May the dream be for those who hate you and its interpretation for your enemies: once again, this parallel structure expresses a single point. Daniel wishes that the bad news of the dream might be for the enemies of King Nebuchadnezzar, but in fact he knows very well that it is for the king himself. The translation must bring out the fact that Daniel is aware of the consequences to Nebuchadnezzar of the interpretation he is about to give. TEV does this by using the verb "I wish" and adding at the end "and not to you." NIV and NEB/REB begin "if only . . . ," and NAB uses "should be . . . ." But it may be necessary to say more than this in some languages and say at the end of the verse something like "but I know it concerns you" (compare verse 22 below).

4.20   RSV   TEV
[4.17]
The tree you saw, which grew and   **The tree, so tall that it reached the**
became strong, so that its top   **sky, could be seen by everyone in**
reached to heaven, and it was visi-   **the world.**
ble to the end of the whole earth;

This is very similar to verse 11, but here the writer adds the fact that the tree was seen by King Nebuchadnezzar.

4.21   RSV   TEV
[4.18]
whose leaves were fair and its fruit   **Its leaves were beautiful, and it had**
abundant, and in which was food for   **enough fruit on it to feed the whole**
all; under which beasts of the field   **world. Wild animals rested under it,**
found shade, and in whose branch-   **and birds made their nests in its**
es the birds of the air dwelt—   **branches.**

This verse is almost a word-for-word repetition of verse 12 above. However, in place of the verb rendered **found shade** in verse 12, this verse actually has a more general word meaning "to live" or "to rest" for the **beasts**. And for the birds, instead of **dwelt** this verse has a term of slightly different meaning. Note that NRSV translates the verb in verse 12 "were fed," while the verb in this verse is rendered "had nests." The same sort of meaning difference is distinguished in NIV. It may or may not be possible to reflect these shades of meaning in the translation. But if it is possible to do so naturally, then it should be done.

4.22   RSV   TEV
[4.19]
it is you, O king, who have grown   **"Your Majesty, you are the**
and become strong. Your greatness   **tree, tall and strong. You have**
has grown and reaches to heaven,   **grown so great that you reach the**
and your dominion to the ends of   **sky, and your power extends over**
the earth.   **the whole world.**

It is you: the Aramaic text does not mention the tree here, but it is clearly in mind. And this is brought out in a number of modern versions. In some languages it will be possible to heighten the suspense by using a structure similar to that of FRCL: "This tree, your Majesty, it is you!" Compare also REB, "that tree, your majesty, is you."

O king: this is not the same word as rendered "my lord" in verse 19, but in some languages it may have to be translated in the same way.

The remainder of this verse draws on verse 11 for its terminology, but the reference is now clearly to the king rather than to the tree.

The words **greatness** and **dominion** refer to the power and authority of the king, which are described as reaching proportions that are difficult to describe. Some possible models for the last part of this verse are "You have become so great that you have power over the heavens; your authority reaches to the end of the earth" or "You are now so great that there is no limit to your power; your authority reaches over the whole world." It will be important in many languages not to translate the conjunction **and** that joins these two statements in such a way as to lead readers to believe that two complete separate matters are being talked about. They are really two ways of talking about the same thing. NCV attempts to tie these statements more closely to the image of the tree, and that version may provide a helpful model to other translators: "You have become great and powerful. You are like the tall tree that touched the sky. And your power reaches to the far parts of the earth."

4.23   RSV   TEV
[4.20]

RSV	TEV
And whereas the king saw a watcher, a holy one, coming down from heaven and saying, 'Hew down the tree and destroy it, but leave the stump of its roots in the earth, bound with a band of iron and bronze, in the tender grass of the field; and let him be wet with the dew of heaven; and let his lot be with the beasts of the field, till seven times pass over him';	While Your Majesty was watching, an angel came down from heaven and said, 'Cut the tree down and destroy it, but leave the stump in the ground. Wrap a band of iron and bronze around it, and leave it there in the field with the grass. Let the dew fall on this man, and let him live there with the animals for seven years.'

And whereas . . . : the form used here may be taken simply to introduce the next in a series of events, "Next . . ." with a full stop at the end of this verse. Or it may be understood as in RSV, introducing (or reintroducing) the vision that is to be explained in the following verse. AB begins with "As for the king's vision . . . ." The RSV translation reflects the structure of the Aramaic in making verses 23-25 one very long sentence. But in most languages it is probably better to make two or more sentences of these verses. See also comments at the beginning of verses 24 and 25.

The king: instead of using the third person reference to the king, it will be much more natural in many languages to use the second person singular pronoun "you," or perhaps the phrase "you, O king." On the grammatical change of person, see comments on 2.10.

A watcher, a holy one coming down from heaven: see verse 13.

Destroy it: this is a way of summarizing the meaning of that part of verse 14 which used several different verbal expressions, including "cut off," "strip off," and "scatter."

Most of the rest of this verse is a repetition of the essential content of verses 15 and 16 above.

4.24　　　　　RSV　　　　　　　　　　　　　　　TEV
[4.21]

| this is the interpretation, O king: It is a decree of the Most High, which has come upon my lord the king, | "This, then, is what it means, Your Majesty, and this is what the Supreme God has declared will happen to you. |

Since this is again a kind of summary or conclusion, a paragraph break is made in TEV and a number of other English versions. Such a break is also recommended to translators.

O king: see verse 22.

A decree: see verse 17.

The Most High: see comments on this term in verse 17.

My lord the king: as in 1.10, it may be more natural to translate this whole expression by a simple pronoun, as is done in TEV.

4.25　　　　　RSV　　　　　　　　　　　　　　　TEV
[4.22]

| that you shall be driven from among men, and your dwelling shall be with the beasts of the field; you shall be made to eat grass like an ox, and you shall be wet with the dew of heaven, and seven times shall pass over you, till you know that the Most High rules the kingdom of men, and gives it to whom he will. | You will be driven away from human society and will live with wild animals. For seven years you will eat grass like an ox and sleep in the open air, where the dew will fall on you. Then you will admit that the Supreme God controls all human kingdoms and that he can give them to anyone he chooses. |

RSV continues the sentence begun in the previous verse to describe the decree. But it will probably be better in most languages to begin a new sentence as in TEV.

You shall be driven from among men: the passive formulation of RSV is really a third person plural indefinite construction in Aramaic: "They will chase you . . . ." In some languages this will be better translated as "People will chase you from among them" or something similar. And, of course, **men** here refers to human beings in general and not just males.

Beasts of the field: see 2.38 and 4.12.

You shall be made to eat grass: literally "they (indefinite) will make you to eat (will feed you) grass." This kind of rendering avoids the passive of RSV. But it is not appropriate to say "people will make you eat grass," because at this point the king will have no other human beings around him.

You shall be wet with the dew of heaven: literally "they (indefinite) will wet you . . . ." GECL has interpreted this to mean that Nebuchadnezzar would have to get his drinking water from the dew, but the interpretation of TEV above seems more likely.

Till you know: another way of translating this idea is to begin a new sentence with "At the end of this time you will know (or acknowledge)."

The Most High: see 3.26 and 4.17.

Kingdom of men: to be taken as a plural as in verse 17. Similarly the singular pronouns that follow should also be pluralized.

Seven times shall pass over you: to be understood as "seven years" as in verse 16 above.

Gives it: or better "can give it" as in verse 17.

4.26
[4.23]

RSV	TEV
And as it was commanded to leave the stump of the roots of the tree, your kingdom shall be sure for you from the time that you know that Heaven rules.	The angel ordered the stump to be left in the ground. This means that you will become king again when you acknowledge that God rules all the world.

As it was commanded: the RSV passive reflects another third person plural indefinite form in Aramaic, "they commanded (or said)." But in verse 15 it was clearly the angel who gave the order. For this reason TEV has translated "The angel ordered." The force of the word **as** in the beginning of this verse is rendered at the beginning of the second sentence in TEV, "This means . . . ." Another way of handling this is to structure the translation as has been done in NJV: "The meaning of the command to leave the stump of the tree with its roots is . . . ."

The stump of the roots of the tree: see verse 15.

Your kingdom shall be sure for you: some better ways of saying this may be "the kingdom will surely be returned to you," "it is certain that you will become king again," or "God will undoubtedly restore the kingdom to you."

Know: that is, "acknowledge," "confess," or "admit."

That Heaven rules: in chapter 2 there is reference to "the God of heaven" or "God in heaven" (2.18, 19, 28, 37, 44), but here we find the only Old Testament example of a euphemism (an expression for avoiding the name of God) that became common in the intertestamental period and in New Testament times. The text is literally "your kingdom shall be restored when you acknowledge that heaven rules." Here, as in 1 Maccabees 3.19, and later in the story of the Prodigal Son (Luke 15.18, 21), "heaven" stands for God. Most English versions retain the euphemism "heaven," sometimes beginning with an upper case letter (RSV, NRSV, and REB); but TEV has simply "when you acknowledge that God rules . . . ." Perhaps a better solution is that of FRCL, "that the God of Heaven is master (ruler) . . . ."

4.27   RSV   TEV
[4.24]

Therefore, O king, let my counsel be acceptable to you; break off your sins by practicing righteousness, and your iniquities by showing mercy to the oppressed, that there may perhaps be a lengthening of your tranquillity."

So then, Your Majesty, follow my advice. Stop sinning, do what is right, and be merciful to the poor.[g] Then you will continue to be prosperous."

[g] Stop sinning . . . to the poor; *or* Make up for your sins by doing what is right and by being merciful to the poor.

O king: see 2.4.

Let my counsel be acceptable to you: the translation should make it clear that the advice being talked about is found in the words that follow. In some cases this can be made clear by the use of a colon to introduce the actual advice. In others it will be better to say "please comply with this (following) advice," "I beg you to accept what I am about to say," or simply "take my advice" (NAB and AB).

Break off your sins by practicing righteousness, and your iniquities by showing mercy to the oppressed: once again the parallel structure of the original is driving at a single point. The verb **break off** carries over to the second part, where **your iniquities** is parallel to **your sins** in the first part. It may be difficult to find two different words for **sins** and **iniquities** that are natural in some languages. Also, **practicing righteousness** and **showing mercy** are roughly equivalent, although the addition of **to the oppressed** is an important new element. Where the resources of the language permit, these items should be distinguished. It will be noted that a TEV footnote indicates that this whole phrase may possibly be translated "Make up for your sins by doing what is right and by being merciful to the poor," or as NRSV has it, "atone for your sins with righteousness." But this interpretation is not recommended. Also the translation of **the oppressed** by "the poor" in TEV is not recommended, since it will very likely carry different connotations.

Perhaps: the Aramaic text is not as strongly affirmative as the TEV rendering would suggest; and the element of doubt conveyed by this particle should be retained in translation. REB begins a new sentence for the last part of this verse: "It may be that you will enjoy long contentment."

A lengthening of your tranquility: the word translated **tranquility** has a somewhat broader meaning. It is perhaps more accurately rendered "prosperity" (NRSV, NAB, and Mft, as well as TEV).

4.28   RSV   TEV
[4.25]

   All this came upon King Nebu-   All this did happen to King
chadnezzar.   Nebuchadnezzar.

This verse serves as a kind of introduction to the fulfilling of what Daniel had predicted in his explanation of the dream. These events are described in the verses that follow (28-33).

All this: some languages may require something more here. Translators should consider "All these things" or "All that had been predicted."

4.29   RSV   TEV
[4.26]

At the end of twelve months he was   Only twelve months later, while he
walking on the roof of the royal   was walking around on the roof of
palace of Babylon,   his royal palace in Babylon,

At the end of twelve months: in some languages it will be much more natural to say simply "a year later" (FRCL). And in a few cases it may be necessary to refer to the event from which the time was counted. This would be the time of the dream and its interpretation by Daniel. The idea is that of a relatively short period of time; this is why TEV begins with "Only . . . ."

Walking on the roof: literally "on the palace." In some languages a literal translation of the RSV phrase without further explanation may give readers the impression that Nebuchadnezzar had already lost his mind. The idea of walking on a roof is totally foreign to many cultures; so this custom may have to be explained in a footnote. However, in the translation itself it is legitimate to say something like "walking around on the roof-top porch (of his palace)" or "wandering about on the flat-topped roof."

Of the royal palace: in some languages where royalty as described in the Bible is unknown, this may have to be rendered simply "of his (the king's) big house."

4.30   RSV   TEV
[4.27]

and the king said, "Is not this great   he said, "Look how great Babylon
Babylon, which I have built by my   is! I built it as my capital city to
mighty power as a royal residence   display my power and might, my
and for the glory of my majesty?"   glory and majesty."

The king said: literally "speaking the king said." But the content of the quotation that follows may make it necessary to use a stronger verb here. NJV and NEB/REB have "exclaimed." Other versions prefer to take this as a thought process, "said to himself" (AT); but this is unlikely, since the following verse seems to indicate that he actually uttered these words aloud.

Is not this great Babylon . . . : the rhetorical question of the original is both lengthy and negative in form. This may make it very difficult to translate literally in a large number of languages. The idea is "Just look at this great city (called Babylon) that I have built for my residence!" It is probably a good idea to break this down into two separate sentences. TEV should serve as a good model at this point.

The words translated **royal residence** refer to the place where the king lives. It has the same essential meaning as **royal palace** in the previous verse and may have to be translated identically in many languages. But it may also be rendered "the center of my government."

The glory of my majesty is an abstract notion that will be difficult to translate in some languages. Note that TEV speaks of "my capital city to display my power and might, my glory and majesty." Another way of saying this is "the center of my government which shows that I am great and strong. My power and glory (or honor) can be seen here."

4.31 RSV	TEV
[4.28]	
While the words were still in the king's mouth, there fell a voice from heaven, "O King Nebuchadnezzar, to you it is spoken: The kingdom has departed from you,	Before the words were out of his mouth, a voice spoke from heaven, "King Nebuchadnezzar, listen to what I say! Your royal power is now taken away from you.

Although there is no break in the text of RSV, it may be helpful to the reader to begin a new paragraph here as in TEV.

While the words were still in the king's mouth: there may be many other ways of saying this that are more natural in other languages. Some possibilities are "Just as the king was saying these words" (FRCL); "The words were still on the king's lips, when . . ." (NJV), or "Before he had finished what he was saying."

There fell a voice from heaven: in most languages this will be quite unnatural. It may be preferable to say "someone spoke from heaven," "a voice from heaven said . . . ," or "he heard a voice from heaven saying . . . ." This voice is, of course, the voice of God, and in some languages it will be necessary to make this clear in translation. Some may say "God spoke from heaven . . . ."

To you it is spoken: these words may also be considered strange and artificial if translated literally. The meaning is clearly "I am telling you," or "Listen to what I am about to tell you," or perhaps better, "This is what has been decided concerning you." Mft says "here is your sentence: . . . ," and NAB has "it has been decreed for you."

The kingdom has departed from you: it may prove quite unnatural in many languages to make **the kingdom** the subject of the sentence here. The TEV rendering may be equally difficult because it is passive in form. Some more workable models may be "You have now lost your royal power" (making Nebuchadnezzar the subject) or "God has now taken your royal power from you" (making God the subject). But since it is God who is speaking, it will be more natural in most languages to say "I have now taken your royal power from you."

4.32 RSV .TEV
[4.29]

and you shall be driven from among men, and your dwelling shall be with the beasts of the field; and you shall be made to eat grass like an ox; and seven times shall pass over you, until you have learned that the Most High rules the kingdom of men and gives it to whom he will."	You will be driven away from human society, live with wild animals, and eat grass like an ox for seven years. Then you will acknowledge that the Supreme God has power over human kingdoms and that he can give them to anyone he chooses."

You shall be driven: as in verse 25 this passive form reflects an indefinite third person plural form and should be translated to correspond with the earlier reference.

The remainder of this verse is also very close to the wording of verse 25. But it should be noted that there is no mention of the dew in this case.

4.33 RSV TEV
[4.30]

Immediately the word was fulfilled upon Nebuchadnezzar. He was driven from among men, and ate grass like an ox, and his body was wet with the dew of heaven till his hair grew as long as eagles' feathers, and his nails were like birds' claws.	The words came true immediately. Nebuchadnezzar was driven out of human society and ate grass like an ox. The dew fell on his body, and his hair grew as long as eagle feathers and his nails as long as bird claws.

Immediately: literally "At that moment." Compare "At that very moment" (REB), "Instantly" (Mft), "There and then" (NJV), "At once" (NAB), and "At that same instant" (FRCL).

The word was fulfilled: the word is singular in form but has a collective meaning and should therefore be translated as a plural in many languages. REB translates "this judgement came upon Nebuchadnezzar." Another way of saying this may be "what had been predicted actually happened."

He was driven from among men: see verse 25.

Till his hair grew as long as eagles' feathers: the figurative language used here may be more naturally translated by a different image or by an emphatic non-figurative statement such as "very, very long" or "remarkably lengthy." However, some languages may natural similes that would be appropriate to describe the length or fullness of a person's hair.

His nails were like bird claws: it may be important in some instances to say in what way the king's nails resembled the claws of birds. As in the case of the **hair**, the focus is probably on their length rather than the sharpness or danger they may be to others.

It may be noted that NEB reads "until his hair grew long like goat's hair and his nails like eagles' talons." This, however, is not a rendering of the Aramaic but of a conjecture of what the original text might have been, and it has been rejected by REB. Translators are therefore advised to stay with the traditional reading reflected in REB and most other versions.

King Nebuchadnezzar praises God: 4.34-37 [4.31-34]

RSV

34 At the end of the days I, Nebuchadnezzar, lifted my eyes to heaven, and my reason returned to me, and I blessed the Most High, and praised and honored him who lives for ever;

for his dominion is an everlasting dominion,
and his kingdom endures from generation to generation;
35 all the inhabitants of the earth are accounted as nothing;
and he does according to his will in the host of heaven
and among the inhabitants of the earth;
and none can stay his hand or say to him, "What doest thou?"
36 At the same time my reason returned to me; and for the glory of my kingdom, my majesty and splendor returned to me. My counselors and my lords sought me, and I was established in my kingdom, and still more greatness was added to me. 37 Now I, Nebuchadnezzar, praise and extol and honor the King of heaven; for all his works are right and his ways are just; and those who walk in pride he is able to abase.

TEV

Nebuchadnezzar Praises God

34 "When the seven years had passed," said the king, "I looked up at the sky, and my sanity returned. I praised the Supreme God and gave honor and glory to the one who lives forever.

"He will rule forever,
and his kingdom will last for all time.
35 He looks on the people of the earth as nothing;
angels in heaven and people on earth
are under his control.
No one can oppose his will
or question what he does.
36 "When my sanity returned, my honor, my majesty, and the glory of my kingdom were given back to me. My officials and my noblemen welcomed me, and I was given back my royal power with even greater honor than before.
37 "And now, I, Nebuchadnezzar, praise, honor, and glorify the King of Heaven. Everything he does is right and just, and he can humble anyone who acts proudly."

TEV Section Heading: Nebuchadnezzar praises God

Some other possible wordings for this section heading are "The healing of Nebuchadnezzar" (FRCL), or "Restoration and thanksgiving" (NEB), which suggests the reason for Nebuchadnezzar's praise; this may also be expressed as "King Nebuchadnezzar thanks God for his restoring him."

4.34　　　　　RSV　　　　　　　　　　　TEV
[4.31]

At the end of the days I, Nebu-chadnezzar, lifted my eyes to heaven, and my reason returned to me, and I blessed the Most High, and praised and honored him who lives for ever;

for his dominion is an ever-lasting dominion,
and his kingdom endures from generation to generation;

"When the seven years had passed," said the king, "I looked up at the sky, and my sanity returned. I praised the Supreme God and gave honor and glory to the one who lives forever.

"He will rule forever,
and his kingdom will last for all time.

I, Nebuchadnezzar: the text now returns to the first person account of the king, as in verses 4-18.

At the end of the days: this phrase indicates that the time mentioned in verses 16, 23, 25, and 32 had come to an end. A literal translation of **days** may in many cases give the wrong idea of the length of time involved. Mft has "When the time was over," and REB "At the end of the appointed time." But it is probably better in many languages to translate "When the seven years had passed," as in TEV.

Lifted up my eyes to heaven: that is, toward God in heaven. The translation does not necessarily have to use the name of God here, but it should certainly not limit itself to indicating a simple gesture of looking up at the sky. It should suggest a change in the attitude of the king toward God.

My reason returned to me: since it may not be natural to make **reason** the subject of a verb like **returned**, translators may consider "I returned to my right mind" (NEB), "I was restored to my right mind" (REB), or something similar. Languages usually have a variety of ways of speaking of sanity and insanity. Translators should look for the most natural equivalent to speak of a return to sanity.

In this verse the pagan king breaks forth in another hymn of praise to the God of Daniel (compare 4.1-3). It will be important for translators to render what follows as poetry, if this is can be done in their language. There is, however, some disagreement with regard to the precise place where the actual hymn begins. Most versions, however, take the first half of this verse as a kind of introductory statement and consider the hymn as starting with the words **his dominion . . . .**

Blessed the Most High: on this name for God, see 3.26 and 4.2. In many languages the verb "to bless" is not appropriate in this context, since blessing is something that can only be done by a superior to an inferior. The meaning here is quite similar to **praised and honored** in the next phrase but may also be rendered "thanked" as in FRCL. The cumulative effect of using a number of different words having approximately the same meaning is important. So different terms should be found if at all possible.

The parallelism of the last part of this verse ("dominion" = "kingdom" and "everlasting" = "from generation to generation") recalls the very similar wording in verse 3.

4.35   RSV   TEV
[4.32]

| all the inhabitants of the earth are accounted as nothing; and he does according to his will in the host of heaven and among the inhabitants of the earth; and none can stay his hand or say to him, "What doest thou?" | He looks on the people of the earth as nothing; angels in heaven and people on earth are under his control. No one can oppose his will or question what he does. |

All the inhabitants of the earth: the word **all** is omitted from TEV, but it should be included in the translation unless there are very strong reasons for omitting it.

Are accounted as nothing: the passive verb here should probably be rendered as an active one in order to make clear the fact that God is the agent. But some languages may prefer "all people on earth are as nothing in his eyes," retaining a structure similar to the passive but insuring that the subject is understood. The verb **accounted** has the idea of evaluation, showing that God considers the population of the world as utterly insignificant, for they cannot oppose his will.

The host: in the Bible the word **host** sometimes stands for the armies of Israel, sometimes for the stars and other heavenly beings (Isa 40.26; Psa 33.6), and sometimes for angels (Psa 103.21; Luke 2.13). In this context, where the term is joined with **of heaven**, the context favors the last meaning, and it is good to make this clear in the translation in order to avoid the term being taken in a military sense.

Note that TEV restructures the middle of this verse so that the phrase **he does according to his will** is translated by "are under his control," and instead of making God the grammatical subject, "angels" and "people" are used.

None can stay his hand: since **hand** is often used to represent "power" in Scripture (1.2; 2.38; 3.17), it is often better to give this meaning directly in the translation. In some cases it may be appropriate to say simply "no one can stop him."

Or say to him, "What doest thou?" This direct question is better rendered as indirect speech in most languages. Some models are "question what he does" (TEV, REB) or, very similarly, "ask him what he is doing" (Mft).

4.36 RSV TEV
[4.33]

At the same time my reason returned to me; and for the glory of
my kingdom, my majesty and splendor returned to me. My counselors
and my lords sought me, and I was
established in my kingdom, and still
more greatness was added to me.

"When my sanity returned, my
honor, my majesty, and the glory of
my kingdom were given back to me.
My officials and my noblemen welcomed me, and I was given back my
royal power with even greater honor
than before.

At the same time: or "At that time."

My reason returned: see verse 34 and comments.

My majesty and splendor returned to me: such nouns may not fit with
a verb like **returned** in some languages. This may therefore be reworded "I
received my majesty and splendor once again." Possibly translators may find
it more natural to say "God gave back my majesty and splendor." In some
languages these abstract nouns may have to be rendered "honor and power"
or "respect and greatness."

My counselors and my lords: see 3.24. The root of the second of these
two terms comes from the Aramaic word for "great," and the term is used to
refer to important individuals in the royal court. The word "nobles" is
sometimes used to translate it. Some languages may have to speak of "my
advisors and the leaders in my kingdom" or "the great ones who confer with
me."

I was established in my kingdom: the verb here obviously has the
meaning "established again" or "reestablished," as in NRSV and REB, since
Nebuchadnezzar had been firmly established as king before his illness.

And still more greatness was added to me: this indicates that, in spite
of the magnificence he enjoyed before his illness, Nebuchadnezzar received
even more prominence.

4.37 RSV TEV
[4.34]

Now I, Nebuchadnezzar, praise and
extol and honor the King of heaven;
for all his works are right and his
ways are just; and those who walk
in pride he is able to abase.

"And now, I, Nebuchadnezzar,
praise, honor, and glorify the King
of Heaven. Everything he does is
right and just, and he can humble
anyone who acts proudly."

Praise and extol and honor: it is neither necessary nor desirable to
spend time searching for shades of difference in meaning to distinguish these
three verbs. It is the cumulative effect of these three synonyms that is
important. Translators should not be concerned if they find only two verbs to
translate the three in the original at this point.

The King of heaven: in some languages it may be necessary to say "God,
who is the king of heaven."

His works are right and his ways are just: this parallelism may be retained as long as the reader does not think of the two statements as representing two completely different facts. It is simply a matter of saying the same thing two different ways. In some cases the two statements may legitimately be reduced to one.

Those who walk in pride: the verb **walk** is often used for behavior in general and so may be translated "live" or "act" in this context. REB speaks of "those whose conduct is arrogant."

The verb **abase** stands in contrast with **those who walk in pride**. In some languages it will be rendered "humble" or "bring low," or "cause to be submissive."

Belshazzar's Banquet

Daniel 5.1-31

The handwriting on the wall: 5.1-12

RSV

TEV
Belshazzar's Banquet

1 King Belshazzar made a great feast for a thousand of his lords, and drank wine in front of the thousand. 2 Belshazzar, when he tasted the wine, commanded that the vessels of gold and of silver which Nebuchadnezzar his father had taken out of the temple in Jerusalem be brought, that the king and his lords, his wives, and his concubines might drink from them. 3 Then they brought in the golden and silver vessels which had been taken out of the temple, the house of God in Jerusalem; and the king and his lords, his wives, and his concubines drank from them. 4 They drank wine, and praised the gods of gold and silver, bronze, iron, wood, and stone.

5 Immediately the fingers of a man's hand appeared and wrote on the plaster of the wall of the king's palace, opposite the lampstand; and the king saw the hand as it wrote. 6 Then the king's color changed, and his thoughts alarmed him; his limbs gave way, and his knees knocked together. 7 The king cried aloud to bring in the enchanters, the Chaldeans, and the astrologers. The king said to the wise men of Babylon, "Whoever reads this writing, and shows me its interpretation, shall be clothed with purple, and have a chain of gold about his neck, and shall be the third ruler in the kingdom." 8 Then all the king's wise men came in, but they could not read the writing or make known to the king the interpretation. 9 Then King Belshazzar was greatly alarmed, and his color changed; and his lords were perplexed.

10 The queen, because of the words of the king and his lords, came into the banqueting hall; and the queen said, "O king, live for ever! Let not your thoughts alarm you or your color change. 11 There is in your kingdom a

1 One night King Belshazzar invited a thousand noblemen to a great banquet, and they drank wine together. 2 While they were drinking, Belshazzar gave orders to bring in the gold and silver cups and bowls which his father(H) Nebuchadnezzar had carried off from the Temple in Jerusalem. The king sent for them so that he, his noblemen, his wives, and his concubines could drink out of them. 3 At once the gold cups and bowls were brought in, and they all drank wine out of them 4 and praised gods made of gold, silver, bronze, iron, wood, and stone.

5 Suddenly a human hand appeared and began writing on the plaster wall of the palace, where the light from the lamps was shining most brightly. And the king saw the hand as it was writing. 6 He turned pale and was so frightened that his knees began to shake. 7 He shouted for someone to bring in the magicians, wizards, and astrologers. When they came in, the king said to them, "Anyone who can read this writing and tell me what it means will be dressed in robes of royal purple, wear a gold chain of honor around his neck, and be the third in power in the kingdom." 8 The royal advisers came forward, but none of them could read the writing or tell the king what it meant. 9 In his distress King Belshazzar grew even paler, and his noblemen had no idea what to do.

10 The queen mother heard the noise made by the king and his noblemen and entered the banquet hall. She said, "May Your Majesty live forever! Please do not be so disturbed and look so pale. 11 There is a man in your kingdom who has the spirit of the holy gods(I) in him. When your father was king, this man showed good sense, knowledge, and wisdom like the wisdom of the gods. And King

129

man in whom is the spirit of the holy gods. In the days of your father light and understanding and wisdom, like the wisdom of the gods, were found in him, and King Nebuchadnezzar, your father, made him chief of the magicians, enchanters, Chaldeans, and astrologers, 12 because an excellent spirit, knowledge, and understanding to interpret dreams, explain riddles, and solve problems were found in this Daniel, whom the king named Belteshazzar. Now let Daniel be called, and he will show the interpretation."

Nebuchadnezzar, your father,(J) made him chief of the fortunetellers, magicians, wizards, and astrologers. 12 He has unusual ability and is wise and skillful in interpreting dreams, solving riddles, and explaining mysteries; so send for this man Daniel, whom the king named Belteshazzar, and he will tell you what all this means."

TEV Section Heading: Belshazzar's Feast

NEB gives the subheading "The Judgement on Sacrilege" after the more general title identical with that of TEV. NIV and REB have "The Writing on the Wall," focusing on a particular aspect of the story.

Those translators following the outline provided in the introduction to this handbook (page 10) will have a subheading following the main heading above. Verses 1-12 deal with "The handwriting on the wall."

5.1	RSV	TEV

King Belshazzar made a great feast for a thousand of his lords, and drank wine in front of the thousand.

One night King Belshazzar invited a thousand noblemen to a great banquet, and they drank wine together.

The beginning of this chapter may be considered rather abrupt in some languages. In order to indicate to the reader that a new subject has been introduced, TEV adds the words "One night," under the influence of verse 30. It is, however, not altogether certain that the feast actually began at night. For this reason some translators may prefer the more neutral "One day" (see FRCL), indicating any time during a twenty-four hour period. Where the word "day" refers only to the time when there is sunlight translators may prefer "One time" or simply "Once."

In chapter 4 Nebuchadnezzar was king, but here a new king is named without any indication of the transition. Some languages may require that this chapter begin with words like "In the time when Belshazzar was king, he . . ." or "After Belshazzar had become king, he . . . ."

Belshazzar: this name is an Aramaic corruption of the Akkadian *bel-sharra-usur*, meaning "O Bel, protect the king." Belshazzar is presented in this story as the son and successor of Nebuchadnezzar (see verses 2 and 11). In fact, the name of the immediate successor of Nebuchadnezzar as Babylonian ruler was Evilmerodach (2 Kgs 25.27; Jer 52.31). The only person by the name Belshazzar known to Babylonian history is the son of the king Nabonidus (556-539 B.C.), and he was only the regent of the kingdom (person acting as king) during the absence of his father. According to the best available information on Babylonian history, he was not actually a descendant of Nebuchadnezzar. These historical suppositions, however, cannot influence the translator dealing with the text of Daniel. The text must be translated as it stands and not "corrected" on the basis of what we think we know from secular history.

A great feast: this would be what we might call a "state banquet" today. The word translated **feast** here originally meant "food" in general. For agricultural people this would mean "bread," and for pastoral people it may suggest "meat." The more common word for banquet comes from the verbal root "to drink." In languages that do not have a term for "feast" or "banquet," it may be necessary to speak of a "big eating and drinking."

Lords: see 4.36 and comments.

Wine: the Aramaic word used here is equivalent to the Hebrew in 1.5, 8, 16. Translators should therefore refer to the comments in chapter 1 on the rendering of this term.

In front of the thousand: the writer almost certainly does not mean that the king was the only one to drink wine at the banquet while all the invited guests looked on. If a literal translation gives this impression, it should be modified. The TEV rendering is one model, but in order to maintain the focus on the king, it is possible to say something like "he was drinking wine with the thousand guests."

5.2 RSV	TEV
Belshazzar, when he tasted the wine, commanded that the vessels of gold and of silver which Nebuchadnezzar his father had taken out of the temple in Jerusalem be brought, that the king and his lords, his wives, and his concubines might drink from them.	While they were drinking, Belshazzar gave orders to bring in the gold and silver cups and bowls which his father[h] Nebuchadnezzar had carried off from the Temple in Jerusalem. The king sent for them so that he, his noblemen, his wives, and his concubines could drink out of them.

[h] *There were several kings of Babylonia between Nebuchadnezzar and Belshazzar.* Father *may mean predecessor, or the name* Nebuchadnezzar *may be used for Nabonidus.*

When he tasted the wine: in spite of the RSV wording, this does not mean that, after sipping only a small amount of wine, the following events occurred. On the contrary the meaning is more likely "after having become slightly drunk." FRCL has "under the influence of the alcohol," and similarly NAB, NJV, REB, and AB all have "under the influence of the wine." NRSV also uses this formulation. Some other renderings are "carried away by the wine" (Mft), "warmed by the wine" (NEB), and "inflamed by the taste of the wine" (AT).

Vessels: the meaning of this term is simply "containers," but since they were to be used for drinking wine, the TEV rendering "cups and bowls" is a good common language equivalent in English.

Had taken out of the temple: for the historical account of this event, see 2 Kgs 25.15. The word **temple** refers to the structure in Jerusalem built by the people of Israel under Solomon for the worship of God (1 Kgs 6–8). It was modeled after the tabernacle but differed from it in size, complexity, permanence and location. The term used in the translation should refer to this particular building. If necessary a comprehensive explanation may be included in a glossary entry.

Be brought: the passive form will have to be made active in many languages. The active formulation may read "ordered his servants to bring" or "commanded his men to pick up [fetch]." And in some languages it will be necessary to state where these cups and bowls were to be brought. So translators may want to add "to him" or "to the banquet."

His father Nebuchadnezzar: while the footnotes in some versions indicate that the term for **father** used here may be understood to mean "ancestor" or "predecessor," no English version puts this interpretation in the text. As noted above, Nebuchadnezzar was not, in fact, the literal father of Belshazzar (see also verses 11, 13, and 18; and compare verse 22 "you his son").

That . . . might drink from them: literally "and . . . will drink . . . ." This indicates the purpose of having the cups and bowls brought to the banquet. In many cases it will be a good idea to express this purpose clause in a separate sentence, as in TEV.

Wives and concubines: the two Aramaic terms probably referred to two distinct categories of legitimate spouses that made up the royal harem. The second term, however, is the subject of considerable debate. Some commentators take it to refer to some sort of "entertainers" rather than to **concubines**. NJB translates it "the women who sang for him," and NAB has "his entertainers." However, the generally accepted meaning is probably the correct one. These women were probably members of the royal court but having some kind of inferior status when compared to the first group. Therefore the FRCL translation, "his wives and his second rank spouses," may not be a bad model if the translator has suitable terms available. Another possibility is "his royal wives and his service wives" (compare TOB). The same terms are repeated in verses 3 and 23 of this chapter.

5.3 RSV TEV

Then they brought in the golden and silver vessels^j which had been taken out of the temple, the house of God in Jerusalem; and the king and his lords, his wives, and his concubines drank from them.

At once the gold cups and bowls were brought in, and they all drank wine out of them

^j Theodotion Vg: Aramaic *golden vessels*

Then: the connection between the order (in verse 2) and its being obeyed is indicated by this transition word. Some versions take the relationship to be a logical one ("So" in NEB/REB as well as NRSV), while others make it a time relationship (**Then** in RSV and others, or "At once" in TEV). What is important is that the relationship be clear and natural in the translation.

They: it is not clear who this pronoun refers to, but probably something like "the king's servants" should be in the mind of the reader.

Golden and silver vessels: while both gold and silver are mentioned in the order given in the previous verse, it is questionable whether both types of containers were actually brought in to the banquet. Although RSV and a number of other English versions indicate that there were containers made of both gold and silver, the Aramaic text here has only "golden vessels." The addition of silver vessels comes from the Greek translation of Theodotion. However, a number of modern versions (including TEV, NIV, and NJV in English) prefer to retain the reading of the Aramaic text and omit the mention of "silver." This is also the reading recommended by HOTTP and CTAT. REB and certain other versions leave out any reference to gold or silver, saying only "those vessels."

Temple: see verse 2 and comments.

Lords, wives, and concubines: see comments on verse 2 above.

5.4

RSV	TEV
They drank wine, and praised the gods of gold and silver, bronze, iron, wood, and stone.	and praised gods made of gold, silver, bronze, iron, wood, and stone.

They drank wine: since the concluding words of the previous verse are "drank from them," these words in verse 4 may be considered an unnecessary repetition, depending on the structure of the translation. They are thus omitted by TEV. But if this repetition is not troublesome in the receptor language, it may be retained; it serves to highlight the relationship between the drinking and the praise offered to the false gods. Some translations begin this verse "While drinking, they praised. . ."

Gods of gold . . . : in this context some languages will require the word for "idols" rather than "gods." The relationship between these objects and the various materials listed afterward should be made clear: the **gods** or "idols" were made of these materials. Note that the most expensive material is mentioned first, followed by materials of decreasing value.

Immediately the fingers of a man's hand appeared and wrote on the plaster of the wall of the king's palace, opposite the lampstand; and the king saw the hand as it wrote.

Suddenly a human hand appeared and began writing on the plaster wall of the palace, where the light from the lamps was shining most brightly. And the king saw the hand as it was writing.

Immediately: the sudden and surprising character of the event described in the following verses is marked by this introductory word. Most languages will have a special way of introducing a startling occurrence. Whatever this method is, it should be used here.

The fingers of a man's hand: there is no particular emphasis on the **hand** being the hand of a male. For this reason it will be better to say simply "a human hand" as in NJV, NJB, NRSV, and NEB/REB, as well as TEV. Also it is evident that the writer did not intend to give the picture of fingers detached from the hand but of the hand as a whole. This is made clear by the wording at the end of this verse.

Plaster: the corresponding Aramaic word is used only here in the Old Testament, but the Hebrew equivalent is related to the word for "lime," which was used in making plaster. It is found in Lev 14.41-48. In some languages it may be necessary to resort to a general term meaning "covering" or "stucco."

Opposite the lampstand: this would be in the most clearly illuminated part of the banquet hall. This should probably be stated clearly in most languages. In addition to the TEV model, translators may consider "where the light was strongest" or "where people could see very clearly."

And the king saw . . . : in some languages it may be more natural to introduce this sentence by a time clause ("when the king saw . . .") rather than by a simple conjunction. Some commentators think that the writing was visible only to the king, but this is not stated in the text and in fact it is not necessarily the meaning. So it would be a mistake to translate "the king alone saw it." At the same time translators should avoid saying too much in the other direction. "The king and his guests saw it" would probably also be wrong unless the language excludes everyone that is not specifically included.

The hand: literally the Aramaic text has "the hand of the hand." In Aramaic there are two different words used for the hand, and they are found together here. The first, sometimes translated "palm" (AT, Mft, and REB), is usually applied to the hand as such below the wrist. The second may refer to the entire arm from the elbow to the tips of the fingers. NAB has "the wrist and hand," and NEB translates "the back of the hand." Such a rendering seems logical, since this is what is actually seen when a person is writing. One commentary has suggested that the two terms together actually mean "a detached hand." Even KJV may be helpful in this case: "the part of the hand."

5.6 RSV	TEV
Then the king's color changed, and his thoughts alarmed him; his limbs gave way, and his knees knocked together.	He turned pale and was so frightened that his knees began to shake.

If a time clause is used at the end of verse 5, this verse will be a continuation of the sentence started there: "When the king saw . . . he turned pale . . . ." The appearance of the hand caused four simultaneous reactions in the king. Two were visible: (a) paleness and (d) trembling; and the other two were internal: (b) dread and (c) exhaustion or loss of strength. In each case the structure of the phrase may be awkward in some languages, since the subject of the verb is a part of the king (his color, thoughts, limbs, or knees) but not the king himself. The structure will have to be changed if this is the case.

The king's color changed: the word for **color** is actually plural in form in the original. As an equivalent for this expression, translators should look for the most natural way of describing the change in physical appearance that comes over a person when he is paralyzed with fear. It is interesting to note that, while many English translations speak of Belshazzar's face turning pale, NJV renders the same expression "the king's face darkened."

His thoughts alarmed him: the meaning is simply "he became very frightened."

His limbs gave way: literally "the joints of his loins/hips were loosened" (compare KJV). But the word for loins or hips may, in fact, refer to the entire midsection of the body, which was the source of physical strength, according to ancient thinking. Sudden and extreme anxiety can cause the loss of physical force. So the meaning of this expression is something like "his hips gave way" or "he became extremely weak all over." But in some languages it will be possible to stay close to the form of the original.

His knees knocked together: this refers to an observable trembling in the legs. It may or may not be natural in a given language to speak of the knees actually coming together as a result of this shaking.

5.7 RSV	TEV
The king cried aloud to bring in the enchanters, the Chaldeans, and the astrologers. The king said to the wise men of Babylon, "Whoever reads this writing, and shows me its interpretation, shall be clothed with purple, and have a chain of gold about his neck, and shall be the third ruler in the kingdom."	He shouted for someone to bring in the magicians, wizards, and astrologers. When they came in, the king said to them, "Anyone who can read this writing and tell me what it means will be dressed in robes of royal purple, wear a gold chain of honor around his neck, and be third in power in the kingdom."

The king: the pronoun "He" may be more natural here in some languages.

To bring: if it is necessary to say who the order was given to, translators may follow the vague rendering of TEV, "someone," or say more specifically "his servants."

The enchanters, the Chaldeans and the astrologers: see the earlier comments on such lists in 2.2, 27. Later in this verse the more general term **wise men** (see chapter 2) is used to summarize the list. The text does not actually say that these advisors did come in to present themselves before the king, but this may be included as in TEV if necessary.

Interpretation: this word occurs more than thirty times in the Book of Daniel. See comments on 2.4.

Clothed with purple: purple or crimson (a deep red) clothing was extremely expensive due to the nature of the dye involved. So only the most fortunate and wealthy people could afford it. Consequently clothing of this color was symbolic of a very high social status and this is what should be brought out in the translation. TEV attempts to do this with "robes of royal purple." In some languages there is a special vocabulary to describe clothing worn by a chief or other dignitaries. In other cases the addition of an adjective meaning "expensive" or "luxurious" may be considered.

Have a chain of gold about his neck: this is another sign of wealth and high status. According to some commentators this was not actually a chain but more like a solid metal collar. NAB has "golden collar," and AB uses the more difficult English word "torque." In some languages a single verb can be used for wearing purple clothing and the golden collar. But in others it will be more natural to use two separate verbs for "wearing" clothing and for "wearing" an ornament like a chain or collar around the neck.

Be the third ruler in the kingdom: this RSV rendering may possibly be misunderstood as referring to the third in a succession of rulers, or possibly even the ruler of one-third of the kingdom. The meaning, however, is either "third in rank [after the king and the queen mother]" (compare NRSV) or "the third highest ruler in the kingdom" (NIV), or possibly "one of the three men who govern the country" (NJB). In some languages it may be more natural to say something like "shall become the third most powerful person in the country" or "be promoted to the third highest office in the land" or "one of the three rulers of the kingdom."

Certain commentators feel that the word usually translated **third** has lost its numerical value in this context. If this is the case it will be legitimate to translate "one of the principal rulers in the kingdom," as FRCL has done.

5.8 RSV | TEV

Then all the king's wise men came in, but they could not read the writing or make known to the king the interpretation.	**The royal advisers came forward, but none of them could read the writing or tell the king what it meant.**

All the king's wise men: the more general word for the royal advisors is used here as in 2.12 and other places. Note that TEV omits the detail **all**, but this should be retained in the translation.

Came in: since the king was already speaking to the royal advisors—or at least some of them—in the previous verse, this presents logical difficulties. One commentary notes that the participial force of the verb here gives the idea "were coming in" and indicates that the arrival of the advisors happened over a period of several hours. TEV takes it to mean that these men "came forward" or drew closer to the king. NJB carries a similar meaning. But NAB has "though all the king's wise men came in," meaning that even after the arrival of the last of the advisors there was no solution to the problem. This is probably the best interpretation. Some may wish to translate "When all the royal advisors had arrived" or "After all of the king's advisors had finished coming in."

5.9 RSV	TEV
Then King Belshazzar was greatly alarmed, and his color changed; and his lords were perplexed.	In his distress King Belshazzar grew even paler, and his noblemen had no idea what to do.

Was greatly alarmed: this indicates an increase in the fear that was already strong in the mind of the king in verse 6. Translators may want to say "became even more afraid" or something similar.

His color changed: since the color of the king had already changed in verse 6, it may be more natural to say "changed again" or something similar. TEV attempts to cover this by saying "grew even paler." REB also indicates a greater degree of paleness in this verse by saying ". . . drove all colour from (his) cheeks."

His lords: translators should be careful to translate in such a way that the reader knows that this group is the noblemen referred to in verse 1 and not the royal advisors who had been called in later. See also 4.36.

5.10 RSV	TEV
The queen, because of the words of the king and his lords, came into the banqueting hall; and the queen said, "O king, live for ever! Let not your thoughts alarm you or your color change.	The queen mother heard the noise made by the king and his noblemen and entered the banquet hall. She said, "May Your Majesty live forever! Please do not be so disturbed and look so pale.

Both RSV and TEV make a paragraph break here because a new subject is introduced. Some versions place a section heading at this point, since this is the beginning of the section where Daniel interprets the writing on the wall. But other versions, like TEV, place this title before verse 13 below.

The queen: the text clearly implies that this person was not originally a member of the banquet group. She **came into the banqueting hall** later. It is very likely that the term used here refers to the "queen-mother" (the mother of the king) rather than to the queen herself. The queen mother occupied a very influential position in Babylonia as well as in Israel and Judah at the time. Mft, AT, TEV, and FRCL all translate "queen mother." In many languages it may be necessary to say something like "the mother of the king." The second reference to this woman may be represented by the pronoun "she" if the reference is clear; but in languages where there is no distinction between masculine and feminine, this may cause confusion. In this case, some languages will accept "that woman."

Because of the words . . . : a literal rendering of this phrase might give the impression in some languages that the king and his noblemen had sent a message to the queen mother. But the meaning is rather that the sound of the commotion caused by the events was so loud that she came into the banquet hall to find out what was the matter. Having learned the details of the problem she then went on to try to calm her son.

The banqueting hall: or "the place where people were eating the feast."

O king, live for ever: see 2.4.

Thoughts alarm . . . color change: see verses 6 and 9.

5.11   RSV   TEV

There is in your kingdom a man in whom is the spirit of the holy gods.[k] In the days of your father light and understanding and wisdom, like the wisdom of the gods, were found in him, and King Nebuchadnezzar, your father, made him chief of the magicians, enchanters, Chaldeans, and astrologers,[l]

There is a man in your kingdom who has the spirit of the holy gods[i] in him. When your father was king, this man showed good sense, knowledge, and wisdom like the wisdom of the gods. And King Nebuchadnezzar, your father,[j] made him chief of the fortunetellers, magicians, wizards, and astrologers.

[k] Or *Spirit of the holy God*
[l] Aramaic repeats *the king your father*

[i] gods; *or* God.
[j] your father *(see 5.2).*

The spirit of the holy gods: see 4.8.

In the days of your father: or "during the time when your father ruled."

Light and understanding and wisdom: the three corresponding Aramaic terms have more or less the same meaning. While the first contains the idea of "light," it is to be taken in a figurative sense and probably not translated literally in most languages. The second gives the idea of a kind of intelligence that enables a person to avoid errors or miscalculation. The third word in the list carries the notion of discernment or good judgment. If possible the translator should try to find three similar terms that include these concepts.

But in some languages he or she may be forced to reduce the number of terms to two. This is comparable to the three synonymous verbs found at the end of the previous chapter (4.37).

Were found in him: this passive formulation will be plainly impossible in some languages. Some other ways to communicate this idea are "people saw in him," "he demonstrated," or possibly "he was known for" (NJB), although this is also a passive.

King Nebuchadnezzar, your father: see the comments on verse 1 above. Following this expression the Aramaic text repeats the words "your father, the king" (compare KJV, NIV, and NASB), although some ancient versions omit them. HOTTP and CTAT indicate that this was very probably a part of the original and may have a vocative meaning. While these words should not be rejected for text-critical reasons, many translators may find the repetition very awkward and will have to omit them for translation reasons.

Made him chief: see 2.48.

Magicians, enchanters, Chaldeans, and astrologers: see verse 7 as well as 2.2.

5.12 RSV	TEV
because an excellent spirit, knowledge, and understanding to interpret dreams, explain riddles, and solve problems were found in this Daniel, whom the king named Belteshazzar. Now let Daniel be called, and he will show the interpretation."	He has unusual ability and is wise and skillful in interpreting dreams, solving riddles, and explaining mysteries; so send for this man Daniel, whom the king named Belteshazzar, and he will tell you what all this means."

This subordinate clause is attached to verse 11 in RSV and a few other versions to explain why Daniel had been made chief of the wise men. This is certainly a grammatical possibility. But the majority of modern versions (NJB, NJV, NEB, and TEV) begin a new sentence here and thus make this clause the reason for the appeal to call for Daniel at the end of the verse.

An excellent spirit: it is better to understand the word translated **spirit** as being equivalent to something like "mind" in English. NAB translates the two words together as "an extraordinary mind," and NIV has "a keen mind." Others take it in the sense of ability: "rare ability" (Mft), "surpassing ability" (AT), "exceptional ability" (REB), or "unusual ability" (TEV). But it would probably be a mistake to use the literal equivalent for "spirit" in most languages.

Knowledge: this is yet another term similar in meaning to those in the previous verse. But in some languages it may be necessary to repeat one of the words already used.

Understanding: the last of these three words here is the same as the second of the list in the previous verse.

To interpret dreams, explain riddles, and solve problems: these infinitives are really verbal nouns, and they all serve to explain what Daniel's knowledge and understanding involved. On **interpret dreams** see chapter 4. The words **explain riddles** may be rendered "explain enigmas" (AB and NAB) or "hidden things to reveal" (Knox). The noun refers to a mystery that puzzles the ordinary person. The expression **solve problems** literally means "to untie knots," indicating an ability to find solutions to seemingly impossible problems. Some commentators see in this expression some kind of reference to the literal untying of knots in the context of Aramaic magical practices. AT, for example, has "unraveling knots." But this is unlikely. NJB retains something of the image with "unravelling difficult problems" (compare REB).

Were found: this is once again a passive form that should be made active in many languages. This idea may be expressed by beginning the verse "he possesses" followed by the list of qualities.

Let Daniel be called: it should be made clear in translation that this is a command of the king. NAB is correct in rendering it "summon Daniel . . . ." Some other ways of saying this are "call for Daniel" (NIV) or simply "send for him" (NJB).

Show the interpretation: see 2.4. In some languages it may be appropriate to state clearly what is to be interpreted, as in "the interpretation of the writing on the wall" or "the meaning of the written message that appeared." The writing has not been mentioned since verse 8.

Daniel explains the writing: 5.13-31

RSV

13 Then Daniel was brought in before the king. The king said to Daniel, "You are that Daniel, one of the exiles of Judah, whom the king my father brought from Judah. 14 I have heard of you that the spirit of the holy gods is in you, and that light and understanding and excellent wisdom are found in you. 15 Now the wise men, the enchanters, have been brought in before me to read this writing and make known to me its interpretation; but they could not show the interpretation of the matter. 16 But I have heard that you can give interpretations and solve problems. Now if you can read the writing and make known to me its interpretation, you shall be clothed with purple, and have a chain of gold about your neck, and shall be the third ruler in the kingdom.

17 Then Daniel answered before the king, "Let your gifts be for yourself, and give your rewards to another; nevertheless I will read the writing to the king and make known to him the interpretation. 18 O king, the Most

TEV

Daniel Explains the Writing

13 Daniel was brought at once into the king's presence, and the king said to him, "Are you Daniel, that Jewish exile whom my father the king brought here from Judah? 14 I have heard that the spirit of the holy gods(K) is in you and that you are skillful and have knowledge and wisdom. 15 The advisers and magicians were brought in to read this writing and tell me what it means, but they could not discover the meaning. 16 Now I have heard that you can find hidden meanings and explain mysteries. If you can read this writing and tell me what it means, you will be dressed in robes of royal purple, wear a gold chain of honor around your neck, and be the third in power in the kingdom."

17 Daniel replied, "Keep your gifts for yourself or give them to someone else. I will read for Your Majesty what has been written and tell you what it means.

18 "The Supreme God made your father Nebuchadnezzar a great king and gave him dignity and majesty. 19 He was so great that

High God gave Nebuchadnezzar your father kingship and greatness and glory and majesty; 19 and because of the greatness that he gave him, all peoples, nations, and languages trembled and feared before him; whom he would he slew, and whom he would he kept alive; whom he would he raised up, and whom he would he put down. But when his heart was lifted up and his spirit was hardened so that he dealt proudly, he was deposed from his kingly throne, and his glory was taken from him; he was driven from among men, and his mind was made like that of a beast, and his dwelling was with the wild asses; he was fed grass like an ox, and his body was wet with the dew of heaven, until he knew that the Most High God rules the kingdom of men, and sets over it whom he will. 22 And you his son, Belshazzar, have not humbled your heart, though you knew all this, 23 but you have lifted up yourself against the Lord of heaven; and the vessels of his house have been brought in before you, and you and your lords, your wives, and your concubines have drunk wine from them; and you have praised the gods of silver and gold, of bronze, iron, wood, and stone, which do not see or hear or know, but the God in whose hand is your breath, and whose are all your ways, you have not honored.

24 "Then from his presence the hand was sent, and this writing was inscribed. 25 And this is the writing that was inscribed: MENE, MENE, TEKEL, and PARSIN. 26 This is the interpretation of the matter: MENE, God has numbered the days of your kingdom and brought it to an end; 27 TEKEL, you have been weighed in the balances and found wanting; 28 PERES, your kingdom is divided and given to the Medes and Persians."

29 Then Belshazzar commanded, and Daniel was clothed with purple, a chain of gold was put about his neck, and proclamation was made concerning him, that he should be the third ruler in the kingdom. 30 That very night Belshazzar the Chaldean king was slain. 31 And Darius the Mede received the kingdom, being about sixty-two years old.

people of all nations, races, and languages were afraid of him and trembled. If he wanted to kill someone, he did; if he wanted to keep someone alive, he did. He honored or disgraced anyone he wanted to. 20 But because he became proud, stubborn, and cruel, he was removed from his royal throne and lost his place of honor. 21 He was driven away from human society, and his mind became like that of an animal. He lived with wild donkeys, ate grass like an ox, and slept in the open air with nothing to protect him from the dew. Finally he admitted that the Supreme God controls all human kingdoms and can give them to anyone he chooses.

22 "But you, his son, have not humbled yourself, even though you knew all this. 23 You acted against the Lord of heaven and brought in the cups and bowls taken from his Temple. You, your noblemen, your wives, and your concubines drank wine out of them and praised gods made of gold, silver, bronze, iron, wood, and stone—gods that cannot see or hear and that do not know anything. But you did not honor the God who determines whether you live or die and who controls everything you do. 24 That is why God has sent the hand to write these words.

25 "This is what was written: 'Number, number, weight, divisions.' 26 And this is what it means: number, God has numbered the days of your kingdom and brought it to an end; 27 weight, you have been weighed on the scales and found to be too light; 28 divisions, your kingdom is divided up and given to the Medes and Persians."(L)

29 Immediately Belshazzar ordered his servants to dress Daniel in a robe of royal purple and to hang a gold chain of honor around his neck. And he made him the third in power in the kingdom. 30 That same night Belshazzar, the king of Babylonia, was killed; 31 and Darius the Mede, who was then sixty-two years old, seized the royal power.

TEV Section Heading: Daniel explains the writing

Many versions do not have a section heading at this point. They prefer to see the whole of chapter 5 as a single unit. However, it will probably be more helpful to the reader if the dream and its interpretation are separated into two different sections, as TEV has done. Some translators may prefer to say "The meaning of the writing on the wall."

5.13   RSV   TEV

Then Daniel was brought in   Daniel was brought at once
before the king. The king said to   into the king's presence, and the
Daniel, "You are that Daniel, one of king said to him, "Are you Daniel,
the exiles of Judah, whom the king   that Jewish exile whom my father
my father brought from Judah.   the king brought here from Judah?

Then: the transition word used here often introduces a new stage in a narrative and adds special emphasis. TEV has attempted to get at this by using "at once." In other versions a simple paragraph break without any other obvious marker is used to show the transition (NJB, for example).

Was brought in: this passive formulation will have to be made active in many languages. Sometimes it is possible to say "someone brought Daniel in"; in other cases it will be more natural to use a third person plural indefinite pronoun "they brought Daniel in."

The king said: literally "the king speaking said." See 2.5. But in this context it is quite acceptable to use the verb "asked" as in AB and NAB.

You are that Daniel: the punctuation of RSV makes this a simple declaration of fact. But since Belshazzar had not known Daniel before the queen mother's explanation that led to his being summoned, it is much more logical that this should be translated as a question. This is done in many versions. Others seem to assume that the king would have been told who Daniel was when he came into his presence. Thus the rendering "So you are Daniel" (NEB/REB and NRSV).

One of the exiles of Judah . . . : literally "one of the sons of the exile of Judah." In order to avoid the RSV repetition of the geographical reference **Judah**, TEV and REB use the adjective "Jewish" here. Compare 2.25.

If the translator follows the recommendation of rendering Belshazzar's words as a question, the language may require a response that is not given in the text. If this is the case, it will be perfectly legitimate to insert the words " 'Yes,' replied Daniel" at the end of this verse, and then "Then the king continued" or similar words at the beginning of the next verse. Another way of handling the problem may be to replace the straightforward interrogative form with one that may not require an answer: "You are Daniel . . . , aren't you?" Making the translation sound natural should dictate the exact form here.

5.14   RSV   TEV

I have heard of you that the spirit of   I have heard that the spirit of the
the holy gods[k] is in you, and that   holy gods[k] is in you and that you
light and understanding and excel-   are skillful and have knowledge and
lent wisdom are found in you.   wisdom.

[k] Or *Spirit of the holy God*   [k] gods *or* God.

The spirit of the holy gods: while both RSV and TEV have the adjective **holy** in this verse, the majority of versions omit it. This word is clearly found in verse 11 above, but it is not recommended by HOTTP/CTAT that it be repeated here. The king would not necessarily have repeated the words of verse 11 exactly.

Light and understanding and excellent wisdom: this is a repetition of the same three words used in verse 11.

Are found in you: the passive expression will have to be made active in many languages. A possible model is "and I know that you are (have)."

5.15	RSV	TEV
	Now the wise men, the enchanters, have been brought in before me to read this writing and make known to me its interpretation; but they could not show the interpretation of the matter.	The advisers and magicians were brought in to read this writing and tell me what it means, but they could not discover the meaning.

Now: the probable meaning is "at the present moment," indicating a very recent happening. This may be reflected in the verb phrase in some languages ". . . were just now brought in." Compare REB "have just been brought in," but note that NJB reads "have already been brought in."

The wise men, the enchanters: note that only two terms (the more general terms for the royal advisors) are used in this verse. Compare 1.20; 2.2, 12.

Have been brought in: this passive may be better translated in some languages as "I have called in," "I have caused to come in," "my men have brought in," or something of this nature. Or the indefinite third person plural pronoun may be used: "they have brought into my presence."

The interpretation of the matter: literally "the interpretation of the word." Instead of the more general term **matter**, it may be preferable to say what **the matter** is; for example, "the writing" or "the message written on the wall." But if the previous reference in this verse to **interpretation** has already made clear what is being referred to, perhaps a pronoun can be used here at the end of the verse.

5.16	RSV	TEV
	But I have heard that you can give interpretations and solve problems. Now if you can read the writing and make known to me its interpretation, you shall be clothed with purple, and have a chain of gold about your	Now I have heard that you can find hidden meanings and explain mysteries. If you can read this writing and tell me what it means, you will be dressed in robes of royal purple, wear a gold chain of honor around

neck, and shall be the third ruler in the kingdom.	your neck, and be the third in power in the kingdom."

But: in some languages a rather strong contrastive conjunction like this will be required, because there is a contrast between the other "wise men" and Daniel. Mft, AT, and AB have "However."

Give interpretations: literally "interpret interpretations," where the verb and the noun have the same root. This is a common type of construction in Aramaic as in Hebrew, but it should not be imitated in other languages unless it is natural.

Solve problems: although the construction is a bit different from that in verse 12, the same Aramaic words are involved. They speak literally of "untying knots" but are intended in a figurative sense.

You shall be clothed: the three things offered to Daniel are the same as the rewards that would have been given to the other wise men in verse 7, if they had succeeded in explaining the mystery. But once again the passive construction will have to be made active in many languages.

5.17 RSV	TEV
Then Daniel answered before the king, "Let your gifts be for yourself, and give your rewards to another; nevertheless I will read the writing to the king and make known to him the interpretation.	Daniel replied, "Keep your gifts for yourself or give them to someone else. I will read for Your Majesty what has been written and tell you what it means.

Let your gifts be for yourself: Daniel's answer may sound impudent in some languages if translated using the imperative form, as in TEV and several other versions. Probably no such arrogance is intended, and the answer may have to be softened in some languages. Many English versions make the discourse sound less harsh by beginning with "You may keep . . ." instead of the imperative (NJB and NAB). In some cases it may be possible to say "It is good for you to keep . . . ." However, it should be noted that some scholars think that the author intentionally uses strong language here to show that Daniel is a messenger of divine judgment. This is in keeping with the tone of judgment that is found in the rest of the speech.

And give your rewards to another: the use of the conjunction **and** makes it appear that the **gifts** and **rewards** refer to two different sets of objects, one of which Belshazzar would keep and the other which would be given to someone else. This, however, is not the intention of the writer. So the conjunction should be "or." Daniel is saying that the three rewards (the royal clothing, the royal collar, and royal power mentioned at the end of verse 16) may either be kept by the king or given away to other people. In addition to TEV, those versions using the conjunction "or" are NEB, NAB, NRSV, and AB. REB restructures the two phrases and joins them with a semicolon: "I do not look for gifts from you; give your rewards to another." Another possible model is "I don't want to receive your gifts. If you want to, give them to someone else."

Nevertheless: this adverb stresses the fact that, even without any reward, Daniel intends to clear up the mystery of the writing on the wall.

To the king . . . to him: since Daniel is speaking directly to the king, it will be very unnatural in most languages to use this third person reference. It will be much more natural to say something like "I will read the writing to you, your Majesty, and tell you what it means." On the use of the third person in place of the second, see 2.10 and comments.

5.18 RSV TEV

O king, the Most High God gave Nebuchadnezzar your father kingship and greatness and glory and majesty;

"The Supreme God made your father Nebuchadnezzar a great king and gave him dignity and majesty.

O king: the formal address is left out by TEV but should be included in translation if an appropriately natural way is found to do this. See 2.4. The Aramaic actually has an emphatic expression ("You, O king"), calling attention to the long accusation that follows. AB translates "Hear, O king!" Some translators may prefer to begin with "Listen, O king!"

The Most High God: see 3.26.

Nebuchadnezzar your father: see verses 2 and 11.

Gave . . . kingship: while the verb to give may be appropriate to the other three nouns in this list, it may not be suitable for the word **kingship**. In many languages it will be better to use an expression like "make king," or there may be a special word for "enthrone." Another way of handling the problem may be to say "gave your father this kingdom with all its greatness and glory and majesty" (similarly Mft). While the dignity and majesty may be given by the people of the kingdom in the first place, in the ways in which they show respect to the king, the writer sees it as ultimately coming from God.

On the synonymous terms **greatness and glory and majesty**, compare 2.37; 4.30, 36.

5.19 RSV TEV

and because of the greatness that he gave him, all peoples, nations, and languages trembled and feared before him; whom he would he slew, and whom he would he kept alive; whom he would he raised up, and whom he would he put down.

He was so great that people of all nations, races, and languages were afraid of him and trembled. If he wanted to kill someone, he did; if he wanted to keep someone alive, he did. He honored or disgraced anyone he wanted to.

. . . he gave him: in some cases it may be important to translate the pronoun **he** by the noun "God" to avoid possible confusion in the mind of the reader.

Peoples, nations, and languages: see 3.4, 7; 4.1.

Trembled and feared: these two terms are very similar in meaning and may have to be translated by a single verb in some languages.

Whom he would he slew: the NRSV gives the same information in more common English word order and vocabulary: "He killed those he wanted to kill."

Whom he would he kept alive: both the RSV and the TEV rendering "if he wanted to keep someone alive, he did" sounds as if the king may have been a great physician with exceptional healing powers, but this is not the meaning of the text. So this meaning should be avoided. It will be much better to say "allow to live" instead of "keep alive." Another possibility is "spared whom he pleased" (NJB).

Raised up . . . put down: the translation of these terms should not give the impression of physical lifting up and its opposite. Very often in Scripture these words are used in a figurative sense to speak of promotion and demotion, or of distinction and dishonor. This meaning is conveyed here by TEV, "honored or disgraced." NEB has "promoted . . . and . . . degraded," and NAB reads "exalted or humbled."

5.20   RSV   TEV

| But when his heart was lifted up and his spirit was hardened so that he dealt proudly, he was deposed from his kingly throne, and his glory was taken from him; | But because he became proud, stubborn, and cruel, he was removed from his royal throne and lost his place of honor. |

But: the initial conjunction contrasts the king's glory and majesty with his humiliation after being dethroned.

The structure of this verse may be simplified by taking the first two clauses, which are subordinate in Aramaic, and making an independent clause of them. The third clause may then be introduced by something like "Therefore" or "Consequently."

His heart was lifted up: this expression indicates a state of arrogance and conceit. See comments on "heart" at 1.8; 2.30; 4.16. In some languages it may be acceptable to translate this literally, but in others a literal rendering will have a totally different meaning. Some possible models are "his heart became proud" (AB), "his heart became arrogant" (NIV), or "he grew (became) haughty" (NJV and REB). Some languages have figures of speech such as "his heart swelled up" or "he acted with a big head" to indicate such arrogance.

His spirit was hardened: this expression refers to stubbornness and inflexibility. Other versions have "willfully presumptuous" (NJV), "his spirit stiff with arrogance" (NJB), and "stubborn" (REB).

So that he dealt proudly: literally "until arrogance." This has been translated in a variety of ways: "presumptuous" (NEB and NJV); "insolence" (NAB); and "so that he bore himself haughtily" (Mft). The cumulative effect of the last three phrases is more important than the details of each expression. Extreme pride and arrogance are in view.

He was deposed: this is the main clause of this verse and should probably be introduced by something like "Therefore" to show the relationship with the previous statements. In many languages restructuring will be required by the fact that it is passive in form. Translators may say "he lost his royal authority" or identify the agent by saying something like "God deposed him" or "God caused him to fall."

His glory was taken from him: although this is passive in RSV, the text literally reads "they (indefinite) took away his glory." A literal rendering of the Aramaic may be acceptable in some cases. Or some may have to say "his glory disappeared completely."

5.21	RSV	TEV
	he was driven from among men, and his mind was made like that of a beast, and his dwelling was with the wild asses; he was fed grass like an ox, and his body was wet with the dew of heaven, until he knew that the Most High God rules the kingdom of men, and sets over it whom he will.	He was driven away from human society, and his mind became like that of an animal. He lived with wild donkeys, ate grass like an ox, and slept in the open air with nothing to protect him from the dew. Finally he admitted that the Supreme God controls all human kingdoms and can give them to anyone he chooses.

He was driven from among men: literally "from among the sons of men he was driven." The expression "sons of men" speaks of human society in general. The passive must be made active in some languages by saying something like "they (indefinite) drove him out," or possibly "God drove him out."

Most of the rest of this verse is also a repetition of the account in 4.25. But the passive forms will have to be made active in many languages. Also, while this verse has **wild asses**, the text in chapter 4 has only "wild animals." The mention of the particular kind of animal (**asses**) rather than the more general expression of chapter 4 should be retained here.

On **asses**, see *Fauna and Flora*, pages 5-7. The wild ass of the Orient is quite different from the smaller and less intelligent modern European ass. But the important point in this context is that they are untamed. The text therefore focuses on the uncivilized character of the king's behavior.

Until he knew . . . : or "until he learned . . . ," or "until he came to acknowledge" (REB). The remainder of this verse can well be translated as a separate sentence, as in TEV: "Finally he admitted . . . ."

147

The Most High God: see 3.26.

Kingdom of men: as in 4.25 the singular **kingdom** may be translated as a plural. And **men** in this context clearly refers to human beings in general.

5.22	RSV	TEV

And you his son, Belshazzar, have not humbled your heart, though you knew all this,	"But you, his son, have not humbled yourself, even though you knew all this.

And: the conjunction used in RSV indicates simple coordination. But it should mark contrast as in NJB, NJV, NIV, and REB, as well as TEV.

Belshazzar: note that TEV does not include the proper name here but simply says "you, his son." Making the translation sound natural will determine which model should be followed on this point.

Have not humbled your heart: the heart in this context stands for the whole person. This is why NJV as well as TEV say "have not humbled yourself." In some languages it is possible to say "refused to be modest" or "failed to recognize God."

Even though you knew all this: it is quite possible that the order of the two clauses in this verse should be switched in many languages. This will probably constitute a more natural structure; for example, "You are his son, and you knew all this. But you didn't humble yourself."

5.23	RSV	TEV

but you have lifted up yourself against the Lord of heaven; and the vessels of his house have been brought in before you, and you and your lords, your wives, and your concubines have drunk wine from them; and you have praised the gods of silver and gold, of bronze, iron, wood, and stone, which do not see or hear or know, but the God in whose hand is your breath, and whose are all your ways, you have not honored.	You acted against the Lord of heaven and brought in the cups and bowls taken from his Temple. You, your noblemen, your wives, and your concubines drank wine out of them and praised gods made of gold, silver, bronze, iron, wood, and stone—gods that cannot see or hear and that do not know anything. But you did not honor the God who determines whether you live or die and who controls everything you do.

In Aramaic, as in RSV, this verse constitutes a single long sentence. It should be broken down into smaller units in most languages.

Lifted yourself against the Lord of heaven: this can also be understood to mean "you have lifted yourself up above the Lord of heaven." The whole verbal expression has been variously translated "exalted yourself against"

(NJV), "set yourself up against" (NEB), "defied" (NJB and FRCL), and "rebelled against" (NAB). Another possibility is "you have placed yourself above the Lord of heaven." In languages where the same word is used for "chief" and "Lord," it may be necessary to make the expression **Lord of heaven** more precise by saying "the Lord God of heaven." FRCL has simply "the God of heaven."

Vessels: see verses 2 and 3.

His house: while verse 3 has the very full expression "the temple, the house of God in Jerusalem," here the text has only the ordinary word for "house" and the attached third person singular possessive pronoun. The pronoun refers back to **the Lord of heaven**, which is another way of talking about God. **His house** clearly refers to the Temple, and it should be made equally clear in the translation.

Silver and gold: the order of the Aramaic text is the reverse of that found in verse 4. But on translation grounds TEV has switched to the more natural English order.

Lords: see 4.36. And compare also verses 1 and 3 above.

Wives, . . . concubines: see verse 2.

Gods: or "idols" as in verse 4. These objects of worship are further defined in the text as things **which do not see or hear or know**. Since these gods are utterly incapable of seeing, hearing, or knowing anything, TEV and REB capture the meaning better by saying "that can not . . ." instead of "do not . . . ."

The God in whose hand is your breath: as is seen often in the Old Testament, the **hand** stands for power, and this expression simply means that it is God who has power over whether or not a person breathes, that is, whether he lives or dies. This phrase stands in very close relationship with the one that follows, and the two should be considered together.

And whose are all your ways: God also has power over everything that happens in Belshazzar's life. AB speaks of "the whole course of your life." NJV renders the two phrases above as "God who controls your lifebreath and every move you make."

You have not honored: this returns to the same theme as the first verbal expression in this verse (**lifted yourself up against . . .**) but states the same sort of thing in negative form. In rebelling against God, the king had also failed to honor him.

5.24	RSV	TEV
	"Then from his presence the hand was sent, and this writing was inscribed.	That is why God has sent the hand to write these words.

RSV makes a paragraph break at the beginning of this verse, but this seems to spoil the relationship between this verse and the previous verse. The word translated **Then** in RSV, which may be understood as a simple adverb of time, is rendered as an adverb of purpose by TEV and NJB: "That is why."

Similarly, NEB/REB has "This is why . . . ," and AB "Therefore." This meaning seems to fit the context better.

From his presence the hand was sent: this expression may be difficult to translate literally, because it is awkward and includes a passive form. In Aramaic it actually includes the two words for hand as seen in verse 5 above. But the meaning is simply "God sent the hand."

And this writing was inscribed: this expression involves another passive construction, while the conjunction **and** may also be misleading. The relationship between the hand and the writing may be unclear if **and** is translated literally. The hand was sent for the purpose of writing the inscription. So one way of expressing the two clauses together is "God sent the hand in order to write the message." Another model is that of NJB: "he has sent the hand that has written these words."

5.25	RSV	TEV

And this is the writing that was inscribed: MENE, MENE, TEKEL, and PARSIN.

"This is what was written: 'Number, number, weight, divisions.'

The Aramaic words written on the wall were not foreign to King Belshazzar. They were quite ordinary words. The mystery lay in their brevity and the fact that they could be read either as nouns or as verbs. Consequently, although most English versions transliterate the Aramaic terms, translators are advised to give the meaning following the TEV model. **MENE** may be translated "number," "measure," or "quantity." **TEKEL** concerns a "weight" or a "load." **PARSIN** has to do with "division," "split," "partition," or "separation." Note that the first word is repeated while the others occur only once. Although several ancient versions omit the second occurrence of the first word, it is found in the Aramaic text and should be included in the translation.

According to certain commentators the words could have been used to designate three different pieces of money in Aramaic: the mina, the shekel and the half-mina. While this is possible, it plays no role in the narrative and does not even have to be mentioned in a footnote. The meaning of the words is given in detail in the following verses.

5.26	RSV	TEV

This is the interpretation of the matter: MENE, God has numbered the days of your kingdom and brought it to an end;

And this is what it means: *number,* God has numbered the days of your kingdom and brought it to an end;

MENE: although the first word was apparently written twice, it is explained only once. The cryptic word meaning "number," "measure," or "count" is explained in greater detail by Daniel. It is taken as a verb with God as the subject. What has been numbered, measured, or counted is the days from the beginning to the end of Belshazzar's rule.

And brought it to an end: the use of the past tense here reflects the writer's conviction that an unchangeable decision has already been made, even if it has not yet been fully accomplished. The grammar of some languages will make it impossible to use a past tense here, but a present progressive may convey the same idea.

5.27	RSV	TEV

TEKEL, you have been weighed in the balances and found wanting;

weight, you have been weighed on the scales and found to be too light;

TEKEL: as indicated in the TEV rendering, this word means "weigh" or "weight," depending on whether it is taken as a verb or a noun. Here it is taken as a verb, with God once again as the intended subject.

You have been weighed in the balances: if this passive and the one in the following expression have to be made active, God should certainly be the subject of the verb. It is God who examines Belshazzar and reaches the conclusion that there is something lacking. The idea of **balances** may be foreign to some cultures, but there is probably some kind of rough equivalent that can be used here. Within the commercial system of most groups, there is a system of measuring weight or quantity that can be employed here.

And found wanting: on the passive formulation, see above. Some possible models are "he (God) has seen that you are insignificant," or "he has determined that you are incompetent," or "he has decided that you are inadequate to rule." If it is desirable to retain the metaphor in the receptor language, translators may consider "he saw that you weighed too little" or "he found that you were not heavy enough."

5.28	RSV	TEV

PERES, your kingdom is divided and given to the Medes and Persians."

divisions, your kingdom is divided up and given to the Medes and Persians."[1]

[1] PERSIANS: *In Aramaic the word for "Persians" sounds like the word for "division."*

PERES: this is the singular form of the plural *parsin* found in verse 25. The word comes from a root meaning "divide," "dissect," or "cut in two." But there is a play on words in this verse, so that it is also related to the **Persians** mentioned at the end of the verse. While NJB and REB have the plural form, this is not recommended. In fact, with all three terms, it will be better to translate the meaning rather than retain the transliterated form of the Aramaic.

Your kingdom is divided: once again the passive may have to be transformed into an active form with God as the agent: "God has divided . . . ," or in some languages "God is about to divide . . ." or "God is dividing . . . ."

And given to the Medes and the Persians: if God is made the subject of the verb "divide" in the previous phrase, this one may continue "so that he might give it to . . ." or "in order to hand it over to . . . ." The two names are actually singular in form in the Aramaic, "the Mede and the Persian," but they have a collective meaning and should be translated as plurals in most cases. The Aramaic word for "Persian" constitutes a play on words with *parsin* in verse 25 and *peres* here. But it is inevitable that the wordplay will be lost if the meaning is translated in verses 25 and 28 instead of being transliterated. If judged indispensable for the reader, this information can be provided in a footnote.

5.29   RSV   TEV

Then Belshazzar commanded, and Daniel was clothed with purple, a chain of gold was put about his neck, and proclamation was made concerning him, that he should be the third ruler in the kingdom.	Immediately Belshazzar ordered his servants to dress Daniel in a robe of royal purple and to hang a gold chain of honor around his neck. And he made him the third in power in the kingdom.

Then: see comments on this same transition word in verse 13. Here TEV translates "Immediately."

Commanded . . . : since many languages will require an object following this verb, it will be good to follow the model of TEV and clearly say "his servants."

Was clothed: if "servants" have been clearly mentioned as the object of the previous verb, the pronoun "they" can be used as the subject of this one and will refer back to the servants: "and they dressed Daniel . . ."; or in other cases the TEV use of the infinitive may be a good model.

Purple, a chain of gold: see verses 7 and 16.

Proclamation was made: the implied agent of this action is clearly King Belshazzar. Where necessary this may be made explicit. Since the king has already been mentioned by name in the verse, a simple pronoun, or possibly "the king" (without the proper name), will be adequate in most languages.

The discrepancy between Daniel's statement that he would not accept the rewards (verse 17) and his eventual acceptance of them can probably be explained by the insistence of King Belshazzar. But this should not concern the translator.

5.30   RSV   TEV

That very night Belshazzar the Chaldean king was slain.

That same night Belshazzar, the king of Babylonia, was killed;

That very night: in some languages it will be more natural to say "During the night that followed." This indicates that Belshazzar's death took place after he had gone to bed and immediately following the events described in this chapter. It does not necessarily mean that the banquet itself took place or started after dark (see comments on the TEV rendering of 1.1).

Chaldean: or "Babylonian." The Aramaic word used here is to be taken in its geographical sense as in 1.4, and not in its cultural sense as in 2.2.

Was killed: the agent of this passive form is not clear. In some languages it will be better to say simply "died." But it is also possible to say "someone killed" or "they (impersonal) killed." What is important is not the identity of the assassin but the fact that what Daniel predicted actually did happen.

We know from ancient history that the city of Babylon was conquered in the night of October 11 in the year 539 B.C. It was probably during the course of the taking of this city that King Belshazzar died.

At the time when the Aramaic text was divided into chapters and verses, between the 13th and 16th centuries A.D., the following verse was unfortunately attached to the story of chapter 6 and became verse 1 of that chapter. But because it is a part of the account of Belshazzar's Feast, most English versions follow another ancient tradition of chapter and verse division and include it as verse 31 of this chapter. Note, however, that NJV, NJB, and NAB follow the numbering system of the Aramaic text. The relationship between the two ways of numbering the verses is shown below:

Traditional English system	NJB NAB NJV
5.31	6.1
6.1-28	6.2-29

5.31   RSV   TEV
[6.1]

And Darius the Mede received the kingdom, being about sixty-two years old.

and Darius the Mede, who was then sixty-two years old, seized the royal power.

Darius the Mede: this person is not mentioned anywhere else in ancient history. Three different men bearing the name Darius ruled over the Persian Empire, but at later dates. Furthermore, secular history tells us that the city of Babylon was captured by Cyrus, King of the Persians. Nevertheless the translator must respect the text as we have it today. It should not be "corrected" on the basis of modern knowledge. See also the comments on the father of Belshazzar in 5.1. But note the remarks on the relationship between Darius and Cyrus in 6.28.

Received the kingdom: translators may prefer to say simply "became king," or "started to rule," but TEV has "seized royal power." Some languages, however, will require some kind of object for the verb "rule" or "become king." In those cases translators may use a rather vague object such as "the country" or the actual name "Babylonia."

Daniel in the Pit of Lions

Daniel 6.1-28

Commentators often point out numerous similarities in structure and theme between the account of the blazing furnace in chapter 3 and that of the lion's den in this chapter. The parallel even includes a great deal of common vocabulary. For example, the list of officials (3.2, 3 and 6.7), the charge that the Jews "pay no heed to you" (3.12 and 6.13), and "I make a decree" (3.29 and 6.26). It should also be noted that there is considerable similarity between the hymn of praise to the living God in 4.3, 34-35 and the one in 6.26-27. Both accounts contain a great deal of repetition and the general outline of the two stories is also similar:

The king orders the worship of false gods	3.1-9	=	6.1-8
Faithful Jew(s) refuse the order	3.10-13	=	6.9-18
Faithful Jew(s) sentenced to death	3.14-18	=	6.19-24
Deliverance of the faithful and repentance of the king	3.19-28	=	6.25-28

Daniel's enemies set a trap for him: 6.1-9 [6.2-10]

RSV

1 It pleased Darius to set over the kingdom a hundred and twenty satraps, to be throughout the whole kingdom; 2 and over them three presidents, of whom Daniel was one, to whom these satraps should give account, so that the king might suffer no loss. 3 Then this Daniel became distinguished above all the other presidents and satraps, because an excellent spirit was in him; and the king planned to set him over the whole kingdom. 4 Then the presidents and the satraps sought to find a ground for complaint against Daniel with regard to the kingdom; but they could find no ground for complaint or any fault, because he was faithful, and no error or fault was found in him. 5 Then these men said, "We shall not find any ground for complaint against this Daniel unless we find it in connection with the law of his God."

TEV

Daniel in the Pit of Lions

1 Darius decided to appoint a hundred and twenty governors to hold office throughout his empire. 2 In addition, he chose Daniel and two others to supervise the governors and to look after the king's interests. 3 Daniel soon showed that he could do better work than the other supervisors or the governors. Because he was so outstanding, the king considered putting him in charge of the whole empire. 4 Then the other supervisors and the governors tried to find something wrong with the way Daniel administered the empire, but they couldn't, because Daniel was reliable and did not do anything wrong or dishonest. 5 They said to each other, "We are not going to find anything of which to accuse Daniel unless it is something in connection with his religion."

6 So they went to see the king and said, "King Darius, may Your Majesty live forever!

6 Then these presidents and satraps came by agreement to the king and said to him, "O King Darius, live for ever! 7 All the presidents of the kingdom, the prefects and the satraps, the counselors and the governors are agreed that the king should establish an ordinance and enforce an interdict, that whoever makes petition to any god or man for thirty days, except to you, O king, shall be cast into the den of lions. 8 Now, O king, establish the interdict and sign the document, so that it cannot be changed, according to the law of the Medes and the Persians, which cannot be revoked." Therefore King Darius signed the document and interdict.

7 All of us who administer your empire—the supervisors, the governors, the lieutenant governors, and the other officials—have agreed that Your Majesty should issue an order and enforce it strictly. Give orders that for thirty days no one be permitted to request anything from any god or from any human being except from Your Majesty. Anyone who violates this order is to be thrown into a pit filled with lions. 8 So let Your Majesty issue this order and sign it, and it will be in force, a law of the Medes and Persians, which cannot be changed." 9 And so King Darius signed the order.

TEV Section Heading: Daniel in the pit of lions

While TEV provides a single heading for this entire chapter, some versions divide it into two or three subsections. NRSV, for example, breaks it down with the following headings:

1-9	The Plot against Daniel
10-18	Daniel in the Lions' Den
19-28	Daniel Saved from the Lions

FRCL divides the chapter similarly but gives even more explicit fuller section headings: "The enemies of Daniel set a trap for him" (verses 1-9); "Daniel is thrown into a pit of lions" (verses 10-18); "Daniel leaves the pit of lions unharmed" (verses 19-28).

In some languages it may be more helpful to the reader to subdivide this chapter as in NRSV or FRCL, rather than to give it a single section heading as in TEV.

6.1   RSV   TEV
[6.2]

It pleased Darius to set over the kingdom a hundred and twenty satraps, to be throughout the whole kingdom;

Darius decided to appoint a hundred and twenty governors to hold office throughout his empire.

As at the first verse of chapter 5, it may be necessary in some languages to introduce transition material here, since this is the beginning of a new chapter, a new section, and a new story. Many people may start reading at this point without reference to the previous chapters. In some cases it will be possible to begin "One day King Darius . . ." or "After he became king, Darius . . . ."

It pleased Darius: another way of saying this is "Darius was pleased." However, the focus is not on his pleasure but on his will. It will be more natural in most languages to say something like "Darius decided," ". . . ordered the appointment," or ". . . made a decree appointing" (compare 4.2 and comments). The **Darius** of this story may have been Darius I, who ruled over the Persian Empire from 522 to 486 B.C.

Satraps: the term thus translated in RSV is the same as in 3.2. See comments at that point. The English word "satrap" comes from the Persian (through Greek) for the title of the highest authority over a "satrapy," or a particular administrative subdivision of the Persian Empire. The word has become a part of the English language as a technical term of Persian history, but it is not common language. Consequently a more general term will have to be sought in common language translations, such as "governors" (TEV).

To be throughout the whole kingdom: the verb **to be** in this context carries the meaning "to exercise power," "to be in charge" (REB), or to "hold office" (TEV), and should probably be so translated in most languages.

A possible model for restructuring this verse is something like GECL: "Darius subdivided his kingdom into one hundred and twenty provinces and named a governor over each one of them."

6.2   RSV   TEV
[6.3]

and over them three presidents, of whom Daniel was one, to whom these satraps should give account, so that the king might suffer no loss.

In addition, he chose Daniel and two others to supervise the governors and to look after the king's interests.

Presidents: it will be advisable in many languages to begin a new sentence here in order to simplify the structure and make the meaning clearer. The one hundred and twenty **satraps**, or "governors" (TEV), were in turn managed or presided over by three higher officers, one of whom was Daniel. The equivalent for the word **president** may not be suitable in many languages, because it would be unthinkable that there could be more than one president in the country. This term has been translated "chief ministers" by REB. These three, in turn, were answerable to the king. Another way of wording this is "He also appointed three higher officials to watch over the work of these governors . . . and Daniel was one of these three," placing the statement about Daniel at the very end of the verse.

Suffer no loss: the idea here is that the three overseers would guarantee the supervision of the king's affairs so that he would not have to worry. In some languages it may be possible to say something similar to the NJV rendering, "in order that the king not be troubled." REB, however, translates "so that the king's interests might not suffer."

6.3   RSV   TEV
[6.4]

| Then this Daniel became distinguished above all the other presidents and satraps, because an excellent spirit was in him; and the king planned to set him over the whole kingdom. | Daniel soon showed that he could do better work than the other supervisors or the governors. Because he was so outstanding, the king considered putting him in charge of the whole empire. |

Then: this transition word is rendered "soon" by NRSV as well as TEV.

This Daniel: the demonstrative pronoun **this** with the proper name **Daniel** occurs frequently in this chapter (also in verses 5 and 28, for example). This style is an imitation of the ancient Persian, but it need not be reflected in translation, since it is stylistic rather than carrying any real meaning. In English such a construction might indicate emphasis or have a negative meaning, but this is not the case in Aramaic. It merely means "the man in question." NJV has "this man Daniel."

Became distinguished: Daniel's work was clearly superior to that of all the other officials. The idea of this expression may therefore be expressed according to one of the following models: "Daniel outshone the other ministers" (NEB/REB), "was so evidently superior to the other presidents" (NJB), or "surpassed the other ministers" (NJV).

An excellent spirit was in him: this phrase may be taken as an explanation of the reason for Daniel's surpassing all the other officials, or as a reason for King Darius promoting him. The overall impact is virtually the same, but the structure will differ depending on which interpretation is chosen. The punctuation of RSV favors the first interpretation, while TEV clearly supports the second. The majority of scholars seem to prefer the first.

Planned to set him over the whole kingdom: it should be made clear that this was merely something that the king was thinking about doing, but that it had not actually taken place: compare "it was the king's intention" (REB). It should also be clear that this did not mean that Daniel would replace the king, but rather that he would be the top official in the king's administration.

6.4   RSV   TEV
[6.5]

| Then the presidents and the satraps sought to find a ground for complaint against Daniel with regard to the kingdom; but they could find no ground for complaint or any fault, because he was faithful, and no error or fault was found in him. | Then the other supervisors and the governors tried to find something wrong with the way Daniel administered the empire, but they couldn't, because Daniel was reliable and did not do anything wrong or dishonest. |

Sought to find a ground for complaint: the translation should make clear the fact that there was some kind of inquiry or accusation against Daniel. The expression **ground of complaint** occurs twice in this verse, but this may be awkward in translation. One translation puts it this way: "began to look round for some pretext to attack Daniel's administration" (NEB).

No error or fault was found in him: the Aramaic uses the verb "to find" three times in this verse, but it is unnecessary to reflect this in the translation. The parallel construction **no error or fault** may need to be reduced to a single statement in some languages. Also, the passive construction will have to be made active in many cases: "no one could find any error or fault in him" or "they could discover neither negligence nor malpractice" (REB). The point of this statement does not seem to be that Daniel was absolutely perfect or sinless, but that he was law-abiding and trustworthy.

6.5 [6.6] RSV	TEV
Then these men said, "We shall not find any ground for complaint against this Daniel unless we find it in connection with the law of his God."	They said to each other, "We are not going to find anything of which to accuse Daniel unless it is something in connection with his religion."

These men said: note that TEV makes clear the fact that Daniel's accusers were talking to each other. The verb in Aramaic may have a reciprocal meaning, and this is obviously the case here, since there is no one else to whom they might have addressed these ideas. The inclusive "we" would therefore be used in those languages that distinguish between inclusive and exclusive forms.

Ground for complaint: see verse 4.

This Daniel: see verse 3.

Unless we find it . . . : this clause may be better translated as a separate sentence in some languages. One possibility to consider is "The only thing that will make him do wrong (before the king) will be his obedience to matters of his God."

The law of his God: this is taken to mean "his religion" in NEB/REB as well as TEV, and rightly so, since the usual word for law is not used here. But in many languages of the world the word "religion" is difficult to translate, and it may be better to use an expression like "the affairs of his God" or something similar.

6.6   RSV   TEV
[6.7]

    Then these presidents and satraps came by agreement[m] to the king and said to him, "O King Darius, live for ever!

    So they went to see the king and said, "King Darius, may Your Majesty live forever!

[m] Or *thronging*

    These presidents and satraps: the repetition of the two terms for the Persian administrators may be unnecessary here. The pronoun "they" will be perfectly adequate in most languages.

    Came by agreement: the meaning of this Aramaic expression is uncertain. The verb is used only here and in verses 11 and 15, and has been understood to mean "came together (in a group)" (NIV), "went in a body" (NJB), "rushed in" (NAB), and "watched for an opportunity" (NEB). TEV appears to leave it untranslated. The most probable meaning is "to go together by secret agreement," or as AB translates, "went in collusion." In some languages it may be necessary to express this clearly by saying something like "So they secretly agreed to go to the king, and when they arrived they said . . . ."

    O King Darius, live for ever!: compare 2.4. But note that the use of the proper name **Darius** with the title makes this different from 2.4.

6.7   RSV   TEV
[6.8]

All the presidents of the kingdom, the prefects and the satraps, the counselors and the governors are agreed that the king should establish an ordinance and enforce an interdict, that whoever makes petition to any god or man for thirty days, except to you, O king, shall be cast into the den of lions.

All of us who administer your empire—the supervisors, the governors, the lieutenant governors, and the other officials—have agreed that Your Majesty should issue an order and enforce it strictly. Give orders that for thirty days no one be permitted to request anything from any god or from any human being except from Your Majesty. Anyone who violates this order is to be thrown into a pit filled with lions.

    Presidents . . . prefects, counselors and governors: once again there is a list of government officials, but the order differs from that of 3.3. TEV uses a more summary expression, "all of us who administer your empire," but then goes on to list each title separately.

    Establish an ordinance and enforce an interdict: the wording of RSV may give the impression that the **ordinance** and the **interdict** were two different things, but this is not the case. What the officials were asking was that the king issue a decree and then guarantee that it be enforced.

Makes petition: literally "prays a prayer." This simply means "prays" as indicated in the rendering of NJB, NIV, and NRSV. TEV has "request anything," while Mft has "offer a prayer."

Shall be cast: this passive form may be rendered in some languages by the impersonal third person pronoun "they will cast . . . ," or possibly by using some other indefinite subject such as "your servants."

Into the den of lions: the expression **den of lions** has become well known in English, but in other languages it will probably be necessary to describe what this refers to: "in a big hole where lions are imprisoned" or, more generally, "in a place where they keep lions." But translators should avoid the use of a word like "cage," which is not suitable to the remainder of the story. The definite article of RSV, **the den**, is uncalled for in this first mention of the place where the lions are kept. It has been dropped in favor of the indefinite "a den" in NRSV and NJV, and "a pit" in TEV.

6.8
[6.9]

RSV	TEV
Now, O king, establish the interdict and sign the document, so that it cannot be changed, according to the law of the Medes and the Persians, which cannot be revoked."	So let Your Majesty issue this order and sign it, and it will be in force, a law of the Medes and Persians, which cannot be changed."

O king: see 2.4.

Establish the interdict and sign the document: once again the parallelism should not be understood as talking about two different things. The **document** to be signed is, in fact, the **interdict**, or "order," that would be established. Compare verse 7. NJV translates "So issue the ban, O king, and put it in writing."

So that it cannot be changed: the purpose of putting the ban in writing and signing the document is to make it more binding than a mere verbal decree. The finality of the decree sought by the government officials is emphasized by reference to the laws of the Medes and Persians, which were famous for being very firmly fixed.

The unchangeable character of the **law of the Medes and the Persians** is also attested in the Book of Esther (1.19 and 8.8). The rendering of AB may be helpful to translators, in that it shows clearly that this would be one among many other laws: "so that it will be as irrevocable as the other immutable laws of the Medes and the Persians."

Which cannot be revoked: this is essentially the same as the above expression **cannot be changed**. Instead of the negative statement, NEB gives the same idea more positively: "for the law of the Medes and the Persians stands for ever."

6.9   RSV   TEV
[6.10]
Therefore King Darius signed the   **And so King Darius signed the or-**
document and interdict.   **der.**

Therefore: the corresponding Aramaic word originally meant "Because of all that," indicating a cause and effect relationship. But the expression came to be used more loosely and in a general sense. NJB, NEB, and AT use the English word "Accordingly." NAB, NIV, and Mft translate "So."

Signed: the Aramaic verb here (and in verse 8) may mean "sign" or possibly more generally "write" (see "inscribed" in 5.24-25). Here and in the previous verse, the more restricted sense "to sign" is more appropriate, since it is difficult to imagine the king himself actually writing the decree.

The document and interdict: note that once again the two nouns refer to one directive. If there is a danger that readers will misunderstand two terms joined by the conjunction "and" as referring to two different things, then these two terms should be translated by a single word, as in TEV and REB.

Daniel in the lions' pit: 6.10-18 [6.11-19]

RSV

10 When Daniel knew that the document had been signed, he went to his house where he had windows in his upper chamber open toward Jerusalem; and he got down upon his knees three times a day and prayed and gave thanks before his God, as he had done previously. 11 Then these men came by agreement and found Daniel making petition and supplication before his God. 12 Then they came near and said before the king, concerning the interdict, "O king! Did you not sign an interdict, that any man who makes petition to any god or man within thirty days except to you, O king, shall be cast into the den of lions?" The king answered, "The thing stands fast, according to the law of the Medes and Persians, which cannot be revoked." 13 Then they answered before the king, "That Daniel, who is one of the exiles from Judah, pays no heed to you, O king, or the interdict you have signed, but makes his petition three times a day."

14 Then the king, when he heard these words, was much distressed, and set his mind to deliver Daniel; and he labored till the sun went down to rescue him. 15 Then these men came by agreement to the king, and said to the king, "Know, O king, that it is a law of the Medes and Persians that no interdict or ordinance which the king establishes can be changed."

TEV

10 When Daniel learned that the order had been signed, he went home. In an upstairs room of his house there were windows that faced toward Jerusalem. There, just as he had always done, he knelt down at the open windows and prayed to God three times a day.

11 When Daniel's enemies observed him praying to God, 12 all of them went together to the king to accuse Daniel. They said, "Your Majesty, you signed an order that for the next thirty days anyone who requested anything from any god or from any human being except you, would be thrown into a pit filled with lions."

The king replied, "Yes, that is a strict order, a law of the Medes and Persians, which cannot be changed."

13 Then they said to the king, "Daniel, one of the exiles from Judah, does not respect Your Majesty or obey the order you issued. He prays regularly three times a day."

14 When the king heard this, he was upset and did his best to find some way to rescue Daniel. He kept trying until sunset. 15 Then Daniel's enemies came back to the king and said to him, "Your Majesty knows that according to the laws of the Medes and Persians no order which the king issues can be changed."

16 So the king gave orders for Daniel to be taken and thrown into the pit filled with

16 Then the king commanded, and Daniel was brought and cast into the den of lions. The king said to Daniel, "May your God, whom you serve continually, deliver you!" 17 And a stone was brought and laid upon the mouth of the den, and the king sealed it with his own signet and with the signet of his lords, that nothing might be changed concerning Daniel. 18 Then the king went to his palace, and spent the night fasting; no diversions were brought to him, and sleep fled from him.

lions. He said to Daniel, "May your God, whom you serve so loyally, rescue you." 17 A stone was put over the mouth of the pit, and the king placed his own royal seal and the seal of his noblemen on the stone, so that no one could rescue Daniel. 18 Then the king returned to the palace and spent a sleepless night, without food or any form of entertainment.

Section heading

In those languages where two or more section headings are desirable for this story, it will be appropriate to place one at the beginning of the paragraph that begins in verse 10. Translators may say "Daniel is thrown into a pit of lions," or possibly "Daniel prays from the pit of the lions," emphasizing another aspect of the story.

6.10 RSV	TEV
[6.11]	
When Daniel knew that the document had been signed, he went to his house where he had windows in his upper chamber open toward Jerusalem; and he got down upon his knees three times a day and prayed and gave thanks before his God, as he had done previously.	**When Daniel learned that the order had been signed, he went home. In an upstairs room of his house there were windows that faced toward Jerusalem. There, just as he had always done, he knelt down at the open windows and prayed to God three times a day.**

When Daniel knew: the word translated **When** in RSV and TEV may be better rendered as in NAB and AB, "Even after." NRSV renders it "Although." If this example is followed, then the verb "to know" is logical; but if the translator follows the majority in translating **When**, then the subsequent verb is better rendered "learned" (NJV, NEB/REB) or "heard" (NJB and NAB), or possibly "found out."

That the document had been signed: the passive will have to be translated "that the king had signed the document" in many languages.

Went to his house: the verb here literally means "entered." But since Daniel had surely come from his house before the event described here, some languages will require "went back to his house" or "returned home."

Upper chamber: the idea of an upstairs room such as this may be difficult to communicate in some cultures. In those areas of the world where such multistory construction is traditionally unknown, unconventional expressions have developed. Some examples are "room on top of a room" or "room on top of the house."

Open toward Jerusalem: the Aramaic verb does not necessarily mean that the windows were actually open when Daniel arrived at the house, but rather that when they were opened it was possible to look out in the direction of Jerusalem. NJV captures the idea well with "windows made facing Jerusalem." Compare also NJB "faced toward Jerusalem" and NEB "looking toward Jerusalem." But it is clear that later, when Daniel was praying, the windows were open, because his enemies could observe him praying. It is important that translators show clearly that Daniel **got down on his knees** so that there is obvious physical evidence of his praying that could be observed by others. Certain languages may possibly say something like "assumed the position of prayer."

Prayed and gave thanks to God: while neither of the two verbs used here is identical to what is forbidden in verse 8, it is clear that this is taken as a violation of the order. The first word comes from a root meaning to "bow," and the second conveys the idea of offering praise.

As he had done previously: the RSV wording may seem to indicate something that Daniel had done only once or relatively infrequently in the past, but this is not the meaning. It was his usual custom to pray three times a day in this position. Some may wish to say something like "as was his custom" (REB) or "as he had the habit of doing." And in other languages the form of the verb will convey the habitual meaning.

6.11   RSV   TEV
[6.12]
Then these men came by agreement   **When Daniel's enemies ob-**
and found Daniel making petition   **served him praying to God,**
and supplication before his God.

These men: TEV seeks to make the meaning more precise with "Daniel's enemies." REB likewise has "his enemies," while NRSV has "the conspirators."

Came by agreement: see verse 6 above. Note that this is left out by TEV in both cases. But since this may be intended to emphasize the fact that there was a plot, it should probably be retained in some form.

Found Daniel: the verb "to find" will be misleading in some languages. The idea is that they caught him in the act of praying. Some may say "discovered" or simply "saw."

Making petition and supplication before his God: the text actually has two verbs here. The first is the same as the one used in verse 7, where such action is prohibited. The second carries the idea of asking for help (as in NIV). Both NAB and NJB translate the second "pleading." While these verbs differ from those used in verse 10, the meaning is more or less the same. REB renders the two verbs by a single verb phrase, "at his prayers making supplication to his God."

6.12 RSV

TEV

[6.13]

Then they came near and said before the king, concerning the interdict, "O king! Did you not sign an interdict, that any man who makes petition to any god or man within thirty days except to you, O king, shall be cast into the den of lions?" The king answered, "The thing stands fast, according to the law of the Medes and Persians, which cannot be revoked."

all of them went together to the king to accuse Daniel. They said, "Your Majesty, you signed an order that for the next thirty days anyone who requested anything from any god or from any human being except you, would be thrown into a pit filled with lions."

The king replied, "Yes, that is a strict order, a law of the Medes and Persians, which cannot be changed."

Came near: the structure of RSV may make it questionable on first reading as to whether they came near to Daniel or near to the king. But the meaning is clearly that they approached the king. So the structure should probably be changed in many languages. The TEV rendering also makes it clearer that their purpose was to accuse Daniel.

Concerning the interdict: this indicates that those who came before the king spoke to him about the order that he had given, forbidding the worship of anything other than himself. Other versions have worded this as follows: "and reminded him of the royal prohibition" (AB) or "they talked to him about the law he had made" (NCV).

O king: see 2.4. This formal address is repeated later in the verse, but the repetition is omitted by TEV as being stylistically undesirable.

Did you not sign . . . ? The first part of the discourse of Daniel's accusers before the king is in the form of a rather long and complicated question which is intended merely to remind the king of what he had done. But in some languages it will be more natural to follow the TEV model and make this a simple declarative statement, but followed by a shorter question like "Is that not so?" or something similar. Another possibility is to begin by saying "We remember that you . . ." and then concluding with "Is this not true?"

The thing stands fast: the rather vague word translated **thing** in RSV can also mean "word," "affair," or "utterance" and refers to the decree prohibiting prayers to any deity or human being other than the king. In most cases it will be desirable to state this in the translation. The verb may be rendered "is firm" or "is rigid" in this context. In addition to the above TEV model, translators may also consider the following: "the decree is absolute" (AB), "the decision stands" (NJB), "the matter has been determined" (REB), "the order stands firm" (NJV). Mft says simply "It is true" in answer to the question.

The law of the Medes and the Persians: see verse 8.

6.13   RSV   TEV
[6.14]

Then they answered before the king, "That Daniel, who is one of the exiles from Judah, pays no heed to you, O king, or the interdict you have signed, but makes his petition three times a day."

Then they said to the king, "Daniel, one of the exiles from Judah, does not respect Your Majesty or obey the order you issued. He prays regularly three times a day."

That Daniel: see comments on "this Daniel" in verse 3 above.

The exiles from Judah: compare chapter 1 and 2.25.

Pays no heed to you: see 3.12.

Makes his petition: this is the same verb as in verses 7 and 12. It may be translated "says his prayers" or simply "prays." The ancient Greek translations add "to his God." While this may or may not have been a part of the original text, it is certainly information that may be supplied in the translation if necessary for understanding or if it sounds more natural.

6.14   RSV   TEV
[6.15]

Then the king, when he heard these words, was much distressed, and set his mind to deliver Daniel; and he labored till the sun went down to rescue him.

When the king heard this, he was upset and did his best to find some way to rescue Daniel. He kept trying until sunset.

The king, when he heard . . . : this rather peculiar structure with the relative clause between the subject and the verb is not recommended to translators in most languages. It will probably be more natural to put this relative clause either before the subject, as in TEV, or after the verb "distressed."

Set his mind: literally "set his heart upon" (NJV). But since the heart was considered the seat of intelligence (see comments on 1.8; 2.30; 4.16), it will be more natural in most cases to say something like "tried to think of a way" (NEB), "made up his mind" (NAB), or "thought about a means."

Deliver: since Daniel had not yet been arrested, this is not to be taken in the sense of liberating or freeing from imprisonment. Rather it carries the idea of sparing him from the fate required by the decree. The verb translated **rescue** at the end of the verse is virtually identical in meaning.

He labored . . . : this clause emphasizes the king's persistence in seeking a way to spare Daniel's life. Some other renderings are "continued his efforts" (REB), "made every effort" (NRSV), "racked his brains" (NJB).

6.15 RSV TEV
[6.16]

Then these men came by agreement[m] to the king, and said to the king, "Know, O king, that it is a law of the Medes and Persians that no interdict or ordinance which the king establishes can be changed."

Then Daniel's enemies came back to the king and said to him, "Your Majesty knows that according to the laws of the Medes and Persians no order which the king issues can be changed."

[m] Or *thronging*

Then: a number of translations prefer a stronger contrastive conjunction here, since there is a clear contrast between the determination of the king to save Daniel and the desire of the accusers to see him executed. Several versions have "But" (NJB, NAB, AB, and FRCL).

These men: if necessary this may be translated more precisely as "the enemies of Daniel," "the conspirators," or "Daniel's accusers." Compare verse 11.

Came by agreement: see verses 6 and 11 above, and note that this is again dropped by TEV as an unnecessary repetition. But TEV does add the detail that they returned ("came back") to the king, since this was not the first time they had come before him. Other versions translate this and the verb **said** by a stronger word such as "insisted" (NAB), "reminded the king" (Mft), or "kept pressing the king" (NJB).

Know, O king: the imperative form of this verb in English suggests that the speaker(s) want to inform the hearer of something that he is unaware of. But the Persian king is not ignorant of the fact presented to him (see verse 8). If this is also the case in the translator's language, it will be better to make this a declarative statement in many languages, as in TEV. On the form of address, **O king**, see 2.4.

Interdict or ordinance: as in verse 7, the two words focus on a single item and may therefore be translated by a single noun in order to avoid confusion on the part of the reader.

Can be changed: this passive may be made active as in verse 8. Compare also "be revoked" in verse 12.

6.16 RSV TEV
[6.17]

Then the king commanded, and Daniel was brought and cast into the den of lions. The king said to Daniel, "May your God, whom you serve continually, deliver you!"

So the king gave orders for Daniel to be taken and thrown into the pit filled with lions. He said to Daniel, "May your God, whom you serve so loyally, rescue you."

The first sentence of this verse may be understood in two slightly different ways. In the first case the actual execution of the order is not

mentioned, but only the order (see TEV). And in the second the king's order as
such is not given (see RSV), but the execution of it makes clear what it was.
However, the meaning of these two is essentially the same, so translators
should simply translate in such a way as to make it clear that the order was
given and then carried out.

The king commanded: RSV does not provide the detail that the king
commanded someone to do something. If this information is to be supplied in
the translation, the translator may wish to say that he commanded "them"
(indefinite), or "someone," or "his servants." They were ordered to throw Daniel
into the hole where the lions were.

Was brought and cast: these two passive verbs may be taken care of by
the addition of the information suggested above following the verb **commanded**. The whole first sentence may be translated as two and may say something
like "The king commanded his servants to take Daniel and throw him into the
hole where the lions were. And they did so." Another way of conveying the
same essential meaning is "On orders from the king, some men (they) took
Daniel and threw him into the place where the lions were kept."

Den of lions: see verse 7.

Whom you serve continually: the emphasis should be rather on the
devotion and faithfulness of Daniel rather than on the continuity of his service.
NRSV renders "whom you faithfully serve" (compare also NJB).

May your God . . . deliver you: in Aramaic there is strong emphasis on
the subject **your God**, which is separated from the rest of the sentence at the
beginning and then taken up again by the third person singular pronoun. This
emphasis is brought out in FRCL by saying "Only your God . . . can save you."
NJB attempts to reflect the same idea with "Your God . . . will have to save
you." And NEB has "Your own God . . . will save you." This should probably be
understood as more than a fond hope or mere wishful thinking. Instead, it is
to be seen as a rather firm affirmation of faith.

6.17	RSV	TEV
[6.18]		

RSV	TEV
And a stone was brought and laid upon the mouth of the den, and the king sealed it with his own signet and with the signet of his lords, that nothing might be changed concerning Daniel.	A stone was put over the mouth of the pit, and the king placed his own royal seal and the seal of his noblemen on the stone, so that no one could rescue Daniel.

A stone: the stone in question had to be quite large, since it had to cover
the opening through which a person could enter the pit.

Was brought and laid: these passive forms may be made active by using
agents such as "they" (indefinite), or "some men," or "the king's servants," as
in the earlier references of this kind.

The mouth of the den: this would be like a kind of door or opening to the place where the lions were kept. It is this reference that makes experts believe that the **den** was actually a kind of cave or hole.

The king sealed it with his own signet: it was common practice to put some clay at the place where the stone met the edge of the entrance to the cave or pit. Then an image would be placed in the fresh clay, using a personal seal. In this case it was the seal of the king himself and those of his noblemen. It is not necessary that this entire process be described in the translation, but the reader should at least be made aware that this was a means of guaranteeing that the stone was not moved. If necessary the details of the procedure can be explained in a footnote.

That nothing might be changed concerning Daniel: or "in order that no one might be able to change Daniel's situation." Some consider that the TEV rendering goes too far, but this is clearly the point of sealing the pit. Compare REB. The seal of the officials would effectively prevent the king and his close associates from coming in secret to rescue Daniel. But the king's seal would perhaps also deter the enemies of Daniel from coming in secret to make sure that he was dead, in case the lions did not kill him.

6.18 RSV	TEV
[6.19]	
Then the king went to his palace, and spent the night fasting; no diversions were brought to him, and sleep fled from him.	Then the king returned to the palace and spent a sleepless night, without food or any form of entertainment.

Went to his palace: that is, "returned" or "went back to his palace," since this was certainly not the first time that he had been there.

Spent the night fasting: or "had nothing to eat all night," or "he refused to eat anything throughout the night." The Aramaic actually has an adverb that depends on the verb "spend the night."

No diversions were brought to him: in addition to the difficulty of the passive form, this clause also contains a word that has long troubled commentators. The word here rendered as **diversions** is found nowhere else in Aramaic literature known to the present. It has been understood to refer to "concubines" (NJB), women (NEB and REB), "dancing girls" (Mft), "entertainers" (NAB), and "musical instruments" (NJB note). NRSV takes this clause as an amplification of what comes before it and translates "no food was brought to him." It is, however, probably best to use a more general word for "diversion" or "entertainment."

Sleep fled from him: there are many ways of saying that a person is unable to go to sleep: "He spent a white night," "his eyes would not stay closed," or "sleep would not come to him."

Daniel is unharmed and the king repents: 6.19-28 [6.20-29]

RSV

19 Then, at break of day, the king arose and went in haste to the den of lions. 20 When he came near to the den where Daniel was, he cried out in a tone of anguish and said to Daniel, "O Daniel, servant of the living God, has your God, whom you serve continually, been able to deliver you from the lions?" 21 Then Daniel said to the king, "O king, live for ever! 22 My God sent his angel and shut the lions' mouths, and they have not hurt me, because I was found blameless before him; and also before you, O king, I have done no wrong." 23 Then the king was exceedingly glad, and commanded that Daniel be taken up out of the den. So Daniel was taken up out of the den, and no kind of hurt was found upon him, because he had trusted in his God. 24 And the king commanded, and those men who had accused Daniel were brought and cast into the den of lions—they, their children, and their wives; and before they reached the bottom of the den the lions overpowered them and broke all their bones in pieces.

25 Then King Darius wrote to all the peoples, nations, and languages that dwell in all the earth: "Peace be multiplied to you. 26 I make a decree, that in all my royal dominion men tremble and fear before the God of Daniel,

for he is the living God,
enduring for ever;
his kingdom shall never be destroyed,
and his dominion shall be to the
end.

27   He delivers and rescues,
he works signs and wonders
in heaven and on earth,
he who has saved Daniel
from the power of the lions."

28 So this Daniel prospered during the reign of Darius and the reign of Cyrus the Persian.

TEV

19 At dawn the king got up and hurried to the pit. 20 When he got there, he called out anxiously, "Daniel, servant of the living God! Was the God you serve so loyally able to save you from the lions?"

21 Daniel answered, "May Your Majesty live forever! 22 God sent his angel to shut the mouths of the lions so that they would not hurt me. He did this because he knew that I was innocent and because I have not wronged you, Your Majesty."

23 The king was overjoyed and gave orders for Daniel to be pulled up out of the pit. So they pulled him up and saw that he had not been hurt at all, for he trusted God. 24 Then the king gave orders to arrest all those who had accused Daniel, and he had them thrown, together with their wives and children, into the pit filled with lions. Before they even reached the bottom of the pit, the lions pounced on them and broke all their bones.

25 Then King Darius wrote to the people of all nations, races, and languages on earth:

"Greetings! 26 I command that throughout my empire everyone should fear and respect Daniel's God.

"He is a living God,
and he will rule forever.
His kingdom will never be destroyed,
and his power will never come to
an end.

27   He saves and rescues;
he performs wonders and miracles
in heaven and on earth.
He saved Daniel from being killed by
the lions."

28 Daniel prospered during the reign of Darius and the reign of Cyrus the Persian.

Section heading

In those languages where more than one section heading is desired for this chapter, this will be the point where it may be appropriate to say something like "Daniel comes out of the lions' pit unharmed" or "God protects Daniel." NRSV has "Daniel saved from the lions."

6.19   RSV   TEV
[6.20]
    Then, at break of day, the king   **At dawn the king got up and**
arose and went in haste to the den   **hurried to the pit.**
of lions.

    At the break of day: literally "at dawn, at first light." Compare NEB "At
dawn, as soon as it was light," and NJB "At the first sign of dawn." REB begins
this verse "he was greatly agitated," reordering the elements and transposing
the idea of **haste** to the beginning of the verse. Regarding the expression **went
in haste**, see 2.25 and comments.

6.20   RSV   TEV
[6.21]
When he came near to the den   **When he got there, he called out**
where Daniel was, he cried out in a   **anxiously, "Daniel, servant of the**
tone of anguish and said to Daniel,   **living God! Was the God you serve**
"O Daniel, servant of the living God, **so loyally able to save you from the**
has your God, whom you serve   **lions?"**
continually, been able to deliver you
from the lions?"

    The name of Daniel occurs three different times in the first half of this
verse. Such repetition may be awkward in many languages and can be reduced
as in TEV.
    Cried out . . . and said: the use of both of these verbs may be redundant
in certain languages, and the verbs can be reduced so that the first one is used
exclusively: "shouted" or "called out."
    In a tone of anguish: some ancient translations have "in a loud voice."
But most follow the idea of anguish or sorrow: "anxiously" (NEB/REB and NRSV
as well as TEV), "in a sorrowful voice" (AT), "in a mournful voice" (NJV). One
Aramaic lexicon says that the word means "sad." It is clear in any case that
the king was very distressed over the situation of Daniel.
    The living God: this expression is used frequently in the New Testament
(Matt 26.63; John 6.69; Heb 9.14, for example) and elsewhere in the Old
Testament (Deut 5.26; Josh 3.10; 1 Sam 17.26). But in some languages this
poses serious problems, since the descriptive term **living** is considered
unnecessarily redundant.
    Serve continually . . . : see verse 16, where the same terms are used,
except for **from the lions**.

6.21   RSV   TEV
[6.22]
Then Daniel said to the king, "O   **Daniel answered, "May Your**
king, live for ever!   **Majesty live forever!**

Said: literally the text has "spoke with the king." Compare NJV "talked with." This is different from the expression normally used in such a context (see 2.5). But in this context the verb may be more naturally translated "answered" as in REB and TEV.

O king, live for ever! See verse 6 as well as 2.4. Note, however, that the ancient Greek version has "O king, I am alive!" But none of the well-known versions follow this reading.

6.22   RSV   TEV
[6.23]

| My God sent his angel and shut the lions' mouths, and they have not hurt me, because I was found blameless before him; and also before you, O king, I have done no wrong." | God sent his angel to shut the mouths of the lions so that they would not hurt me. He did this because he knew that I was innocent and because I have not wronged you, Your Majesty." |

My God: the personal pronoun **My** is dropped in TEV. This may be necessary in languages where the possessive form gives the wrong idea. Or in other cases the meaning may be translated by "The God I worship," to avoid the idea of a personal possession of God.

His angel: the same Aramaic term as in 3.28.

Shut the lions' mouths: the subject of the verb here is not indicated in Aramaic. Grammatically it may be either God or his angel, but since the angel was fulfilling the will of God who sent him, there is no real difference between the two. It is probably better to translate so that the angel is the subject of the verb.

And they have not hurt me: the conjunction **and** really gives the reason for the closing of the mouths of the lions. Hence it may be better translated "so that" in many languages. This, in fact, is the reading of NJV and NRSV.

Because . . . . : while the sentence continues in RSV, reflecting the original, it may be advisable to begin a new sentence here, as is done in TEV.

I was found blameless before him: this is technically a passive in RSV and will have to be made active in many cases. The meaning is rather "he considered me innocent." A literal rendering of the Aramaic is "innocence (purity) was found in me before him." Some other models are "I am not guilty in his eyes" or, in legal terms, "he acquitted me."

6.23   RSV   TEV
[6.24]

| Then the king was exceedingly glad, and commanded that Daniel be taken up out of the den. So Daniel | The king was overjoyed and gave orders for Daniel to be pulled up out of the pit. So they pulled him |

was taken up out of the den, and no   up and saw that he had not been
kind of hurt was found upon him,   hurt at all, for he trusted God.
because he had trusted in his God.

Exceedingly glad: in this case translators must search for an expression
that describes happiness that exceeds all bounds and surpasses the imagination.

Commanded: as in similar cases earlier, it may be necessary to say
"commanded his servants" or something of this kind.

Be taken up . . . was taken up: these passive forms will have to be made
active in many languages. The agent of the action will be "the servants," or
"some men," or simply "they."

No kind of hurt was found upon him: compare 3.25, 27; but the
expression is stronger here. Translators may consider "no one could find any
trace of injury on his body," or "he appeared to be in perfect health," or
possibly "it seemed that the lions had not injured him at all."

His God: as in the previous verse, TEV drops the possessive pronoun. But
if the possessive form causes problems, it is probably better to translate it "the
God he worshiped."

6.24   RSV   TEV
[6.25]

And the king commanded, and   Then the king gave orders to arrest
those men who had accused Daniel   all those who had accused Daniel,
were brought and cast into the den   and he had them thrown, together
of lions—they, their children, and   with their wives and children, into
their wives; and before they reached   the pit filled with lions. Before they
the bottom of the den the lions   even reached the bottom of the pit,
overpowered them and broke all   the lions pounced on them and
their bones in pieces.   broke all their bones.

The king commanded, and . . . : once again it may be necessary to state
who received and executed the order. See verse 16.

Were brought and cast: literally "they brought them and they threw
them." Once again these two passive verbs of RSV should probably be made
active, as in verse 16. The first verb may be taken in the sense of "arrest," as
TEV makes clear.

They, their children and their wives: the subject of the passive verbs is
further amplified here. But it will probably be better in most languages to
restructure this verse and make more than one sentence of it. In many
languages it will be more natural to mention **wives** before **children**. Some may
prefer to add a separate sentence after indicating that Daniel's accusers were
cast into the pit: "They (indefinite) also threw the wives and children of these
men into the hole where the lions were."

Reached the bottom: this statement helps us to understand better the
shape of the pit where the lions were kept, since it indicates that there was an

opening at the top. These men apparently fell through the air or slid down a very steep incline.

Broke all the bones: the translation should not give the impression that the lions broke the bones of the men without eating them, as both RSV and TEV can be understood. The idea is that the lions ate them up completely, including their bones. Note that NEB has "crunched them up, bones and all." REB carries the same meaning although using a slightly less vivid verb: "devoured them, bones and all."

6.25   RSV   TEV
[6.26]

Then King Darius wrote to all   **Then King Darius wrote to the**
the peoples, nations, and languages   **people of all nations, races, and**
that dwell in all the earth: "Peace be **languages on earth:**
multiplied to you.   **"Greetings!**

As indicated in the comments on 2.20-23, this passage (through verse 27) includes the fourth of the hymns of praise in the first half of the Book of Daniel (see also 4.3, 34-35). Translators should use the same principles as those used in rendering poetry in the Psalms and elsewhere in the Old Testament.

Then: it is obvious that the royal decree was not written immediately at the entrance of the lions' pit. For this reason the connecting word here may be translated something like "After that" or "Later" (FRCL) in many languages.

Wrote to: in some cases a more formal wording may be appropriate. For example, "addressed the following message" (FRCL).

Peoples, nations, and languages: the same list as found in 3.4, 7, 29; 4.1; 5.19; and later in 7.14.

Peace be multiplied to you: compare 4.1.

6.26   RSV   TEV
[6.27]

I make a decree, that in all my royal   **I command that throughout my**
dominion men tremble and fear   **empire everyone should fear and**
before the God of Daniel,   **respect Daniel's God.**
    for he is the living God,   **"He is a living God,**
      enduring for ever;   **and he will rule forever.**
    his kingdom shall never be   **His kingdom will never be**
      destroyed,   **destroyed,**
    and his dominion shall be   **and his power will never**
      to the end.   **come to an end.**

I make a decree: REB "I have issued a decree." See 3.29.

In all my royal dominion: some other ways of wording this are "everywhere that my power extends" or "among all the people over whom I rule."

174

Men: the decree was not exclusively for males but applied to every individual in the empire. For this reason it is fitting to use more inclusive terminology here such as "everyone" (TEV), "each person," "every inhabitant of the empire," or simply "all people."

Tremble and fear: here the focus is more on the idea of respect and honor of God than on literal trembling and fear.

The God of Daniel: as in the case of "my God" (verse 22) and "his God" (verse 23), the possessive idea may be better rendered as "the God Daniel worships."

The living God: see verse 20. Note that here TEV uses the indefinite article rather than the definite "the" in this case. Whatever the reasons for doing this in TEV, translators should avoid giving the impression that there are many living gods.

Enduring for ever: many languages will have to use a verb such as "remain" or "continue" and follow it up with something like "always" or "which will never end."

Be destroyed: this passive may be translated "no one (no power) will ever be able to destroy his kingdom" or "no one can spoil his rule."

The last two lines of this verse are parallel in structure and meaning, and the parallelism may be retained in those languages where it is natural to do so. But translators should avoid giving the impression that two totally different things are being talked about. In some languages this may be done simply by not using a conjunction like "and."

6.27 [6.28]	RSV	TEV

	He delivers and rescues,
	  he works signs and won-
	    ders
	  in heaven and on earth,
	he who has saved Daniel
	  from the power of the li-
	    ons."
		He saves and rescues;
		  he performs wonders and
		    miracles
		  in heaven and on earth.
		He saved Daniel from being
		  killed by the lions."

Delivers and rescues ... works ... : the habitual verb form will probably be used in those languages that possess such a form. In other languages there will be different means of indicating that this is an action that occurs regularly and not just something that happens once or is simply taking place at present.

Signs and wonders: see 4.2.

Saved: this is the same word as translated **delivers** at the beginning of the verse (compare TEV). But in some languages it may be stylistically desirable to use a different term here. Note, however, that the verb form is different, since this part of the verse talks about the past tense deliverance of Daniel from the lions, while the first part of the verse is a generalization about the nature of God.

175

From the power of the lions: literally "from the hand of the lions"; but as has been pointed out earlier (1.2 and 3.15), the word "hand" often stands for **power**. Translators may also consider "from certain death in the lion's pit" or, more literally, "from the claws (or paws) of the lions."

6.28   RSV   TEV
[6.29]

So this Daniel prospered dur-   Daniel prospered during the
ing the reign of Darius and the reign   reign of Darius and the reign of
of Cyrus the Persian.   Cyrus the Persian.

So: this translates the common, multipurpose conjunction in Aramaic that may be left untranslated as in TEV. But other languages will require some kind of connecting word in this context, since what follows is a kind of conclusion to the story.

This Daniel: see verse 3.

Prospered: the translation of this verb should not focus on physical prosperity. As in 3.30, where the verb is translated "promoted," the verb used here suggests the idea of Daniel's political success. FRCL translates "occupied an important position," and NAB reads "fared well."

During the reign: or "while Darius was ruling," or "at the time when Darius was king."

The reign of Darius and the reign of Cyrus the Persian: the conjunction **and** in the Book of Daniel and elsewhere in the Old Testament may be used in the sense of "namely," or "that is to say . . . ." This has led some scholars to suggest that this phrase is really intended to show that Darius and Cyrus are one and the same person, as indicated in the NIV footnote rendering, "Or *Darius, that is, the reign of Cyrus*." The point would then be to explain the identity of this otherwise unknown ruler. However, the repetition of the phrase **during the reign of** makes this somewhat less likely. In view of the uncertainty of this hypothesis, translators are advised to render the conjunction literally and, if required, a footnote may be added giving this other interpretation. However, many scholars consider the hypothesis too weak to merit a footnote.

Note that the whole verse is restructured by REB as follows: "Prosperity attended Daniel during the reigns of Darius and Cyrus the Persian."

Part Two:
Daniel Describes His Revelations from God
Daniel 7.1–12.13

First Vision:
The Four Beasts and the Heavenly Beings

Daniel 7.1-28

As indicated in the introductory section of this Handbook and at the beginning of chapter 1, TEV divides the Book of Daniel into two major sections. The second section begins here. The TEV heading "DANIEL DESCRIBES HIS VISIONS" in all capital letters marks its beginning. In those languages where two levels of headings are being used, it is wise to follow the example of TEV in marking the shift to the second major section.

Vision: The vision of the four beasts: 7.1-8

RSV

1 In the first year of Belshazzar king of Babylon, Daniel had a dream and visions of his head as he lay in his bed. Then he wrote down the dream, and told the sum of the matter. 2 Daniel said, "I saw in my vision by night, and behold, the four winds of heaven were stirring up the great sea. 3 And four great beasts came up out of the sea, different from one another. 4 The first was like a lion and had eagles' wings. Then as I looked its wings were plucked off, and it was lifted up from the ground and made to stand upon two feet like a man; and the mind of a man was given to it. And behold, another beast, a

TEV
DANIEL DESCRIBES HIS VISIONS
(7.1–12.13)

Daniel's Vision of the Four Beasts

1 In the first year that Belshazzar was king of Babylonia, I had a dream and saw a vision in the night. I wrote the dream down, and this is the record 2 of what I saw that night:

Winds were blowing from all directions and lashing the surface of the ocean. 3 Four huge beasts came up out of the ocean, each one different from the others. 4 The first one looked like a lion, but had wings like an eagle. While I was watching, the wings were torn off. The beast was lifted up and made to stand up straight. And then a human mind was given to it.

second one, like a bear. It was raised up on one side; it had three ribs in its mouth between its teeth; and it was told, 'Arise, devour much flesh.' 6 After this I looked, and lo, another, like a leopard, with four wings of a bird on its back; and the beast had four heads; and dominion was given to it. 7 After this I saw in the night visions, and behold, a fourth beast, terrible and dreadful and exceedingly strong; and it had great iron teeth; it devoured and broke in pieces, and stamped the residue with its feet. It was different from all the beasts that were before it; and it had ten horns. 8 I considered the horns, and behold, there came up among them another horn, a little one, before which three of the first horns were plucked up by the roots; and behold, in this horn were eyes like the eyes of a man, and a mouth speaking great things.

5 The second beast looked like a bear standing on its hind legs. It was holding three ribs between its teeth, and a voice said to it, "Go on, eat as much meat as you can!"

6 While I was watching, another beast appeared. It looked like a leopard, but on its back there were four wings, like the wings of a bird, and it had four heads. It had a look of authority about it.

7 As I was watching, a fourth beast appeared. It was powerful, horrible, terrifying. With its huge iron teeth it crushed its victims, and then it trampled on them. Unlike the other beasts, it had ten horns. 8 While I was staring at the horns, I saw a little horn coming up among the others. It tore out three of the horns that were already there. This horn had human eyes and a mouth that was boasting proudly.

TEV Section Heading: Daniel's vision of four beasts

This section heading should probably be compared with the one at the beginning of chapters 8 and 10, to be sure that they are sufficiently different yet parallel in structure. In order to show that another vision follows, it may be better here to say "Daniel's first vision: The four beasts."

7.1   RSV   TEV

In the first year of Belshazzar king of Babylon, Daniel had a dream and visions of his head as he lay in his bed. Then he wrote down the dream, and told the sum of the matter.

In the first year that Belshazzar was king of Babylonia, I had a dream and saw a vision in the night. I wrote the dream down, and this is the record

In the first year of Belshazzar: a literal reading of this phrase may give the impression that Belshazzar was only a year old at the time. But the sense of the expression is that the vision took place during the first year of the reign of Belshazzar as king. Translators should be sure at this point that the proper name of this king is sufficiently distinguished from the one given to Daniel in 1.7 (see also 5.1 and comments).

King of Babylon: Belshazzar was ruler over all Babylonia and not just the capital city of Babylon. So it is better to translate as in TEV, "king of Babylonia."

Daniel . . . his . . . he: note that the account is transposed from the third person to the first person in TEV. In the original the third person pronouns are used in this verse, but in the following verse there is a shift to a direct quote from Daniel. In some languages it may be advisable to put the entire story in the first person as in TEV, but naturalness in the translation should be the determining factor. If the TEV model is not followed, translators must be careful to see that the pronoun references are clear, since both Daniel and the king are mentioned earlier in this verse.

A dream and visions: the rendering of this phrase should not give the impression that two different things are being talked about here. These are simply two terms used to describe a single event. In some languages the idea of a vision has to be expressed by a phrase like "something happened inside my head" or "I saw something happening in my mind." Compare NIV "visions passed through his mind." For comments on the term "vision," see 2.19.

As he lay in his bed: or "as he lay on his bed." Other languages may express this idea in very different ways, depending on cultural practices. Some may say "as he lay down to go to rest," or "when he stretched himself out for sleeping," or "when he was on his sleeping mat."

Then: it may be better to omit this transition word altogether in some languages. But in others it will be necessary to indicate the sequence of events: first Daniel had the dream, then he wrote it down.

Wrote down the dream and told the sum of the matter: according to some interpreters these two verbal expressions should not be taken as referring to two different actions. The second would be rather an extension of the first. The two are combined in the NIV rendering: "wrote down the substance of his dream." Many versions, however, take the second verb phrase as introducing the actual wording that begins after **Daniel said** in the following verse. NJB, for example, has "he wrote the dream down, and this is how the narrative began: . . . ." And Mft translates "he wrote down the dream, describing all that he had seen." But the oral character of the message (in addition to the fact that it was written) seems to be emphasized by the writer. The verb meaning "tell" or "say" occurs both here and again at the beginning of the following verse.

7.2	RSV	TEV

RSV	TEV
Daniel said, "I saw in my vision by night, and behold, the four winds of heaven were stirring up the great sea.	**of what I saw that night:** **Winds were blowing from all directions and lashing the surface of the ocean.**

Daniel said: literally, "answered and said." This begins the direct quotation from Daniel in the original. However, if first person pronouns have been used from the beginning of this chapter, as in TEV, these words will be redundant and should be omitted. On the other hand, if it is natural to do so, the form of the original may be followed, retaining the third person up to this point.

Behold: this particle is frequently used where visions are involved. See comments on 2.31; 4.10, 13.

The four winds of heaven: a literal rendering of this expression will probably be unnatural in most languages. The figure **four** is a reference to the cardinal points of a compass: north, south, east, and west. In some cases the number four will be meaningless or will distract from the real meaning. In those cases it may be better to speak of "all directions" as in TEV.

Stirring up: other versions use verbs like "churning up" or "agitated." In some languages it will be more natural to use a causative form of a verb meaning "to mix up." NCV offers another possible model using a separate sentence: "these winds made the sea very rough."

The great sea: while the expression "Great Sea" is sometimes used in the Old Testament to refer to the Mediterranean (see, for example, Num 34.6), this is not the case here. The definite article may therefore be misleading. Probably no particular body of water is intended, since this is a vision. It is more likely a reference to the ocean that covered the earth at the time of creation. What is important in translation is to convey the notion of the vastness of this **sea**.

7.3 RSV	TEV
And four great beasts came up out of the sea, different from one another.	Four huge beasts came up out of the ocean, each one different from the others.

Four great beasts: in many languages it will be necessary to say something like "four very large (and frightening) animals." It is generally believed that the four beasts represent the Babylonians (the lion of verse 4), the Medes (the bear of verse 5), the Persians (the leopard of verse 6), and the Greeks (the apocalyptic beast of verses 7 and 8). But this interpretation should not be put into the translation. The character of the vision is that it presents a challenge to the reader to discover what the symbolism stands for, and this character must be maintained. Other interpreters feel that the second beast represents Medo-Persia, so that the third would be Greece and the fourth would then be Rome.

Different from one another: or "each one different from the others" (REB). Every translation team will have to look for the most natural way of communicating the idea that there were no two beasts alike. But in many languages it will be preferable to make this a separate sentence.

7.4 RSV	TEV
The first was like a lion and had eagles' wings. Then as I looked its wings were plucked off, and it was lifted up from the ground and made to stand upon two feet like a man; and the mind of a man was given to it.	The first one looked like a lion, but had wings like an eagle. While I was watching, the wings were torn off. The beast was lifted up and made to stand up straight. And then a human mind was given to it.

Like a lion: translators should make certain that the vision deals with a resemblance, but that what was seen was not actually a real lion. In some cases translators may wish to say "resembled a lion," or "seemed like a lion," or something similar.

And had eagles' wings: it may be better in many languages to use a conjunction like "but" at the beginning of this phrase, since the description of the wings that follows is certainly contrary to what the reader would expect. And here, too, it may be more natural to say that the wings were "like those of an eagle" instead of giving the impression that they were literal eagles' wings.

The words **as I looked** may seem completely unnecessary in some languages, although it is probably intended to serve as a reminder that Daniel kept on watching. For this reason these words may be better translated "while I was still looking" or "I kept on watching, and . . . ."

The passive forms in this verse may present serious problems in many languages. Instead of **were plucked** it may be necessary to say "someone (or something) plucked." In place of **it was lifted up . . . and made to stand**, translators may have to say "they (impersonal) lifted it up . . . and it stood" or possibly "it rose up . . . and stood." The context seems to indicate that the front feet of the animal were lifted up, but in a vision it is not impossible that this expression refers to the lifting up above the ground of all four feet.

Upon two feet: while the Aramaic uses the same term for the feet of a human being and the legs of an animal, in some languages there are totally different words for these two objects. The idea here is that the animal stood up on its hind legs in a manner similar to the position of a man standing up.

The mind of a man was given to it may be translated in some languages as "it received the mind of human being."

7.5	RSV	TEV

And behold, another beast, a second one, like a bear. It was raised up on one side; it had three ribs in its mouth between its teeth; and it was told, 'Arise, devour much flesh.' | The second beast looked like a bear standing on its hind legs. It was holding three ribs between its teeth, and a voice said to it, "Go on, eat as much meat as you can!"

Behold: see verse 2.

Like a bear: since bears are unknown in many parts of the world, translators must either borrow the term or use a more general expression such as "another large and ferocious animal" or something similar.

Was raised up on one side: the meaning of this expression in Aramaic is unclear. The root verb of this passive form is the same as that found in verse 4. However, the emphasis is not on the movement of the animal but on the resulting position. If it is taken to mean "standing on its hind legs," as in TEV, then the command **Arise** later in the verse, if taken literally, becomes meaningless. It is probably better to understand the meaning here as "half crouching" (NEB), in which case the imperative that follows is a command to stand up straight or to get up completely.

Three ribs: in those languages that have different words for the ribs of a human being and those of an animal, it is probably best to use the term for animal ribs in the context of this vision. In fact the word translated "ribs" in most English versions has been understood to refer to "tusks" (NAB and NRSV) or "fangs" (NJV). But translators are advised to retain the meaning "ribs" as in RSV and TEV. This would leave the impression that another creature had just been eaten and that some of the bones were still in the mouth of the beast.

In its mouth between its teeth: part of this expression may be considered redundant in many languages. Whatever is between the teeth is clearly in the mouth. Or in other cases whatever is in the mouth is thought of as being between the teeth.

It was told: in order to avoid the passive, some languages will have to say "it received the order," or "they (impersonal) told it," or "someone commanded it."

Arise: depending on how the earlier part of this verse is translated, this may have to be rendered "Stand up completely" or "Finish rising up."

Devour much flesh: it is more natural in many languages to say "eat a lot of meat" or "consume as much meat as you can."

7.6   RSV   TEV

After this I looked, and lo, another, like a leopard, with four wings of a bird on its back; and the beast had four heads; and dominion was given to it.	While I was watching, another beast appeared. It looked like a leopard, but on its back there were four wings, like the wings of a bird, and it had four heads. It had a look of authority about it.

After this I looked: a literal rendering of these words may give the reader the impression that Daniel had not been looking previously. But the sense is rather "After seeing that I looked again" or "While I was still looking." NRSV has "As I watched," while REB has "As I gazed."

And lo: this is the same particle that is translated "behold" in verses 2 and 5. It will be necessary to leave it untranslated in some languages. But where a language has a similar particle for directing the attention of the hearer, it may be used here.

Like a leopard: the precise identification of this animal is uncertain. The experts are not in complete agreement as to whether this refers to a leopard or to a panther. Most English versions have "leopard," but since this is a comparison in a vision, the precise identification of "panther" or "leopard" is probably of no great importance.

With four wings of a bird on its back: translators should be careful not to give the impression of four little bird wings resting unattached on the back of the animal. The intention of the writer was clearly that they were attached to and a part of the body of the animal, as was the case with the lion in verse 4. In the same way, the **four heads** should be understood as being firmly connected to the body of the beast.

Dominion was given to it: again, the passive form will have to be translated actively in many languages. This seems to be parallel in meaning to the expressions "standing like a man" in verse 4. The upright position is symbolic of power and dominion. But in this case the symbolism appears to be replaced by nonfigurative language. **Dominion** means the power or authority to rule over or impose its will on others; NIV has "authority to rule," and REB "sovereign power."

7.7 RSV	TEV
After this I saw in the night visions, and behold, a fourth beast, terrible and dreadful and exceedingly strong; and it had great iron teeth; it devoured and broke in pieces, and stamped the residue with its feet. It was different from all the beasts that were before it; and it had ten horns.	As I was watching, a fourth beast appeared. It was powerful, horrible, terrifying. With its huge iron teeth it crushed its victims, and then it trampled on them. Unlike the other beasts, it had ten horns.

After this I saw: while the RSV rendering differs here, this verse begins exactly the same way as verse 6 in the original. See the comments on the beginning of the previous verse.

Night visions: this refers back to verse 2 and situates the vision being described. This information is not repeated here in TEV.

Behold: see verse 2.

Terrible and dreadful and exceedingly strong: these three adjectives are used to describe the fourth beast. The first two have almost the same meaning and describe the reaction of awe and fear in those who see the beast. In some languages the two terms may be translated by a single expression such as "which provokes terror" (GECL). The third descriptive term is reinforced by the use of the adverb "very" or "extremely." It relates to the natural physical strength of the beast.

Great iron teeth: while some manuscript evidence adds "and claws of bronze," few modern versions include these words. This is not recommended to translators.

Devoured and broke in pieces: the first of these two verbs carries the idea of eating like an animal, as in 4.33. The idea of eating has not been clearly translated in TEV, but this should not be imitated in the receptor language. The second verb makes readers think of reducing to powder, or to small bits. The same word is found in 2.34, 45; 6.24. It may be rendered something like "shatter," "fragment," or "splinter." This combination of verbs is repeated in verse 19 below.

Stamped . . . with its feet: in some languages this idea may be expressed as "trampled," "stepped on," or "stood on."

The residue: that is, what was left of the victims. NJB has "trampled their remains," NRSV "what was left."

Different from all: or "totally different from the other beasts." The difference is directly related to the fact that the fourth beast had **ten horns**. So in some languages translators may want to say "it was completely different from the other beasts because it had ten horns."

7.8 RSV	TEV
I considered the horns, and behold, there came up among them another horn, a little one, before which three of the first horns were plucked up by the roots; and behold, in this horn were eyes like the eyes of a man, and a mouth speaking great things.	While I was staring at the horns, I saw a little horn coming up among the others. It tore out three of the horns that were already there. This horn had human eyes and a mouth that was boasting proudly.

Considered: the main component of this verb is the idea of looking intently at an object. It may be better translated "looked at," "was gazing upon" (NJV), "examined" (FRCL), "watched" (AT, NJB, and Mft). NIV translates "thinking about," but this is less desirable.

Behold: the particle is used twice in this verse but may be omitted in many languages. See verses 2 and 5-7, as well as 2.31 and 4.10, 13.

Before which . . . were plucked up: the structure of RSV is complex and should probably be transformed in most languages. As in TEV, a new sentence will be required in many cases. The idea is that the small horn that had not been apparent previously now dislodges three of the others. The agent of the passive expression **were plucked up** is not certain. In those languages without passive forms, translators may have to say "someone pulled out" or "they (indefinite) removed by force." But it will be noted that TEV makes the **little horn** the agent here. This does seem to fit the historical description provided in verse 24b.

Speaking great things: the Aramaic term used here has a clearly negative meaning probably indicating pride or arrogance. This meaning should definitely be conveyed in the translation. In addition to the TEV model, compare the following renderings: "spoke boastfully" (NIV), "spoke arrogantly" (NAB, similarly NRSV), "uttered bombast" (REB), "a mouth full of proud words" (Mft).

The Ancient One and the One like a man: 7.9-14

RSV

9 As I looked,
>   thrones were placed
>   and one that was ancient of days
>   took his seat;
>   his raiment was white as snow,
>   and the hair of his head like pure
>   wool;
>   his throne was fiery flames,
>   its wheels were burning fire.
10   A stream of fire issued
>   and came forth from before him;
>   a thousand thousands served him,
>   and ten thousand times ten thou-
>   sand stood before him;
>   the court sat in judgment,
>   and the books were opened.
11 I looked then because of the sound of the great words which the horn was speaking. And as I looked, the beast was slain, and its body destroyed and given over to be burned with fire. 12 As for the rest of the beasts, their dominion was taken away, but their lives were prolonged for a season and a time. 13 I saw in the night visions,
>   and behold, with the clouds of heaven
>   there came one like a son of man,
>   and he came to the Ancient of Days
>   and was presented before him.
14   And to him was given dominion
>   and glory and kingdom,
>   that all peoples, nations, and languag-
>   es
>   should serve him;
>   his dominion is an everlasting domin-
>   ion,
>   which shall not pass away,
>   and his kingdom one
>   that shall not be destroyed.

TEV

*The Vision of the One Who Has Been
Living Forever*

9 While I was looking, thrones were put in place. One who had been living forever sat down on one of the thrones. His clothes were white as snow, and his hair was like pure wool. His throne, mounted on fiery wheels, was blazing with fire, 10 and a stream of fire was pouring out from it. There were many thousands of people there to serve him, and millions of people stood before him. The court began its session, and the books were opened.

11 While I was looking, I could still hear the little horn bragging and boasting. As I watched, the fourth beast was killed, and its body was thrown into the flames and destroyed. 12 The other beasts had their power taken away, but they were permitted to go on living for a limited time.

13 During this vision in the night, I saw what looked like a human being. He was approaching me, surrounded by clouds, and he went to the one who had been living forever and was presented to him. 14 He was given authority, honor, and royal power, so that the people of all nations, races, and languages would serve him. His authority would last forever, and his kingdom would never end.

TEV Section Heading: The vision of the One who has been living forever

Verses 9-14 constitute a change of scene but a continuation of the vision described in verses 1-8. So it may be misleading to use the word "vision" in the section heading here, since this may make the reader think that a totally new vision is about to be described. Some other possible titles are "The judgment of God" (FRCL), "A vision of judgment," "The destruction of human kingdoms."

7.9 RSV	TEV

As I looked,
  thrones were placed
    and one that was ancient
      of days took his seat;
  his raiment was white as
      snow,
    and the hair of his head
      like pure wool;
  his throne was fiery flames,
    its wheels were burning
      fire.
	While I was looking, thrones were put in place. One who had been living forever sat down on one of the thrones. His clothes were white as snow, and his hair was like pure wool. His throne, mounted on fiery wheels, was blazing with fire,

Note that verses 9 and 10 are in poetic format in RSV/NRSV, NIV, NJV, NJB, NEB/REB, and NAB.

As I looked: in Aramaic these words are the same as those translated "I looked" in verse 6 and "I saw" in verse 7.

Thrones were placed: here the Aramaic verb form reverts to the perfect tense in contrast with the use of participles in verses 2-8. The passive construction may be rendered "someone put thrones in place" or "they (indefinite) arranged some thrones." But the **thrones** involved were intended as seats for judges. According to Jewish tradition the holy ones of God have the privilege of sitting in judgment at his side (compare Matt 19.28; Luke 22.30; Rev 3.21; 20.4). Although the level of Mft's rendering is above the common language, it carries the meaning well: "I watched until an Assize was held." Translators may consider "I looked on as they (indefinite) prepared places for the judges to sit" or something similar.

Ancient of days: this expression designates an aged person and one who is therefore, in the biblical culture, considered especially wise. In the language of the vision this "old person" is clearly God himself. But the style of the vision would be betrayed if this were clearly stated in the text (as in LB). This information may be given in a footnote. Some other nonliteral renderings of this expression are "the (or an) Ancient One" (NAB and NRSV), "the Ancient in Years" (REB), "a primeval Being" (Mft), "The Venerable One" (AT), "The-One-Who-Endures" (Lacocque). Some languages will have a similar expression that can be used to refer to God without using his name.

White as snow: the figure of **snow** will, of course, be meaningless where snow is unknown. Since this is clearly figurative language, it is possible to change the figure of snow to one that is commonly used to describe whiteness in the translator's language; for example, "white as egret feathers" or "white as white clouds." But it is probably preferable to drop the image altogether and translate the idea by using a more general expression such as "extremely white" or "very, very white." Compare some other references where "snow" is used as a figure to describe whiteness: Exo 4.6; Num 12.10; 2 Kgs 5.27; Psa 51.7; Isa 1.18. In the New Testament compare Matt 28.3 and Rev 1.14.

The hair of his head: in languages that have a special word for the hair on top of the head as opposed to that on the rest of the body, the words **of his head** are redundant and unnecessary in the translation.

Like pure wool: these words have been variously translated as "lamb's wool" (NJV and REB), "cleanest wool" (NEB), and "white like wool" (NIV). Most English versions focus on the purity of the wool. However, since the wool is being compared with the hair of the being in the vision, it is quite possible that its whiteness is more in focus than its purity.

His throne was fiery flames, its wheels were burning fire: in some languages it may be necessary to establish the fact that the judgment seat had wheels before stating the fiery nature of the wheels. And it may also be more natural to change the metaphors to similes, using the words for "like," "resembled," or "appeared as." The fire suggests the idea of bright light shining out from the one seated on the throne. Compare the visions in Ezek 1 and 10.

7.10	RSV	TEV

	A stream of fire issued
	    and came forth from before
	    him;
	a thousand thousands served
	    him,
	    and ten thousand times ten
	    thousand stood before
	    him;
	the court sat in judgment,
	    and the books were
	    opened.
		and a stream of fire was pouring out from it. There were many thousands of people there to serve him, and millions of people stood before him. The court began its session, and the books were opened.

A stream of fire: since the word **stream** may suggest a rather small or insignificant flow, it may be better to follow the example of REB in translating "a river of fire." And in some languages it will be more natural to express this phrase as "fire was rushing out like the waters of a river." In languages where the idea of fire being in some way like the water of a stream or river would be unthinkable, a different image may have to be used, or perhaps the image may have to be dropped completely. An example of a different figure may be "fire came out like grain being poured out." If the image is removed altogether, the translation may say something like "much fire kept coming out . . . ."

Issued and came forth: in many languages it will be perfectly legitimate to translate these two verbs by a single verb as in TEV.

Before him: this indicates more precisely the place from which the river of fire originated. But the third person singular pronoun may refer either to the throne ("it," TEV) or to the person seated on the throne (**him**, RSV). The majority of versions seem to prefer "before him" or "from his presence."

A thousand thousands . . . ten thousand times ten thousand: these two expressions are in parallel, as are the verbs that accompany them. And the figures are not meant to be taken as mathematically precise. Rather they suggest extremely large or incalculable numbers. If such parallel structure is not considered natural in the translator's language, it is possible to restructure the whole sentence, combining the various elements. FRCL, for example, reads "Millions, even tens of millions of persons stood in his presence in order to serve him." It should be noted also that the word "persons" or "people" (TEV, FRCL) is very likely intended and should probably be made explicit in the translation. However, Mft takes it to be "angels."

Stood before him: translators should avoid giving the impression that there were two groups, one of which was working and the other simply standing around. The expression "to stand before" does not indicate idly standing in the presence of the "Ancient of Days." It is rather in parallel with **served him** in the previous line and indicates that those standing in his presence were prepared to do whatever he required of them. Compare 1.5.

The court sat in judgment: that is, the actual court session began (compare TEV). In some languages translators may wish to say "the court proceedings began."

The books: although almost all English versions have the definite article here, the form of the Aramaic is indefinite. The use of the definite article may be justified by the fact that, according to the understanding of the people of antiquity, there existed heavenly books in which all the deeds of human beings, both good and bad, were recorded. Mft translates "the records were opened." Compare Jer 17.1; Psa 56.8; Mal 3.16; and Rev 20.12.

Were opened: in order to avoid the passive form, it is possible to make the judges the subject of the last two verbs in this verse: "The judges sat down (to begin their work) and opened the books."

7.11	RSV	TEV
	I looked then because of the sound of the great words which the horn was speaking. And as I looked, the beast was slain, and its body destroyed and given over to be burned with fire.	While I was looking, I could still hear the little horn bragging and boasting. As I watched, the fourth beast was killed, and its body was thrown into the flames and destroyed.

I looked then: that is, "I kept on looking," or "I went on watching" (REB). Compare verse 6.

Great words: as in the similar expression in verse 8, this also refers to proud, insolent speech, and this should be made clear in the translation. NRSV has "arrogant words."

The beast: since the text describes four different beasts in the previous verses, it is probably wise to say clearly here that it was "the fourth beast" who was killed (see verse 7).

Was slain: while it may be necessary to avoid the passive here, it is probably better not to state clearly who actually did the killing. In most languages it is possible to say something like "someone killed" or "they (indefinite) killed."

Destroyed and given over: the Aramaic order of the two verbs, which is reflected in RSV, will probably be unnatural in many languages. There would be nothing left to throw into the fire if the beast were already destroyed. And again, the passive forms should be translated in such a way as to avoid stating clearly who performed the action.

Burned with fire: this will be unnecessarily redundant in many languages, and the words **with fire** may be omitted.

7.12 RSV	TEV
As for the rest of the beasts, their dominion was taken away, but their lives were prolonged for a season and a time.	The other beasts had their power taken away, but they were permitted to go on living for a limited time.

The rest of the beasts: that is, the other three beasts that remained after the destruction of the fourth.

Dominion: compare 4.3, 22, 34; 6.26, as well as verse 6 above.

Was taken away . . . were prolonged: once again, in transforming the passive forms to active, the translator should be careful not to name a particular agent. The agent may be "someone" or the indefinite "they."

For a season and a time: the two terms in Aramaic mean virtually the same thing, and together they make up an expression carrying the idea of time limitation. Hence the rendering of TEV. Compare also other versions: "until a specific date and time" (TOB), "until an appointed time and season" (REB), and "for a certain period" (Mft).

7.13 RSV	TEV
I saw in the night visions, and behold, with the clouds of heaven there came one like a son of man, and he came to the Ancient of Days and was presented before him.	During this vision in the night, I saw what looked like a human being. He was approaching me, surrounded by clouds, and he went to the one who had been living forever and was presented to him.

As in verses 9-10, poetic format is used for verses 13-14 in the following versions: RSV/NRSV, NJB, NJV, and NAB. But note that NIV and NEB/REB, which used poetic indentation in verses 9-10, do not do so here.

Night visions: see verse 7 above.

With the clouds of heaven: the words **of heaven** may be omitted in some languages as unnecessarily redundant. And it is probably more natural in most cases to translate the preposition **with** as "in the midst of" (FRCL), or "surrounded by" (TEV), or "on the clouds" (NJB and NAB).

One like a son of man: the words translated "son of man" appear nearly two hundred times in the original languages of Scripture. There are eighty-four occurrences in the Gospels. And Ezekiel is addressed ninety-three times as "son of man." In the Book of Daniel the prophet himself is addressed thus in 8.17, and the expression focuses on his humanity. Here in 7.13 the meaning of the term is also "human being," but the context is quite different. The framework is that of an apocalyptic vision, and the words "son of man" come immediately after the Aramaic particle usually translated by the English adverb "like." This shows that the one referred to resembles a human being but in fact is not mortal. In the New Testament apocalypse the writer intentionally uses words very similar to what we find in this crucial passage (Rev 1.13; 14.14). While the being referred to is anything but human, the expression "son of man" in itself may still be rendered "a human being." Most translators will probably have in their language a particle corresponding to the English "like" which will indicate that, although the being resembled a mortal in some ways, it was different. Mft translates "a figure in a human form." NEB has simply "like a man," AB states categorically that "the Aramaic phrase should not be translated 'one like a son of man' (RSV, JB, NAB) or 'one like the Son of man' (KJV), as if the expression were a proper designation or title of a specific historical or mythological or supernatural person of the male sex. Just as the four horrifying and vile beasts (7.3-7) are not real animals but symbols, pure and simple, of the pagan kingdoms . . . so too the 'one in human likeness' is not a real individual, celestial or terrestrial, but is only a symbol of 'the holy ones of the Most High,' a title given to the faithful Jews—men, women and children . . ." (page 87; see also the article " 'Son of Man' and Contextual Translation" in *The Bible Translator,* April 1989, pages 201-208.)

The Ancient of Days: see verse 9.

Was presented before him: once again the transformation of the passive to an active form will be required in many languages, but the agent should not be identified too clearly. The text literally says "they (indefinite) led him into his presence." Note that the GECL rendering takes this clause as parallel with **he came to the Ancient of Days** and therefore renders the two as a single statement.

7.14 RSV	TEV
And to him was given domin- ion and glory and kingdom, that all peoples, nations, and languages should serve him;	He was given authority, honor, and royal power, so that the people of all nations, races, and languages would serve him. His authority would last forever, and his kingdom would never end.

> his dominion is an everlast-
>   ing dominion,
> which shall not pass away,
> and his kingdom one
>   that shall not be destroyed.

To him was given: in those languages where an active verb form is required, it is possible to make the **Ancient of Days** the subject of the verb and say "The Ancient of Days gave him."

Dominion and glory and kingdom: compare 2.37; 4.3, 34.

Peoples, nations, and languages: see 3.4.

Serve him: this verb is used of worshiping Nebuchadnezzar's gods in chapter 3, and of worshiping the true God in chapter 6. Compare also 1.10 above.

Note that the expressions **everlasting, which shall not pass away**, and **shall not be destroyed** all say essentially the same thing. If there are not enough different terms in the translator's language, these may be reduced to one or two statements. Compare 4.34.

Explanation: The four kingdoms: 7.15-28

RSV

15 "As for me, Daniel, my spirit within me was anxious and the visions of my head alarmed me. 16 I approached one of those who stood there and asked him the truth concerning all this. So he told me, and made known to me the interpretation of the things. 17 'These four great beasts are four kings who shall arise out of the earth. 18 But the saints of the Most High shall receive the kingdom, and possess the kingdom for ever, for ever and ever.'

19 "Then I desired to know the truth concerning the fourth beast, which was different from all the rest, exceedingly terrible, with its teeth of iron and claws of bronze; and which devoured and broke in pieces, and stamped the residue with its feet; 20 and concerning the ten horns that were on its head, and the other horn which came up and before which three of them fell, the horn which had eyes and a mouth that spoke great things, and which seemed greater than its fellows. 21 As I looked, this horn made war with the saints, and prevailed over them, 22 until the Ancient of Days came, and judgment was given for the saints of the Most High, and the time came when the saints received the kingdom.

TEV

The Visions Are Explained

15 The visions I saw alarmed me, and I was deeply disturbed. 16 I went up to one of those standing there and asked him to explain it all. So he told me the meaning. 17 He said, "These four huge beasts are four empires which will arise on earth. 18 And the people of the Supreme God will receive royal power and keep it forever and ever."

19 Then I wanted to know more about the fourth beast, which was not like any of the others—the terrifying beast which crushed its victims with its bronze claws and iron teeth and then trampled on them. 20 And I wanted to know about the ten horns on its head and the horn that had come up afterward and had made three of the horns fall. It had eyes and a mouth and was boasting proudly. It was more terrifying than any of the others.

21 While I was looking, that horn made war on God's people and conquered them. 22 Then the one who had been living forever came and pronounced judgment in favor of the people of the Supreme God. The time had arrived for God's people to receive royal power.

23 This is the explanation I was given: "The fourth beast is a fourth empire that will be on the earth and will be different from all other empires. It will crush the whole earth

23   "Thus he said: 'As for the fourth
         beast,
      there shall be a fourth kingdom on
         earth,
         which shall be different from all
            the kingdoms,
      and it shall devour the whole earth,
         and trample it down, and break it
            to pieces.
24   As for the ten horns,
      out of this kingdom
         ten kings shall arise,
         and another shall arise after them;
      he shall be different from the former
         ones,
         and shall put down three kings.
25   He shall speak words against the
         Most High,
         and shall wear out the saints of
            the Most High,
         and shall think to change the
            times and the law;
      and they shall be given into his hand
         for a time, two times, and half a
            time.
26   But the court shall sit in judgment,
         and his dominion shall be taken
            away,
         to be consumed and destroyed to
            the end.
27   And the kingdom and the dominion
         and the greatness of the kingdoms
            under the whole heaven
         shall be given to the people of the
            saints of the Most High;
      their kingdom shall be an everlasting
         kingdom,
         and all dominions shall serve and
            obey them.'
      28 "Here is the end of the matter. As
for me, Daniel, my thoughts greatly alarmed
me, and my color changed; but I kept the
matter in my mind."

and trample it down. 24 The ten horns are ten kings who will rule that empire. Then another king will appear; he will be very different from the earlier ones and will overthrow three kings. 25 He will speak against the Supreme God and oppress God's people. He will try to change their religious laws and festivals, and God's people will be under his power for three and a half years. 26 Then the heavenly court will sit in judgment, take away his power, and destroy him completely. 27 The power and greatness of all the kingdoms on earth will be given to the people of the Supreme God. Their royal power will never end, and all rulers on earth will serve and obey them."

28 This is the end of the account. I was so frightened that I turned pale, and I kept everything to myself.

TEV Section Heading: The visions are explained

The plural "visions" of TEV can be misleading. It may be better here to use a section heading like "The interpretation of the first vision" or "The explanation of the (vision of) the four beasts," since verses 15-28 actually explain the first of Daniel's visions, the one about the four beasts. His second vision (of the ram and the goat) is found in 8.1-14 and explained in 8.15-27.

7.15   RSV   TEV

    "As for me, Daniel, my spirit
within me was anxious and the
visions of my head alarmed me.

    The visions I saw alarmed me,
and I was deeply disturbed.^{m}

^{m} *Aramaic has two additional words,
the meaning of which is unclear.*

    As for me, Daniel: the very same expression, consisting of an emphatic
first person pronoun followed by the proper name, is used in verse 28 at the
end of this chapter. It serves to remind the reader of the source of the
information and perhaps here marks the point in the vision when the prophet
comes to himself. The pronoun plus proper noun combination may also be
found frequently in the next chapters (8.1, 15, 27; 9.2; 10.2, 7; 12.5). This may
be a literary device to mark important transition points in the discourse
structure of the last half of Daniel.
    Within me: literally "in the midst of the sheath." The last word in
Aramaic is normally used of the leather container into which a sword or knife
is placed when not in use. Compare NAB "within its sheath of flesh." According
to some scholars it is here used as a metaphor for the human body, in which
the spirit resides. If this assumption is accepted, naturalness in the translation
will determine whether translators use the noun "body" or the pronoun "me"
(Mft, NEB, NJV). However, some versions, following the ancient Greek, omit the
two words altogether (NJB as well as TEV). It may also be possible to omit these
words for translation reasons.
    And: the conjunction here is not intended to indicate two totally different
reactions to the vision. The structure is rather parallel, and the two phrases
describe a single emotion. This should be made clear in the translation.

7.16   RSV   TEV

I approached one of those who
stood there and asked him the truth
concerning all this. So he told me,
and made known to me the interpretation of the things.

I went up to one of those standing
there and asked him to explain it all.
So he told me the meaning.

    One of those who stood there: this was presumably one of the multitude
of persons (or possibly angels) mentioned in verse 10 above.
    The truth concerning all this: this wording may possibly be understood
as meaning "what was true in the entire vision" (suggesting that not all of it
was true), but that meaning is to be avoided.
    Told me, and made known to me: once again the same thing is said in
two slightly different ways. But it will be more natural in many languages to
reduce this to a single statement. TEV, in fact, reverses the order of the two
verbs and concludes this verse with a translation of **made known to me the**

interpretation of the things. The first of these two verbs (**he told me**) is then used to introduce the following verse, "He said . . . ."

7.17	RSV	TEV

'These four great beasts are four kings who shall arise out of the earth.	**He said, "These four huge beasts are four empires which will arise on earth.**

Note that TEV here inserts the words "He said" from the previous verse, for better style in English, and also for making it clearer that what follows are the words of the one explaining the vision and not of Daniel himself.

Are: in some languages the verb "to be" may not be appropriate to show the correspondence between the beasts and the kings or kingdoms. In those cases it may be better to say "resemble," "depict," "show," "represent," "stand for," or something similar.

Kings: while the word here is literally **kings**, the individual kings represented the kingdoms over which they ruled. For this reason Mft, NIV, NJV, NAB, and NEB/REB translate "kingdoms," and TEV has "empires." In fact, one Aramaic manuscript as well as the ancient Greek and Latin actually has the word "kingdoms." While this reading may not be adopted for textual reasons, there are valid translation reasons for using "kingdoms" or "empires" in some languages. Both HOTTP and CTAT advocate translating the text that says "kings," but under the "proposed interpretation" of CTAT the following is stated: "One may indicate in a note that each of the 'kings' in fact incarnates one of the empires which followed each other in the Ancient Near East" (page 455).

Shall arise out of the earth: the wording of RSV may possibly be misunderstood as a reference to some kind of resurrection from the grave. But this is certainly not the meaning of the text. The verb **arise** indicates "rise to power," "come into authority," or "take (political) control." And **out of the earth** may be translated "on the earth" (NAB), or the whole expression may be reworded "[four kingdoms] of earthly origin will take power" (FRCL).

7.18	RSV	TEV

But the saints of the Most High shall receive the kingdom, and possess the kingdom for ever, for ever and ever.'	**And the people of the Supreme God will receive royal power and keep it forever and ever."**

But: the connecting word is important here. And in some cases it will have to be strengthened by an accompanying adverb. One possibility is to say "But eventually" or "After them (the four kingdoms)" as in FRCL. NJV has simply "Then."

The saints of the Most High: NRSV renders **saints** as "the holy ones." The reference here is to those who are faithful to the true God, namely, the people of Israel. But within the framework of this apocalyptic vision it is unwise to say this too clearly, although it is probably a good idea to make it clear that "people" are involved. The expression translated **the Most High** is actually a plural ("the most high ones"), but it is most likely a plural of majesty that should be rendered as a singular. Compare 3.26 and 4.17.

Receive . . . and possess: the repetition of the word **kingdom** after each of these two verbs will be unnatural in many languages. But the two verbs do focus on two somewhat different aspects, the first having to do with receiving royal power, and the second with retaining it.

For ever, for ever and ever: the Aramaic formula used here is way of expressing an absolute superlative. These words serve to emphasize the fact that the people of God will always keep the power that he gives to them.

7.19	RSV	TEV
	"Then I desired to know the truth concerning the fourth beast, which was different from all the rest, exceedingly terrible, with its teeth of iron and claws of bronze; and which devoured and broke in pieces, and stamped the residue with its feet;	Then I wanted to know more about the fourth beast, which was not like any of the others—the terrifying beast which crushed its victims with its bronze claws and iron teeth and then trampled on them.

Verses 19 and 20 constitute one long sentence in Aramaic and in RSV. But they have been broken into four separate sentences in TEV. This will probably be a good model to follow in the translation.

To know the truth: this verbal expression in Aramaic ("to be certain") has the same root as the noun in verse 16, "the truth."

The fourth beast: see verse 7 above. The information is not given in the same order as in verse 7, but all the elements are present, and in addition the **claws of bronze** are added to the description here.

Different from all the rest: this is better understood as meaning "different from the other three kingdoms" mentioned in this passage, rather than "different from all other kingdoms" in the world.

On the word **bronze**, see, for example, 2.32; 4.15, and comments there.

The wording of REB may provide a helpful model to some translators: "exceedingly fearsome with its iron teeth and bronze claws, devouring and crunching, then trampling underfoot what was left."

7.20	RSV	TEV
	and concerning the ten horns that were on its head, and the other horn	And I wanted to know about the ten horns on its head and the horn that

which came up and before which three of them fell, the horn which had eyes and a mouth that spoke great things, and which seemed greater than its fellows.	had come up afterward and had made three of the horns fall. It had eyes and a mouth and was boasting proudly. It was more terrifying than any of the others.

This verse in RSV is a continuation of the same sentence begun in the previous verse, but it will probably be wise to begin a new sentence in the translation (as in TEV), repeating the words "I wanted to know about." And in some cases it will be more natural to add a word like "also": "I also wanted to know." Much of this verse is a repetition of material found in previous verses.

Ten horns: see verse 7.

The other horn . . . great things: see verse 8.

Seemed greater: literally "its visibility was greater." This is new information not provided in verse 8. Although this **horn** was small, it appeared to be more imposing than the others. NJB has "looked more impressive," while NJV has "was more conspicuous."

Than its fellows: the Aramaic word translated **fellows** does not imply any particular relationship between the small horn and the ten others, as the English word "fellows" may imply. This is a simple comparison that can easily be rendered by "others," as in NRSV, NIV, and NEB/REB, as well as TEV.

7.21   RSV   TEV

As I looked, this horn made war with the saints, and prevailed over them,	While I was looking, that horn made war on God's people and conquered them.

Commentators are divided on the status of verses 21-22. Some consider it to be a later addition to the text, but it is extremely well attested by the manuscript evidence, and it is essential to the explanation that follows. The problem is that there is an implied question raised in verse 19 ("I desired to know the truth concerning the fourth beast"), but the answer does not come until verse 23. The second implied question ("concerning the ten horns," in verse 20) is answered first. The structure of verses 19-23 may therefore be diagrammed as follows:

Question 1	Question 2	Answer 2	Answer 1
verse 19	verse 20	verses 21-22	verse 23

However, some commentators see verses 21-22 as a continuation of the vision (Baldwin, page 145). Anderson says "Though vv. 21 and 22 interrupt the interpretation, they are not necessarily to be seen as a later addition. In summary form they anticipate the fuller description given in verses 23 to 27, but in a presentation that interlaces vision and interpretation, they may be taken as an extension of the former. There is no neat vision-interpretation sequence in ch. 7" (*Signs and Wonders*, page 88).

Made war with: that is, "fought against."
The saints: see verse 18.

7.22	RSV	TEV

until the Ancient of Days came, and judgment was given for the saints of the Most High, and the time came when the saints received the kingdom.

Then the one who had been living forever came and pronounced judgment in favor of[n] the people of the Supreme God. The time had arrived for God's people to receive royal power.

[n] pronounced judgment in favor of; *or* gave the right to judge to.

It will be important in many languages to begin a new sentence here as TEV has done. And in some cases it may be more natural to begin the sentence with the conjunction "but" (FRCL). Still another possibility is to repeat the earlier verb phrase, "I kept on watching until."

The Ancient of Days: see verse 9. In some languages it will be necessary to avoid giving the impression that **the Ancient of Days** and **the Most High** (later in this verse) refer to two different beings.

Judgment was given for: although most versions take this to mean that the Judge "judged in favor of," there is another possible interpretation. According to some experts the meaning should be "gave the right to judge to." This interpretation finds support in New Testament passages such as Matt 19.28; 1 Cor 6.2; and Rev 20.4. But it seems unlikely in this context.

The saints of the Most High: see verse 18.

Received the kingdom: in this context this means "received the power to rule" or "secured the right to govern." REB has "gained possession of kingly power."

7.23	RSV	TEV

"Thus he said: 'As for the
    fourth beast,
there shall be a fourth king-
    dom on earth,
  which shall be different
    from all the kingdoms,
and it shall devour the whole
    earth,
  and trample it down, and
    break it to pieces.

    This is the explanation I was given: "The fourth beast is a fourth empire that will be on the earth and will be different from all other empires. It will crush the whole earth and trample it down.

English versions differ as to whether verses 23-27 are to be considered poetry. In addition to RSV/NRSV, the following translations use poetic format: NJB, AT, and NAB. On the other hand the prose indentation of TEV is also adopted by NIV, NEB/REB, and NJV. The prose format is probably preferable.

Thus he said: this is a better model than TEV for those languages that do not have passive forms. However, it can be made clearer by saying something like "He explained it in this way . . ." or "He gave me this interpretation . . . ." The pronoun **he** again refers to the person questioned by Daniel in verse 16. But since the antecedent is quite some distance from this verse, some may wish to make the subject explicit, or else to use a verb with a passive meaning like "receive," if one exists in the language. The introductory sentence will then read something like "I received this explanation."

There shall be a fourth kingdom: as in verse 17 above, the verb "to be" may not be the most natural way to speak of the relationship between the beast of the vision and the earthly kingdom. In English the best way to express this relationship may be "As for the fourth beast, it stands for a fourth kingdom" or ". . . it means that there will be a fourth kingdom."

Different from all the kingdoms: while the TEV rendering may be taken to mean "unique in all the world," this is not the focus of this passage. Compare verse 19, "different from all the rest."

And it shall devour the whole earth: it will be wise in many languages to begin a new sentence at this point, and probably to make the subject clearer with something like "this kingdom" instead of the pronoun "it." On the verbs **devour . . . trample . . . break** and their order in the translation, see verses 7 and 19.

7.24	RSV	TEV

RSV	TEV

As for the ten horns,
out of this kingdom
  ten kings shall arise,
  and another shall arise
    after them;
he shall be different from the
  former ones,
and shall put down three
  kings.
	The ten horns are ten kings who will rule that empire. Then another king will appear; he will be very different from the earlier ones and will overthrow three kings.

Ten kings shall arise: on the verb **arise** see verse 17 and comments. It will be essential in most languages to indicate clearly whether these ten kings are seen as ruling at the same time or as coming in succession one after the other. FRCL translates "will succeed each other." Another possible model is "ten kings will rule over that empire one after the other."

And: the connection between the reign of the ten kings and the eleventh should be more clearly established. This may be done by shifting the words

after them forward to the beginning of the sentence about the eleventh king. Or the sentence can be started with "then."

Another: it will be important in the translation to make it clear that this is another king. And some may even prefer to say "an eleventh king," as in FRCL.

Shall put down three kings: it should also be made clear that the three kings referred to here are three of the ten kings mentioned earlier. So this should probably be translated "shall put down three of them" or "shall defeat three of those kings."

Historically this text may be applied quite well to Antiochus IV Epiphanes (175-164 B.C.), who followed a succession of rulers of the Seleucid dynasty and took control only after doing away with several rivals for royal power. This information may be put in a footnote, but it should not be included in the text of the apocalyptic vision.

7.25 RSV	TEV
He shall speak words against the Most High, and shall wear out the saints of the Most High, and shall think to change the times and the law; and they shall be given into his hand for a time, two times, and half a time.	He will speak against the Supreme God and oppress God's people. He will try to change their religious laws and festivals, and God's people will be under his power for three and a half years.

Speak words: this kind of expression will be redundant in many languages. The verb "to speak" is normally sufficient to convey the idea.

Wear out: this verb is ordinarily used of wearing out clothing. But in 1 Chr 17.9 the corresponding Hebrew word is used of oppressing people. It carries the idea of a long drawn-out persecution. NEB/REB attempts to get at this idea with "wear down." But most English versions have something like "oppress" (NIV and NAB as well as TEV), "harass" (Mft and NJV), or "torment" (NJB).

Think to change: that is, make an effort to modify or attempt to change. FRCL has "will make plans to modify."

The times and the law: the first of these two terms refers to the calendar of festivals of the people of Israel. This is seen by some as a reference to the fact that Antiochus Epiphanes banned the observance of the Sabbath and feast days (compare 1 Maccabees 1.41-53). The second term is related to the Jewish law in general. Given the fact that this term is more general, it may be more natural in many languages to reverse the order of the two terms, as in TEV.

For a time, two times, and a half time: as in 4.16 (and Rev 12.14) TEV takes the word for "time(s)" to mean "year(s)." Similarly NAB translates "a year, two years and a half-year" (likewise in AT, and in the notes in NIV anu NJV). But the most natural rendering in English is simply "three and a half years" (Mft as well as TEV and the note in NJB).

7.26

RSV	TEV
But the court shall sit in judgment, and his dominion shall be taken away, to be consumed and destroyed to the end.	Then the heavenly court will sit in judgment, take away his power, and destroy him completely.

But: the RSV rendering of the conjunction seems inappropriate here. The connecting word should rather convey the idea that what follows is the next in a sequence of events. In addition to TEV a number of other English versions have "Then" (NRSV, NEB/REB, NJV, and Mft).

The court: TEV makes it clear that this is the "heavenly" court rather than an earthly one. Compare verse 10.

His dominion shall be taken away: literally "they will take away." The pronoun "they" may refer to the members of the heavenly court, or it may possibly be indefinite—a substitute for a passive form. However, in this context it is more likely to be the members of the heavenly court.

Consumed and destroyed: these two terms mean virtually the same thing and may be rendered by a single verb if necessary. Grammatically the object of destruction may be "him" or "the king" as in TEV and GECL, or "it" (the power of the king). The latter interpretation is adopted by NEB, NIV, and others.

To the end: or "totally" as in NRSV. Some other ways of rendering the two Aramaic words are "completely" (TEV), "for all time" (NJV), and "forever" (NIV). NEB has "in the end," although REB reverts to "for ever."

7.27

RSV	TEV
And the kingdom and the dominion and the greatness of the kingdoms under the whole heaven shall be given to the people of the saints of the Most High; their kingdom shall be an everlasting kingdom,	The power and greatness of all the kingdoms on earth will be given to the people of the Supreme God. Their royal power will never end, and all rulers on earth will serve and obey them."

> **and all dominions shall**
> **serve and obey them.'**

And: NIV and NAB translate "Then." But most English versions rightly leave the conjunction untranslated.

The kingdom and the dominion and the greatness of the kingdoms: this literal rendering of the Aramaic is confusing, since it is unclear what is meant by **the kingdom . . . of the kingdoms**. The three terms may be reduced to two in many languages by redistributing the components of meaning.

The kingdoms under the whole heaven: the words **under the whole heaven**, or literally "under all the heavens," constitute another way of saying "in the whole world" or "on all the earth." The word for **whole** or "all" may legitimately be transposed to qualify "kingdoms." Hence the TEV rendering "all the kingdoms on earth." Compare also "all the kingdoms under heaven" (NJB, NJV, and NEB/REB).

The passive expression **shall be given** will have to be made active in many languages, and God will become the subject. In these cases a possible model for the first part of this verse is "Then the Most High God will give power to rule to those people who belong to him. They will rule over all the kingdoms in the whole world, with power and greatness."

Their kingdom: grammatically the possessive pronoun in Aramaic may refer to "the people" or to "the Most High (God)." But virtually all English versions take the pronoun as referring to "people," as in RSV and TEV. The parallel with verse 14 as well as certain other indications in the context of this chapter argue strongly in favor of this interpretation.

The people of the saints of the Most High: this expression differs from the one in verses 18, 22, and 25 in the addition of the word **people**. This addition may cause problems in some languages, since the **saints** are people, and the translation of the term "saints" may in fact be something like "people of God." It would, of course, be absurd to say "the people of the people of God." The meaning is the same as in the previous verses, where only "the saints of the Most High" occurs.

An everlasting kingdom: devout believers were convinced that, when the Jewish worship was reestablished, the much-acclaimed divine event that would bring in the final age would take place, and that nothing could change the situation after that.

All dominions shall serve and obey them: the two Aramaic verbs corresponding to RSV **serve and obey** have very similar meanings. The first, already used in verse 14, has a slightly broader meaning than the second. And for this reason it is possible to reverse the order as is done in FRCL, "will obey him and will serve him." Naturalness in the translation must be the determining factor.

"Here is the end of the matter. As for me, Daniel, my thoughts greatly alarmed me, and my color changed; but I kept the matter in my mind."	This is the end of the account. I was so frightened that I turned pale, and I kept everything to myself.

Here is the end of the matter: literally "Until here, the end of the word (or thing)." Although the wording seems a bit unusual, the meaning is quite clear. **The end of the matter** signals a transition from Daniel's description of his vision to a comment about his state when he regained consciousness. NRSV makes this clearer with "Here the account ends," and TEV is similar. In many languages people say something like "That is all of what I saw in my dream."

As for me, Daniel: as in verse 15, this combination of the emphatic pronoun followed by the proper name probably emphasizes the fact that the prophet is fully conscious and is no longer seeing the vision. The writer wishes to emphasize the fact that Daniel's spirit is troubled, not merely by the vision itself, but by the reality he faces when he becomes conscious of his surroundings again.

My thoughts greatly alarmed me: see 4.19 and 5.6.

My color changed: compare 5.6.

But: the translation of this conjunction will depend to some extent on which interpretation of the following phrase is accepted. If the words that follow the conjunction present an idea that would be different from what people may expect in this context, then it should be translated "but." If, however, a person would be expected to keep silent and not tell anyone else after being very frightened, then "and" will be a better translation. Or possibly it can be left untranslated.

I kept the matter in my mind: literally ". . . in my heart" as in KJV. On the "heart" as the seat of intelligence, see comments on 1.8 and 2.30. The RSV rendering of this phrase can easily be understood to mean "I did not forget about the matter." (Compare NJV "I could not put the matter out of my mind.") But the majority of the versions seem to agree that the meaning is rather "I did not share the matter with anyone else," "I kept these things to myself" (REB), or "I kept the matter to myself" (NIV, NAB).

With the conclusion of this chapter the Aramaic section of Daniel comes to an end. Beginning with the first word of chapter 8 until the end of the book the text is again in Hebrew (as from 1.1 to 2.4a).

Second Vision: The Ram and the Goat

Daniel 8.1-27

Vision: The ram and the goat: 8.1-14

RSV

1 In the third year of the reign of King Belshazzar a vision appeared to me, Daniel, after that which appeared to me at the first. 2 And I saw in the vision; and when I saw, I was in Susa the capital, which is in the province of Elam; and I saw in the vision, and I was at the river Ulai. 3 I raised my eyes and saw, and behold, a ram standing on the bank of the river. It had two horns; and both horns were high, but one was higher than the other, and the higher one came up last. 4 I saw the ram charging westward and northward and southward; no beast could stand before him, and there was no one who could rescue from his power; he did as he pleased and magnified himself.

5 As I was considering, behold, a he-goat came from the west across the face of the whole earth, without touching the ground; and the goat had a conspicuous horn between his eyes. 6 He came to the ram with the two horns, which I had seen standing on the bank of the river, and he ran at him in his mighty wrath. 7 I saw him come close to the ram, and he was enraged against him and struck the ram and broke his two horns; and the ram had no power to stand before him, but he cast him down to the ground and trampled upon him; and there was no one who could rescue the ram from his power. 8 Then the he-goat magnified himself exceedingly; but when he was strong, the great horn was broken, and instead of it there came up four conspicuous horns toward the four winds of heaven.

9 Out of one of them came forth a little horn, which grew exceedingly great toward the south, toward the east, and toward the glorious land. 10 It grew great, even to the host of

TEV

Daniel's Vision of a Ram and a Goat

1 In the third year that Belshazzar was king, I saw a second vision. 2 In the vision I suddenly found myself in the walled city of Susa in the province of Elam. I was standing by the Ulai River, 3 and there beside the river I saw a ram that had two long horns, one of which was longer and newer than the other. 4 I watched the ram butting with his horns to the west, the north, and the south. No animal could stop him or escape his power. He did as he pleased and grew arrogant.

5 While I was wondering what this meant, a goat came rushing out of the west, moving so fast that his feet didn't touch the ground. He had one prominent horn between his eyes. 6 He came toward the ram, which I had seen standing beside the river, and rushed at him with all his force. 7 I watched him attack the ram. He was so angry that he smashed into him and broke the two horns. The ram had no strength to resist. He was thrown to the ground and trampled on, and there was no one who could save him.

8 The goat grew more and more arrogant, but at the height of his power his horn was broken. In its place four prominent horns came up, each pointing in a different direction. 9 Out of one of these four horns grew a little horn, whose power extended toward the south and the east and toward the Promised Land. 10 It grew strong enough to attack the army of heaven, the stars themselves, and it threw some of them to the ground and trampled on them. 11 It even defied the Prince of the heavenly army, stopped the daily sacrifices offered to him, and ruined the Temple. 12 People sinned there instead of offering the proper daily sacrifices, and true religion was thrown

heaven; and some of the host of the stars it cast down to the ground, and trampled upon them. 11 It magnified itself, even up to the Prince of the host; and the continual burnt offering was taken away from him, and the place of his sanctuary was overthrown. 12 And the host was given over to it together with the continual burnt offering through transgression; and truth was cast down to the ground, and the horn acted and prospered. 13 Then I heard a holy one speaking; and another holy one said to the one that spoke, "For how long is the vision concerning the continual burnt offering, the transgression that makes desolate, and the giving over of the sanctuary and host to be trampled under foot?" 14 And he said to him, "For two thousand and three hundred evenings and mornings; then the sanctuary shall be restored to its rightful state."

to the ground. The horn was successful in everything it did.

13 Then I heard one angel ask another, "How long will these things that were seen in the vision continue? How long will an awful sin replace the daily sacrifices? How long will the army of heaven and the Temple be trampled on?"

14 I heard the other angel answer, "It will continue for 2,300 mornings and evenings, during which sacrifices will not be offered. Then the Temple will be restored."

TEV Section Heading: Daniel's vision of a ram and a goat

Another possible way of wording this section heading is "Daniel's second vision: The ram and the goat." See the remarks under the section heading at the beginning of chapter 7. The ram and the male goat are the respective leaders of flocks of sheep and goats. Here they symbolize the physical and military might of the kings or kingdoms that they represent: the king of Persia and the king of Greece (see verses 20-21). In cultures where sheep and goats are not well known, it may be necessary to resort to footnotes to explain the role of the ram and the male goat as leaders of their flocks.

Translators who follow the outline of this Handbook will need to add a subheading for verses 1-14, possibly similar to the one in the outline. However, to avoid redundantly saying "the ram and the goat" in both heading and subheading, it may be better to reduce the subheading to something like "The vision" or "Daniel sees the vision."

Beginning at this point the remainder of the book is written in Hebrew rather than Aramaic, as is the first part of the book up to 2.4.

8.1   RSV   TEV

In the third year of the reign of King Belshazzar a vision appeared to me, Daniel, after that which appeared to me at the first.

In the third year that Belshazzar was king, I saw a second vision.°

° *Beginning at 8.1, the rest of this book is in Hebrew (see 2.4).*

In the third year of the reign of King Belshazzar: on the name **Belshazzar**, see 5.1 (and 1.7). Since Belshazzar's title has already been given at the beginning of chapter 7, it is possible to drop the word **king** here, if that will yield a more natural-sounding introduction.

A vision appeared to me, Daniel: the use of the pronoun followed by the noun may be a device used by the writer to highlight the fact that a new vision is about to be introduced (see 7.15, 28). Another more straightforward way of stating this is "I saw a vision." And in some languages it may be fitting to say a "new vision" or a "different vision," just to be sure that the reader does not think that the same vision is about to be repeated or somehow continued. On the terms "vision" and "dream," see 1.17 and comments.

After that which appeared to me at the first: this is a rather complex way of saying that Daniel has a second vision. In many languages it will be simpler and more natural to say simply "I had another vision" or "a second vision appeared to me." Since the first vision came in the "first year of King Belshazzar" (7.1), it is possible to translate this verse by saying something like "Two years after the first vision, when Belshazzar was still king, I had another one."

8.2	RSV	TEV
	And I saw in the vision; and when I saw, I was in Susa the capital, which is in the province of Elam; and I saw in the vision, and I was at the river Ulai.	In the vision I suddenly found myself in the walled city of Susa in the province of Elam. I was standing by the Ulai River,

It is important that this verse be translated in such a way as to make clear to the reader that Daniel was not physically in Susa, but only in his vision. The repeated use of the phrase **I saw** . . . underlines this fact. Certain scholars maintain that the second occurrence of **I saw in the vision** is a textual error. Several modern versions leave it out, although it is not always clear whether the omission is for textual or translational reasons.

The capital: while Susa was, in fact, the capital of the province of Elam, it was also a fortified city. The word used here seems to focus more on the fortifications than on the fact of its political importance. For this reason most versions have something like "citadel" (NIV, NJB, NASB, AT, Mft) or "the fortress" (NJV, NAB). The TEV rendering is simply a less complicated way of saying the same thing. The rendering used here should be compared with Nch 1.1 and Est 1.2, where the same term is used.

The province of Elam: this is the region east of the Tigris River, which provided numerous raw materials. Its people are depicted as a ruthless nation whose warriors were skillful in using chariots as well as bows and arrows. Elamites are mentioned in the New Testament as being present in Jerusalem at Pentecost (Acts 2.9).

The river Ulai: this expression is repeated in verse 16 of this chapter, and the word translated **river** occurs again in verses 3 and 6. The Ulai is one of three bodies of water near Susa. Today it is called the Eulaeus. It is actually an artificial canal that joins the other two streams, the Kerkha and the Abdizful. For this reason a more accurate translation may be "canal," as in NIV, REB, and NASB. In those languages where there is no word for canal, it will be better to use something like "stream" (NEB, AT), indicating a less important body of water than the word "river" may signify. Some versions, including NJB and AB, have "the Ulai Gate" at this point. This is a conjectural translation based on the ancient versions, but translators are advised not to adopt this solution.

8.3   RSV   TEV

I raised my eyes and saw, and be-hold, a ram standing on the bank of the river. It had two horns; and both horns were high, but one was high-er than the other, and the higher one came up last.

and there beside the river I saw a ram that had two long horns, one of which was longer and newer than the other.

I raised my eyes and saw: this is a typically Hebrew expression where the first part (**I raised my eyes**) does not imply in Hebrew that the person was at first looking downward, but it marks the beginning of the action and is followed by a second verb (**saw**) indicating the essential part of the action. It is similar to "opened my mouth and spoke" in 10.16. But it may be more natural in other languages to use a single verbal expression to translate both parts, as in TEV.

Behold: this interjection will be considered redundant in some languages and should therefore be omitted. But in other languages where the use of such forms is natural and frequent, it may be retained. Here it serves to make the description more dramatic. Compare 2.31; 4.10; 7.2.

The bank of the river: the word translated **bank** is really a very general term in Hebrew which has a wide variety of meanings depending on the context in which it is used. Here it may be rendered by a preposition like "beside" or "by." Another way of conveying the same basic meaning is that of NJV: "between me and the river." It will be noted that NJB and AB have "before the gate" at this point, but translators are advised against using "gate" in the previous verse.

Both horns were high: the mention of **two horns** and **both horns** so close together may sound strange and unnecessary in some languages. They represent the same Hebrew words. And there is in fact some textual evidence to omit the second occurrence (**both horns**), but this may be done for the sake of naturalness rather than for textual reasons. Each language will have its own way of describing particularly large animal horns, but in English it is much more natural to speak of "long horns" (as in TEV and other versions) rather than "high horns." The two horns represent the Medes and the Persians (see verse 20). It was the Persians who took over the empire from the Medes.

But this information should be restricted to footnotes and not placed in the translation itself.

And the higher one came up last: the conjunction **and** should probably be rendered differently in most languages. Since what follows is contrary to the reader's expectation, it may be more effective to say something like "but" or "however." The word translated **last** in RSV may be understood as meaning later in time (TEV, NJB, NJV, and Mft) or in a position behind the other horn (NEB, AT). NAB handles the whole matter by saying "the one (was) larger and newer than the other." See also TEV.

8.4	RSV	TEV
	I saw the ram charging westward and northward and southward; no beast could stand before him, and there was no one who could rescue from his power; he did as he pleased and magnified himself.	I watched the ram butting with his horns to the west, the north, and the south. No animal could stop him or escape his power. He did as he pleased and grew arrogant.

Westward and northward and southward: that is, in all directions except the east. For the writer, who was located in Judea, Persia was situated to the east. It apparently had no interest in making conquests further east in the direction of India. In those languages where the words for north and south are particularly difficult, the essential meaning may be conveyed by saying something like "on all sides except the direction of the rising sun."

No beast could stand before him: here the verb **stand before** is a way of saying "withstand him (or it)" (NJV and NAB), "resist his power," or "hold its own against him" (Mft).

No one who could rescue from his power: literally "no one who could save from his hand." Compare 1.2 on this use of the word "hand." In some languages it may be necessary to state an object for the verb **rescue**. Translators may say "rescue any of his victims" or something similar. REB rewords this to say "from its power there was no escape."

He did as he pleased: or "he did whatever he wanted to do," or "he did whatever his heart desired."

Magnified himself: this expression, which also occurs in 8.8, 11, 25 as well as in 11.36, 37, 39, is more literally "he grew" or "he became great." But translators and commentators alike are in agreement that this does not mean physical growth. Yet there is not complete agreement as to exactly what kind of growth is indicated. The most widely accepted interpretation is that the reference is to growth in power. NJB has "became strong," and NAB reads "became very powerful." TEV, however, indicates that he "grew arrogant." And AT has "accomplished great exploits."

207

As I was considering, behold, a he-goat came from the west across the face of the whole earth, without touching the ground; and the goat had a conspicuous horn between his eyes.	While I was wondering what this meant, a goat came rushing out of the west, moving so fast that his feet didn't touch the ground. He had one prominent horn between his eyes.

As I was considering: compare 7.8. The TEV rendering gives the impression that Daniel was thinking about what he had already seen, when the goat appeared. But NJB translates "This is what I observed: . . . ," making the verb relate to what follows. Most versions, however, adopt the same solution as TEV and indicate that he was reflecting on what he had already seen. This is the recommended interpretation.

Behold: see verse 3.

He-goat: this is not normal English usage, so TEV drops the **he-**, and the gender is made clear by the use of masculine pronouns. Some languages have a separate word for a male goat. If there is no special term, the fact that the goat was male must be conveyed in the most natural way possible.

From the west: again, the point of reference is that of the writer, writing from Judea. In many languages it may be necessary to say "from the side where the sun sets."

Across the face of the whole earth: this clause contains two potential translation problems. In many languages the earth is not depicted as having a **face**. The obvious meaning is the "surface" of the earth. Also this expression constitutes an exaggeration for dramatic effect. If there is a danger that it will be understood literally in the translator's language, it may have to be reduced. But in the context of an apocalyptic vision, the overstatement may be easily understood. The reference to **the face of the whole earth** implies conquering all nations, but this should not be made explicit in the translation of the vision itself.

Without touching the ground: this is not a reference to the use of airplanes! TEV makes it clear that the animal is "moving so fast" that it appears not to touch the ground as it moves. Most translators should probably adopt a similar solution, to avoid misunderstanding on the part of the readers.

A conspicuous horn: that is, a single horn that was very prominent. The rendering of the word **conspicuous** should make it clear that this was really something quite spectacular that could be seen without any effort. It may be indicated in a footnote that this single horn represents Alexander the Great, the founder and first ruler of the Greek Empire (see verse 21).

He came to the ram with the two horns, which I had seen standing on	He came toward the ram, which I had seen standing beside the river,

| the bank of the river, and he ran at | and rushed at him with all his force. |
| him in his mighty wrath. | |

He: that is, the goat. In some languages the noun may have to be used instead of the pronoun.

With the two horns: since this information has already been given in verse 3, it can be omitted here (as in TEV). However, unless it is really unnatural to repeat the information, it may be a good idea to retain it to emphasize the symbolic importance of the two horns.

River: or better "canal," if the translator's language has such a word. See comments on verse 2.

In his mighty wrath: some other renderings are "with impetuous force" (NEB/REB), "in the full force of its fury" (NJB), "with savage force" (NAB).

8.7	RSV	TEV

| I saw him come close to the ram, and he was enraged against him and struck the ram and broke his two horns; and the ram had no power to stand before him, but he cast him down to the ground and trampled upon him; and there was no one who could rescue the ram from his power. | I watched him attack the ram. He was so angry that he smashed into him and broke the two horns. The ram had no strength to resist. He was thrown to the ground and trampled on, and there was no one who could save him. |

Come close to: this is clearly not a friendly approach. The translation should probably make clear the fact that this is the confrontation of an adversary. NIV, NAB, and TEV use the verb "attack."

Enraged against him: some other possibilities are "was very angry with him" or "was furious with him." Some versions translate this verb as an adverb describing how the goat attacked the ram. NIV has "furiously," and NAB says "with furious blows."

Struck: translators will, of course, look for a verb that fits the context in which a goat is the subject. TEV "smashed" is better, but other languages may have a more specialized vocabulary like "butted" or something similar.

The ram: the word for **ram** is repeated four times in the original, and this is dutifully reflected in RSV. This four-fold repetition may be unnatural and distracting in other languages, where it will be necessary to reduce the number of occurrences, while at the same time making it clear which animal is being described in every instance.

To stand before . . . : that is, to "resist" or "withstand." See verse 4, where the same verb is used to describe the ram.

But he cast him down . . . : the pronoun references in this statement may be easily misunderstood. Translators should insure that readers understand the goat as the subject and the ram as the object of the verb meaning "throw down" or "cause to fall."

8.8	RSV	TEV

Then the he-goat magnified himself exceedingly; but when he was strong, the great horn was broken, and instead of it there came up four conspicuous horns toward the four winds of heaven.	**The goat grew more and more arrogant, but at the height of his power his horn was broken. In its place four prominent horns came up, each pointing in a different direction.**

Modern English versions are almost evenly divided as to whether a new paragraph should come at the beginning of verse 8 or verse 9. RSV, NJB, NIV, NRSV, and FRCL make the break at verse 9, but many good English translations (TEV, NEB/REB, NAB, and AB) start the new paragraph here. Others, such as NJV and TOB, do not make a break at either place. All things being equal, translators should probably make the break here.

Magnified himself exceedingly: NRSV translates simply "grew exceedingly great," while REB says "made a great display of its strength." The latter seems to capture the idea of arrogance a bit better. The same verbal expression is used of the ram in verse 4, but here an additional word is used to make it stronger. On the word **exceedingly**, see comments on the corresponding Aramaic word at 6.23; 7.7, 19.

When he was strong: the goat was obviously already strong when it defeated the ram. So this expression is usually taken to mean something like "at the peak of his power" (NJV), "at the height of his (or its) power" (TEV, NIV, NAB, NRSV, and REB).

The great horn was broken: this indicates an abrupt change in the political situation, in which power is suddenly relinquished. It is probably a good idea to bring out the abruptness of this event in the translation. Some English versions seek to do this by using the verb "snapped" (NEB and NJB). This almost certainly refers to the untimely death of Alexander the Great in 323 B.C. He was succeeded by **four conspicuous horns,** a symbolic reference to the kingdoms of Macedonia, Asia Minor, Syria, and Egypt. For comments on the word **conspicuous**, see verse 5. There is some manuscript evidence that reads "four other horns," but this is followed by few English versions (NAB, for example) and is not recommended to translators.

Toward the four winds of heaven: this expression is used to indicate the four cardinal points of the compass. See comments on 7.2. The same expression is used in 11.4. Compare also Zech 2.6; 6.5; Jer 49.36; Rev 7.1. This may be rendered less literally "toward all directions," or as in TEV, "each pointing in a different direction."

8.9 RSV TEV

Out of one of them came forth a little horn, which grew exceedingly great toward the south, toward the east, and toward the glorious land.

Out of one of these four horns grew a little horn, whose power extended toward the south and the east and toward the Promised Land.

Little: the unusual form of the word here has caused much discussion by commentators. This adjective may be taken as describing the horn that grew out of one of the four horns (as in RSV, TEV, and most other English versions) or as describing the horn out of which it grew (FRCL). The latter interpretation is also adopted by NJB: "From one of these, the small one, sprang a[nother] horn." The majority of English versions follow the same interpretation as RSV and TEV, probably because of 7.8, where mention is made of another horn, a small one, which grew and overcame the three others. But according to some commentators this is not sufficient reason to correct the Hebrew text here. In view of the uncertainty on this point, it may be better to follow the lead of the majority of English versions.

Out of one of them: that is, out of one of these four horns.

Grew exceedingly great: on the verb **grew**, see verses 4 and 8, where the same verb is translated "magnified himself." The writer does not mention each of the earlier successors of Alexander the Great in the Seleucid dynasty who ruled over Syria and Palestine. He jumps directly to Antiochus Epiphanes (175-164 B.C.), who is of greater interest than the others.

South . . . east: Antiochus Epiphanes made war against Egypt to the south and against the Persians and Parthians to the east. However, it is probably better not to overload the translation with too many geographical references.

Toward the glorious land: literally "the beautiful" (compare NRSV, "the beautiful land"). The word **land** is not found in the original text. But on the basis of 11.16 and 41, where the Hebrew has "the beautiful land," RSV, TEV, and most commentators take this to refer to the land also; that is, to the land of Israel. Compare also Jer 3.19 and Ezek 20.6, 15.

8.10 RSV TEV

It grew great, even to the host of heaven; and some of the host of the stars it cast down to the ground, and trampled upon them.

It grew strong enough to attack the army of heaven, the stars themselves, and it threw some of them to the ground and trampled on them.

It grew great: this is the same verb as at the beginning of the previous verse, but there is no qualifying adverb here. The idea is that it grew so powerful that it was able to attack **even to the host of heaven**. For the translator the identification of the **host of heaven** presents serious problems. The answer to this question will determine the rendering of the rest of this verse. Many versions equate it with the stars that are mentioned immediately following. The **host of the stars** are introduced by a simple coordinating conjunction and therefore seem to be in apposition with the **host of heaven**. This will yield a translation like that of TEV, ". . . the army of heaven, the stars themselves." On the other hand NAB translates in such a way as to indicate two separate and distinct groups: "Its power extended to the host of heaven, so that it cast down to earth some of the host and some of the stars"; it then indicates in a footnote that the host of heaven "ordinarily meaning the stars, here refers to the People of God; [compare] 12.3." The same kind of solution is adopted by FRCL. Whichever solution is chosen, the translator must not say more than is necessary in the rendering given, and an explanatory note can give more ample information.

Cast down: see verse 7 above.

Trampled: other possible translations of this verb are "walked on" (NCV), or "stamped on" (REB), or "crushed under foot."

8.11	RSV	TEV
	It magnified itself, even up to the Prince of the host; and the continual burnt offering was taken away from him, and the place of his sanctuary was overthrown.	It even defied the Prince of the heavenly army, stopped the daily sacrifices offered to him, and ruined the Temple.

Magnified itself: see verse 4 above. The image here is one of defiance of a superior authority. The goat showed utter contempt and lack of respect for the Almighty by open rebellion against him. NJB translates "it even challenged the power of the Prince," and NEB/REB has "it aspired to be as great as the Prince."

The Prince of the host: this is sometimes understood as referring to the high priest Onias III, the leader of God's people, who was murdered during the reign of Antiochus Epiphanes in 171 B.C. But it is much more likely that it refers to the ultimate leader of the heavenly army, who is none other than God himself. However, if possible, translators should try to maintain the imagery in the text. In some cases this will mean saying something like "God, the chief of the heavenly army" or "God, the leader of the forces in heaven."

The text then gives two ways in which contempt was shown for the heavenly authority. First, the regular sacrifices that were to be offered to God were stopped. And secondly, the Temple, the house of God, was defiled.

The continual burnt offering was taken away from him: this is the usual reading of the text, but a different tradition is indicated in the margin of some manuscripts. The essential meaning of the two readings is the same; however, it will not be possible in some languages to reproduce the passive construction of RSV. It is probably best to make the goat the subject of all three of the verbs in this verse, to render accurately its meaning: (1) it opposed the leader of the heavenly army; (2) it put a stop to the daily sacrifices to God; and (3) it brought disgrace on the Temple itself.

The place of his sanctuary was overthrown: this is a veiled reference to the profaning of the Temple in 167 B.C., when Antiochus Epiphanes set up the "Awful Horror" in the sanctuary at Jerusalem (11.31 TEV). This was a statue or some sort of representation of the Olympian god Zeus. And an attempt was made to get everyone to worship this deity. The translation should be clear enough to allow the reader to understand the scandalous intervention of the "new horn" but without going into historical details. Since, however, the temple was not destroyed but only profaned, the meaning is something like "defiled the temple," "opened the temple to the public," "made the temple unholy," or "put an end to true worship." TEV "ruined" may be intentionally ambiguous.

8.12   RSV   TEV

And the host was given over to it together with the continual burnt offering through transgression;[n] and truth was cast down to the ground, and the horn acted and prospered.

People sinned there instead of offering the proper daily sacrifices,[p] and true religion was thrown to the ground. The horn was successful in everything it did.

[n] Heb obscure

[p] People . . . sacrifices; *Hebrew unclear.*

As the TEV note indicates, the first part of this verse is unclear in Hebrew. In fact the whole of verses 12 and 13 are difficult, and there are numerous possible interpretations. One or more notes will probably be required.

The word translated **host** has been variously understood as referring to "the host of the saints" (NIV) or "the army of heaven" (LB). But TEV takes it here as referring to "people (in the Temple)." It is the same word as in the previous verse, in the expression "the Prince of the host," but the meaning is not necessarily identical. In this case the meaning is probably less broad than in verse 11, here referring to the pious worshipers in the Temple.

The host was given over to it: the least unsatisfactory solution to the understanding of these words seems to be that of NJB and NAB, which (contrary to RSV and TEV) takes them as the continuation of the sentence begun in verse 11b. The meaning is then "and the host (or army, or people) of God was (were) also delivered to the power of the horn." This seems to indicate the temporary success of the persecutor. REB renders it "the heavenly host were delivered up." The use of the past tense is legitimate, since in an apocalyptic vision the events are at the same time past (in the vision) and future (in reality). Considerations of the translator's own language, however, will have to determine which tense is natural in such a context. In those cases where the passive form has to be rendered actively, it may be best to say something like "God allowed the horn to have power over his people," or possibly "the people of God began to turn away from him and gave themselves to (the power of) the horn."

Together with the continual burnt offering: the preposition translated **together with** may be understood to mean "at the same time" (FRCL), "while" (NAB), "in addition," or simply "and" (NEB). The expression that follows is extremely difficult and may possibly be understood to mean (a) that the **transgression**, referring to the "Awful Horror," is substituted for the normal Temple sacrifice, or (b) that the regular offering of sacrifice was pronounced a crime by the persecutor. The latter solution is followed by NEB/REB, "it raised itself impiously against the regular offering." But the first solution is more likely and more commonly adopted. It is worded as follows in some English versions: "sin replaced the daily sacrifice" (NAB), or "thus was the daily sacrifice profanely treated" (Mft). Translators may even say "in the place of the daily sacrifice it established something outrageously evil." The words **through transgression** have been translated in a variety of ways including "because of rebellion (wickedness)" (NIV/NRSV), "iniquity" (NJB), and the adverb "impiously" (REB). Experts do not agree on whose "wickedness" is meant here. It may be that of the horn or of the "host." Or possibly AB is correct in slightly correcting the text so that the term actually refers to the offense or abomination that is set up in place of the regular sacrifice. This conforms to the statement in the following verse.

Truth was cast down: this refers not to abstract truth but to religious truth as contained in the Torah (Law). The passive formulation may be made active with the horn as the agent, "the horn threw true religion down," or in those languages where the word for religion is especially difficult, "it slandered the truth about the things of God."

Acted and prospered: these two verbs simply indicate that the horn was successful in all that it attempted to do.

While AB has no less than nine textual notes on verses 11 and 12, the actual AB translation of this passage may be worth noting:

> Even over the Prince of the host it exalted itself; it removed the daily sacrifice from its stand and defiled the sanctuary and the pious ones; and on the stand of the daily sacrifice it set up an offense. It cast truth to the ground and was successful in its undertaking.

8.13 RSV	TEV
Then I heard a holy one speaking; and another holy one said to the one that spoke, "For how long is the vision concerning the continual burnt offering, the transgression	Then I heard one angel ask another, "How long will these things that were seen in the vision continue? How long will an awful sin replace the daily sacrifices? How long

that makes desolate, and the giving over of the sanctuary and host to be trampled under foot?"° | **will the army of heaven and the Temple be trampled on?"**

° Heb obscure

Like the previous verse, this one is full of problems. Commentaries generally regard it as containing several glosses.

A holy one: most commentators agree that this is a reference to an angel, as in 4.13, and not to a member of the people of God (the Israelites).

Another holy one: some commentators maintain that the second **holy one** is the same as the first one, and that the unknown **one that spoke** represents Daniel himself. But this interpretation is very unlikely. In his vision the prophet overhears the conversation of two "holy ones" or two angels. The whole thing may be greatly simplified without altering the meaning if it is translated "I heard two angels conversing. And one of them asked." In many languages it will be more natural to use the verb "ask," since what follows is a question and in fact a rather long one. Note that TEV breaks the question down into three more manageable parts and also makes their meaning clearer.

How long is the vision . . . ? The wording of the question in RSV is misleading. The real question is not how long the actual vision will last but relates rather to the duration of the terrible events seen in the vision. This should be made clear in the translation, as in TEV. It should also be noted that TEV separates the complex question into three parts and repeats the key words "how long" in each case. This may serve as a good model in many other languages that find the three-part question too complicated as presented in RSV.

The continual burnt offering: this brief expression carries the whole idea of the suppression of the daily sacrifice referred to in the previous verse. In most languages it will probably be wise to fill it out according to the TEV model.

Some manuscript evidence adds the qualifying phrase ". . . which is suppressed," but this reading is not adopted by many modern English versions.

The transgression that makes desolate: although the wording is different, this seems to be the same as the "abominations" of "one who makes desolate" in 9.27.

The giving over: the Hebrew verb here is in the infinitive form and is not grammatically attached to anything. It brings to mind the verb used in verse 12 ("was given over") and should probably be attached to the following noun (**the sanctuary**). In this context it may be legitimate to leave it implicit in translation, as has been done in numerous versions such as TEV. But the idea is that God has temporarily abandoned the army of heaven and the Temple, allowing them to be overrun by those who oppose the practices of the Jewish religion. So some may say "How long will you [God] allow the heathen to trample . . . ?"

The sanctuary: or, more precisely, the Temple, as in verse 11. Note that TEV reverses the order of **sanctuary** and **host**.

The host: TEV reverts to the meaning understood in verse 11 ("army of heaven") rather than the idea of the pious worshipers in verse 12. But the latter seems more likely here.

An additional model for this verse as a whole is found in NCV:

> How long will the things in this vision last? The vision is about the daily sacrifices. It is about the turning away from God that brings destruction. It is about the Temple being pulled down. It is about the army of heaven being walked on.

8.14   RSV   TEV

And he said to him,[p] "For two thou-   I heard the other angel answer,
sand and three hundred evenings   "It will continue for 2,300 mornings
and mornings; then the sanctuary   and evenings, during which sacrific-
shall be restored to its rightful   es will not be offered. Then the
state."   Temple will be restored."

[p] Theodotion Gk Syr Vg: Heb *me*

He said to him: the RSV rendering does not follow the Hebrew text but adopts the reading found in the Greek, Syriac, and Latin versions. The Hebrew has "said to me," and this is adopted by KJV, NIV, and NJV. Some versions do not express the object pronoun and say simply "answered" or "replied" (NEB/REB as well as TEV). But in some languages an object will be required. In those cases it is probably better to adopt the rendering of the versions and translate "answered him." Daniel is merely listening in on a dialogue between two heavenly beings. The explanation of the vision to him does not come until the following verses.

Two thousand three hundred evenings and mornings: this can be understood in two ways. It can mean either 2,300 days or 1,150 days, depending on how the mornings and evenings are counted. **Evenings and mornings** can be counted as pairs, each pair forming one day, the total being 2,300 days; or else they can be counted as separate units of 1,150 each, bringing the total to 2,300 units occurring within 1,150 days. The smaller figure agrees with the three and a half years mentioned in 7.25. It should be made clear that this refers to the number of occasions for offering sacrifices, one in the morning and one in the evening. There will be 2,300 sacrifices (two for each day) that will not be offered. While this interpretation may seem more logical, few modern versions adopt it. It will be noted that earlier editions of TEV had ". . . for 1,150 days, during which evening and morning sacrifices . . . ." The latest edition of TEV restores the number 2,300 in a way that makes it possible to interpret it as 1,150 days of two sacrifices each, but this may not be clear to the reader without close examination of the wording.

Then the sanctuary shall be restored to its rightful state: literally "and the sanctuary will be justified." The verb form used here is unique in all the

Old Testament, and its precise meaning is uncertain. Some take it to mean "purified" or "cleansed" (NJV). Others have the idea of rededication; NIV reads "reconsecrated." Still others have a more general statement: "then shall the wrongs of the sanctuary be righted" (AT) or ". . . have its rights restored" (NJB). The term probably contains the ideas of purification from ritual defilement as well as restoration to its former physical state. The ritual side would, however, be more important.

Explanation: The angel Gabriel explains the vision: 8.15-27

RSV

15 When I, Daniel, had seen the vision, I sought to understand it; and behold, there stood before me one having the appearance of a man. 16 And I heard a man's voice between the banks of the Ulai, and it called, "Gabriel, make this man understand the vision." 17 So he came near where I stood; and when he came, I was frightened and fell upon my face. But he said to me, "Understand, O son of man, that the vision is for the time of the end."

18 As he was speaking to me, I fell into a deep sleep with my face to the ground; but he touched me and set me on my feet. 19 He said, "Behold, I will make known to you what shall be at the latter end of the indignation; for it pertains to the appointed time of the end. 20 As for the ram which you saw with the two horns, these are the kings of Media and Persia. 21 And the he-goat is the king of Greece; and the great horn between his eyes is the first king. 22 As for the horn that was broken, in place of which four others arose, four kingdoms shall arise from his nation, but not with his power. 23 And at the latter end of their rule, when the transgressors have reached their full measure, a king of bold countenance, one who understands riddles, shall arise. 24 His power shall be great, and he shall cause fearful destruction, and shall succeed in what he does, and destroy mighty men and the people of the saints. 25 By his cunning he shall make deceit prosper under his hand, and in his own mind he shall magnify himself. Without warning he shall destroy many; and he shall even rise up against the Prince of princes; but, by no human hand, he shall be broken. 26 The vision of the evenings and the mornings which has been told is true; but seal up the vision, for it pertains to many days hence."

TEV

The Angel Gabriel Explains the Vision

15 I was trying to understand what the vision meant, when suddenly someone was standing in front of me. 16 I heard a voice call out over the Ulai River, "Gabriel, explain to him the meaning of what he saw." 17 Gabriel came and stood beside me, and I was so terrified that I fell to the ground.

He said to me, "Mortal man, understand the meaning. The vision has to do with the end of the world." 18 While he was talking, I fell to the ground unconscious. But he took hold of me, raised me to my feet, 19 and said, "I am showing you what the result of God's anger will be. The vision refers to the time of the end.

20 "The ram you saw that had two horns represents the kingdoms of Media and Persia. 21 The goat represents the kingdom of Greece, and the prominent horn between his eyes is the first king. 22 The four horns that came up when the first horn was broken represent the four kingdoms into which that nation will be divided and which will not be as strong as the first kingdom.

23 "When the end of those kingdoms is near and they have become so wicked that they must be punished, there will be a stubborn, vicious, and deceitful king. 24 He will grow strong—but not by his own power. He will cause terrible destruction and be successful in everything he does. He will bring destruction on powerful men and on God's own people. 25 Because he is cunning, he will succeed in his deceitful ways. He will be proud of himself and destroy many people without warning. He will even defy the greatest King of all, but he will be destroyed without the use of any human power. 26 This vision about the evening and morning sacrifices which has been explained to you will come true. But keep it

27 And I, Daniel, was overcome and lay sick for some days; then I rose and went about the king's business; but I was appalled by the vision and did not understand it.

secret now, because it will be a long time before it does come true."

27 I was depressed and ill for several days. Then I got up and went back to the work that the king had assigned to me, but I was puzzled by the vision and could not understand it.

TEV Section Heading: The angel Gabriel explains the vision

It may be fitting in some cases to make it clearer that it is the second vision that is to be explained by Gabriel. See comments at 7.15.

8.15   RSV   TEV

When I, Daniel, had seen the vision, I sought to understand it; and behold, there stood before me one having the appearance of a man.

I was trying to understand what the vision meant, when suddenly someone was standing in front of me.

I, Daniel: compare "me, Daniel" in 7.15, 28; 8.1. Once again this use of the emphatic pronoun followed by the proper name seems to establish the fact that the prophet is emerging from the vision to the real world; thus it marks an important point in the discourse of the book.

When I had seen the vision, I sought to understand it: it may be important in some languages to alter the verb tenses to make the meaning clearer. The idea is something like "after having seen the vision I was making an effort to understand it," or "while I was thinking about the vision I had seen and trying to figure it out."

Behold: in this case the Hebrew particle is translated as "suddenly" in TEV (as well as REB and Mft) because the context seems to require some such word in English. Many other languages will have similar ways of marking a surprising turn of events.

One having the appearance of a man: in spite of the similarity in English between this expression and the one in 7.13, the Hebrew here is in reality quite different from the Aramaic expression in the previous chapter. Consequently it here designates a being that is different from the "son of man" in the previous chapter. Here the word for **man**, *gever,* signifies an adult male person and not the more generic "human being." The Hebrew word has the same root as the proper name "Gabriel," one of the angels in the service of God, who is named in the following verse (compare 9.21 and Luke 1.19, 26).

8.16   RSV   TEV

And I heard a man's voice between the banks of the Ulai, and it called,

I heard a voice call out over the Ulai River, "Gabriel, explain to him the

"Gabriel, make this man understand   meaning of what he saw."
the vision."

A man's voice: the word for **man** here is not the same as in the previous verse. There is no special emphasis on the male quality of the voice. The meaning is rather "a person's voice." In some languages it will be more natural to say simply "I heard someone calling out."

Between the banks of the Ulai: it will be recalled that the proper name here refers to a river, or more accurately to a "canal" (see verse 2). But the reader may need to be reminded of this fact by adding the classifier term. However, the real problem here is in the understanding of the preposition. Where is the speaker located? The Hebrew is literally "between the Ulai." A literal understanding of RSV seems to indicate that the speaker was standing in the middle of the river, or "from the middle of the Ulai" (NJV). NRSV has simply "by the Ulai." Other versions seem to have the speaker floating above the river, "from between the banks of the Ulai" (AT). NEB/REB have "across the bend of the Ulai." Still others have a rather vague "on the Ulai" (NAB) or "from the Ulai" (NIV). But it is probably better to consider the preposition as describing the position of the sound rather than of the speaker. The translation would can then be something like Mft's "I heard a human voice over the water of the Ulai."

Make this man understand the vision: or "help this person to understand what he has seen (in the vision)," or "explain the vision to this man" (REB). It is possible to translate the noun phrase **this man** by the pronoun "him," if the reference will be clear in the translator's language; see, for example, TEV, or else NJB "tell him the meaning of the vision!"

8.17	RSV	TEV
	So he came near where I stood; and when he came, I was frightened and fell upon my face. But he said to me, "Understand, O son of man, that the vision is for the time of the end."	Gabriel came and stood beside me, and I was so terrified that I fell to the ground. He said to me, "Mortal man, understand the meaning. The vision has to do with the end of the world."

So: the connecting word here has been similarly rendered in Mft and AT, but other versions have translated "Then" (AB), "As" (NIV), and "When" (NAB), while many others like TEV and REB leave it untranslated. Naturalness in the flow of the story will have to determine how this is rendered in the translation.

He came near: the third person singular pronouns in this verse refer to Gabriel, and not the other actor in the previous scene. Therefore in many languages it will be important to use the proper name or another device to make this clear. Compare TEV.

When he came: since the text has already stated **he came near**, this will be considered redundant in many languages and may therefore be omitted as in TEV.

I was frightened and . . . : the Hebrew language frequently resorts to simple coordination of propositions where other languages express the logical relationships more precisely. Here the relationship between fear and falling to the ground is one of cause and effect. This may be expressed as in TEV, or as in REB "I prostrated myself in terror."

Fell on my face: in many Old Testament passages where this expression is used, it indicates an involuntary fall (1 Sam 17.49), but in other contexts the idea of an intentional movement from a standing to a lying position is indicated (1 Sam 25.23). Here it should not be translated in such a way as to suggest an accidental fall. Daniel intentionally threw himself on the ground as a sign of his respect for the angel and his awe of the situation in general. Compare also 2.46.

Understand: the use of the imperative with this particular verb in some languages may sound strange in this context. The idea is something like "I would like for you to understand." And in some languages it may be necessary to add something like "nevertheless," "however," or "but" to show the contrast between the fact that Daniel is mortal and yet considered worthy of receiving the revelation. In that case the translation may refer first to Daniel as a mere **son of man**, followed by this imperative. FRCL, for example, has "Daniel, you are nothing but a human; know, however, that . . . ." Other languages may say something like "nevertheless I want you to understand . . . ."

Son of man: this represents the Hebrew equivalent of the Aramaic expression found in 7.13. But in this context it is the prophet who is addressed as **son of man**. This is very different from the passage in 7.13, where someone is described as being "like a son of man." Since Daniel is here addressed in this way, the speaker is stressing his humanity. It is therefore almost identical with the way this expression is used in the Book of Ezekiel, where it occurs ninety-three times. Here FRCL translates "you are only a human being." AT, like TEV, attempts to convey the same idea with "O mortal man," and NRSV has simply "O mortal." Other versions that reject a thoughtless literal rendering of the original are satisfied with "O man" (REB, NJV, and AB).

For the time of the end: the preposition **for** may be translated "concerns" (NIV), "points to" (REB), "relates to" (Mft and AT), or "refers to" (NJV). **The time of the end** will have to be expressed in very differently in other languages. Frequently "the end of the world" will be the most natural equivalent. But other languages may speak of "the final days" or "the time when this world is finished."

8.18   RSV   TEV

    As he was speaking to me, I
fell into a deep sleep with my face

    While he was talking, I fell to the
ground unconscious. But he took

to the ground; but he touched me and set me on my feet.	hold of me, raised me to my feet,

Fell into a deep sleep: this indicates a loss of consciousness but not necessarily what would be considered normal sleep. The verb used refers rather to an unusual, supernatural state of unconsciousness. It is the same root used of Adam in the creation story (Gen 2.21), and it occurs again in Daniel at 10.9. NRSV translates here "fell into a trance." The word "trance" is also used in the NEB/REB rendering.

With my face to the ground: the TEV repetition of "fell to the ground" is curious and illogical here, since this fact was already established in the previous verse. The meaning of the Hebrew seems to be rather that, while already lying face down on the ground as a result of having thrown himself down (verse 17), Daniel was then overcome by the **deep sleep**. NJV, for example, translates "I was overcome by a deep sleep as I lay prostrate on the ground."

Touched me: the context seems to require more than a mere light touch of the hand. NEB has "he grasped me," which is very similar in meaning to the TEV rendering.

Set me on my feet: literally "made me stand on my standing." It is appropriate for a person about to receive an angelic message to be alert and standing to obey orders.

8.19	RSV	TEV

He said, "Behold, I will make known to you what shall be at the latter end of the indignation; for it pertains to the appointed time of the end.	and said, "I am showing you what the result of God's anger will be. The vision refers to the time of the end.

Behold: see verse 15.

What shall be at the latter end of the indignation: the word for **indignation** refers to God's outrage against sin, **the latter end** is literally "in the afterward" and indicates the time when people will be able to see that outrage take effect. In the perspective of the vision, the end of the world is the time when God, in his anger, will punish human beings for their sins. This will be followed by the restoration of the people of God, who will be reconciled with their creator and master after having received their own chastisement. NRSV translates "what shall take place later in the period of wrath."

Appointed: this element seems to be missing from TEV but it is important. **Appointed time** is one word in the Hebrew, often used for fixed dates on a calendar, as for regular feast days, for example. Thus the time of the end of the persecutions is already fixed and definite. Knox reads "be sure the end for them is fixed."

Pertains to: this RSV rendering carries the same meaning as the preposition "for" in verse 17. The whole clause may then be rendered "the vision refers to the time of the end, which God has already established."

8.20	RSV	TEV

As for the ram which you saw with the two horns, these are the kings of Media and Persia.

"The ram you saw that had two horns represents the kingdoms of Media and Persia.

The actual explanation of the vision begins with this verse. The meaning of the text is fairly straightforward, and translators should refer back to the vision itself for the basic vocabulary.

Ram . . . with two horns: see verse 6.

Kings: on the question of "kings" versus "kingdoms," see comments on 7.17.

The kings of Media and Persia: while these two proper names are singular in form, the meaning is, of course, collective, referring to the Persian and Median kingdoms rather than to the individuals who ruled over them. Some languages may speak more naturally of "the kingdoms called Media and Persia," or even "the governments of Media-land and Persia-land."

8.21	RSV	TEV

And the he-goat^q is the king of Greece; and the great horn between his eyes is the first king.

The goat represents the kingdom of Greece, and the prominent horn between his eyes is the first king.

^q Or *shaggy he-goat*

He-goat: in contrast with verse 5, where a single term is used, here the text has both a Hebrew word and the corresponding Aramaic word placed in apposition. For this reason NJV reads "the buck, the he-goat." Since the Hebrew term is from the same family as the word for "hair," certain translations have felt it necessary to say something like "shaggy goat" (NIV) or "hairy he-goat" (NJB). But this is unnecessary since the second term is probably not intended as a description of the animal. It is rather a means of more precise identification. And in any case, to speak of a "hairy goat" may be considered redundant in some languages.

King: since there is reference at the end of this verse to the first king as in a series of kings, the first use of this word seems to signify the "kingdom," that is, the totality of the kings who ruled. Compare also verse 20 and 7.17.

Greece: literally "Javan" as in NJB. But this is clearly the meaning, since Javan is the Hebrew word for Greece, and a transliteration of the Hebrew would hide the meaning from the ordinary reader.

8.22 RSV	TEV
As for the horn that was broken, in place of which four others arose, four kingdoms shall arise from his[r] nation, but not with his power. [r] Theodotion Gk Vg: Heb *the*	The four horns that came up when the first horn was broken represent the four kingdoms into which that nation will be divided and which will not be as strong as the first kingdom.

The structure of RSV is difficult at this point. It may be simplified in the translation by following the TEV model.

As for the horn that was broken: literally "And the broken one." See verse 8.

His nation: literally "a nation." The Hebrew has no possessive pronoun. The RSV reading comes from the ancient versions, but it is not clear which noun the pronoun refers back to. The context requires something like "that nation" (REB) or "the Greek nation" (Mft). This may be done for translation reasons without recourse to the ancient versions to correct the Hebrew text.

But not with his power: this has been amplified in TEV, since the concise expression of the Hebrew reflected in RSV may be difficult for the modern reader to understand. The four kingdoms into which the empire of Alexander the Great was divided did not actually cover all the territory that he had conquered. So the combined power of the four kingdoms would not be as great as that of Alexander.

8.23 RSV	TEV
And at the latter end of their rule, when the transgressors have reached their full measure, a king of bold countenance, one who understands riddles, shall arise.	"When the end of those kingdoms is near and they have become so wicked that they must be punished, there will be a stubborn, vicious, and deceitful king.

NJB, REB, and NRSV set forth as poetic the section beginning here and going through the end of verse 26, because the Hebrew text breaks into a kind of metrical form. But most other versions retain the prose format, since it is questionable whether the kind of meter used in the Hebrew should be so represented.

At the latter end of their rule: this refers to the four successors to Alexander the Great. Two of these kingdoms disappeared from the political scene fairly quickly. But the other two continued for about a century and a half, each directed by its own dynasty. The Ptolemys ruled in Egypt, and the Seleucids in Syria and Babylonia. The writer's main interest, however, is in one particular ruler of the Seleucid dynasty—Antiochus IV Epiphanes.

The transgressors: while the Hebrew literally speaks of **transgressors**, this whole clause is problematic, and the ancient versions have "transgressions" rather than **transgressors**. Since it is unclear who these **transgressors** were, many modern English translations adopt the reading of the ancient versions: "transgressions" (NJV and NRSV), "sins" (NJB), and "crimes" (AT and AB).

Reached their full measure: the idea here is something like "when they have gone as far as they can go in committing sin." Another way of translating this is "when their sin is at its height" (REB). The ancient notion seems to have been that God waited for sin to reach a certain level of gravity before intervening with punishment. Compare Gen 15.16, where the iniquity of the Amorites is said to be incomplete. See also Matt 23.32, where Jesus speaks of the Scribes and Pharisees completing the measure of their ancestors.

A king of bold countenance: literally "of stern faces." This description of the new king who was to come to power seems to focus on his physical appearance. But the appearance of a person is related to his character. The two Hebrew words have been variously translated as "stern-faced" (NIV), "proud faced" (NJB), "defiant" (Mft), "of grim aspect" (REB), "impudent" (NJV).

One who understands riddles: this gives a very inadequate idea of the meaning of the text. NJB has "ingenious-minded man," but this likewise sounds too much like praise. The idea here is one of an evil genius—a thoroughly malicious, spiteful, and devious person. He was seen as a shrewd expert in cunning and deception. NRSV translates "skilled in intrigue." TEV apparently translates this by the two nouns "vicious and deceitful."

Arise: that is, "rise to power" or "take control" or "begin to govern." See 7.17.

8.24	RSV	TEV

His power shall be great,^s and he shall cause fearful destruction, and shall succeed in what he does, and destroy mighty men and the people of the saints.

He will grow strong—but not by his own power. He will cause terrible destruction and be successful in everything he does. He will bring destruction on powerful men and on God's own people.

^s Theodotion and Beatty papyrus of Gk: Heb repeats *but not with his power* from verse 22

His power shall be great: RSV adds a footnote indicating that it follows the Greek text at this point, but that the Hebrew repeats "but not with his power" from the end of verse 22 (see TEV). And many modern versions include these words in translation. Their interpretation, however, is the subject of much debate. GECL interprets the whole passage as meaning "his strength . . . will not be as great as that of his predecessors," but this is unlikely to be the intended meaning. The writer may be attempting to state that the power of the ruler in question, Antiochus Epiphanes, does not rest in himself, but that he is under the authority of God, whether he likes it or not. Mft translates parenthetically "by no force of arms shall he gain his great power." The interpretation of LB ("but it will be satanic strength and not his own") is hardly intended by the author of the text, as the LB footnote would have its readers believe. Translators are advised to formulate a rendering that gives the following idea: "he will gain strength, but not through any power of his own" or "he will become more and more powerful, although it will not be because of his own actions."

He shall cause fearful destruction: or "he will cause amazing devastation." However, NJB slightly alters the text and understands it to mean "he will plot incredible schemes."

Shall succeed in what he does: some other models for this expression are "will be able to do all the things he wants to do" or "anything he starts to do he will complete."

The people of the saints: a veiled reference to the persecution of the Jewish people. See 7.25, 27 and comments. **Of the saints** does not mean "who belong to the saints" but "who are the saints." Note that in this case there is no mention of "the Most High" as in chapter 7. This phrase has been joined more closely to the previous one in the NCV rendering: "he will destroy powerful people and even God's people."

8.25	RSV	TEV
	By his cunning he shall make deceit prosper under his hand, and in his own mind he shall magnify himself. Without warning he shall destroy many; and he shall even rise up against the Prince of princes; but, by no human hand, he shall be broken.	Because he is cunning, he will succeed in his deceitful ways. He will be proud of himself and destroy many people without warning. He will even defy the greatest King of all, but he will be destroyed without the use of any human power.

Cunning: the corresponding Hebrew term usually has a positive sense of "wisdom" or "intelligence," but in this context it can only have a negative meaning, since it is used for destructive purposes. Knox speaks of "crafty scheming."

He will make deceit prosper: or "he will make treachery succeed." Although technically a causative form, most English versions drop the causative idea. The meaning is simply that he will be very effective in the use of deceit.

Under his hand: literally "in his hand." Stylistically there may be an intentional contrast with the expression that follows, "in his heart." The expression really adds nothing to the meaning of the text and is therefore dropped in many versions.

In his own mind he will magnify himself: literally "and in his heart he will grow big." That is, his own evaluation of his importance will be highly exaggerated. This may be expressed in a wide variety of ways in other languages. In those languages that use the word for "heart" as the seat of intelligence (as in Hebrew), it may be possible to preserve the use of this term. Some will say, for example, "his heart will swell up" or, changing the image, "his head will become big."

Without warning: literally, "in security." This word may be taken to mean (1) that the evil king acts without fear of resistance, or (2) that the people destroyed by the king thought they were completely safe. The TOB rendering, "in complete peace," seems to follow the first, while NJV, "taking them unawares,"adopts the second meaning. The translation **without warning** also takes the second meaning as the correct one. This is probably best, but other languages may render it "when they think they are safe . . . ."

The Prince of princes: this literal rendering presents two serious problems. First, the English word "prince" does not mean the ruler himself but rather the son of the ruler, while the Hebrew term always designates a ruler, not at all implying son of a ruler. See verse 11, where the text speaks of the "Prince of the host." Second, this kind of construction is a common Hebrew way of communicating the superlative idea. Compare "king of kings" in 2.37, where TEV translates "the greatest of all kings." And note that the book title "Song of Songs" actually means "The Greatest of All Songs." So this expression should probably be translated "the greatest of all kings" or something similar. But in this case the expression is a euphemism for God himself.

By no human hand: the word **hand** is often used in the Old Testament to indicate power. In most languages it is inadvisable to translate it literally in such contexts.

He shall be broken: in those languages where it is necessary to transform the passive formulation to an active one, it is not recommended that the agent be named. It will probably be better to say something like "he will fall" or "he will suffer punishment." If required, a more radical restructuring may name the agent: "God will break (or destroy) him without the help of any human being."

8.26   RSV   TEV

RSV	TEV
The vision of the evenings and the mornings which has been told is true; but seal up the vision, for it pertains to many days hence."	This vision about the evening and morning sacrifices which has been explained to you will come true. But keep it secret now, because it will be a long time before it does come true."

The vision of the evenings and the mornings: this refers to the evening and morning sacrifices referred to in verse 14 above. But it really involves the time when it would be impossible to offer those sacrifices. In most languages it will be a good idea to make the idea of sacrifice clear again in this verse, as in TEV. Another possibility is "the vision about the time (or about the things that will happen during the time) when people (or the priests) cannot offer the morning and evening sacrifices."

Which has been told: this is almost certainly a reference to the explanation given in verses 15-25. NJV expresses the first part of the verse as follows: "What was said in the vision about evenings and mornings is true." To avoid the passive, translators may consider "The explanation about the morning and evening sacrifices is true" or "You have heard the interpretation of the morning and evening sacrifices. It is true."

Is true: this is a validation of the explanation given in the previous verses. But it also implies that the fulfillment is certain. So instead of ". . . is true," translators may say ". . . will surely happen (or take place)."

Seal up the vision: this is clearly not intended as a permanent sealing up of the truth revealed in the vision. For this reason TEV adds the information "now." Something like this may be required in many other languages. Many languages will have difficulty with the verb "to seal," since there is nothing corresponding in their culture. A seal usually indicated ownership of objects or the authenticity of documents. Sealing was done by means of some sort of stone or other object making an impression in wax or clay. It also was placed on the outside of a closed document so that the document could not be opened and read without breaking the seal. In this context it may be better to say something like "keep the vision secret . . ." as in TEV.

For it pertains to many days hence: this gives the reason for the command to keep the vision secret for the time being. In some languages the words **many days** may suggest a time period that is altogether too short. In place of **days** many will prefer to use "years," although there may be other ways of expressing this idea: "the distant future" (AT and NIV), "the far future" (Mft), "to far-off days" (NJV).

8.27	RSV	TEV
	And I, Daniel, was overcome and lay sick for some days; then I rose and went about the king's business; but I was appalled by the vision and did not understand it.	I was depressed and ill for several days. Then I got up and went back to the work that the king had assigned to me, but I was puzzled by the vision and could not understand it.

I, Daniel: the use of this formula once again serves as a discourse marker showing boundaries in the story. In this case it seems to mark the beginning of the conclusion to this section. Compare verses 1 and 15.

Was overcome: the translation of the Hebrew word here is much disputed, but the context seems to require something like "weak" (NAB), "faint" (AT), "exhausted" (NIV), "my strength failed" (REB). NJB "lost consciousness" goes back to verse 18, where a different word is used.

Rose: since the context clearly shows that recovery from an illness was involved, some languages may find it more natural to say something like "then I got well" or "my health improved." The meaning is not that Daniel got up while he was still sick.

Went about the king's business: since Daniel had obviously taken some time off from work when he received the vision, TEV includes the idea that he "went back to work." It also makes clear that Daniel did not actually replace the king in performing his duties, but simply returned to carrying out the job assigned to him by the king. These refinements may also be helpful in other languages.

Appalled: this seems to be a poor choice of words in English, although it is followed by NIV, NAB, and Mft. The meaning is rather something like "disquieted" (AT), "dismayed" (NJV), or "perplexed" (NEB).

Did not understand it: literally "and there was no one understanding." The two corresponding Hebrew words may be interpreted in three different ways: (1) "I (Daniel) did not understand it (the vision)" (Mft and the majority of English versions); (2) "No one could explain it (the vision)"; this is the solution followed by NJV, REB, and also by NIV when it says "it was beyond understanding"; (3) "No one could understand (why the vision was to be kept secret or why I was so upset)"; this solution is apparently adopted by TOB, which uses the masculine pronoun—such a pronoun in French cannot refer to the word "vision," which is feminine. The first of these three possibilities is the most commonly accepted and the most likely to be the correct understanding of the text. It is unlikely that the text would focus on the inability of others to understand the vision or why it was to be kept secret, since at this point no one else knew about it.

The Revelation from Jeremiah

Daniel 9.1-27

Vision: Daniel ponders Jeremiah's prophecy: 9.1-3

RSV	TEV
	Daniel Prays for His People
1 In the first year of Darius the son of Ahasuerus, by birth a Mede, who became king over the realm of the Chaldeans—2 in the first year of his reign, I, Daniel, perceived in the books the number of years which, according to the word of the LORD to Jeremiah the prophet, must pass before the end of the desolations of Jerusalem, namely, seventy years.	1 Darius the Mede, who was the son of Xerxes, ruled over the kingdom of Babylonia. 2 In the first year of his reign I was studying the sacred books and thinking about the seventy years that Jerusalem would be in ruins, according to what the LORD had told the prophet Jeremiah. 3 And I prayed earnestly to the Lord God, pleading with him, fasting, wearing sackcloth, and sitting in ashes.
3 Then I turned my face to the Lord God, seeking him by prayer and supplications with fasting and sackcloth and ashes.	

TEV Section Heading: Daniel prays for his people.

Another section heading giving less detail can be simply "The prayer of Daniel." This covers verses 1-19 in TEV, but those translators following the outline at the beginning of this Handbook may prefer to place an additional heading at verse 4, where the idea of praying will be more appropriate. In this case the heading here should be "Daniel reflects on what Jeremiah said," or "Daniel thinks about Jeremiah's words," or something similar. It will be noted that NAB has "Gabriel and the seventy weeks," applying to the entire chapter.

Translators who wish to provide a major heading for the entire chapter may use the heading of the outline, "The revelation from Jeremiah," or "Words written by the prophet Jeremiah," or "Jeremiah's words about the years when Jerusalem was to lay desolate."

9.1	RSV	TEV
	In the first year of Darius the son of Ahasuerus, by birth a Mede, who became king over the realm of the Chaldeans—	Darius the Mede, who was the son of Xerxes, ruled over the kingdom of Babylonia.

The first year of Darius: literally "in the year one of Darius." It is understood that this is talking about the first year of the reign of Darius. Since this information is repeated at the beginning of verse 2, it may be left out in one of the two places. TEV elects to omit it here and also slightly restructures the remaining elements. This may be a suitable model for other languages to follow.

According to some commentators the king already named in 5.31 and in chapter 6 is here distinguished from Darius Hystaspes, who began to rule in 522 B.C. and is mentioned in Ezra 4.24. Others point out that **Darius** may be an old Iranian title rather than a proper name. But the translator is required to translate the text as it stands.

Ahasuerus: this is the Hebrew equivalent of the better known Greek name "Xerxes." The Greek form of the name is used in several modern translations including TEV, NIV, AT, and Mft, as well as in the ancient Greek version. NJB, however, has "Artaxerxes." It is recommended that translators use the Greek form "Xerxes" as the basis for transliteration into other languages, since it is better known by people who have studied this history of the area.

Secular history indicates that King Xerxes of Persia was the son of Darius I of Persia. This has given rise to much speculation about the precise identification of the person referred to here. But translators need not try to solve all these problems of identification.

By birth a Mede: literally "of the race of the Medes." These words stress the ethnic background of the Darius under discussion. And in most languages there should be little difficulty in finding a natural equivalent.

Became king: literally "was made king" as in NJV. REB has "was appointed ruler." Because this is the only case in biblical Hebrew where this particular verb form is used, some scholars have felt that the text must be corrected to say **became king**, as in RSV and most other versions. The essential meaning of the two forms is, however, the same. And in languages where the passive is impossible, translators will have to say "became king" in any case. Most translators should not worry about this slight difference.

The realm of the Chaldeans: as in 1.4; 3.8; 5.30, the term **Chaldeans** refers to the better-known "Babylonians" and should be so translated.

9.2   RSV   TEV

in the first year of his reign, I, Daniel, perceived in the books the number of years which, according to the word of the LORD to Jeremiah the prophet, must pass before the end of the desolations of Jerusalem, namely, seventy years.

In the first year of his reign I was studying the sacred books and thinking about the seventy years that Jerusalem would be in ruins, according to what the LORD had told the prophet Jeremiah.

In the first year of his reign: this is a repetition of the information given in the previous verse, but it seems to fit better in this context than earlier.

I, Daniel: as in 8.15, 27, this form seems to mark a new section in the story. Compare also 7.15, 28; 8.1.

Perceived: the verb used here usually means "understand," but this meaning is hardly suitable to the present context. NAB has attempted to adjust to the context by translating "tried to understand," but it is probably better to take the verb in the sense of "was studying" (TEV, NJB) or "carefully considering." There is no problem in understanding the number of years, since this is clearly stated in Jer 25.11-12; 29.10.

The books: the term is used here in the technical sense of the holy books known to Daniel—including the book of the prophet Jeremiah. For this reason it is legitimate to translate "the Scriptures" (AT, REB, NAB, and NIV).

The word of the LORD to Jeremiah: it will be more natural in some languages to say "what the LORD had revealed to Jeremiah" or something similar.

The prophet: while it is true that the prophets of the Old Testament did sometimes foretell the future, this is not the primary focus of the term. What is more important about the function of the prophets is that they communicated to people in behalf of God. Many languages have special terms to refer to the spokesman or herald of a chief. And it is often possible to use this term in an expression meaning "herald (or spokesman) for God" or "one who proclaims God's message." In other languages it is possible to say "a person sent by God." But translators are advised to avoid the idea of "foreteller of the future."

The end of the desolations of Jerusalem: the writer seems to be suggesting that the years of devastation were fulfilling some purpose and had to be completed before any rebuilding could take place. Seventy years was considered the divinely established period (see 2 Chr 36.21). Translators should not, however, give the impression of seventy consecutive years of acts of destruction. Rather, this period should be understood as the time during which Jerusalem remained in a desolate state. REB speaks of "seventy years which . . . were to pass while Jerusalem lay in ruins."

9.3 RSV	TEV
Then I turned my face to the Lord God, seeking him by prayer and supplications with fasting and sackcloth and ashes.	And I prayed earnestly to the Lord God, pleading with him, fasting, wearing sackcloth, and sitting in ashes.

In some languages it will be more natural to restructure this verse in such a way as to place the **fasting and sackcloth and ashes** at the beginning, before the mention of prayer to God, since these actions were started before the prayer began.

Turned my face to the Lord God: a literal rendering of the verb phrase **turned my face** will probably sound strange in many languages. It simply focuses on the beginning of the action of earnestly praying to God. The word for **Lord** here is not the same as in the previous verse. In the tradition of most

English versions the distinction is made in RSV and TEV only by the use of capital letters for *Yahweh* (in verse 2) as opposed to only the initial upper case letter when translating the Hebrew term *'adonai* (as in this verse). The term found here is used both for God and for highly respected human beings—as in Gen 23.6.

By prayer and supplications: these two terms combined simply refer to sincere prayer and not to two different actions. They may be translated by a single verb in many languages. See comment on "supplication" in 6.11.

Fasting: together with the two terms that follow, this indicates Daniel's attitude of humility in his prayer to God. On the term **fasting**, see 6.18.

Sackcloth and ashes: it will be important in most languages to include the appropriate verb with each of these two nouns. **Sackcloth** was worn around the waist, and people usually sat in **ashes** or put them on their heads (or both). In Jewish culture these two practices were ways of showing sadness, either caused by a calamity such as the death of someone (Gen 37.34 and Amos 8.10), or as a sign of distress and repentance for sin committed (Jonah 3.6). The context shows very clearly that in this case it was because of sin, since verse 5 says clearly "we have sinned." Because of the context it may not be necessary to add the information here, that Daniel wore sackcloth and sat in ashes because he was distressed over the sins of Israel, but this will certainly be legitimate if the translators believe it to be necessary here. The term **sackcloth** has sometimes been rendered "a rough, coarse cloth around the waist" (it was usually made of the hair of a goat or camel), and it is important in the translation of **ashes** to be sure that the reader understands the term used as referring to cold ashes and not hot coals.

Daniel prays for his people: 9.4-19

RSV	TEV
4 I prayed to the LORD my God and made confession, saying, "O Lord, the great and terrible God, who keepest covenant and steadfast love with those who love him and keep his commandments, 5 we have sinned and done wrong and acted wickedly and rebelled, turning aside from thy commandments and ordinances; 6 we have not listened to thy servants the prophets, who spoke in thy name to our kings, our princes, and our fathers, and to all the people of the land. 7 To thee, O Lord, belongs righteousness, but to us confusion of face, as at this day, to the men of Judah, to the inhabitants of Jerusalem, and to all Israel, those that are near and those that are far away, in all the lands to which thou hast driven them, because of the treachery which they have committed against thee. 8 To us, O Lord, belongs confusion of face, to our kings, to our princes, and to our fathers, because we have sinned against thee. 9 To the Lord our	4 I prayed to the LORD my God and confessed the sins of my people. I said, "Lord God, you are great, and we honor you. You are faithful to your covenant and show constant love to those who love you and do what you command. 5 "We have sinned, we have been evil, we have done wrong. We have rejected what you commanded us to do and have turned away from what you showed us was right. 6 We have not listened to your servants the prophets, who spoke in your name to our kings, our rulers, our ancestors, and our whole nation. 7 You, Lord, always do what is right, but we have always brought disgrace on ourselves. This is true of all of us who live in Judea and in Jerusalem and of all the Israelites whom you scattered in countries near and far because they were unfaithful to you. 8 Our kings, our rulers, and our ancestors have acted shamefully and sinned against you, Lord.

God belong mercy and forgiveness; because we have rebelled against him, 10 and have not obeyed the voice of the LORD our God by following his laws, which he set before us by his servants the prophets. 11 All Israel has transgressed thy law and turned aside, refusing to obey thy voice. And the curse and oath which are written in the law of Moses the servant of God have been poured out upon us, because we have sinned against him. 12 He has confirmed his words, which he spoke against us and against our rulers who ruled us, by bringing upon us a great calamity; for under the whole heaven there has not been done the like of what has been done against Jerusalem. 13 As it is written in the law of Moses, all this calamity has come upon us, yet we have not entreated the favor of the LORD our God, turning from our iniquities and giving heed to thy truth. 14 Therefore the LORD has kept ready the calamity and has brought it upon us; for the LORD our God is righteous in all the works which he has done, and we have not obeyed his voice. 15 And now, O Lord our God, who didst bring thy people out of the land of Egypt with a mighty hand, and hast made thee a name, as at this day, we have sinned, we have done wickedly. 16 O Lord, according to all thy righteous acts, let thy anger and thy wrath turn away from thy city Jerusalem, thy holy hill; because for our sins, and for the iniquities of our fathers, Jerusalem and thy people have become a byword among all who are round about us. 17 Now therefore, O our God, hearken to the prayer of thy servant and to his supplications, and for thy own sake, O Lord, cause thy face to shine upon thy sanctuary, which is desolate. 18 O my God, incline thy ear and hear; open thy eyes and behold our desolations, and the city which is called by thy name; for we do not present our supplications before thee on the ground of our righteousness, but on the ground of thy great mercy 19 O LORD, hear; O LORD, forgive; O LORD, give heed and act; delay not, for thy own sake, O my God, because thy city and thy people are called by thy name."

9 You are merciful and forgiving, although we have rebelled against you. 10 We did not listen to you, O LORD our God, when you told us to live according to the laws which you gave us through your servants the prophets. 11 All Israel broke your laws and refused to listen to what you said. We sinned against you, and so you brought on us the curses that are written in the Law of Moses, your servant. 12 You did what you said you would do to us and our rulers. You punished Jerusalem more severely than any other city on earth, 13 giving us all the punishment described in the Law of Moses. But even now, O LORD our God, we have not tried to please you by turning from our sins or by following your truth. 14 You, O LORD our God, were prepared to punish us, and you did, because you always do what is right, and we did not listen to you.

15 "O Lord our God, you showed your power by bringing your people out of Egypt, and your power is still remembered. We have sinned; we have done wrong. 16 You have defended us in the past, so do not be angry with Jerusalem any longer. It is your city, your sacred hill. All the people in the neighboring countries look down on Jerusalem and on your people because of our sins and the evil our ancestors did. 17 O God, hear my prayer and pleading. Restore your Temple, which has been destroyed; restore it so that everyone will know that you are God. 18 Listen to us, O God; look at us and see the trouble we are in and the suffering of the city that bears your name. We are praying to you because you are merciful, not because we have done right. 19 Lord, hear us. Lord, forgive us. Lord, listen to us, and act! In order that everyone will know that you are God, do not delay! This city and these people are yours."

Section Heading: Daniel prays for his people.

As indicated at verse 1, this section heading will be more appropriate here if verses 1-3 are a separate section with their own heading. In some languages it will be more natural to say simply "The prayer of Daniel."

9.4   RSV   TEV

I prayed to the LORD my God and made confession, saying, "O Lord, the great and terrible God, who keepest covenant and steadfast love with those who love him and keep his commandments,	I prayed to the LORD my God and confessed the sins of my people. I said, "Lord God, you are great, and we honor you. You are faithful to your covenant and show constant love to those who love you and do what you command.

The prayer in verses 4-19 appears to be composed of phrases taken from older passages of Scripture (especially Deuteronomy, 1 Kings, Ezra, Nehemiah, and Jeremiah). According to some commentators this accounts for the apparently unnecessary repetitions and certain other anomalies in the prayer, such as the shifts from "my" to "our," and from "you" and "your" to "he" and "his."

The wording of verse 4 is almost the same as Neh 1.5, which ultimately comes from Deut 7.21, 9.

The first occurrence of **LORD** (outside the quotation) in this verse represents *Yahweh,* and the second **Lord** (within the quotation) reflects the Hebrew *'adonai,* as in 1.2. Throughout this chapter there is constant switching from one term to the other. The Hebrew *'adonai* is represented by **Lord** in RSV and TEV, while *Yahweh* is written **LORD** (all capital letters). In this chapter we find the Hebrew for **LORD** here and in verses 2, 4, 8 (where RSV and TEV have "Lord"), 10, 13, 14 (twice), and 20. The Hebrew for **Lord** occurs in verses 3, 4, 7, 9, 15, 16, and 17, and three times in verse 19. However, there have apparently been some scribal modifications of the divine names at certain points—especially in verses 8 and 19, where RSV does not follow the standard Hebrew text.

My God: if the first person singular possessive pronoun is understood in the translator's language as indicating exclusive possession, then it may be better to say "our God." Daniel does not intend to convey the idea that Yahweh is his God alone. However, the singular does emphasize a personal relation with God.

Prayed . . . and made confession: the two verbs used here are not intended to highlight two separate activities. The prayer is a prayer of confession. So it will be possible to render the two by an expression like "confessed in prayer," or simply "confessed to God." Some languages require an object for the verb "confess," such as "sins," but it is unnatural to speak of confessing someone else's sins. In such a case it may be necessary to have Daniel identify himself more closely with the sins of the people by saying something like "confess our sin as a people." The idea of confessing may have to be translated "acknowledge our wrong doing" or "admit that we have sinned."

Great and terrible: the word **terrible** has negative connotations in English and does not accurately reflect the idea of immense respect (rather than fear) that is in the original. It has been translated "awesome" (NJV, NIV, NAB and NRSV), "revered" (AT), "to be feared" (NJB), and "we honor you" (TEV).

Keepest covenant: the **covenant** refers to a kind of relationship or agreement between two parties. In this context **covenant** calls to mind the agreement between God and his people. This phrase indicates that God has kept his word and has fulfilled what was expected of him in the relationship. Some languages may translate in this context "you keep your promises," or "you do what you agree to do," or "you fulfill your responsibilities."

Steadfast love: the corresponding term (*chesed*) is one of the more difficult single Hebrew words to translate. It carries the idea of sustained loyalty and love at the same time. Some suggested translations are "constant love" (TEV), "faithful love" (NJB), "unchanging love," or "trustworthy love." This term is used twenty-six times in Psalm 136 (once in each verse) and in Exo 20.6. (There are two important articles dealing with this term in *The Bible Translator*: April 1980, pages 201-207, and July 1985, pages 317-326.)

Many scholars take the combined terms **covenant** and **steadfast love** as a figure of speech in which two words joined by a conjunction are used to describe a single fact. For this reason NIV translates "keeps his covenant of love," and AB has "loyally keep your covenant." Mft speaks of keeping the "compact of kindness."

Him . . . his: the use of third person pronouns when addressing the Lord directly will be very unnatural in many languages. As in TEV (as well as REB, NAB, NRSV, and NJB), they may have to be changed to the second person singular to comply with the style of the receptor language.

Who love . . . and keep . . . commandments: the structure of the Hebrew at the end of this verse is literally "[A] keeping covenant and [B] steadfast love towards [B'] those who love him and [A'] who keep his commandments." Some interpreters see in this what is called a "chiastic" structure: that is, a structure in which the four parts are crossed, so that the first and last parts go together (A and A') and the middle two parts (B and B') are also matched. If this is true, the real meaning is "keeping covenant with those who keep his commandments" (the two words translated "keep" have the same root in Hebrew) and "showing steadfast love toward those who love him" (the two words translated "love" are not the same in Hebrew). But it is also possible to take the whole section as a general affirmation without separating out and restructuring the various parts.

9.5 RSV	TEV
we have sinned and done wrong and acted wickedly and rebelled, turning aside from thy commandments and ordinances;	"We have sinned, we have been evil, we have done wrong. We have rejected what you commanded us to do and have turned away from what you showed us was right.

This verse begins with four parallel verbs followed by a fifth verb that has two dependent nouns. These five affirmations have more or less the same meaning, but it is the piling up of these verbs that results in the strong impact of the verse as a whole, rather than the precise shades of meaning of the individual forms. The following list attempts to show the shades of difference in meaning between these near synonyms:

Sinned (repeated in verses 8, 11, and 15): this is a very common term to indicate a break in a right relationship with God. The basic meaning is that of missing a target (or goal) or losing the way. To sin is to fail to meet God's standards.

Done wrong: only this verb is not found elsewhere in this chapter. It is related to the verb meaning "bend," "twist," or "make crooked." It is the opposite of doing what is right or "straight." In 1 Kgs 8.47 it is used along with two other words in this list and is translated "acted perversely."

Acted wickedly (repeated in verse 15): this term is especially common in the wisdom literature of the Old Testament (Job, Psalms, and Proverbs). It has to do with something that is abnormal, disjointed, or outside the realm of accepted behavior. In some cases it may have to be translated "done what we should not have done."

Rebelled (repeated in verse 9): in the Old Testament people may rebel against unwanted human authority (Gen 14.4; 2 Kgs 18.7) or against divine authority (Num 14.9; Josh 22.16). The same word can be used figuratively of not accepting the light (Job 24.13). To translate this term some languages will use verbs or verbal expressions like "resist," "defy," "show no respect for," or something similar. But it will be important in some cases to make it clear that it is God's authority that the people had challenged. In the context of this prayer, some may translate "we have refused you [God]," or as TEV puts it, "we have rejected what you commanded."

Turning aside . . . (repeated in verse 11): the verb literally carries the idea of turning away from something. It is the two words that follow that make this ordinary word into a more technical expression for disobeying God.

Each of these terms portrays the idea of a break in normal relations between God and his people. If the translator cannot find five different terms more or less equivalent in the receptor language, it is possible to limit the rendering to three or four verbs. But since the cumulative effect is important, it may be worth the effort to try to find an equivalent for each one.

Commandments and ordinances: these two nouns also represent two different ways of talking about the same thing. They may be reduced to a single noun or noun phrase, or they may be rendered separately.

9.6   RSV   TEV

we have not listened to thy servants the prophets, who spoke in thy name to our kings, our princes, and

We have not listened to your servants the prophets, who spoke in your name to our kings, our rulers,

our fathers, and to all the people of   our ancestors, and our whole na-
the land.   tion.

We have not listened: this may be seen as a continuation of the series
of verbs of confession in the previous verse. But it is also a kind of climax. In
some languages a literal rendering of the verb "listen" in the negative will be
misleading. The idea is not that they did not hear the words of the prophets,
but rather that the people failed to follow or obey what they said. Since this
is a prayer of confession addressed to God, those languages distinguishing
between inclusive and exclusive first person plural pronouns should definitely
use the exclusive forms throughout this passage.

Thy servants the prophets: on the word for **prophets** see verse 2 above.
It will be acceptable in some languages to say simply "your prophets." The
word **servants** indicates that the prophets are in the service of God, and the
pronoun "your" may fulfill the same function.

In thy name: this may be translated "in your behalf" or "for you."

Our princes: this is a general term for "chief," "ruler," or "leader"
(civilian or military) and does not mean sons of a king in Hebrew.

Our fathers: this expression is not to be taken literally but rather refers
to "our ancestors." Compare also 2.23.

All the people of the land: this expression is all-inclusive and is intended
to designate especially the ordinary citizen in opposition to the leaders of the
nation (**kings, princes**, and others).

9.7   RSV   TEV

To thee, O Lord, belongs righteous-   You, Lord, always do what is right,
ness, but to us confusion of face, as   but we have always brought dis-
at this day, to the men of Judah, to   grace on ourselves. This is true of
the inhabitants of Jerusalem, and to   all of us who live in Judea and in
all Israel, those that are near and   Jerusalem and of all the Israelites
those that are far away, in all the   whom you scattered in countries
lands to which thou hast driven   near and far because they were
them, because of the treachery   unfaithful to you.
which they have committed against
thee.

The structure of this verse and of the two following is unusual in English
and perhaps in many other languages. Each of these verses begins with "To
. . . ." By shifting the pronominal expression (**To thee**) forward to the beginning
of the sentence, it is given special importance or emphasis. In some languages
the same effect may be achieved by the use of emphatic pronouns or some
other device stressing such prominence.

Lord: this translates *'adonai* and not *Yahweh*. See comments on verses
3 and 4 above.

Belongs righteousness: literally, "to you Yahweh righteousness" (with no verb, since the verb "to be" is understood). As in the case of the Aramaic equivalent in 4.27, the noun translated **righteousness** conveys the idea of "justice" or "acting correctly." And some experts feel that the idea of salvation is also an important element in this context and should be clearly stated. As indicated in *Harper's Dictionary of the Bible,* "righteousness also refers to God's saving actions . . . . In the Dead Sea Scrolls and its 'teacher of righteousness,' God's righteousness offers hope for redemption from sin" (page 871). If translators decide to choose this option, NJB, which speaks of "saving justice," provides a possible model. The word **belongs** is not found in the Hebrew but was supplied by the RSV translators. The point is that God has been true to his covenant promise to Israel, but that they have failed him shamefully. The whole idea may be translated by a verbal expression in many languages. Some possible models in addition to TEV are "you are righteous" (NIV) and "justice (right, righteousness) is on your side" (NAB, REB, NRSV).

But to us: this marks a very strong contrast in Hebrew coming after **to thee** at the beginning of this verse. It will be possible in some cases to say something like "but as for us, we," using emphatic pronouns.

Confusion of face: the word here rendered **confusion** is translated elsewhere in RSV as "shame" (Psa 44.16), and this is much closer to the meaning in modern English. NRSV translates here "open shame." The term has to do with a feeling of disgrace. And in some languages it will be necessary to say something about what has caused their shame: "as for us, we are terribly ashamed because of what we have done." Some languages may be able to retain something of the terminology used in Hebrew with "for our part, we have lost face."

As at this day: most understand this to mean "even to this (very) day" (NAB, NJV and AB). REB has "now as ever." In some languages it may be possible to leave this unstated, or else implied, as in TEV "This is true . . . ," but only if to state it would be unnatural.

To the men of Judah: the singular noun translated **men** has a collective meaning and does not refer exclusively to the male sex. It will have to be translated "people of Judah" in most languages. It may also be more natural in some languages to change the order of this phrase and of the two phrases **to the inhabitants of Jerusalem, and to all Israel**. And instead of **all Israel** some languages will require "all the rest of Israel" or "all the other Israelites," since the **men of Judah** and **inhabitants of Jerusalem** were also a part of the whole people of Israel.

Those who are near and those that are far away: this phrase is based on 1 Kgs 8.46 (also found in Isa 57.19 and Jer 25.26). And in the context of this verse it is another way of saying "all Israel," focusing on those who were able to remain in the land (**those who are near**) and those who were forced to go into exile (**those who are far away**). According to some scholars this seems to indicate that the original author of this part of Daniel was in Jerusalem and not in Babylon or Susa (Lacocque, page 183). Only a Judean author would have been able to affirm in these terms that the dispersion was a divine punishment.

Because of the treachery which they have committed against thee: in the original the noun **treachery** and the verb, meaning "to commit treason," have the same root. This kind of construction is very frequent in Hebrew. In those languages that use similar constructions naturally in such a context, the form of the original may be reflected in the translation. The basic meaning of the verb "commit treason" and the noun "treachery" involves acting in an unfaithful manner and thereby breaking a relationship. The violation of the covenant relationship with God is the ultimate act of treason. Some languages may say something like "because they have broken the agreement and destroyed their relationship with you" or "because they have not kept faith with you."

9.8   RSV   TEV

To us, O Lord, belongs confusion of face, to our kings, to our princes, and to our fathers, because we have sinned against thee.	Our kings, our rulers, and our ancestors have acted shamefully and sinned against you, Lord.

This verse is largely a repetition of the previous one. It should be noted, however, that the third person plural pronoun "they" at the end of verse 7 becomes a first person plural (**we**) in this verse, so that Daniel identifies himself more closely with those who have sinned.

Confusion of face: see comments on the previous verse.

Our fathers: that is, "our ancestors," as in verse 6 above.

We have sinned: the same as the first verb in verse 5.

9.9   RSV   TEV

To the Lord our God belong mercy and forgiveness; because we have rebelled against him,	You are merciful and forgiving, although we have rebelled against you.

To the Lord our God: since this is a prayer addressed to God, it will be advisable in most languages not use the third person forms as in the original. If the structure of RSV is retained, it will be necessary to say something like "to you, O Lord our God." Note that TEV shortens this considerably.

Mercy and forgiveness: the first of these two nouns refers concretely to the intestines (often translated "bowels" in KJV). For the Israelites this was considered the seat of the emotions of goodness, love, and affection. The two terms together speak of compassion that forgives wrongs.

Because: this conjunction in RSV gives the wrong impression that the rebellion and sin of the people of Israel were the cause of God's mercy. But it is rather in spite of their disobedience that God forgave them. It is therefore advisable to use a connecting word like "although" (TEV), "even though" (NIV), or "since" (NJV). In other languages translators may prefer to begin a completely new sentence using the words "In spite of that."

Rebelled: see verse 5.

Against him: this verse and the following one speak of God in the third person singular, but in verses 8 and 11 Daniel addresses him in the second person. Such changes of grammatical person are not unusual in Hebrew, but they do not indicate that the writer is passing from dialogue (here a prayer) to narrative. Since Daniel is praying directly to God, it will be unnatural in most languages to use a third person pronoun here. It is much more natural to say "against you." Compare verse 4b.

9.10 RSV	TEV
and have not obeyed the voice of the LORD our God by following his laws, which he set before us by his servants the prophets.	We did not listen to you, O LORD our God, when you told us to live according to the laws which you gave us through your servants the prophets.

Have not obeyed: while the verb used here is literally "listened," in this context it has to do with obedience or actually following the instructions that one hears. In many languages the equivalent for "listen" naturally carries the sense of obedience; but in other languages where this is not the case, RSV provides a better model than TEV.

The voice of the LORD our God: or, more naturally, "your voice, O LORD our God," since the prayer is being made directly to the Lord. And in many languages it will be more natural to say "have not obeyed you" rather than "obeyed your voice."

His . . . he . . . his: as in verse 4 and the end of the previous verse, these third person pronouns should be changed to second person in the context of the prayer to God.

Which he set before us: or "which he communicated to us," or simply "gave us" (NAB and NIV, as well as TEV).

By: literally "through the hand of." This is the Hebrew equivalent of "by means of."

His servants the prophets: see verse 6 above.

9.11 RSV	TEV
All Israel has transgressed thy law and turned aside, refusing to obey thy voice. And the curse and oath which are written in the law of Mo-	All Israel broke your laws and refused to listen to what you said. We sinned against you, and so you brought on us the curses that are

ses the servant of God have been poured out upon us, because we have sinned against him. written in the Law of Moses, your servant.

All Israel: that is, all the people of Israel.

Turned aside: see verse 5. The verb is used here in parallel with **transgressed** (violated or broken).

Thy law: the use of the singular to refer to the whole range of God's commands may be natural in some languages, but in others the plural form will be required.

Obey thy voice: see verse 10 on the expression as a whole. And note the comment in the previous verses on the pronoun usage and on the terms "listen" and "obey."

The curse and oath: this is another case of the figure of speech where two Hebrew nouns joined by "and" are used to convey a single idea. It has been rendered "the sworn malediction" (NAB, AB), "the curse embodied in the oath" (AT), and "the curse . . . which was solemnly threatened" (Mft). Since the terms **curse** and **oath** are singular in the Hebrew, the TEV plural "curses" may be seen as a translation of both. Many languages will not have two different terms to use here that have approximately the same meaning. On the curses referred to, see Deut 27.14-26 and 28.15-68.

Which are written in the law of Moses: since the passive form may be troublesome to some translators, this may be rendered "which the Law of Moses talks about," "which the Law of Moses describes," or possibly even "which we can read in the Law of Moses."

The servant of God: or "your servant, O God," which will probably be more natural in the context of this prayer. Compare verse 6, where the prophets are also specifically described as God's servants.

Have been poured out upon us: this is obviously figurative language. The image of pouring curses may not be at all natural in many languages. In English it has been rendered "rained down on us" (REB) and "vented on us" (Mft), but these are still figurative and may not be helpful in other languages. In some cases translators may prefer to say "caused to fall on us" or simply "made happen to us."

The whole second sentence of this verse can possibly be restructured as follows: "So because of our disobedience, you have caused us to receive the curses that are described in the Law of Moses, your servant."

9.12	RSV	TEV

He has confirmed his words, which he spoke against us and against our rulers who ruled us, by bringing upon us a great calamity; for under the whole heaven there has not You did what you said you would do to us and our rulers. You punished Jerusalem more severely than any other city on earth,

been done the like of what has been
done against Jerusalem.

He: since Daniel is praying to the Lord, the use of the third person pronoun will once again be clumsy in most languages. See the earlier notes on pronoun usage in Daniel's prayer.

Confirmed his words: some other ways of expressing this idea are "fulfilled all that he said" (NEB), "made good the warning" (REB), "fulfilled his word" (AT), "carried out the threat" (NJV; similarly NJB, NAB, and Mft).

Our rulers who ruled us: literally "the judges who judged us." This is the same word as used for the leaders in the Book of Judges (2.16-18). But as in the case of the Book of Judges, the sense of the term is far larger than its simple judicial meaning. It has to do with governing or leading in its broadest sense. Here the redundant statement may be expressed more naturally in most languages by omitting the words **who ruled us**.

A great calamity: in Hebrew, literally "a great evil."It is clear that the reason for what happened to Jerusalem was punishment for the sins of the people. Therefore TEV has restructured by substituting the verb "punished." The usage in the following two verses supports this translation.

Under the whole heaven: here this expression is used to indicate universality. It is almost the same expression as the Aramaic equivalent in 7.27. Compare also Job 28.24; 41.11. In some languages the equivalent is "in the whole world."

Been done: this passive idea occurs twice at the end of this verse and will have to be translated actively in many languages. The agent of the activity (punishment) is clearly God himself.

9.13	RSV	TEV
	As it is written in the law of Moses, all this calamity has come upon us, yet we have not entreated the favor of the LORD our God, turning from our iniquities and giving heed to thy truth.	giving us all the punishment described in the Law of Moses. But even now, O LORD our God, we have not tried to please you by turning from our sins or by following your truth.

As it is written in the law of Moses: or "as the Law of Moses says." Compare verse 11. Note that TEV takes this clause and the next as the completion of the sentence begun in verse 12.

Calamity: as in the previous verse, "punishment."

Yet; most languages will require a rather strong contrastive conjunction or expression here. In spite of the divine punishment, the people of Israel failed to respond properly. In addition to the TEV model, translators may consider "even so" (NJB), "nevertheless," or "but in spite of that."

We have not entreated the favor of: literally "we have not softened the face of," meaning to appease, placate, or mollify. This phrase is used with either God or human beings as the object, and it occurs in Psa 119.58 and 2 Chr 33.12, among other places. Translators should look for a verb meaning "appeased" (NAB, NJB), or "sought the favor of" (NIV), or "tried to please" (TEV) in their language. The addition of the negation **not** indicates an intentional refusal. In some languages people speak of "cooling the heart" or "causing the heart to sit down." But others may be able to retain the image of the face found in Hebrew, even though the expression may be something like "calming the face" or "brightening the face."

Giving heed to thy truth: the verb used here evokes the idea of "concentrating one's attention" to a particular object or task, or "examining with care." The Hebrew noun translated **truth** has as its primary component of meaning the idea of firmness or solidity. The **truth** is a firm reality on which a person may count and which does not deceive. In this verse there is no question of abstract intellectual truth but of a firm decision made by God. NAB speaks of God's "constancy," and AB of "his resoluteness." REB has "that you are true to your word." It will be possible in some languages to translate "your will." Some languages may require a restructuring of the last part of this verse along the following lines: "but we have not yet stopped committing sin. We still fail to acknowledge your firm attachment to the truth." Or, as REB has it, "we have neither repented of our wrongful deeds, nor remembered that you are true to your word."

9.14 RSV TEV

RSV	TEV
Therefore the LORD has kept ready the calamity and has brought it upon us; for the LORD our God is righteous in all the works which he has done, and we have not obeyed his voice.	You, O LORD our God, were prepared to punish us, and you did, because you always do what is right, and we did not listen to you.

Once again this verse speaks of God in the third person, and this will have to be transposed into the second person in many languages for the sake of naturalness and clarity.

Therefore: the Hebrew has only the simple conjunction most often translated "and." TEV leaves it untranslated. However, several English versions see the need of a strong transition word here. AT and Mft follow RSV with "Therefore," NJV has "Hence," while NAB and REB have "So."

Kept ready the calamity: the verb here is usually translated "watched" in the sense of keeping a vigil. The phrase appears to be quoted from Jer 1.12; 31.28; 44.27, where the LORD is said to "watch over them to pluck up and break down, to overthrow, destroy, and bring evil" (Jer 31.28). NJB retains the idea of "watching" as it renders "Yahweh has watched for the right moment to bring disaster on us." NEB also focuses on this element with "the LORD has been biding his time and has now brought this calamity on us."

Righteous: see the discussion of **righteousness** in verse 7.
Obeyed his voice: see verses 10 and 11.

9.15	RSV	TEV

And now, O Lord our God, who didst bring thy people out of the land of Egypt with a mighty hand, and hast made thee a name, as at this day, we have sinned, we have done wickedly.	"O Lord our God, you showed your power by bringing your people out of Egypt, and your power is still remembered. We have sinned; we have done wrong.

And now: this transition is frequently used at the opening of a new thought or a new section. Here it marks the beginning of Daniel's supplication, or appeal for mercy, following his confession in verses 5-14. In some languages a paragraph break may serve to communicate the same meaning. An identical transition is used at the beginning of verse 17, but in that case it seems to mark a less prominent transition.

Who didst bring thy people out of the land of Egypt: this is a reminder of the single most dramatic evidence of God's mercy to the people of Israel. A new act of deliverance would not only free the Jews again, but would also be a vindication of God's own reputation (see verse 19).

With a mighty hand: as seen elsewhere in Daniel and other books of the Old Testament, the **hand** stands for power, and it is often better translated in this way. Compare 2.38 and 3.15.

Hast made thee a name: that is, God gained a good reputation among people. NJV has "winning fame for Yourself." Another way of stating this is "you made your name known to many peoples."

As at this day: the idea here is that, even up to the time that the writer penned these words, people remembered and spoke of God's intervention. TEV attempts to convey this by concluding the sentence with "is still remembered." REB has "winning for yourself a name that lives on to this day."

Sinned . . . done wickedly: the two verbs (the same as the first and third in the list found in verse 5 above) are not intended to describe two different actions. Rather they are expressions more or less the same in meaning and describing essentially the same event. In many languages it may be more natural to begin the last sentence of this verse with a contrastive conjunction like "but." The first part of the verse speaks of people remembering the powerful display of God's deliverance from Egypt, while commission of sin in the second part surely stands in contrast with such remembrance.

9.16	RSV	TEV

O Lord, according to all thy righteous acts, let thy anger and thy	You have defended us in the past, so do not be angry with Jerusalem

wrath turn away from thy city Jerusalem, thy holy hill; because for our sins, and for the iniquities of our fathers, Jerusalem and thy people have become a byword among all who are round about us.

any longer. It is your city, your sacred hill.[q] All the people in the neighboring countries look down on Jerusalem and on your people because of our sins and the evil our ancestors did.

[q] SACRED HILL: *Mount Zion (see Zion in Word List).*

Note that TEV sees no need to repeat the address, **O Lord**, found in the original and reflected in RSV. Naturalness in the translation will have to determine how frequently such forms are repeated.

According to all thy righteous acts: **righteous acts** is literally "righteousnesses," the same term as in verse 7. The basis of the plea for mercy is the faithful actions of the past. Daniel is reminded of the way in which God previously intervened in favor of his people, and he requests that he be moved by the same sentiments once again. Some other renderings are "saving deeds" (NEB) or "vindicating deeds" (AB). See comments on "righteousness" in verse 7.

Thy anger and thy wrath: the two words in Hebrew mean virtually the same thing, and they reinforce each other. It is quite possible in many languages to translate them by a single noun, or a noun modified by an adjective, as in "violent anger," "fierce anger" (AB), or "wrathful fury" (NJV).

Thy holy hill: this refers to Mount Zion, the hill on which the Temple was constructed in Jerusalem, and by extension it refers to the city itself. It is therefore in apposition with **thy city Jerusalem**, which comes just before it in the text. The term for **hill** or "mountain" is often associated with deities in ancient Israel and among neighboring peoples. If in the translator's culture hills are bound with other themes that are different and contradictory, translators are advised to speak here of a "holy place" or "the place where you (God) manifest yourself."

A byword: in the traditional English versions the term **byword** translates several different Hebrew words (see Deut 28.37; Job 17.6; 30.9; Psa 44.14). The term used here comes from a verbal root meaning "reproach" and indicates something or someone that is mocked or made fun of by others. Some modern renderings are "mockery" (NJV), "reproach" (NAB and AT), "derision" (Mft), "objects of scorn" (NJB and NIV).

A possible reformulation of the whole verse is:

> O Lord, in the past you demonstrated your faithfulness to Israel, so now please stop being angry with the city of Jerusalem. It belongs to you, and it is on the hill where sacrifice is made. All the other tribes (people) who live around us despise your city and your people because of the sins of our ancestors and because of our sins also.

9.17 RSV	TEV
Now therefore, O our God, hearken to the prayer of thy servant and to his supplications, and for thy own sake, O Lord,[t] cause thy face to shine upon thy sanctuary, which is desolate.	O God, hear my prayer and pleading. Restore your Temple, which has been destroyed; restore it so that everyone will know that you are God.

[t] Theodotion Vg Compare Syr: Heb *for the Lord's sake*

This verse contains two vocative expressions that are widely separated in RSV. In many languages it may be advisable to combine **O our God** at the beginning of the verse with **O Lord**, which is found toward the end. It may be more natural to say "O Lord our God" toward the beginning of the verse.

Now therefore: literally "and now" as in NJB. This is the same transition word used at the beginning of verse 15. But here it seems to make a less prominent transition from the condition of the people, verse 16b, to the appeal in verse 17.

The prayer of thy servant . . . his supplications: here Daniel refers to himself in the third person in order to show his submission to God (compare 2.4, where the wise men speak of themselves in this way before the king). But in most languages such a third person reference in this context would only confuse the reader. It will be better to say "hear my prayer, for I am your servant" or something similar.

For thy own sake, O Lord: the traditional Hebrew text has "for the Lord's sake" at this point, making the statement indirect rather than direct discourse. But several ancient versions read as RSV, "for your own sake, Lord," and this is followed by many other modern translations. This may be done because of translation principles if not for textual reasons. If the traditional reading is followed, the meaning will be something like "so that people may know that you are the Lord" or "for your benefit, Lord." This is the interpretation followed by TEV, but for some unknown reason "God" is substituted for **Lord**. This change, however, is not recommended.

Cause thy face to shine upon: this unusual idiomatic expression is familiar because of the well-known benediction in Num 6.25. The idea is to "look with favor on" (NIV) or "deal kindly with" (AB). NJB attempts to retain something of the form of the original with the expression "let your face smile again on," and a very similar turn of phrase is used by Mft, but somehow these sound a bit unnatural.

Thy sanctuary: as in 8.11, 13, 14, this refers to the Temple, and in most languages it is probably advisable to say this clearly.

Which is desolate: that is, "which has been devastated" or "which is in ruins."

9.18 RSV TEV

O my God, incline thy ear and hear; open thy eyes and behold our desolations, and the city which is called by thy name; for we do not present our supplications before thee on the ground of our righteousness, but on the ground of thy great mercy.

Listen to us, O God; look at us and see the trouble we are in and the suffering of the city that bears your name. We are praying to you because you are merciful, not because we have done right.

Incline thy ear and hear: literally "give your ear and hear." This double expression is clearly parallel to the following double expression, **open thy eyes and behold**. The two together are the equivalent of "please listen attentively and please look carefully." Compare 2 Kgs 19.16. In those languages that require an object for the verbs "listen" and "look," the meaning to be conveyed is "listen to us" and "look at our troubles."

Our desolations, and the city which is called by thy name: these two expressions, joined by the conjunction "and," do not refer to two different things that God is asked to look at, but to the city of Jerusalem that is in ruins. The idea **which is called by your name** may be conveyed in some languages by "which belongs to you."

Present our supplications: this expression focuses on the pleading nature of the requests made to God. See also comments on verse 3 above as well as 6.11.

On the ground of: or "on the basis of," or "because of." This expression occurs twice. The first time it is negative in form, indicating that Daniel does not presume to make his request in behalf of the people of Israel because of their good deeds. The basis of the request is rather God's goodness and mercy. FRCL translates "we are not counting on our merits but on your infinite love." The order of these two elements may have to be reversed (as in TEV) for the sake of naturalness in some languages. Translators may consider "it is because you are merciful that we make this plea, not because we are good," or "we beg you to do this because we know that you are very compassionate, and not because we think we are just."

9.19 RSV TEV

O Lord, hear; O Lord, forgive; O Lord, give heed and act; delay not, for thy own sake, O my God, because thy city and thy people are called by thy name."

Lord, hear us. Lord, forgive us. Lord, listen to us, and act! In order that everyone will know that you are God, do not delay! This city and these people are yours."

This verse constitutes a summary and conclusion to the prayer that started in verse 4. The threefold repetition of **O Lord** in RSV (following the Hebrew) may be unnatural in some languages and should therefore be reduced to one or two occurrences. The verbs **hear** and **give heed** are parallel, as are **forgive** and **act**. Since Daniel is praying in behalf of the people of Israel, it may be more natural in many languages to say "hear us," "give heed to us," and possibly even "act for us."

For thy own sake: see verse 17.

My God: the singular possessive is not intended to be exclusive. If it is likely to be understood in this way in the language of translation, some kind of adjustment will be required. See verse 4.

Thy city and thy people are called by thy name: the expression **are called by thy name** simply means that the city of Jerusalem and the nation of Israel have been chosen by God and belong to him. See verse 18.

Explanation: Gabriel explains the prophecy: 9.20-27

RSV

TEV

Gabriel Explains the Prophecy

20 While I was speaking and praying, confessing my sin and the sin of my people Israel, and presenting my supplication before the LORD my God for the holy hill of my God; 21 while I was speaking in prayer, the man Gabriel, whom I had seen in the vision at the first, came to me in swift flight at the time of the evening sacrifice. 22 He came and he said to me, "O Daniel, I have now come out to give you wisdom and understanding. 23 At the beginning of your supplications a word went forth, and I have come to tell it to you, for you are greatly beloved; therefore consider the word and understand the vision.

24 "Seventy weeks of years are decreed concerning your people and your holy city, to finish the transgression, to put an end to sin, and to atone for iniquity, to bring in everlasting righteousness, to seal both vision and prophet, and to anoint a most holy place. 25 Know therefore and understand that from the going forth of the word to restore and build Jerusalem to the coming of an anointed one, a prince, there shall be seven weeks. Then for sixty-two weeks it shall be built again with squares and moat, but in a troubled time. 26 And after the sixty-two weeks, an anointed one shall be cut off, and shall have nothing; and the people of the prince who is to come shall destroy the city and the sanctuary. Its end shall come with a flood, and to the end there shall be war; desolations are decreed. 27 And he shall make a strong covenant with many for one week; and for half of the week he shall cause sacrifice and offering to cease; and upon the wing of abominations shall come one

20 I went on praying, confessing my sins and the sins of my people Israel and pleading with the LORD my God to restore his holy Temple. 21 While I was praying, Gabriel, whom I had seen in the earlier vision, came flying down to where I was. It was the time for the evening sacrifice to be offered. 22 He explained, "Daniel, I have come here to help you understand the prophecy. 23 When you began to plead with God, he answered you. He loves you, and so I have come to tell you the answer. Now pay attention while I explain the vision.

24 "Seven times seventy years is the length of time God has set for freeing your people and your holy city from sin and evil. Sin will be forgiven and eternal justice established, so that the vision and the prophecy will come true, and the holy Temple will be rededicated. 25 Note this and understand it: From the time the command is given to rebuild Jerusalem until God's chosen leader comes, seven times seven years will pass. Jerusalem will be rebuilt with streets and strong defenses, and will stand for seven times sixty-two years, but this will be a time of troubles. 26 And at the end of that time God's chosen leader will be killed unjustly. The city and the Temple will be destroyed by the invading army of a powerful ruler. The end will come like a flood, bringing the war and destruction which God has prepared. 27 That ruler will have a firm agreement with many people for seven years, and when half this time is past, he will put an end to sacrifices and offerings. The Awful Horror will be placed on the highest

248

who makes desolate, until the decreed end is poured out on the desolator."

point of the Temple and will remain there until the one who put it there meets the end which God has prepared for him."

TEV Section Heading: "Gabriel explains the prophecy"

If a more detailed section heading is preferred, translators may consider "Gabriel explains about the seven times seventy years" or "The seventy weeks are explained." The heading will depend on how the text is translated, especially in verses 24 and 25.

9.20	RSV	TEV

While I was speaking and praying, confessing my sin and the sin of my people Israel, and presenting my supplication before the LORD my God for the holy hill of my God;

I went on praying, confessing my sins and the sins of my people Israel and pleading with the LORD my God to restore his holy Temple.

While I was speaking and praying: this does not refer to two different actions. Compare "while I was speaking in prayer" in the following verse. The two expressions are slightly different, but the meaning is identical. Here, however, it is better to understand the word translated **While** as meaning "I was still speaking" or something of this nature, focusing on the continuity of the action of the verb. Otherwise this verse will not be a complete sentence.

Confessing my sin: see comments on "confession" in verse 4.

Presenting my supplication: see comments on this expression in verse 18.

The LORD my God: on the use of the first person singular possessive pronoun, see comments on verses 4 and 19 above.

The holy hill: this, of course, refers to the hill on which the Temple was located. But the prophet is not simply praying for the mound of earth. He is praying about the Temple and, in this context, its restoration in particular.

9.21	RSV	TEV

while I was speaking in prayer, the man Gabriel, whom I had seen in the vision at the first, came to me in swift flight at the time of the evening sacrifice.

While I was praying, Gabriel, whom I had seen in the earlier vision, came flying down to where I was. It was the time for the evening sacrifice to be offered.

While I was speaking in prayer: this is only slightly different from the initial clause in the previous verse, but here it sets the stage for the appearance of Gabriel.

The man Gabriel: the writer does not intend to deny that Gabriel is an angel, but he focuses on the fact that Gabriel looked like a man. When Gabriel is first introduced it was said that he was **one having the appearance of a man** (see 8.15). Consequently, AB translates "the manlike Gabriel." It is also possible to say "the angel Gabriel, who looked like a man." Perhaps because of the danger of misunderstanding a literal rendering, TEV has chosen to leave this information out.

Had seen . . . at the first: the idea here is simply "had seen previously." Some other ways of translating this are "had originally seen" (NJB) and "had already seen" (REB).

In swift flight: according to some interpreters, the traditional Hebrew text here can only mean "wearied in weariness," but this is not very meaningful in the present context. Most others read it as "flying in flight," and this is taken to mean "in rapid flight."

The time of the evening sacrifice: this is a reference to the daily schedule of sacrifices in the Temple, which consisted of one in the morning and one in the late afternoon (see Exo 29.38-41; Num 28.4; 1 Kgs 18.29, 36). If the word **evening** is understood as referring to the period after dark, it will be necessary to select a different word indicating the time just before the sun sets.

9.22	RSV	TEV
	He came[u] and he said to me, "O Daniel, I have now come out to give you wisdom and understanding.	He explained, "Daniel, I have come here to help you understand the prophecy.

[u] Gk Syr: Heb *made to understand*

He came and he said: literally "he explained (caused to understand) and he spoke to me and he said." This series of three verbs having almost the same meaning in the Hebrew is reduced to two in the ancient Greek and Syriac versions, where the object pronoun is also lacking. NJB, like RSV, indicates in a note that it follows these ancient versions. But such a redundant expression can be simplified for translation reasons without recourse to textual decisions. Some languages, however, will definitely require the object pronoun.

O Daniel: the use of the proper name marks the beginning of the interpretation provided by Gabriel.

Come out: this verb has been translated in a variety of ways: "come down" (NJB); "come forth" (NJV and AB); "now come" (NAB and NIV). There is no special emphasis on movement from inside to outside, as the RSV rendering may suggest. But if it is necessary to say where the angel comes from, translators can say "from heaven."

Wisdom and understanding: the context makes it clear that this does not refer to general knowledge and discernment. It refers in particular to enlightenment concerning the prophecy of Jeremiah mentioned in verse 2 above. Note that TEV makes this clear.

At the beginning of your supplications a word went forth, and I have come to tell it to you, for you are greatly beloved; therefore consider the word and understand the vision.	**When you began to plead with God, he answered you. He loves you, and so I have come to tell you the answer. Now pay attention while I explain the vision.**

At the beginning of your supplications: or "When you started to pray," or better, "As soon as you began your petition" (AB). In many languages it will be appropriate to indicate that the pleading or petition was made "to God."

A word went forth: this literal rendering of the Hebrew does not really convey the meaning of the text. The meaning is rather "an answer (to the supplications) was given" (NAB and NIV). Others may say "a message was sent out." In order to avoid a passive construction, translators may say "he (God) gave an answer."

I have come to tell it to you: HOTTP/CTAT recommends a Hebrew text that does not include the object pronoun, **to you**. But both RSV and TEV (as well as NIV) include it. It is worthy of note that TOB, which is normally very close to the recommendations of HOTTP/CTAT, has the object pronoun in this case. In the some languages such a pronoun may be required for the sake of naturalness regardless of the textual decision.

You are greatly beloved: literally "you are preciousness." The Hebrew word carries the idea of affection or profound attachment of someone to another person or thing. To avoid a passive formulation it may be better to say "he (God) loves you very much." Or it will not be too far from the meaning to say "you are like a precious treasure (to God)."

Consider the word: the **word** here is God's word, or answer, earlier in this verse (**a word went forth**), which was given to explain the prophecy of Jeremiah. The meaning of this expression is something like "pay attention to the answer," or "listen carefully the response that God has given," or taken together with the words **understand the vision**, which is parallel, "make an effort to understand the answer."

The vision: while the prophecy of Jeremiah is not normally considered a vision, it is a kind of revelation from God, and the use of this word here indicates that for Daniel it was in the same category as the visions. It was the means by which God revealed something to Daniel. It may legitimately be translated "revelation" (AD).

"Seventy weeks of years are decreed concerning your people and your holy city, to finish the transgression, to put an end to sin, and to atone for iniquity, to bring in	"Seven times seventy years is the length of time God has set for freeing your people and your holy city from sin and evil. Sin will be forgiven and eternal justice estab-

everlasting righteousness, to seal both vision and prophet, and to anoint a most holy place.

lished, so that the vision and the prophecy will come true, and the holy Temple[r] will be rededicated.

ʳ Temple; *or* altar.

Verses 24-27 are written in a kind of rhythmic prose and are set off as poetry by NJB and NAB. But this is not recommended to translators unless poetry is the normal form for this kind of discourse.

Seventy weeks of years: literally "seventy sevens" or "seventy weeks." Verse 2, quoting Jeremiah, speaks of "seventy years." When Gabriel speaks of **seventy weeks**, he is clearly not suggesting periods of seven days, but seven years per week, or 490 years. This must somehow be expressed in the translation, since the modern reader will certainly not understand a literal rendering. Some see in the wording of TEV a change in the focus of the original and suggest that it would be better to say "a period of seventy times seven years" as in FRCL. This would show more clearly the relationship to the prophecy of Jeremiah.

Are decreed: the verb used here does not occur elsewhere in the Old Testament, but it does appear in other Jewish literature, and the meaning is clearly "to decide" or "resolve." The passive form may be rendered actively with God as subject. It is God who has decreed or decided the time period in question. Note TEV "the length of time God has set."

Your people and your holy city: the possessive pronoun **your** appears to refer to Daniel in this context. While it seems proper to say **your people**, it seems odd to say **your holy city**, although some commentators indicate that this shows the extent to which Daniel, as representative of the people of Israel, was revered by the supposed author or editors. Some have suggested the following model translation: "the people to whom you belong and the holy city where you live." But this would be a contradiction, since Daniel was living in Babylon, and **holy city** refers to Jerusalem. It may be best to omit the possessive pronoun in the second case and translate simply "the holy city" as in FRCL and GECL.

Finish the transgression: the traditional written text has "to seal the transgressions" (NJB "placing a seal on sin"). But another tradition indicated in the margin of the manuscripts by ancient Jewish scholars proposes a different reading. This tradition is what RSV and most other English versions follow. It appears that at some point a scribe may have introduced an error. However, it is possible that the verb "seal" was used in the sense of "putting an end to" sin. Since the two Jewish textual traditions can have virtually the same meaning, the translator should not be unduly concerned about the problem. What is important is to avoid a literal rendering of the verb "to seal" that will very likely mislead the reader. But it may also be important in some language to avoid the impression that the people are being given permission to keep on sinning until they have finished the action. The idea is to put a stop to sin immediately.

To put an end to sin: this has essentially the same meaning as the statement before it (**to finish the transgression**) and the one that follows (**to atone for iniquity**). Just as words and expressions for sin were piled up in verse 5, here there is a piling up of phrases involving the elimination of sin. The cumulative effect is important.

To atone for iniquity: literally "to eliminate sin." The verb used here is frequent in Leviticus (see, for example, Lev 4.20; 14.18-21). It evokes the idea of the ritual by which the priest atones for and "covers" sin. That is, he eliminates it by means of pardon. It is not a question of "expiation" in the sense of the guilty party being punished in order to be considered acquitted of his wrongdoing.

To bring in everlasting righteousness: or "to establish eternal justice." It will be suitable in many languages to make the real subject explicit by saying something like "that God will set up eternal justice."

To seal: if this means "to seal up" or "to hide away" as in 8.26, then it will be very difficult to make sense of this verse. The other two elements given here are positive and in the nature of fulfillment. There are two different textual traditions at this point, one meaning "seal" and the other meaning "fulfill" or "put an end to." The latter is followed by FRCL, but most English versions follow the meaning "seal," which may be understood in the sense of "ratify." This is the verb found in REB, NAB, Mft, and NJV. AT and AB use the verb "confirm," which gives essentially the same idea.

Both vision and prophet: while the second of these nouns is literally **prophet**, the context seems to require that it be taken to mean "prophecy"—the prophet's message—and it should be so translated.

A most holy place: literally "a holy of holies." This may refer to the altar, to the Temple in general, or to the high priest ("the most holy place," or "the most holy thing," or "the most holy person"). Although some scholars understand 1 Chr 23.13 to refer to Aaron, the High Priest, as "the most holy one," this is not generally accepted and should not trouble the translator here. Most versions that make the meaning of this verse clearer have "the Most Holy Place" (NEB) or "the holy Temple" (TEV). Here Gabriel is probably referring to the ceremony of reconsecration of the Jerusalem sanctuary after the place had been profaned by Antiochus Epiphanes (see 8.14). But intentional ambiguity cannot be ruled out. The reestablishment of the priesthood would coincide with the restoration of the altar and the Temple. Perhaps the writer had all three in mind. But if the translator must choose, then it is probably better to speak of the Temple.

9.25 RSV	TEV
Know therefore and understand that from the going forth of the word to restore and build Jerusalem to the coming of an anointed one, a prince, there shall be seven weeks.	Note this and understand it: From the time the command is given to rebuild Jerusalem until God's chosen leader comes, seven times seven years will pass. Jerusalem will be

Then for sixty-two weeks it shall be built again with squares and moat, but in a troubled time.	**rebuilt with streets and strong defenses, and will stand for seven times sixty-two years, but this will be a time of troubles.**

Know: it will be considered strange if not impossible in some languages to use the imperative of the verb "to know." In some cases this can be avoided by saying "I want you to know . . ." or "I would like for you to be aware of this . . . ." But others will choose a different verb such as "learn" (NCV) or "note" (TEV).

Therefore: this RSV rendering is much stronger than the ordinary conjunction in the original. It is left untranslated by NAB, NJV, NIV, as well as TEV. And this is certainly justifiable.

From the going forth of the word: that is, from the time the order is given. This is a reference to the prophecy pronounced by Jeremiah (see comments on verse 2).

An anointed one, a prince: here the word **prince** refers to a ruler or leader, and not the son of a ruler, which is the normal meaning of the English rendering. Compare 8.25 and comments. The word translated **anointed one** is the origin of our term "Messiah," and it evokes the idea of consecration. But in the present context it is not used with all the theological meaning that the word "Messiah" has in Christian thought. Some scholars have identified this "anointed one" with Cyrus the Great, who is in fact called "the LORD's anointed one" in Isa 45.1, and who did permit the first Jews to go back to Jerusalem. Others think that it is Zerubbabel, who is referred to by messianic titles in Haggai 2 and Zechariah 4. But the most likely candidate is Jeshua, the son of Jehozadak, who was a high priest during this period (see Ezra 2.2, 36 and Neh 7.7, 39). This man is referred to as Joshua in Hag 1.1 and Zech 6.11. In any case, this information should only be given in a footnote if at all, and the rendering should be ambiguous enough to be applied to any of the candidates. Some English versions use capital letters in the text as a way of indicating that this term refers to Christ (NIV), and others translate "Messiah" (NASB), but neither of these solutions is recommended.

Seven weeks: the expression used here means seven periods of seven years each. On the meaning of **weeks** see the previous verse. Since it may sound strange in some languages to say "seven times seven years," it is legitimate to make the calculation and render the whole expression as "forty nine years." However, it may be preferable to retain the number "seven" as a number signifying completeness for the Jews.

Sixty-two weeks: again the word **weeks** indicates a period of seven years. Hence the TEV rendering "seven times sixty-two years." However, in keeping with the discussion of the previous verse, it may be better to say "sixty-two times seven years." In those languages where this is unnatural, it will be possible to say "four hundred and thirty-four years." But many feel that this is too direct and precise in the context of an apocalyptic vision, in which the number "seven" plays a symbolic role.

It shall be built: the pronoun refers to the city of Jerusalem, and the passive construction as a whole may be rendered actively by means of an indefinite subject: "they shall rebuild the city."

With squares and moat: the Hebrew equivalent of the first of these two words usually designates a "plaza" or a space just inside the city gate, used as a forum, a market, and place for deciding court cases. But here it may be taken in the more general sense of "streets" (NAB, NIV, AB, as well as TEV). The second word, rendered **moat** by RSV, is literally the word for "cut" and refers to a trench cut into the rock on the exterior walls of a city in order to make the wall a more difficult obstacle for those who would attempt to attack from the outside. This is the only time in the Old Testament where the word is used in this sense. It is translated "ramparts" by NJB and more generally as "strong defenses" in TEV.

In a troubled time: given the present context, the translation of this expression will probably have to conserve a certain amount of vagueness, but in some languages it may be necessary to state who will experience the trouble. If this is the case, translators may consider saying "at a time when God's people will be troubled" or ". . . when God's people will suffer."

9.26 RSV	TEV
And after the sixty-two weeks, an anointed one shall be cut off, and shall have nothing; and the people of the prince who is to come shall destroy the city and the sanctuary. Its end shall come with a flood, and to the end there shall be war; desolations are decreed.	And at the end of that time God's chosen leader will be killed unjustly.ˢ The city and the Temple will be destroyed by the invading army of a powerful ruler. The end will come like a flood, bringing the war and destruction which God has prepared.

ˢ *One ancient translation* unjustly; *Hebrew unclear.*

The Hebrew text of verses 26 and 27 is uncertain and obscure in several places.

After the sixty-two weeks: instead of repeating the actual time period from the previous verse, it is possible to make a more general reference to this period, as in TEV "at the end of that time."

An anointed one: see verse 25.

Shall be cut off: the verb translated **cut off** is not used previously in Daniel but is frequent elsewhere in the Old Testament. In some contexts it means "excommunicated from the people of God." But here and in many other places it means "be put to death" or "be destroyed" (Gen 9.11, for example). Also, where necessary the passive formulation may be made active by using something like "disappear" (NJV) or simply "die."

And shall have nothing: these words have given rise to a great deal of guesswork as to what the writer really meant. KJV translated them "but not for himself." Other interpretations are (1) "leaving no one to succeed him" (AT and Mft); (2) "when the city is no longer his" (NAB and AB); (3) "with no one to take his part" (NEB); (4) "and vanish" (NJV); (5) "unjustly" (TEV); and (6) "his Kingdom still unrealized" (LB). This wide variety of possible translations simply shows that no one knows what this passage means. Nevertheless the translator is forced to make a choice. The textual change proposed by NAB and AB is quite appealing. The translator can therefore possibly translate the idea "when he does not possess the city."

The people of the prince who is to come: in this context the word translated **people** refers to "troops" or "soldiers," as in Judges 5.2 and 2 Sam 10.13. NJV rightly translates "the army of a leader."

Its end shall come with a flood: literally "his (or its) end is a flood." It is unclear what the intended antecedent of the pronoun is. It can be either the leader with his invading army or the city with its sanctuary. If the latter interpretation is adopted, it may be necessary to translate "they (the city and the sanctuary) will come to an end like a flood" or "the city with its Temple will be destroyed as in a flood." The **flood** is to be understood figuratively and not in its literal sense. The former interpretation, which is perhaps more likely, can be rendered as in NJB, "The end of that prince will be catastrophe." This solution is also preferred by NJV and FRCL.

To the end there shall be war: this will have to be reworded in a number of languages, and in some cases it will be necessary to state more specifically the meaning of **the end**. A possible model is "war will continue until the end of that period of time [referring to the sixty-two weeks]."

Desolations are decreed: in a number of languages it will be necessary to reformulate this passive expression and make it clear that it is God who decreed the destruction.

9.27   RSV   TEV

And he shall make a strong cove-nant with many for one week; and for half of the week he shall cause sacrifice and offering to cease; and upon the wing of abominations shall come one who makes desolate, until the decreed end is poured out on the desolator."

That ruler will have a firm agree-ment with many people for seven years, and when half this time is past, he will put an end to sacrifices and offerings. The Awful Horror[t] will be placed on the highest point of the Temple and will remain there until the one who put it there meets the end which God has prepared for him."

[t] THE AWFUL HORROR: *A pagan image set up in the Jerusalem Temple by*

foreign   conquerors   (see   1 Macc 1.54-61).

He: the pronoun refers to the ruler or leader mentioned in the previous verses. In view of the confusion in verse 26, it may be a good idea to make this clear in the translation, as in TEV.

A strong covenant: the meaning is very likely that the leader will make a binding agreement with other groups of people in order to strengthen his position. Some other renderings are "make a firm league" (NEB) and "strike a firm alliance" (NJB). AT, however, understands this to mean that "the covenant will be abandoned by many." This interpretation is not recommended.

With many: other versions understand this to mean "with the mighty" (NEB). But it is generally agreed that it means "many peoples."

One week . . . half of the week: once again the meaning of the word for **week** is a period of seven years. Some prefer to translate the second time reference as "in the middle of the 'seven' (years)" (NIV). Compare NEB "the week half spent." The problem of "weeks" in this case may be avoided by saying more generally "half of the time" or "in the middle of the period." But in the first occurrence of **week** it is unavoidable and should probably be rendered "seven years."

Cause sacrifice and offering to cease: both nouns are singular in form but have a collective meaning and should be translated by a plural in many languages. The term translated **sacrifice** involves the killing of animals in the worship of God, while the word for **offering** relates to giving of such things as grain, wine, and oil. In 167 B.C. the Jews were forbidden to practice their religion, and the sacrificing of animals was especially prohibited (compare 8.11 and comments).

The end of this verse is very obscure, and a variety of corrections of the text have been proposed. A literal rendering of the Hebrew text yields something like "on the wing abominations desolations until the end and what was decreed is poured on the desolator." Obviously it requires some ingenuity to make sense of this text without relying on textual changes.

Upon the wing of abominations: the words are badly connected in RSV and the meaning is unclear. The word translated **wing** is understood in TEV as referring to the pinnacle, or highest point, of the Temple. NAB, NIV, and NJB adopt a similar solution. (Compare Matt 4.5.) Others understand it to mean "at the corner of the altar" (NJV) or "in the train of these abominations" (NEB). The idea of the "wing" or "pinnacle" of the Temple is probably best here.

In Hebrew the two words meaning **abominations** and **desolations** are placed side by side. This proximity has given birth to the expression "the abomination that makes desolate" found in 11.31, and the nearly identical Hebrew expression in 12.11. Compare these two passages. Compare also Matt 24.15.

Until the decreed end is poured out: on the image of "pouring out" anger or punishment, see comments on verse 11. The **decreed end** is the end decided by God. This may have to be stated directly, as in TEV.

In view of all the problems listed above, the following wording may be suggested:

> For one seven-year period that leader will make a steadfast agreement with many peoples. For half of that time he will abolish all sacrifice and offering. And he will put something very terrible on the high point of the Temple, and it will remain there until God does away with him (who placed it there), just as he has planned.

The Great Vision:
The Man Dressed in Linen

Daniel 10.1–12.4

Vision: The One Dressed in Linen: 10.1–11.2a

RSV

TEV

Daniel's Vision by the Tigris River

1 In the third year of Cyrus king of Persia a word was revealed to Daniel, who was named Belteshazzar. And the word was true, and it was a great conflict. And he understood the word and had understanding of the vision. 2 In those days I, Daniel, was mourning for three weeks. 3 I ate no delicacies, no meat or wine entered my mouth, nor did I anoint myself at all, for the full three weeks. 4 On the twenty-fourth day of the first month, as I was standing on the bank of the great river, that is, the Tigris, 5 I lifted up my eyes and looked, and behold, a man clothed in linen, whose loins were girded with gold of Uphaz. 6 His body was like beryl, his face like the appearance of lightning, his eyes like flaming torches, his arms and legs like the gleam of burnished bronze, and the sound of his words like the noise of a multitude. 7 And I, Daniel, alone saw the vision, for the men who were with me did not see the vision, but a great trembling fell upon them, and they fled to hide themselves. 8 So I was left alone and saw this great vision, and no strength was left in me; my radiant appearance was fearfully changed, and I retained no strength. 9 Then I heard the sound of his words; and when I heard the sound of his words, I fell on my face in a deep sleep with my face to the ground. 10 And behold, a hand touched me and set me trembling on my hands and knees. 11 And he said to me, "O Daniel, man greatly beloved, give heed to the words that I speak to you, and stand upright, for now I have been sent to you." While he was speaking this word to me, I stood up trembling. 12 Then he said to me, "Fear not, Daniel, for from the first day that you set your mind to understand and

1 In the third year that Cyrus was emperor of Persia, a message was revealed to Daniel, who is also called Belteshazzar. The message was true but extremely hard to understand. It was explained to him in a vision. 2 At that time I was mourning for three weeks. 3 I did not eat any rich food or any meat, drink any wine, or comb my hair until the three weeks were past. 4 On the twenty-fourth day of the first month of the year I was standing on the bank of the mighty Tigris River. 5 I looked up and saw someone who was wearing linen clothes and a belt of fine gold. 6 His body shone like a jewel. His face was as bright as a flash of lightning, and his eyes blazed like fire. His arms and legs shone like polished bronze, and his voice sounded like the roar of a great crowd. 7 I was the only one who saw the vision. Those who were with me did not see anything, but they were terrified and ran and hid. 8 I was left there alone, watching this amazing vision. I had no strength left, and my face was so changed that no one could have recognized me. 9 When I heard his voice, I fell to the ground unconscious and lay there face downward. 10 Then a hand took hold of me and raised me to my hands and knees; I was still trembling. 11 The angel said to me, "Daniel, God loves you. Stand up and listen carefully to what I am going to say. I have been sent to you." When he had said this, I stood up, still trembling. 12 Then he said, "Daniel, don't be afraid. God has heard your prayers ever since the first day you decided to humble yourself in

259

humbled yourself before your God, your words have been heard, and I have come because of your words. 13 The prince of the kingdom of Persia withstood me twenty-one days; but Michael, one of the chief princes, came to help me, so I left him there with the prince of the kingdom of Persia 14 and came to make you understand what is to befall your people in the latter days. For the vision is for days yet to come."

15 When he had spoken to me according to these words, I turned my face toward the ground and was dumb. 16 And behold, one in the likeness of the sons of men touched my lips; then I opened my mouth and spoke. I said to him who stood before me, "O my lord, by reason of the vision pains have come upon me, and I retain no strength. 17 How can my lord's servant talk with my lord? For now no strength remains in me, and no breath is left in me."

18 Again one having the appearance of a man touched me and strengthened me. 19 And he said, "O man greatly beloved, fear not, peace be with you; be strong and of good courage." And when he spoke to me, I was strengthened and said, "Let my lord speak, for you have strengthened me." 20 Then he said, "Do you know why I have come to you? But now I will return to fight against the prince of Persia; and when I am through with him, lo, the prince of Greece will come. 21 But I will tell you what is inscribed in the book of truth: there is none who contends by my side against these except Michael, your prince. *[Chapter 11:]* 1 And as for me, in the first year of Darius the Mede, I stood up to confirm and strengthen him.

2 "And now I will show you the truth.

order to gain understanding. I have come in answer to your prayer. 13 The angel prince of the kingdom of Persia opposed me for twenty-one days. Then Michael, one of the chief angels, came to help me, because I had been left there alone in Persia. 14 I have come to make you understand what will happen to your people in the future. This is a vision about the future."

15 When he said this, I stared at the ground, speechless. 16 Then the angel, who looked like a human being, reached out and touched my lips. I said to him, "Sir, this vision makes me so weak that I can't stop trembling. 17 I am like a slave standing before his master. How can I talk to you? I have no strength or breath left in me."

18 Once more he took hold of me, and I felt stronger. 19 He said, "God loves you, so don't let anything worry you or frighten you."

When he had said this, I felt even stronger and said, "Sir, tell me what you have to say. You have made me feel better."

20-21 He said, "Do you know why I came to you? It is to reveal to you what is written in the Book of Truth. Now I have to go back and fight the guardian angel of Persia. After that the guardian angel of Greece will appear. There is no one to help me except Michael, Israel's guardian angel. *[Chapter 11:]* 1 He is responsible for helping and defending me. 2 And what I am now going to tell you is true."

TEV Section Heading: Daniel's vision by the Tigris River

In contrast with the headings at 7.1 and 8.1, the TEV heading here tells nothing about the content of the vision but focuses on its location. To make it more parallel to the others, it is possible to say something like "The vision of the man dressed in linen." Compare the NIV Study Bible heading, "Daniel's vision of a man." NJB entitles this section simply "The great vision," while NAB has "Vision of the Hellenistic Wars."

If translators follow the pattern of the Handbook outline, there will be both a major heading for the two chapters and a subheading for the vision itself, 10.1–11.2a. To avoid useless repetition in the subheading, the major heading can be simply "The great vision" or "Daniel has an important vision." Or the major heading can include the information about the man dressed in linen, and the subheading can be shortened to "The vision," "This is what Daniel dreamed," or "Daniel dreamed this."

This third vision is by far the longest one; with its explanation it continues to chapter 12. Chapter 10 contains the first part of the vision, while the second part is found in chapter 12. Chapter 11 is therefore seen by some writers as breaking up the actual vision by giving a long description of the historical events in which the people of Israel were involved, including the period of the Persian Empire (at the end of the 6th century B.C.) and the time of Antiochus Epiphanes (until about 165 B.C.).

10.1 RSV TEV

In the third year of Cyrus king of Persia a word was revealed to Daniel, who was named Belteshazzar. And the word was true, and it was a great conflict. And he understood the word and had understanding of the vision.

In the third year that Cyrus was emperor of Persia, a message was revealed to Daniel, who is also called Belteshazzar. The message was true but extremely hard to understand.[u] It was explained to him in a vision.

[u] but extremely hard to understand; *or* and it was about a great war.

In the third year of Cyrus king of Persia: the ancient Greek translation reads "In the first year of King Cyrus," but modern English versions do not follow this reading. Compare 7.1 and comments.

A word was revealed: this clearly refers to more than a single word (KJV has "a thing"). Mft translates "a revelation was made." In some languages it may be wise to follow the TEV model and translate "a message was revealed"; but in those cases where passive forms cause difficulties, it will be better to restructure the sentence and say "a revelation came to Daniel" (REB), "God revealed a matter to Daniel," or something similar. Translators should understand that the **word . . . revealed** and the **vision** mentioned at the end of this verse are not identical. The vision came later in order to explain the revelation.

Who was named Belteshazzar: see 1.7; 2.26; 4.8. In order to avoid the passive, it is fitting to say "whom the king had named Belteshazzar."

The word was true: literally "the word was sealed." In ancient times the use of a seal was a guarantee that a document was legitimate. It served to confirm the truth of what was contained in the writing. So this phrase emphasizes the fact that what God revealed to Daniel was authentic. If **word** is translated "message" earlier, then the same rendering should probably be used again to insure that the reader understands that the reference is to the "word that was revealed."

And it was a great conflict: the meaning of the two Hebrew words translated by this clause is unclear. Some have taken them as a description of the war waged by the angels in verses 12-21 at the end of the chapter. They have thus been translated "it concerned a great war" (NIV) or "it concerned a great conflict" (NRSV). While this meaning is certainly possible, it is more likely that the two difficult words refer to the struggle involved in understanding the message. These words may be taken, as in TEV, to mean that the matter revealed to Daniel required a real mental struggle to understand; that is, it was extremely difficult to comprehend. REB translates "yet only after much struggle (did understanding come to him in the course of the vision)." And NJV renders the same expression "it was a great task (to understand the prophecy)."

He understood the word and had understanding of the vision: this literal rendering of the original is not very natural in English. The meaning is stated more clearly in the following renderings: "he paid heed to the revelation and understood the vision" (Mft); "understanding came to him through the vision" (NJV); "He paid attention to the oracle, so that he understood the revelation" (AB).

This verse is clearly different from what follows, since Daniel is here referred to by a third person singular pronoun. In the verses that follow, the first person singular pronoun is used. For this reason some early editions of TEV placed this verse within parentheses. But this is not necessary. It will be sufficient to set it off as a separate paragraph, as in the later editions of TEV and in most other versions.

10.2   RSV   TEV

In those days I, Daniel, was   At that time I was mourning
mourning for three weeks.   for three weeks.

In those days: that is, "at that time." This presumably refers to the time established at the beginning of the chapter.

I, Daniel: see 7.15, 28; 8.1, 15, 27.

Mourning: this term does not indicate that one of Daniel's close relatives had died. Among the Jewish people mourning rituals were practiced, not only at the death of a relative, but also during times of national crisis. The same rituals were sometimes performed with the purpose of showing repentance and asking God to pardon national sins (see 9.3), or as a kind of spiritual preparation to receive a revelation from God (compare Exo 34.28). A more detailed explanation of what the mourning practices were is given in the following verse. Here it seems that Daniel's actions were intended to prepare himself for the understanding of God's revelation. Some other translations of this verb are "doing. . . penance" (NJB), "afflicted myself" (AB) and "had been very sad" (NCV). In those languages where the verb "mourn" is used exclusively of the action that follows the death of relatives or close friends, another verb should be chosen.

For three weeks: literally "three weeks of days." The added information "of days" in Hebrew is important in the overall context of the Book of Daniel. In contrast with the "weeks of years" in chapter 9, here it is ordinary seven-day weeks that are intended. Further, this precision shows that it was not "approximately three weeks" but precisely three full weeks or twenty-one days. NJV, Mft, and NAB express this clearly by translating "three full weeks." AT and REB have the same idea, with "three whole weeks."

10.3 RSV	TEV
I ate no delicacies, no meat or wine entered my mouth, nor did I anoint myself at all, for the full three weeks.	I did not eat any rich food or any meat, drink any wine, or comb my hair until the three weeks were past.

Ate no delicacies: the word here rendered **delicacies** is literally "bread of delightfulness." It has been variously translated "agreeable food" (NJV); "tasty food" (NJV); "choice food" (NIV and REB); "savory food" (NAB); "appetizing food" (AT); "rich food" (TEV and NRSV). Most languages will have a way of describing pleasant food in contrast with ordinary food taken merely to stay alive. Perhaps there is even a deliberate contrast here with "bread of affliction" (Deut 16.3).

No meat or wine entered my mouth: a literal rendering may be unnatural in some languages, since it may give the impression that the meat and wine could act of their own will. Some languages will require two separate verbs as in TEV, but some other models are "never tasted flesh or wine" (Mft) and "took no meat or wine" (NAB). This mourning was not a matter of fasting as such but of the refusal of certain types of food and drink that were normally much sought after and considered a luxury.

Nor did I anoint myself at all: the idea of anointing in this context is that of using perfumed oil on the hair and face. It has nothing to do with anointing in the religious sense of consecration to God, but rather relates to ordinary care for skin and hair. TOB translates "did not perfume myself"; NIV says "I used no lotions at all." Note that TEV renders the same expression "did not . . . comb my hair." Compare the rendering of the same kind of expression in the New Testament in Matt 6.17, for example.

10.4 RSV	TEV
On the twenty-fourth day of the first month, as I was standing on the bank of the great river, that is, the Tigris,	On the twenty-fourth day of the first month of the year I was standing on the bank of the mighty Tigris River.

The actual vision of Daniel begins with this verse. Verses 2 and 3 should be seen as preparation for the vision but not as a part of the vision itself.

The first month: this does not refer to the month of January, as may be understood in many languages. The first month in the Jewish calendar is Nisan, which corresponds approximately to mid-March to mid-April in our present system. According to some commentators the dating is significant because of the two great celebrations, Passover and Unleavened Bread (Exo 12.1-20), which occurred during this month. These celebrations were associated with Israel's past deliverance, and Daniel is thinking about future deliverance of his people. This information can be given in a footnote. It is also wise to provide the reader with a complete table of Old Testament calendar systems along with other readers' helps or as a part of the glossary. Good models for this are provided in NJB (page 2076) or in the footnote at Exo 12.4 in the *NIV Study Bible* (pages 102-103), although permission from the copyright holder is required to simply copy such tables.

That is, the Tigris: this is taken by some commentators as a later addition to the text. But since the "great river" in the Old Testament is usually the Euphrates (see, for example, Josh 1.4), this clarification is necessary for translation reasons in any case. The Hebrew name for this river is *Hiddekel* (as in KJV here and at Gen 2.14), but most versions adopt the better known Persian name "Tigris."

10.5	RSV	TEV

RSV	TEV
I lifted up my eyes and looked, and behold, a man clothed in linen, whose loins were girded with gold of Uphaz.	I looked up and saw someone who was wearing linen clothes and a belt of fine gold.

Lifted up my eyes: this expression in English will normally indicate a movement of the eyes from looking downward toward the ground to a position straight ahead. However, the Hebrew idiom simply indicates that Daniel began the action of looking carefully, intently. The translation should avoid giving the impression that he began looking up into the sky. See comments on "raised my eyes" in 8.3, where the same Hebrew verb is used. The imagery that follows is very similar to that found in chapters 2 and 3 of Ezekiel.

Behold: see comments on 2.31 and 4.10.

Clothed in linen: that is, "wearing clothing made of linen." The biggest problem for most translators, however, will be the rendering of the word **linen**. This refers to a white cloth material made from the fibers of flax (see *Fauna and Flora,* pages 119-121) and known for its strength and relative coolness. In those areas where flax is unknown, translators may have to use a more generic expression such as "fine white cloth." Note that this expression appears again in 12.6 and 7.

His loins were girded: this archaic English expression reflects the Hebrew original, which conveys the idea "his waist was encircled." But this is probably better expressed "with a belt . . . around his waist," as in NRSV and many other English versions.

With gold of Uphaz: the word translated **Uphaz** is usually taken as a proper name referring to an otherwise unknown place where gold was found (see also Jer 10.9). However, the Hebrew text is uncertain here, and many scholars take this as a scribal error for "Ophir" (NEB/REB, AT, and Mft), which is mentioned in 1 Kgs 9.28. A few Hebrew manuscripts, in fact, have this reading. Still other scholars suggest that **Uphaz** is a misspelling of the Hebrew word for "refine" (*muphaz*) and should therefore be translated "pure" or "fine" as in 1 Kgs 10.18 and Song 5.11. This is the solution of NJB, NAB, NJV, and NIV, as well as TEV, and is commended to translators.

10.6	RSV	TEV
	His body was like beryl, his face like the appearance of lightning, his eyes like flaming torches, his arms and legs like the gleam of burnished bronze, and the sound of his words like the noise of a multitude.	His body shone like a jewel. His face was as bright as a flash of lightning, and his eyes blazed like fire. His arms and legs shone like polished bronze, and his voice sounded like the roar of a great crowd.

This entire verse contains one simile after another. Except for the last one, which refers to sound rather than appearance, they all have in common the fact that they are visually dazzling and radiant. If possible it is good to find a series of verbs of similar meaning such as "glowed . . . shone . . . flamed . . . glittered." (REB).

Like beryl: the body as a whole is, first of all, compared to the precious stone called **beryl** in RSV. Other English versions render this stone as "chrysolite" (NAB and TOB) or "topaz" (Mft, AT, and NEB/REB). The exact identity and qualities of this stone are uncertain, but the focus here is on its brightness and not its color. This jewel was one of the twelve stones in the high priest's breastplate (Exo 28.20) and is also mentioned as a part of the wall in the heavenly Jerusalem (Rev 21.20). Where such gemstones are unknown, it will probably be wise to use a more general term such as "jewel" or "valuable stone" in this context.

Like the appearance of lightning: the face of the man in the vision is compared to **lightning**. Since this is something that people all over the world know about, there is usually no problem in translating the word. However, in some languages it will be important to add a verb to make the image more forceful and natural. Some will say that his face "dazzled (or shone) like lightning" or that it "looked as bright as lightning."

Like flaming torches: the man's eyes are compared to **flaming torches**, which are also well known and present few problems. Here also the addition of a verb may make the translation more natural and interesting. For example, one may say that the man's eyes "sparkled like flaming torches" or that they "blazed like fire."

Like the gleam of burnished bronze: the arms and legs are compared to **bronze**, which is a shiny alloy of copper and tin. The word **burnished** indicates that the metal has been brightened or polished (KJV, TEV).

The sound of his words simply refers to the sound one heard when he spoke. TEV represents this with "his voice sounded," and other variations are possible.

Like the noise of a multitude: the voice of the one in the vision is compared to the uproar made by a large crowd of people. Knox translates "when he spoke, it was like the murmur of a throng."

Verses 5 and 6 apparently served as the inspiration for the formulation of the descriptions in Rev 1.13-15; 2.18; 19.12.

10.7 RSV	TEV
And I, Daniel, alone saw the vision, for the men who were with me did not see the vision, but a great trembling fell upon them, and they fled to hide themselves.	I was the only one who saw the vision. Those who were with me did not see anything, but they were terrified and ran and hid.

I, Daniel: see verse 2 as well as the earlier references.

Vision: the word thus translated here differs very slightly from the usual word for a "vision," and some commentators feel that the difference is intentional because it refers, not to an internal impression on the imagination, but to a real (although extraordinary) external display. For this reason some versions render it differently: "the sight" (AB); "the apparition" (NJB). Most versions, however, make no such distinction.

Alone: this qualifies the verb **saw** and is not intended to describe Daniel's circumstances as a whole. As the context indicates, there were others with him, but he was the only one to see the vision. Note the similarity of this account with the experience of Paul recorded in Acts 9.

The men who were with me: NRSV revises this to "the people who were with me," while REB has "those who were near me." There is no special emphasis on the maleness of those accompanying Daniel at this point.

A great trembling fell upon them: the context seems to suggest that this fearful reaction may have occurred before the vision actually fully appeared. So in some languages it may be necessary to make this clear by saying something like "at the very beginning of the vision, they were very frightened" or "before I actually saw the vision, the men ran away and hid because they were very much afraid." In some languages the way of expressing great fear will be quite idiomatic: "their stomachs were up high," "their livers were agitated," or "they saw great terror."

They fled to hide themselves: the purpose of their running away was to hide. Some will say, however, "they ran away and concealed themselves."

10.8   RSV   TEV

So I was left alone and saw this great vision, and no strength was left in me; my radiant appearance was fearfully changed, and I retained no strength.

I was left there alone, watching this amazing vision. I had no strength left, and my face was so changed that no one could have recognized me.

So: as a result of the others running away, Daniel found himself all alone. The particular transition word to be used in the translation will be determined by a consideration of what is most natural in such a context as this.

Saw: the translation should avoid giving the impression that Daniel saw something new at this point. He kept on looking (or gazing) at what had already begun to take place.

Great vision: the adjective should not focus so much on the size or length of the vision as on the impression it made on Daniel. In some languages translators may prefer to say something like "this fantastic sight" or "this astounding revelation." Knox translates "this high vision."

No strength was left in me: this has essentially the same meaning as **I retained no strength** at the end of the verse. In many languages it will probably be awkward style to repeat the idea.

My radiant appearance was fearfully changed: more literally "my splendor . . . ," referring to Daniel's appearance, which was radically altered. Since the most obvious manifestation of a person's appearance is seen on the face, several versions have translated this term using the word "face": "my face turned deathly pale" (NIV). But REB renders the phrase "I became a sorry figure of a man." And NJB has "my appearance was changed and contorted."

Was fearfully changed: literally "was overturned upon me to destruction." The Hebrew expression suggests the idea of passing from life to death. NIV renders the last part of the verse "my face turned deathly pale," and NAB has "I turned the color of death."

10.9   RSV   TEV

Then I heard the sound of his words; and when I heard the sound of his words, I fell on my face in a deep sleep with my face to the ground.

When I heard his voice, I fell to the ground unconscious and lay there face downward.

The structure of the first part of this verse is awkward in English, and the two occurrences of the phrase **I heard the sound of his words** may easily be reduced to one as in TEV and translated simply "I heard his voice."

Fell on my face in a deep sleep: literally "I had become entranced on my face, with my face to the ground." In this context the "fall" is clearly unintentional and in contrast with 2.46 and 8.17, where it is voluntary. In fact, the verb "to fall" is not actually found in the original here, but most readers of the Hebrew would supply it. NJV avoids it by saying "overcome by sleep, I lay prostrate on the ground." Another way of saying it is "I fainted and lay unconscious with my face to the earth." On the idea of the **deep sleep**, see comments at 8.18.

10.10   RSV   TEV

> And behold, a hand touched me and set me trembling on my hands and knees.

> Then a hand took hold of me and raised me to my hands and knees; I was still trembling.

Behold: see verse 5 as well as 2.31 and 4.10.

A hand: there is no indication of whose hand this was. It is therefore unwise to make it "the hand of the man dressed in linen," although it is possible that this is what was intended. It is better to leave it vague, but translators should also avoid the suggestion of a detached hand. The best solution may be to say "someone's hand."

Touched me: the verb thus translated is a very general term, but in this context it is probably more than a light touch, because the result was that Daniel was raised from a lying position to one on his hands and knees. Translators may wish to say "grasped me" (NEB) or, as in TEV, "took hold of me."

Set me trembling: literally "caused me to waver (tremble)." Although the primary meaning of this verb is "to totter" or "to waver," it is used in a variety of senses. Here it is taken by many scholars to mean "caused me to rise up." This, in fact, is the same as the rendering of the ancient Greek versions. And one of the manuscripts found at Qumran has a different Hebrew word meaning "moved me." It is therefore better in this case to translate the idea "raising me" (NAB) or "lifting me." Note that NRSV revises RSV to "and roused me to my hands and knees."

On my hands and knees: literally "on my knees and the palms of my hands." On the word used twice referring to the hands, see 5.5. Daniel was apparently in a crawling position prior to getting up completely (verse 11).

10.11   RSV   TEV

And he said to me, "O Daniel, man greatly beloved, give heed to the words that I speak to you, and stand upright, for now I have been sent to you." While he was speaking this word to me, I stood up trembling.

The angel said to me, "Daniel, God loves you. Stand up and listen carefully to what I am going to say. I have been sent to you." When he had said this, I stood up, still trembling.

He said to me: since the subject pronoun refers to the angel, it may be better in some languages to say this clearly, using a noun as in TEV.

Man greatly beloved: this is very similar to the expression found in 9.23, but here the noun **man** is added. The meaning is that Daniel is a person considered very precious in God's sight. The passive idea can mean loved by other people or loved by God, but in this context the latter is clearly much more likely. TEV expresses it in an active way, and this will serve as a good model for many other languages.

The order of the commands has been changed in TEV, and this also may be a good model in other languages. It is more natural that a person would be required to **stand upright** in order to be able to listen attentively (**give heed to the words**). Daniel's attention is to be focused on what follows. For this reason TEV says clearly "what I am going to say."

Trembling: the root of this word is not the same as the one translated similarly and discussed under the previous verse. Nevertheless, if the idea of "trembling" is introduced earlier, then it may be more natural to say "still trembling" here, as in TEV.

10.12	RSV	TEV
	Then he said to me, "Fear not, Daniel, for from the first day that you set your mind to understand and humbled yourself before your God, your words have been heard, and I have come because of your words.	Then he said, "Daniel, don't be afraid. God has heard your prayers ever since the first day you decided to humble yourself in order to gain understanding. I have come in answer to your prayer.

Fear not: Daniel's trembling was due to his fear because of the appearance of the heavenly being. He is therefore instructed to abandon his fear. This may be better translated in some languages as "stop being afraid" or "leave your apprehension."

Set your mind to understand: in many languages it will be necessary to state clearly what it was that Daniel was trying to understand. If this is the case, translators may wish to say something like "ever since you started trying to understand the message (revelation, vision, oracle)," using the same term as in verse 1.

Humbled yourself: in some languages it is possible to use an idiomatic expression like "lower your heart" or "abase yourself." The reference is probably to Daniel's self-denial described in verse 3. In many cases it will be more natural to reverse the order of the two verbs "understand" and "humbled yourself." Logically, humbling yourself comes before the attempt to gain understanding.

Your words have been heard: this clearly means that the words that were spoken to God in prayer had been heard by him. It is therefore better in many languages to express the idea of prayer directly and transform the passive to an active form. A good model for this is the TEV rendering above.

I have come because of your words: or, as NIV has it, "I have come in response to them." Another model is "I have come to bring the answer (to your prayer)."

10.13	RSV	TEV

RSV	TEV
The prince of the kingdom of Persia withstood me twenty-one days; but Michael, one of the chief princes, came to help me, so I left him there with the prince of the kingdom of Persia	The angel prince of the kingdom of Persia opposed me for twenty-one days. Then Michael, one of the chief angels, came to help me, because I had been left there alone in Persia.

Prince: in the context this seems to refer to some sort of supernatural being like Gabriel and Michael (see verses 20-21). Each nation was thought to have its own angel who served as its protector. For this reason TEV and NEB have made it clear that the reference is to "the angel prince." Translators may also consider an expression like "The protecting angel" or "The guardian angel" (Mft and REB).

Withstood me: in some languages translators will want to know whether the term thus translated in RSV involves physical resistance or some other kind of opposition. The word has the basic meaning of "to stand" or "to take up a position," and here it means "stood in my way" (NAB).

Twenty-one days: this corresponds to the same period of time ("three weeks") of Daniel's self-denial as described in verses 2 and 3. But this is probably not very significant. However, if it is more natural in the translator's language to say "three weeks" than **twenty-one days** here, then this may be done.

Michael: this is the guardian angel of the people of God. Compare Zech 3.1-2, where the angel of the LORD resists Satan, and Jude 9, where Michael is mentioned by name. Here Michael is further described as **one of the chief princes**, or "a prince of the first rank" (NJV), or "one of the archangels" (AT and Mft).

I left him there: the RSV rendering comes from a proposed correction in the Hebrew text, based on the ancient Greek. The Hebrew text actually has a passive verb form, "I was (had been) left there." This text is followed by NIV, "I was detained there," and by TEV and certain other English versions. Some commentators feel that this does not make good sense, because the guardian angel did not remain with the angel of Persia but came to Daniel as a result of Michael's help. However, it is quite possible to adopt the reading of the traditional Hebrew text, in the sense that Michael came after the guardian angel had been detained there for a while. The change proposed by RSV is therefore unnecessary.

With the prince of the kingdom of Persia: literally "with prince of the kings of Persia," but RSV takes this as having the same meaning as the initial clause in this verse. It is true that in Daniel "kings" and "kingdoms" are frequently interchanged (compare 7.17; 8.21, and comments). Some versions (NJB, for example) follow a different text that says "with the kings of Persia." This, in fact, is the reading recommended by HOTTP/CTAT. It is, however, interesting to note that the proposed interpretation of CTAT allows for an explanatory note indicating that the "king" in fact represents the empire, as in 7.17 and 8.21.

10.14	RSV	TEV
	and came to make you understand what is to befall your people in the latter days. For the vision is for days yet to come."	I have come to make you understand what will happen to your people in the future. This is a vision about the future."

Note that in RSV this is a continuation of the sentence started in verse 13. But it will probably be better to begin a new sentence, as in TEV, REB, and others.

Came: or "have come" (NRSV), or "now I am here" (Mft and Knox).

To make you understand: that is, "to help you to comprehend" or "to enable you to know." There is no thought of forcing Daniel against his will to understand.

In the latter days: this phrase and the one that follows in the next sentence, **for days yet to come**, both refer to the future. The word translated **yet** in RSV has been revised in NRSV to "a further vision." It is understood as meaning "new" in NJB: "This is a new vision about those days." NAB has similarly followed this interpretation, applying the word **yet** to the verb rather than to the noun **days**. The result is "for there is yet a vision concerning those days." This interpretation is probably to be preferred.

The rendering of this verse may be compared with Hab 2.3, from which it is thought by some scholars to be borrowed.

10.15	RSV	TEV
	When he had spoken to me according to these words, I turned my face toward the ground and was dumb.	When he said this, I stared at the ground, speechless.

When he had spoken to me according to these words: this is an awkward expression and can be rendered much more naturally in most languages. It may be better also to alter the verb tense: "While he was speaking these words to me" (NRSV); "While he was saying these things to me" (NJV); "While he was speaking thus to me" (NAB).

Turned my face toward the ground: literally "I placed my face to the ground." But this does not mean that Daniel prostrated himself again. While he remained standing he looked down in an attitude of humility. As far as the physical movement is concerned, this is the opposite of "lifted up my eyes" (verse 5).

Was dumb: the Hebrew verb here expresses the idea of being incapable of speaking and is not a voluntary refusal to talk. The rendering "kept silent" (NAB and NVSR) may therefore be misleading. In many languages the best way to say this is "was speechless" (NRSV) or "was unable to speak" (REB).

10.16

RSV	TEV
And behold, one in the likeness of the sons of men touched my lips; then I opened my mouth and spoke. I said to him who stood before me, "O my lord, by reason of the vision pains have come upon me, and I retain no strength.	Then the angel, who looked like a human being, reached out and touched my lips. I said to him, "Sir, this vision makes me so weak that I can't stop trembling.

Behold: see verses 5 and 10 above. REB translates here "Suddenly." It may be more natural at this point in many languages to insert a transition word that indicates the continuation of a sequence of events. Translators may consider "Next . . ." or "Then . . ." (AT, NAB, NIV, NRSV, as well as TEV).

One in the likeness of the sons of men: this is similar in meaning to the Aramaic expression translated "one like a son of man" in 7.13, but it differs in form because the word for "son" is plural here. This may be taken to refer to the same being as the one mentioned in verse 15, in which case it is wise to translate "that person (angel) was like a human being." This is the solution followed by TEV. Or the phrase may be understood as pointing to another (different) heavenly being. If this interpretation is adopted, translators should probably say "another being, who was like a person" (FRCL) or "then someone (else) looking like a man" (NJB). The majority of versions seem to prefer this second interpretation.

Touched my lips: this gesture confirms the fact that Daniel was incapable of speaking (verse 15). Compare Isa 6.7 and Jer 1.9. There is nothing in the text corresponding to the TEV "reached out and," although this expression is used in Jer 1.9, and this is probably what readers will assume here.

Opened my mouth and spoke: this typically Hebrew expression comes out very awkward in most languages if translated literally. The meaning is simply that he began to talk again (compare Matt 5.2). In some languages it will be better to say "I was able to speak again." REB renders this as follows: "then I broke my silence and addressed him."

To him who stood before me: this may sound strange in some languages, even if the meaning is clearly understood, since readers know without being told that the person who is being addressed is standing there.

O my lord: the term translated **my lord** here is one of great honor and is in fact the same in form as used for God in 1.2 and nine times in chapter 9. Translators should seek an equivalent in their languages that is appropriate for any person who is greatly respected. In some cases this may be a term appropriate only for humans, while in other cases it could refer to beings human or divine.

By reason of the vision: or "because of the vision." In many languages this part of the verse should probably be restructured, making the vision the subject of the sentence: "this vision has caused me to have pains."

Pains have come upon me: literally "my pangs (as those of a woman in childbirth) have overpowered me." The corresponding Hebrew terms would make people think of both anxiety and suffering—as in the case of childbirth (1 Sam 4.19). In some languages it will be natural to speak of the stomach being upset or of the liver being disturbed.

And I retain no strength: the conjunction **and** does not really introduce a second separate fact. The idea is rather that the **pains** resulted in the lack of strength and the feeling of helplessness. The two things are very closely associated. For this reason NRSV revises RSV to say "such pains have come upon me that I retain no strength."

10.17	RSV	TEV
	How can my lord's servant talk with my lord? For now no strength remains in me, and no breath is left in me."	I am like a slave standing before his master. How can I talk to you? I have no strength or breath left in me."

The initial question in this verse is extremely awkward because Daniel refers to himself (**my lord's servant**) and to the angel (**my lord**) in the third person. TEV attempts to simplify the structure by separating the question from the servant-master comparison and by expressing that comparison clearly. The first sentence shows Daniel's understanding of his status relative to the angel with whom he is speaking. Then it has Daniel asking how he can possibly speak with someone whose rank or standing is so different from his own. It would be possible to use a more general expression like "I am completely insignificant in your eyes" or "I am without worth before you," if the image of the servant does not convey this idea.

My lord: see comments on this term in the previous verse.

No breath is left in me: if a literal rendering of this clause will be understood to refer to death, then it is certainly to be avoided. Translators may have to resort to "I can hardly breathe" (NIV) or "I am as good as dead." The Hebrew word translated **breath** is *nefesh,* which may be rendered "life," "soul," or "desire," as well as "breath."

10.18   RSV   TEV

    Again one having the appear-   Once more he took hold of me,
ance of a man touched me and   and I felt stronger.
strengthened me.

    One having the appearance of a man: see verse 16. If this is taken as
a second being in verse 16 and not the angel of verses 5-9, then it should be
made clear that the same being is performing the action here.
    Touched me: or "grasped me" (compare verse 10).
    Strengthened me: or "caused me to feel stronger again."

10.19   RSV   TEV

And he said, "O man greatly be-   He said, "God loves you, so don't
loved, fear not, peace be with you;   let anything worry you or frighten
be strong and of good courage."   you."
And when he spoke to me, I was   When he had said this, I felt
strengthened and said, "Let my lord   even stronger and said, "Sir, tell me
speak, for you have strengthened   what you have to say. You have
me."   made me feel better."

    He: if a second heavenly being has been introduced in verse 16, it should
be made clear which one is intended here. It is the same being as mentioned
in that verse.
    O man greatly beloved: see verse 11 and 9.23. TEV goes on to use a very
important connecting word, "so," showing the relationship between the fact of
God's love for Daniel and the advice, once again, that he should abandon his
fear.
    Four common exhortations found frequently in the Old Testament are
given to Daniel here. TEV reduces these to two and thus loses something of the
cumulative force of the original. Unless it is really unnatural, the four different
admonitions should be retained in the translation.
    Fear not: see verse 12.
    Peace be with you: this reflects the familiar Hebrew word *shalom,* which
contains the idea of wholeness or total well-being. REB translates it "all will be
well with you" (compare FRCL).
    Be strong and of good courage: literally "be strong and be strong"
repeating the exact same word for the sake of emphasis. This kind of repetition
does not occur frequently in Hebrew but is certainly acceptable. However, in
many other languages, including English, such repetition is stylistically
unacceptable. And even in some Hebrew manuscripts the second term has been
replaced by another verb of similar meaning, "be strong and be courageous,"
which is an expression found frequently in the Old Testament (Deut 31.7; Josh
1.6-7; 1 Chr 22.13, for example). From a textual point of view, the repetition
of the same verb is preferable, and in those languages where this is acceptable,

it should be used. However, where such an expression would be unacceptable style, two different verbs with the same meaning should be used, or else a single verb used in an emphatic manner; for example, "be the strongest of the strong" or "be very big-strong."

Note that TEV makes a paragraph break in middle of this verse. This is done, however, because of the change in speaker at this point; translators should follow their own established principles regarding paragraph breaks. TEV is virtually the only English version to make a break here.

Let my lord speak: the use of the third person here, as in verses 16 and 17, is again difficult to follow in most languages. The TEV rendering should serve as a good model here.

You have strengthened me: this confirms the fact that Daniel, who had lost his strength (see verses 8 and 16), now regains it as a result of the angel's intervention.

10.20-21   RSV   TEV

20 Then he said, "Do you know why I have come to you? But now I will return to fight against the prince of Persia; and when I am through with him, lo, the prince of Greece will come. 21 But I will tell you what is inscribed in the book of truth: there is none who contends by my side against these except Michael, your prince.

20-21 He said, "Do you know why I came to you? It is to reveal to you what is written in the Book of Truth. Now I have to go back and fight the guardian angel of Persia. After that the guardian angel of Greece will appear. There is no one to help me except Michael, Israel's guardian angel.ᵛ

ᵛ *Probable text* guardian angel; *Hebrew* guardian angel. And I, in the first year of Darius the Mede.

The clauses in these two verses are in an unusual order. Several translations and commentaries decide that they must be rearranged in order to make good sense. The most common restructuring consists of transposing verse 20b ("But . . . Greece will come") to the middle of verse 21. This makes the answer follow the question of verse 20a more closely (as in TEV, NJB). Some versions, however, move verse 21a to a position at the end of the first verse in chapter 11 and omit the date there. Another possibility is to place 10.21b and 11.1 in parentheses (NIV). But the restructuring of TEV and NJB will probably be best for most languages.

The prince of Persia: as in verse 13, this refers to the angel designated to protect Persia.

When I am through with him: this seems to be a deliberately vague expression for giving somebody a bad time; there are similar idiomatic expressions in many languages which may be used here. In some languages, however, what is meant may have to be made clearer by saying something like "when I have defeated him" or "after he is subdued."

Lo: see comments on the Aramaic equivalent for this term at 7.6.

The prince of Greece: literally "the prince of Javan." As seen above, the word for **prince** is used here in the sense of an angel who watches over and protects the area mentioned. See 8.21 for comments on the word "Javan."

I will tell you: in this context the verb in Hebrew has the sense of "explain," "reveal, or "make known" something that is not generally known or that has not been known before, or something hidden or mysterious. REB "expound" and TEV "reveal" express this sense better than the more general term **tell**.

What is inscribed: this is not the usual word for "what is written," since it occurs only here in all the Old Testament. But it is very similar to an Aramaic word having to do with writing. The main translation problem here will be the passive form for many languages. In this case translators should not make the subject too definite, since we do not know who did the writing. It will be better to say something like "someone wrote" or "they (indefinite) wrote."

The book of truth: literally "the writing of truth." It is not known exactly what this refers to. In 9.2 there was the reference to the "(holy) books," which contained the revelation of God to human beings, including among others the Book of Jeremiah. Here the Hebrew expression is different. It may refer to a heavenly book in which, according to an ancient notion, God wrote in advance the destiny of individuals and of nations. Knox translates "the book of doom." It is, however, better not to give such details in translation, since the meaning is not certain. If the translators see a need, this kind of information can be included in a footnote on this passage.

None who contends by my side against these: the would-be adversaries are the protecting angels of Persia and Greece. Another possible wording is "no one supported me in my struggle with them."

Your prince: while the English pronoun **your** may be singular or plural, the Hebrew form on which it is based is plural in this case and is taken to refer to the people of Israel as a whole rather than just to Daniel. This is why TEV and FRCL say clearly "Israel's guardian angel." This plural form should be clearly reflected in the language of translation.

This is one of the most difficult chapter transitions in all the Bible. The chapter division is badly placed, and there are problems as to the relationship and proper arrangement of the verses at the end of chapter 10 and the beginning of chapter 11. See comments on 10.20-21. NIV puts 10.21b and 11.1 in parentheses. In any case, the end of chapter 10 and the beginning of chapter 11 are very closely tied together, and there should under no circumstances be a new paragraph or new section heading at this point. The comments on the first verse of this chapter should help the translator to understand the problem better.

11.1 RSV	TEV
And as for me, in the first year of Darius the Mede, I stood up to confirm and strengthen him.	**He is^w responsible for helping and defending me.**

^w *One ancient translation* He is; *Hebrew* I am.

Several commentators think that this verse is a late addition to the text of Daniel, so some correct it, and others transfer all (REB) or parts (TEV) of it to a footnote. As indicated in HOTTP/CTAT, there are three separate textual problems in this verse alone:

(a) Are the words "and I, in the first year of Darius the Mede" a part of the original text?
(b) Did the original text have "my standing up (was)," translated **I stood up** (RSV), or did it have "with me" (NEB and NJB)?
(c) Is the pronoun at the end of the verse "for him" or "for me"?

HOTTP recommends that: (1) the dating be retained, (2) translators render the words "my standing up" in the sense of "my intervention (took place)," and (3) the final pronoun be translated "(to strengthen) him." It will be noted that TEV does the opposite in every case, since it follows the reading of the ancient Greek version on problems (b) and (c), and makes a change in the text with regard to problem (a).

While it is impossible to make firm recommendations where the text is so jumbled, it is suggested that it may be possible to make sense of the Hebrew text as follows:

a1. Take the words "and I" as emphatic and translate them something like "I myself" or, as in RSV, **as for me . . . .**

a2. Take the phrase **in the first year of Darius the Mede** as adverbial, describing the time in which the action of support or defense took place. On the dating, see comments on 6.1 and 9.1.

b. Follow the interpretation suggested by HOTTP, so that the words "my standing up" can be translated in the sense "I supported" or "I stood firm."

c. Translate the pronoun as "him" at the end of the verse. This may require a relative clause construction such as "whom I supported" or "whom I strengthened" in some languages. The pronoun refers, of course, to Michael, who is named in 10.21.

The resulting translation can be something like the following: "As for me, I supported and strengthened him in the first year of the rule of Darius the Mede" or "I myself helped and strengthened him during the first year when Darius the Mede was King." Taken together with the previous verse (10.21), the rendering may come out something like "no one helps me to combat these enemies except for Michael, the guardian angel of Israel, [11.1] whom I myself helped and supported during the first year of Darius, the Mede" (FRCL). In some languages this will be better rendered as a separate sentence: "I myself strengthened and helped him during the first year that Darius was chief of the Medes."

It will be noted that many English versions omit the time reference because they feel that its insertion makes very awkward style (TEV, NEB, NAB, and NJB). See the TEV footnote on 10.20-21. On the other hand, certain versions are able to make sense of the text along the lines indicated above (NIV and NJV, as well as RSV).

11.2a   RSV   TEV

"And now I will show you the   **And what I am now going to tell you**
truth.   **is true."**

And now: in some languages this wording may indicate that he had not been telling the truth up to this point. If this is the case, such meaning is definitely to be avoided. The idea is "here and now" (REB), which is the normal introduction to a letter or a speech. In this case it marks the beginning of the long speech that continues to the end of this chapter.

I will show you the truth: these words, which introduce the long description of verses 2b-45, are a return to the wording of 10.21: "I will tell you what is inscribed in the book of truth." The verb translated **show** here is the same as the one translated **tell** in 10.21; its meaning may be "announce, report" or "declare, make known" something previously hidden or misunderstood. This seems to be more appropriate to the context here. On the word for **truth** see comments on 8.12, 26 and 9.13, although the context is quite different here.

Explanation: The kingdoms of Egypt and Syria: 11.2b-20

RSV

TEV

The Kingdoms of Egypt and Syria

2b Behold, three more kings shall arise in Persia; and a fourth shall be far richer than all of them; and when he has become strong through his riches, he shall stir up all against the kingdom of Greece. 3 Then a mighty king shall arise, who shall rule with great dominion and do according to his will. 4 And when he has arisen, his kingdom shall be broken and divided toward the four winds of heaven, but not to his posterity, nor according to the dominion with which he ruled; for his kingdom shall be plucked up and go to others besides these.

5 "Then the king of the south shall be strong, but one of his princes shall be stronger than he and his dominion shall be a great dominion. 6 After some years they shall make an alliance, and the daughter of the king of the south shall come to the king of the north to

2b The angel said, "Three more kings will rule over Persia, followed by a fourth, who will be richer than all the others. At the height of his power and wealth he will challenge the kingdom of Greece.

3 "Then a heroic king will appear. He will rule over a huge empire and do whatever he wants. 4 But at the height of his power his empire will break up and be divided into four parts. Kings not descended from him will rule in his place, but they will not have the power that he had.

5 "The king of Egypt will be strong. One of his generals, however, will be even stronger and rule a greater kingdom. 6 After a number of years the king of Egypt will make an alliance with the king of Syria and give him his daughter in marriage. But the alliance will not last, and she, her husband, her child, and

make peace; but she shall not retain the strength of her arm, and he and his offspring shall not endure; but she shall be given up, and her attendants, her child, and he who got possession of her.

7 "In those times a branch from her roots shall arise in his place; he shall come against the army and enter the fortress of the king of the north, and he shall deal with them and shall prevail. 8 He shall also carry off to Egypt their gods with their molten images and with their precious vessels of silver and of gold; and for some years he shall refrain from attacking the king of the north. 9 Then the latter shall come into the realm of the king of the south but shall return into his own land.

10 "His sons shall wage war and assemble a multitude of great forces, which shall come on and overflow and pass through, and again shall carry the war as far as his fortress. 11 Then the king of the south, moved with anger, shall come out and fight with the king of the north; and he shall raise a great multitude, but it shall be given into his hand. 12 And when the multitude is taken, his heart shall be exalted, and he shall cast down tens of thousands, but he shall not prevail. 13 For the king of the north shall again raise a multitude, greater than the former; and after some years he shall come on with a great army and abundant supplies.

14 "In those times many shall rise against the king of the south; and the men of violence among your own people shall lift themselves up in order to fulfil the vision; but they shall fail. 15 Then the king of the north shall come and throw up siegeworks, and take a well-fortified city. And the forces of the south shall not stand, or even his picked troops, for there shall be no strength to stand. 16 But he who comes against him shall do according to his own will, and none shall stand before him; and he shall stand in the glorious land, and all of it shall be in his power. 17 He shall set his face to come with the strength of his whole kingdom, and he shall bring terms of peace and perform them. He shall give him the daughter of women to destroy the kingdom; but it shall not stand or be to his advantage. 18 Afterward he shall turn his face to the coastlands, and shall take many of them; but a commander shall put an end to his insolence; indeed he shall turn his insolence back upon him. 19 Then he shall turn his face back toward the fortresses of his own land; but he shall stumble and fall, and shall not be found.

the servants who went with her will all be killed. 7 Soon afterward one of her relatives will become king. He will attack the army of the king of Syria, enter their fortress, and defeat them. 8 He will carry back to Egypt the images of their gods and the articles of gold and silver dedicated to those gods. After several years of peace 9 the king of Syria will invade Egypt, but he will be forced to retreat.

10 "The sons of the king of Syria will prepare for war and gather a large army. One of them will sweep on like a flood and attack an enemy fortress. 11 In his anger the king of Egypt will go to war against the king of Syria and capture his huge army. 12 He will be proud of his victory and of the many soldiers he has killed, but he will not continue to be victorious.

13 "The king of Syria will go back and gather a larger army than he had before. When the proper time comes, he will return with a large, well-equipped army. 14 Then many people will rebel against the king of Egypt. And some violent people from your nation, Daniel, will rebel because of a vision they have seen, but they will be defeated. 15 So the king of Syria will lay siege to a fortified city and capture it. The soldiers of Egypt will not continue to fight; even the best of them will not have enough strength. 16 The Syrian invader will do with them as he pleases, without opposition. He will stand in the Promised Land and have it completely in his power.

17 "The king of Syria will plan an expedition, using his whole army. Then, in order to destroy his enemy's kingdom, he will make an alliance with him and offer him his daughter in marriage; but his plan will not succeed. 18 After that he will attack the nations by the sea and conquer many of them. But a foreign leader will defeat him and put an end to his arrogance; indeed he will turn the arrogance of Syria's king back on him. 19 The king will return to the fortresses of his own land, but he will be defeated, and that will be the end of him.

20 "He will be followed by another king, who will send an officer to oppress the people with taxes in order to increase the wealth of his kingdom. In a short time that king will be killed, but not publicly and not in battle."

20 "Then shall arise in his place one who shall send an exactor of tribute through the glory of the kingdom; but within a few days he shall be broken, neither in anger nor in battle.

TEV Section Heading: The kingdoms of Egypt and Syria

On the question of whether to use the names "Egypt and Syria" as opposed to "the kingdoms of the North and South," see the comments on verse 5.

The translator will have to make a decision about the level of clarity to use when translating this section of Daniel. On the one hand, every detail mentioned covers a detail of history. Yet the writer uses vague language, and often it is difficult to know which pronoun refers to what person. Readers are left wondering whether the writer was attempting to keep details vague in order to preserve the style of a vision—even though the readers knew exactly what details he was referring to—or whether he needed to avoid persecution by authorities if they discovered what he was writing about. Therefore the translator has three choices:

1) Make everything as clear as possible; for example, by referring to "Antiochus Epiphanes" directly when he is "king of the north" in the Hebrew text.
2) Make references moderately clear without destroying the vision quality of the discourse; for example, in study Bibles, adding a footnote about characters such as Antiochus Epiphanes, but in all Bibles translating "king of Syria" for "king of the north."
3) Retain the vagueness of the original text throughout.

As will be seen, this Handbook favors the second choice. The first choice is not faithful to the vision character of the discourse, while the third choice prevents today's readers from understanding the message that the original readers did clearly understand.

11.2b

RSV	TEV
Behold, three more kings shall arise in Persia; and a fourth shall be far richer than all of them; and when he has become strong through his riches, he shall stir up all against the kingdom of Greece.	The angel said, "Three more kings will rule over Persia, followed by a fourth, who will be richer than all the others. At the height of his power and wealth he will challenge the kingdom of Greece.

The meaning of this verse is not easy to understand, since it summarizes in a few words more than two centuries of Persian history (538-333 B.C.). The identification of the four Persian kings is uncertain, because there were in fact nine kings in succession who governed the empire during that period, and the apparent historical references are not precise enough to give us any positive confirmation.

Behold: see comments on 2.31; 4.10.

Shall arise: the verb used here has a different root from the ones in 2.39; 7.17, but the meaning is not radically different. The root here means rather "to stand," and here the idea is that they will govern or be in command. NJV restructures the whole sentence to say "Persia will have three more kings."

And a fourth shall be far richer than all of them: literally "a fourth shall be rich with great richness more than all." It is to be made clear that this fourth ruler will be wealthier than all those kings who ruled before he came to power.

When he has become strong through his riches: this reflects only two Hebrew words, literally "in-his-power by-his-wealth." This statement whose meaning is not very clear has been rendered "strengthened by riches" (NAB), "by the power he obtains through his wealth" (NJV), and "(when) by his wealth he has extended his power" (REB), to give only a few examples.

Stir up all against the kingdom of Greece: the corresponding Hebrew text is not completely clear. It can mean "he will agitate all, *namely* the kingdom of Greece," or "he will agitate all (others) *against* the kingdom of Greece." NAB follows the former interpretation with "he will rouse all the kingdom of Greece," but most English versions adopt the latter. REB, for example, says "he will mobilize the whole empire against the kingdom of Greece." The word **Greece** is literally "Javan," as in 8.21 and 10.20.

11.3	RSV	TEV
	Then a mighty king shall arise, who shall rule with great dominion and do according to his will.	"Then a heroic king will appear. He will rule over a huge empire and do whatever he wants.

A mighty king: the Hebrew word translated **mighty** in RSV may be rendered as an adjective meaning "valiant" or "strong." But it may also be taken as a noun referring to a "warrior." FRCL translates "a warrior will become king." Several English versions also include the idea of warrior in their renderings: "a warrior king" (NJV, NRSV, and NEB/REB); "a warlike king" (AT); "a warrior of a monarch" (Mft). Such a rendering simply makes clear what most commentators agree the text means. The reference here is to the king of Greece, Alexander the Great, who was indeed a conqueror or warlike king.

Shall arise: see comments on verse 2b.

Rule with great dominion: literally "rule (with) a great ruling." This kind of construction, where the verb and noun have the same root, is quite frequent in Hebrew and is often an emphatic way of stating something. Compare 9.7 and comments on "treachery." If this kind of repetition is natural, translators may wish to imitate it in their own languages.

Do according to his will: the same expression is applied in 8.4 to the "ram" that is symbolic of the Persian Empire. The idea is that he will be subject to no one and will do as he himself pleases.

11.4	RSV	TEV

RSV	TEV
And when he has arisen, his kingdom shall be broken and divided toward the four winds of heaven, but not to his posterity, nor according to the dominion with which he ruled; for his kingdom shall be plucked up and go to others besides these.	But at the height of his power his empire will break up and be divided into four parts. Kings not descended from him will rule in his place, but they will not have the power that he had.

And: since what follows is contrary to what people expect of such a great ruler, TEV prefers to render the conjunction by the English "But." So also REB, NJV, NJB, and AB. This may be the most natural rendering in a number of other languages.

When he has arisen: the verb is again "stand up" as in verses 2 and 3, but here it conveys the idea of being firmly "established" (REB) or "grown strong" (AT). A slightly modified meaning is given in NRSV, which interprets the verb tense differently: "while still rising in power." But this is less likely.

Shall be broken and divided: Mft renders these two verbs "shattered and scattered," while NJB has "broken up and parcelled out." The passive forms may be rendered actively as "his kingdom shall break up and divide" or, using an indefinite agent, "they (or someone) will destroy and separate his kingdom."

Toward the four winds of heaven: this Hebrew metaphor may be rendered less figuratively as "in the four directions under heaven" (NAB) or "split up north, south, east, and west" (NEB). But given the difficulty in translating the points of the compass in many languages, it is possible to say simply "in all directions" or "on all sides." See comments on 8.8, 22. Some writers see the number **four** as significant enough to be retained here, in view of 7.4-7, where the same number is used: note TEV "into four parts." The empire of Alexander the Great was, in fact, divided into four sections after his death.

Not to his posterity: in some languages the expression "who are not his children (or grandchildren)" or "whom he did not produce" will be appropriate here, since the term "children" or "grandchildren" will be understood in the broad sense of any descendant. The words **not to** relate back to the verb **divided** and indicate those who will (or will not in this case) receive the parts into which the empire will be split. AB translates ". . . but not among his descendants"; NIV says "It will not go to his descendants," REB "It will not pass to . . . ." TEV takes this phrase with what follows: "Kings not descended from him will rule in his place."

Nor according to the dominion with which he ruled: literally "and not as the ruling which he ruled." Compare "ruled with great dominion" in the previous verse. This indicates that the successors' kingdom would be unlike that of the "warrior king" (Alexander the Great). In some languages it may be necessary to state in what way future kingdoms will be unlike that of the great king. If this is the case, it is probably better to focus on the manner of ruling: "it will not be ruled as he ruled it" (NJB). To be more precise, it has to do with the degree of power: "nor will its power be comparable to his" (REB); "nor shall it be so powerful as it was in his hands" (Mft).

Shall be plucked up: while the basic meaning of the verb here is "rooted up," the meaning in this context is probably "torn to pieces" (NAB) or "torn up" (Mft), although a number of versions maintain the more literal translation "uprooted" (NIV, NJV, REB, and NRSV). Once again, if the passive has to be made active, it is probably best to use an indefinite agent as subject. Note that TEV omits this last part of the verse as being a repetition of the same idea expressed in the beginning.

Others besides these: the demonstrative pronoun **these** refers to the descendants of Alexander the Great. It therefore has the same meaning as **not of his posterity**. For this reason it may be unnecessary to translate the idea twice (compare TEV). When Alexander the Great died, he was succeeded by his military leaders rather than by his sons.

11.5 RSV	TEV
"Then the king of the south shall be strong, but one of his princes shall be stronger than he and his dominion shall be a great dominion.	"The king of Egypt will be strong. One of his generals, however, will be even stronger and rule a greater kingdom.

Then: naturalness in the receptor language will require such a transition word in many cases. And it will be essential to begin a new paragraph at this point, since a new topic is being dealt with. Note that TEV and REB have no transition word here.

The king of the south: in verse 8 "Egypt" is referred to by name in the Hebrew text. The ancient Greek version does so consistently throughout this passage. If **south** is not identified as "Egypt" in this verse, the reader will very likely understand the clear reference to Egypt in verse 8 as referring to a different king. It is therefore advisable to make this identification clear from the beginning, as in TEV. The "king of the north" in the following verse (and the rest of the chapter) should also be clearly identified as "the king of Syria." This chapter is quite difficult to understand, but the identification of the two opposing forces by more precise geographical terms should provide some help to the reader.

One of his princes: this refers to one of the generals in the army of the king of Egypt. Since the word "prince" may be understood as a son of the king, it will be advisable in most cases to translate as "one of his generals" (TEV,

FRCL and REB) or possibly "one of his officers" (NJV and NRSV). Given the meaning in the modern military, the rendering "one of his captains" (AT and Mft) is not recommended, since the rank is not high enough.

His dominion shall be a great dominion: this reading of RSV reflects the traditional Hebrew text, which is recommended by HOTTP and CTAT. TEV, however, follows a slightly different text that contains the comparative idea "greater than (his dominion)" in parallel with **stronger than** in the first part of the verse. Many other versions, including NJB, NEB/REB, NAB, NRSV, and TOB, adopt this form of the text, which seems to fit the context better.

This verse is an intentionally obscure reference to Ptolemy I Soter of Egypt (323-285 B.C.) and to one of his officers, Seleucus I Nicator (305-281 B.C.), who became the ruler of Syria and gave his name to the ensuing Seleucid dynasty.

11.6	RSV	TEV

After some years they shall make an alliance, and the daughter of the king of the south shall come to the king of the north to make peace; but she shall not retain the strength of her arm, and he and his offspring shall not endure; but she shall be given up, and her attendants, her child, and he who got possession of^y her.	After a number of years the king of Egypt will make an alliance with the king of Syria and give him his daughter in marriage. But the alliance will not last, and she, her husband, her child,^{x} and the servants who went with her will all be killed. ^{x} *Some ancient translations* her child; *Hebrew* her father.

^{y} Or *supported*

After some years: literally "at the end of years," meaning an indefinite period of time extending beyond two or three years.

They shall make an alliance: the pronoun here seems to refer forward to the two kings mentioned later in the verse. It may be wise to clearly identify them early in the verse, as in TEV. The idea of a covenant, compact, or **alliance** may be depicted by a variety of idioms, depending on the language. In some languages translators may say "cut an agreement" or "eat an agreement."

The daughter of the king of the south shall come to the king of the north to make peace: a literal rendering to this part of the text will almost certainly be misunderstood. The king's daughter is not so much the negotiator of the peace as a kind of guarantee that the peace should last, because the two kingdoms will be united by marriage. The Hebrew expression **come to** suggests marriage in this context. This sense should be made clear if a literal rendering would be meaningless or misunderstood. REB rightly translates "to seal the agreement the daughter of the king of the south will be given in marriage to the king of the north." Although this guarantee did not actually work, it was the intention of the arrangement.

The king of the north: that is, "Syria." See comments on **the king of the south** in the previous verse.

To make peace: literally "to make straight things." Intermarriage between members of royalty in different kingdoms often led to the conclusion of peace treaties. Since this has essentially the same meaning as **make an alliance**, it is possible to translate the two expressions by a single phrase in the receptor language.

The strength of her arm: the word **arm** is often used to convey the idea of physical might or power, and it is so translated in NIV. But in TEV it is taken to mean that the alliance between Egypt and Syria will not be permanent. That is, her power to hold things together will prove inadequate.

The two phrases **she shall not retain the strength of her arm** and **he and his offspring will not endure** have been rendered in TEV by a single statement, "but the alliance will not last." This may be a valid model for several other languages. Translators may also consider "but the plan will fail" or "but the scheme will not succeed." But REB provides a more complete model: "but she will not maintain her influence and their line will not last."

He and his offspring: the traditional Hebrew text literally reads "he and his arm (meaning power)." But by changing the vowels it can mean **he and his offspring** as in RSV. This is the meaning found in the Greek Septuagint and in other ancient versions. And it is also adopted by most modern translations.

She shall be given up: many interpreters take this to mean "surrendered" or "handed over." If it means "be killed," this is an unusual usage of the verb involved. REB translates more generally "will . . . be victims of foul play." But ultimately it is death that seems to be suggested.

Her child: the traditional text literally has "the one who begot her" (NJV), presumably meaning "her father." But a slight change in the vowels of the Hebrew gives the meaning "the one she begot" or **her child**, and this is followed by the Latin Vulgate and the Syriac. HOTTP/CTAT advises against following this change in the text, but it is adopted by the majority of modern versions (NEB, NJB, TOB, NAB, FRCL, AT, Mft). It is therefore permissible to follow this option, if translators wish to do so.

He who got possession of her: in addition to the pronoun **she** (that is, the daughter of the king) and **her child**, the text also mention another person who would be a victim; literally "the one supporting her." This is generally seen to mean "her husband."

This verse is a veiled reference to the marriage of Bernice, the daughter of the Egyptian King Ptolemy II, to Antiochus II of Syria (grandson of Seleucus) around 250 B.C. Bernice, her husband, and her son died by poisoning.

11.7 RSV	TEV
"In those times a branch^z from her roots shall arise in his place; he shall come against the army and enter the fortress of the king of the	Soon afterward one of her relatives will become king. He will attack the army of the king of Syria, enter their fortress, and defeat them.

**north, and he shall deal with them
and shall prevail.**

z Gk: Heb *from a branch*

In those times: as the verse numbering of NRSV indicates, these words actually represent the last word in the Hebrew text of verse 6, literally "in the days." As interpreted by RSV, NRSV, and many others, it indicates an additional lapse of time following the alliance mentioned at the beginning of the previous verse. But this period is shorter than the period referred to there. NJB renders it "In due time," while NAB has "But later." Note, however, that NJV and NIV attach these words to the last sentence of the previous verse, to give a time frame to the execution of the Egyptian king's daughter and those surrounding her.

A branch from her roots: the image of the "family tree" with its roots and branches may be unfamiliar to readers in some languages. If this is the case, it is probably better to drop the image altogether. In addition to the TEV model, translators may consider "a member of her family" or "someone from the same parents (as her)."

Shall arise in his place: the pronoun **his** should probably be taken to refer to the father or predecessor of the person in question. It refers back to the "king of the south" mentioned in verses 5 and 6, who would, of course, be the father of the daughter given in marriage to the king of the north. TEV leaves this information to be understood from the wider context, but it is possible to translate "in succession to his father" (Mft) or "will appear in his father's place" (REB).

Against the army: some manuscript evidence would be translated "against the fortifications (or defenses)." Although followed by NJB, NAB, and REB, this is not recommended by HOTTP/CTAT, and translators should probably retain the idea of **the army**.

Enter the fortress: the singular noun **fortress** is probably collective, referring in general to the strongholds or defenses of Syria. REB translates "he will penetrate the defences."

He shall deal with them and shall prevail: the two verbs used here may easily be rendered by a single verbal expression in some languages. Some possible models are "will win a decisive victory" (REB), "conquer them" (NAB), or "succeed in overcoming them" (NJB). But in other cases it will be perfectly natural to use two verbs, as in NJV "fight and overpower them."

The historical reference in this verse is to the intervention of Ptolemy III, the brother of Bernice, who took revenge for the death of his sister in a military expedition against Seleucus II of Syria, son of Antiochus II, in 246 B.C. As indicated in the following verse, he took considerable spoils back to Egypt.

11.8   RSV   TEV

He shall also carry off to Egypt their   He will carry back to Egypt the im-
gods with their molten images and   ages of their gods and the articles
with their precious vessels of silver   of gold and silver dedicated to
and of gold; and for some years he   those gods. After several years of
shall refrain from attacking the king   peace
of the north.

Also: it may be better to drop the conjunction here. It indicates that the
carrying away of treasures is in addition to attacking and defeating the enemy.
It does not mean that they carried off items other than those mentioned in the
verse.

Carry off: the corresponding Hebrew expression is often used in the Old
Testament with regard to prisoners of war taken captive, but this is not the
only usage. Here it is clearly a matter of objects such as metal statues and
valuable utensils. It is therefore unnecessary and misleading to translate
"carry captive" (AT and KJV). The meaning is rather to "carry away as booty"
(NAB and REB).

To Egypt: this is one of the few places where the Hebrew text actually
gives a geographic name.

Their gods with their molten images: this is not intended as representing two distinct categories of objects, as the RSV rendering may seem to
indicate. Rather the victor took away the gods of Syria, which were in the form
of **molten images** or statues. Note TEV "images of their gods."

Precious vessels of silver and of gold: compare 5.2 and comments.

For some years: note that TEV begins a new sentence with "after several
years" at the end of this verse and continues it into the next verse.

Refrain from attacking: or, more literally, "allow to stand," or "leave
alone." But the expression indicates not only a lack of contact but also the
absence of conflict. This may be expressed in a variety of ways: "there will be
several years without war" or "during some years he will not fight with . . . ."
NAB translates "for years he shall have nothing to do with . . . ," NJV has "for
some years he will leave . . . alone," and TEV "After several years of peace."

11.9   RSV   TEV

Then the latter shall come into the   the king of Syria will invade Egypt,
realm of the king of the south but   but he will be forced to retreat.
shall return into his own land.

Then: depending on how the end of the previous verse is structured, it
may be possible to drop the transition word here. But if a new sentence is
started here, it may begin with "After that . . . ."

The latter: this clearly refers to the "king of the north," or the king of
Syria, and this should probably be made clear in the translation.

The two expressions **come into the realm** and **shall return into his own land** are rather neutral in meaning. Historical documents make no mention of a corresponding Syrian invasion into Egypt. Furthermore the neutral vocabulary of this verse does not necessarily mean that there was hostile intent. It is therefore impossible for us to know with certainty what the purpose of this visit may have been: military revenge as TEV indicates, or political negotiation. Nor is it clear whether it was a success or a failure. Therefore it may be better to leave the translation as neutral as possible. FRCL provides a model for this type of rendering: "the king of the north will go into the kingdom of the south and then return to his own country." Since it is highly unlikely that the king went alone, it may be misleading in some languages to use the verbs "go" and "return" without giving any further information. It may be necessary to choose a plural subject like "the king and his men." It should be noted, however, that most modern English versions use the loaded term "invade," implying hostile military action (NIV, NJB, NJV, REB, NAB, AT, and Mft, in addition to TEV). NEB carries the same meaning with "overrun" and "retreat." If this interpretation is followed, an explanatory footnote may be given, stating that this is not necessarily the only possible interpretation.

The subject of the phrase **shall return into his own land** can theoretically refer either to the king of the north or the king of the south. But it is more probable that the king of the north (Syria) is intended.

11.10 RSV	TEV
"His sons shall wage war and assemble a multitude of great forces, which shall come on and overflow and pass through, and again shall carry the war as far as his fortress.	"The sons of the king of Syria will prepare for war and gather a large army. One of them will sweep on like a flood and attack an enemy fortress.

His sons: that is, the sons of the king of Syria ("the king of the north"). It is important to insure that the persons referred to by the pronoun be made clear. This will mean using a noun phrase like "the king's sons" in place of the pronoun. This is especially important at the beginning of a new paragraph.

Wage war and assemble a multitude: if the first verb is taken to mean "make war," as the RSV rendering so indicates, then this expression is not in logical order. But the meaning here is rather "prepare for war" as in TEV and NIV. Compare also NAB, which is more literal: "But his sons shall prepare and assemble a great armed host." The most important element in preparing for war is the gathering together of a large group of warriors. The **multitude of great forces** consists therefore of soldiers, and it will be important to make this clear in most languages.

The second half of this verse switches the subject abruptly from a plural subject, **His sons**, to the third person singular masculine pronoun. It is confusing to say "he" without a singular noun that it can refer back to (as in NJV and NJB), and misleading to use the relative pronoun **which** (NIV and NRSV) referring to the assembled armies. Some versions attempt to reflect the singular pronoun by saying "one of them" (NEB/REB and TEV), referring to one of the sons of the Syrian king. This is probably the best solution to a difficult problem.

The Hebrew text that follows contains no less than five different verbs in series. The first is repeated in the infinitive form. A literal rendering of these verbs is:

    (a) he will come on to come on and
    (b) he will overflow and
    (c) he will pass along and
    (d) he will turn and
    (e) he will do battle

In the following comments, discussions of these verbs are marked by letters within brackets for the sake of easier reference.

(a) The duplication of the first verb, **come on**, serves as a kind of emphasis. The KJV rendering "shall certainly come" is not bad. The verb translated **come on** is the ordinary word "come" used several times in the verses immediately preceding. The translation **come on** is repeated in verse 13, but there is no reason to translate by any verb other than "come." It is the repetition here that requires a more emphatic translation.

(b) The verb **overflow** gives a picture of flowing water that spills over the banks of its normal course. Since this is incompatible with a singular subject, it is possible to shift the subject once again and add "and with his soldiers, he will . . . ." The imagery of an army as a flood is taken from Isa 8.8. The flood image is retained in most English versions.

(c) The verb translated **pass through** can also mean "cross over" and possibly refers to crossing over the border into the other country, but this can also be taken as a part of the flood imagery.

(d) The next verb is the subject of considerable debate. It may mean "carry on" or "turn back," or simply **again**. NAB, TOB, and KJV take it to mean "return," "turn back," or "retreat." NIV, NEB, AT, and Mft prefer the meaning "press forward" or "carry on." And NJV and NASB, as well as RSV/NRSV, translate the same term "again." The meaning "press forward" is probably to be preferred.

(e) According to the traditional written text, this verb has a plural subject, "they will attack (or do battle)," but the ancient specialists in the Jewish holy books noted in the margin of the manuscripts that it should be read as a singular, "he will attack." This suggestion is followed by most modern versions.

His fortress: the possessive pronoun **his** in this case refers back to the king of Egypt. The reference here is probably to "the fortress of Gaza" (Mft), which was the strongest fortification in southern Judea. However, it is probably better not to be as precise as this in translation. It can be rendered "the enemy's strongest town" or something similar. NJB has "the southern stronghold," while REB has simply "the enemy stronghold."

11.11   RSV   TEV

Then the king of the south, moved with anger, shall come out and fight with the king of the north; and he shall raise a great multitude, but it shall be given into his hand.	In his anger the king of Egypt will go to war against the king of Syria and capture his huge army.

Then: once again, this translates the multi-purpose Hebrew conjunction that may be best left untranslated in many languages.

The king of the south: the king of Egypt, as confirmed by verse 8. Similarly, the **king of the north** in this verse should again be rendered "the king of Syria."

Moved with anger: the position of this element in the sentence will be determined by what is most natural in the translator's language. But it is clearly in a prominent position in the Hebrew. Note that NRSV, like TEV, has shifted it to the beginning of the sentence.

Come out and fight: or "go forth to battle." The use of two verbs in this manner is a frequent Hebrew way of describing the initiation of an action followed by the essential meaning. Compare comments on the construction "answered and said" in 2.5. In those languages where such a formula is unnatural, it will be better to use a single verbal expression such as "launch an offensive" (FRCL), or an expression indicating purpose, "march out to do battle" (NEB).

He shall raise a great multitude: the third person pronoun here may refer to the **king of the south** (Egypt) or to the **king of the north** (Syria). But it is much more likely that it refers to the Syrian ruler. The **great multitude** is, as in verse 10, a very large army.

But it shall be given into his hand: the subject pronoun, **it**, refers back to the **great multitude** or army that the Syrian king mustered. And as often in Scripture, the word **hand** represents "power." The third person singular possessive pronoun, **his**, in this case refers to the **king of the south** (Egypt). The restructuring of TEV clarifies all these pronouns and makes the meaning comprehensible. It should serve as a good model for other languages.

This verse is thought to refer to the battle at Raphia, where Ptolemy IV (King of the South) fought Antiochus III in 217 B.C. Antiochus was defeated and his army suffered considerable loss as Judea was rejoined to Egypt.

11.12   RSV   TEV

And when the multitude is taken, his heart shall be exalted, and he shall cast down tens of thousands, but he shall not prevail.	He will be proud of his victory and of the many soldiers he has killed, but he will not continue to be victorious.

When the multitude is taken: this is understood by some commentators as a later addition to the text or a variant reading of the last statement in verse 11. But it may equally well be understood as an intentional repetition of the previous idea, with the meaning "and when he has finished defeating this great army . . . ," or as in NEB, "when this horde has been captured . . . ."

His heart shall be exalted: the essential element in this expression is the pride of the Egyptian king. The languages of the world have various ways of communicating this idea. Some will say "his heart swelled up," and others, "he thought he was great" or "he was lifted up." Translators should search for the most natural equivalent in their own language.

Cast down tens of thousands: the number is probably intended to be taken not literally but rather as a reference to a very great (uncountable) number of enemy soldiers. And in most languages it is a mistake to translate the verb **cast down** literally. The meaning is to exterminate or cause to die.

But: the conjunction marks the beginning of an unexpected thought. In spite of his achievements this ruler will not continue to be successful. In some cases it will be good to find an equivalent for "yet" (NJB), "however," or "nevertheless."

He shall not prevail: it may be necessary in some languages to say something like "he will not go on winning," "he will have no enduring strength" (NJB), or "he will not remain triumphant" (NIV).

11.13 RSV	TEV
For the king of the north shall again raise a multitude, greater than the former; and after some years[a] he shall come on with a great army and abundant supplies.	"The king of Syria will go back and gather a larger army than he had before. When the proper time comes, he will return with a large, well-equipped army.

[a] Heb *at the end of the times years*

Shall again raise a multitude: once again the term **multitude** refers to a large military unit. The Hebrew actually uses two different verbs, literally "return and raise." But the word sometimes translated "return" is the same word as used in verse 10, which may also be rendered "again." Here, however, it may be better to translate it "return" or possibly "revive." The second verb is the same as in verse 11. But in some languages it will be natural to add "more troops" or "new troops."

After some years: literally "at the end of the times, of the years." NJV retains something of the form with "after a time, a matter of years." But the idea is simply "after an indefinite and rather lengthy period of time."

Come on: see comments on verse 10.

Abundant supplies: the noun in Hebrew usually refers to personal possessions that may be moved from one place to another (such as furniture, domestic animals, sheep, goats). Depending on the context, it may also mean "wealth" or "riches" in general. But this meaning is improbable in the present context, since people do not go off to war with "riches." This context requires a meaning like "war material" or "equipment for fighting." The expression "fully equipped" (NIV) is a good English equivalent.

The probable historical reference of verse 13 is to the military campaign of Antiochus III against Egypt in 205 B.C. He took advantage of the death of Ptolemy IV, whose son and successor (Ptolemy V) was only four or five years old when he began to reign.

11.14   RSV   TEV

"In those times many shall rise against the king of the south; and the men of violence among your own people shall lift themselves up in order to fulfil the vision; but they shall fail. | Then many people will rebel against the king of Egypt. And some violent people from your nation, Daniel, will rebel because of a vision they have seen, but they will be defeated.

In those times: or "At that time" (Mft and NJB). This may also be translated by the adverb "Then" as in TEV.

Many: the noun translated **many** is a term often used in the Qumran writings for the ordinary members of the community as distinct from the leaders. Here it seems to refer to the masses. Most versions, however, use a more general expression like "many people" (TEV), and this is probably the best solution for most languages.

Rise against: or "rebel against," or "resist."

The men of violence among your own people: literally "sons of the violent ones of your people." This refers to Jewish people who were impatient and could not wait for divine intervention. They actively encouraged recourse to armed struggle. But the writer of the Book of Daniel could not accept this perspective, because he was expecting action by God himself. This is why he uses rather hard words with negative connotations (**men of violence**) in referring to those who would resort to armed struggle to liberate Israel. The idea is conveyed in some English translations as "some hotheads" (NEB), "renegades" (REB), "outlaws" (NAB), "the lawless" (NRSV), "some wild spirits" (Mft).

Lift themselves up: the verb here conveys essentially the same notion of resistance or rebellion as **rise against** earlier in the verse. In many languages it may be necessary to state clearly who it is they are rebelling against. If this is the case, translators should repeat the idea contained earlier in the verse, **against the king of the south**. But where such repetition is unacceptable, the phrase "against him" will probably be satisfactory.

In order to fulfill the vision: literally "to make vision stand." The use of the definite article **the** with the noun **vision** in RSV is misleading. There is no such article in the Hebrew and the reference is unclear. It is therefore unwise to translate with Mft "the prediction of the vision," as if it referred unambiguously to Daniel's vision. It is preferable to speak of "a (indefinite) vision that they have had," similar to the TEV rendering; compare REB "to give substance to a vision," and AB "in fulfillment of vision."

But they shall fail: literally "they will stumble (stagger)." This may also be stated negatively, "they will not succeed," or possibly in other languages, "will end badly," or as in NEB, "will come to disaster."

During the conflicts between Syria and Egypt, Israel's geographical location between the two meant that it was crossed by military troops from the north and from the south. It is not surprising that the Jews wished to be liberated from Egyptian domination and therefore even made a pact with Antiochus III in the hope of eventually gaining total independence for their country.

11.15 RSV	TEV
Then the king of the north shall come and throw up siegeworks, and take a well-fortified city. And the forces of the south shall not stand, or even his picked troops, for there shall be no strength to stand.	So the king of Syria will lay siege to a fortified city and capture it. The soldiers of Egypt will not continue to fight; even the best of them will not have enough strength.

Then: once again this reflects the common Hebrew conjunction and should be rendered in such a way that the transition is natural in the translation. The connection seems to be temporal rather than logical, that is, it introduces the next event in a sequence of events. The TEV rendering "so" may therefore be misleading.

Throw up siegeworks: the noun used in Hebrew refers to a large mound or ramp of earth that an attacking army built up against the wall of a fortified city. Such a mound enabled the archers to reach their targets inside the city and at the same time provided them with some protection. The Hebrew verb used here usually means "spill" or "pour out" (the earth was brought in baskets and "poured out" at the base of the city wall). In languages where walled cities and sieges are completely unknown, translators may have to resort to a less direct expression, such as "pile up earth against the wall in order to be able to attack the city" or something similar.

And take a well-fortified city: this refers to the military capture of a city that had strong defenses and was well protected.

The forces of the south: as in the expression **king of the south**, the word **south** is a reference to Egypt. The first word is literally "arms" (see KJV) but refers to the "armed forces" or the military personnel of Egypt stationed in the fortress.

Shall not stand: the verb in this context has the sense of standing firm in resistance of the enemy, but it is, of course, made negative in this verse. Translators may say "will not be able to hold out," or "will not stand up to him" (REB), or "will be powerless to resist" (NJV and NIV).

Even his picked troops: or "the elite of his army" (NJV), "their best troops" (NIV), or "even though its best warriors engage him" (Knox).

There shall be no strength to stand: many languages will require a clearer statement of the real subject of this sentence. Who is it that will lack strength? Although the structure of the original is unusual, it is clearly **his picked troops** that is intended.

The probable historical reference of verse 15 is to the siege of the coastal fortress town of Sidon by Antiochus III in 198 B.C. This city was held by Egyptian troops under General Scopas.

11.16 RSV	TEV
But he who comes against him shall do according to his own will, and none shall stand before him; and he shall stand in the glorious land, and all of it shall be in his power.	The Syrian invader will do with them as he pleases, without opposition. He will stand in the Promised Land and have it completely in his power.

He who comes against him: the pronoun references are unclear in RSV. Translators should probably use a noun as the subject, "the king of the north" or "the king of Syria," depending on how precise the translation is in the previous verses. Another possibility is to say "the invading king." The object pronoun, **him**, refers to the king of the south represented by his besieged army. It will therefore be better in most cases to use a plural pronoun "them," or perhaps better still, a phrase like "his enemies" or "the invader" (REB).

Shall do according to his own will: that is, "do whatever he pleases." See verses 3 and 36.

None shall stand before him: or "no one will be able to stand against him," "he shall meet no resistance," or "no one will dare to oppose him."

He shall stand: while the two words in this verse translated **stand** in RSV are the same in Hebrew, the contexts require very different renderings. Here the meaning is "he will establish himself" (NIV and REB) or "he will occupy" (AB). The singular pronoun refers to the king, but he represents his entire army in this case. Some languages may require that this be translated "he and his army" or "with his army he shall stand."

The glorious land: this, of course, refers to the land of Israel, but the expression has a very positive meaning. It is unwise to use a name like Mft, "the fair land of Palestine." But translators should probably say something like "the fairest of all lands" (NEB) or "the Land of Splendour" (NJB). This is not exactly the same expression as in 8.9, where only the noun "beauty" is found with the definite article, meaning "the beautiful one." Here the word for "land" with the definite article is included. The basic meaning is, however, the same in both cases. Compare also verse 41.

All of it shall be in its power: literally, the Hebrew text has "and destruction shall be in his hand" (see NIV, NJB and NJV). HOTTP/CTAT recommends this reading rather than the one followed by RSV and TEV. Although a number of modern versions adopt the emended reading, the Hebrew text makes sense as it is, and there is no strong reason to deviate from it. Translators are therefore advised to say something like "he will have the power to destroy it [the Land]."

The taking of the fortress at Sidon by Antiochus III assured his total conquest of Judea. Thus the land passed from Egyptian to Syrian domination.

11.17	RSV	TEV

RSV	TEV
He shall set his face to come with the strength of his whole kingdom, and he shall bring terms of peace[b] and perform them. He shall give him the daughter of women to destroy the kingdom;[c] but it shall not stand or be to his advantage.	"The king of Syria will plan an expedition, using his whole army. Then, in order to destroy his enemy's kingdom, he will make an alliance with him and offer him his daughter[y] in marriage; but his plan will not succeed.
[b] Gk: Heb *upright ones* [c] Heb *her* or *it*	[y] his daughter; *or* a young woman.

He shall set his face: once again the subject pronoun should probably be rendered by "the king of Syria" or "the king of the north" (see the previous verse). And the idiomatic expression **set his face** will probably not be rendered literally. It carries the sense of making a firm decision or "making up one's mind." Some translations use verbs like "determine" (NIV) and "resolve" (REB). See the comparable New Testament expression in Luke 9.51.

With the strength of his whole kingdom: this expression may mean either (a) "using the might of his (the king of the north's) entire kingdom" or (b) "conquering his (the king of the south's) entire kingdom." Solution (a) is followed by NIV, REB, TOB, AT, and Mft, as well as RSV and TEV. On the other hand, solution (b) is preferred by NEB, NJB, NJV, and AB. Translators will find themselves in good company whichever solution they adopt; but perhaps solution (a) is the better choice.

Bring terms of peace and perform them: the Hebrew equivalent is so ambiguous that there are several possible interpretations. There is also a significant textual problem to consider. The traditional Hebrew text says literally "and right intentions with him, and he makes . . . ." This is taken by NEB to mean "he will come to fair terms with him." However, the addition of a single Hebrew consonant yields the meaning "he will make a treaty with him." But the meaning of the two alternatives is not radically different. Since most versions include the idea of an alliance or "coming to terms" (NJB, TEV, TOB, NAB, NJV, NIV, and AT), this is the idea that should probably be conveyed in the translation.

He shall give him: translators should be careful to identify the participants more precisely in their own languages. The subject is the king of Syria (king of the north), and the object pronoun represents the king of Egypt or "the

king of the south." If the persons referred to are not clearly understood, it will
be important to make this clear in translation.

The daughter of women: there is no definite article in Hebrew before the
word "daughter." This expression seems to be the feminine equivalent of "son
of man" (see 7.13) and therefore means simply "a woman." The interpretation
of TEV, "his daughter," corresponds with the historical event, and this same
interpretation is followed by AB and AT. Mft even has "the princess of Egypt."
However, this is perhaps too precise in an account that seems to be intentionally vague. It is probably better to use a more general expression like "a
woman's hand" (NJB), "a woman" (NRSV), or possibly "a daughter" (NIV, NJV,
NAB). But it is unnecessary to emphasize youth as in "a young woman" (NEB)
or "young daughter" (REB).

To destroy the kingdom: literally "to overthrow (destroy) her (it)."
Grammatically the final pronoun in Hebrew can refer to **the daughter of
women** or to the "land (of Egypt)," which is also feminine in Hebrew. RSV
rightly takes it to be the latter and makes this clear in translation.

But it shall not stand or be to his advantage: literally "but she (it) will
not stand, she (it) will not happen to him." This can be understood to mean
either "she will fail" or "the plan will fail," but the sense is the same.

This verse is an apparent reference to the marriage of Cleopatra, the
daughter of Antiochus III, to Ptolemy V. The Syrian king counted on this
alliance to dominate little by little the Egyptian kingdom, but Cleopatra took
the side of her husband against her father.

11.18 RSV	TEV
Afterward he shall turn his face to the coastlands, and shall take many of them; but a commander shall put an end to his insolence; indeed[d] he shall turn his insolence back upon him.	After that he will attack the nations by the sea and conquer many of them. But a foreign leader will defeat him and put an end to his arrogance; indeed he will turn the arrogance of Syria's king back on him.[z]
[d] Heb obscure	[z] *Probable text* his arrogance . . . on him; *Hebrew unclear.*

Turn his face: or "turn his attention" (NIV), or simply "turn," as in many
English versions. But since his turning or his attention inevitably means
hostility, it may be better in some languages to use a more precise verb like
"attack," as in TEV.

The coastlands: the corresponding Hebrew term means "regions with
borders on the sea." In Gen 10.5 the inhabitants of these areas are described
as people "who live along the coast and on the islands" (TEV). Here the word
is translated "coasts and islands" by NEB/REB and NJB, and this may be a good
model for other languages. In other cases it will be more natural to speak of

"nations by the (big) water," "peoples (or tribes) living by the (salt) water," or something similar.

Shall take many of them: this refers to the capturing of many of the lands or peoples just mentioned. Some may prefer to translate "he will take control of many of these lands" or "he will capture many of those peoples."

A commander: the Hebrew word used here is an archaic and poetic word similar in meaning to the more usual term for "judge" or military leader found in Josh 10.24; Judges 11.6; Isa 10.1. It has been variously rendered "consul" (NJV), "leader" (NAB), "magistrate" (NJB and AB), and even "a certain Roman general" (Mft). NEB, FRCL, and GECL as well as TEV all retain the idea of a **commander** but add a qualifying word meaning "foreign," since the reference is to a Roman consul.

Insolence: the corresponding Hebrew word denotes the "contempt" with which a person may be treated, and by extension the "shame" or "dishonor" that the victim feels. It may also be used for the "insults" that are poured out on the despised person. On the other hand, in this context the term seems to qualify the attitude of the person who treats others contemptibly. It is therefore probably best translated "insolence" as in RSV, or "arrogance" (TEV), or "impudence."

He shall turn his insolence back on him: the meaning of the Hebrew text is uncertain at this point. Several textual changes have been proposed. NEB follows one of them with "by wearing him down." But it is best to understand this expression in the way suggested by CTAT: "a ruler will cause his insolence to cease. It will be only his insolence that will pay him back." It is also possible to translate "make him suffer the consequences of his arrogance." The expression seems to contain the idea of retribution for arrogance. Some other possible models are "put an end to his insults, nay pay him back for his insults" (NJV) and "put a stop to his defiant insults and pay him back for them" (Mft).

This verse seems to refer to the conquests of Antiochus III along the coast of Asia Minor and Greece. The **commander** is probably the Roman Consul Lucius Cornelius Scipion, who defeated Antiochus between 191 and 189 B.C.

11.19	RSV	TEV
	Then he shall turn his face back toward the fortresses of his own land; but he shall stumble and fall, and shall not be found.	The king will return to the fortresses of his own land, but he will be defeated, and that will be the end of him.

Turn his face back: this reflects exactly the same words found at the beginning of the previous verse, but the context requires the addition of the word **back**. It will be more natural in many languages to use a verb like "return" (TEV), "retreat" (REB), or "retire" (Mft). NEB uses an English expression having a military sense ("fall back"), which is appropriate in this context.

The fortresses of his own land: or "the well-protected cities in his country," or "the strong, walled cities of his own country" (NCV).

Stumble and fall: if these verbs may be understood in their literal sense by some readers, translators should replace them with an expression indicating defeat in battle. The first verb is the same as the one translated "fail" in verse 14.

Shall not be found: this is a veiled reference to death. The passive construction may have to be rendered actively as "he will disappear." But if such an expression will be understood literally, then it will be better to look for a euphemism that unquestionably refers to death.

Antiochus III, deprived of his eastern conquests (Asia Minor and Greece) and condemned to pay an enormous tax to Rome, returned to **his own land**, where the inhabitants turned against him and assassinated him in 187 B.C., when he tried to pillage the temple of one of their gods.

11.20   RSV   TEV

"Then shall arise in his place one who shall send an exactor of tribute through the glory of the kingdom; but within a few days he shall be broken, neither in anger nor in battle.

"He will be followed by another king, who will send an officer to oppress the people with taxes in order to increase the wealth of his kingdom. In a short time that king will be killed, but not publicly and not in battle."

Then shall arise in his place one: in some languages the most natural and economical way to express this will be simply "his successor," as in FRCL.

Who shall send an exactor of tribute through the glory of the kingdom: literally "one sending over an exactor of splendor of kingdom." This part of the verse is loaded with difficulties. AB takes the whole expression to mean "one suffering a loss of dominion, glory and sovereignty." On the other hand it may mean "a tax collector to maintain royal splendor" (NIV) or "a tax collector through the glorious kingdom" (NAB). FRCL follows yet another possibility, with "a man to pillage the most glorious edifice of the kingdom" (that is, the Temple). The interpretation of TEV, NIV, and NJV involving the "tax collector" is recommended.

A literal translation of the word **glory** may be misleading. In certain contexts the same word means "wealth," and this seems to be the case here.

Within a few days: this expression is not necessarily to be taken literally as referring to a period of time less than a week or two. It simply means "after a (relatively) short period of time" (see NEB/REB and AB, as well as TEV) or "(very) soon" (NAB and Mft). NIV has "in a few years."

He shall be broken: the meaning is undoubtedly "will be killed," and a literal rendering of RSV may be misleading in many languages. Where the passive construction is unnatural or impossible, translators may say "he will die" or use a less direct but equivalent expression that will be clearly understood. REB has "will meet his end." Compare 8.25 and comments on the same verb there.

Neither in anger nor in battle: literally "not by the nose (nostrils) and not in battle." The first of the two nouns here may be taken, by extension, to refer to the face as a whole or as a figure of speech for **anger**. This gives rise to two different interpretations, both of which are attested by the ancient versions. In the first case the expression means "not to the face of people" or "not publicly" (NJB, NEB/REB, AB, and FRCL, as well as TEV). The second interpretation is translated as in RSV, **not in anger** (similarly in NIV, NJV, NAB, and TOB). AT seems to combine the two ideas with "not in open violence." But in view of the probable Aramaic background of the Hebrew text, the first interpretation is to be preferred. It may be rendered positively as "in secret," if it is desirable to avoid the negative form.

Seleucus IV, one of the sons of Antiochus III, succeeded him on the throne of Syria. He sent his finance minister, Heliodore, to Jerusalem to capture the temple treasure. But Heliodore was unsuccessful in his attempt, and later he assassinated the king.

The evil king of Syria: 11.21-45

RSV

21 In his place shall arise a contemptible person to whom royal majesty has not been given; he shall come in without warning and obtain the kingdom by flatteries. 22 Armies shall be utterly swept away before him and broken, and the prince of the covenant also. 23 And from the time that an alliance is made with him he shall act deceitfully; and he shall become strong with a small people. 24 Without warning he shall come into the richest parts of the province; and he shall do what neither his fathers nor his fathers' fathers have done, scattering among them plunder, spoil, and goods. He shall devise plans against strongholds, but only for a time. 25 And he shall stir up his power and his courage against the king of the south with a great army; and the king of the south shall wage war with an exceedingly great and mighty army; but he shall not stand, for plots shall be devised against him. 26 Even those who eat his rich food shall be his undoing; his army shall be swept away, and many shall fall down slain. 27 And as for the two kings, their minds shall be bent on mischief; they shall speak lies at the same table, but to no avail; for the end is yet to be at the time appointed. 28 And he shall return to his land with great substance, but his heart shall be set

TEV

The Evil King of Syria

21 The angel went on to explain: "The next king of Syria will be an evil man who has no right to be king, but he will come unexpectedly and seize power by trickery. 22 Anyone who opposes him, even God's High Priest, will be swept away and wiped out. 23 By making treaties, he will deceive other nations, and he will grow stronger and stronger, even though he rules only a small nation. 24 He will invade a wealthy province without warning and will do things that none of his ancestors ever did. Then he will divide among his followers the goods and property he has captured in war. He will make plans to attack fortresses, but his time will soon run out.

25 "He will boldly raise a large army to attack the king of Egypt, who will prepare to fight back with a huge and powerful army. But the king of Egypt will be deceived and will not be successful. 26 His closest advisers will ruin him. Many of his soldiers will be killed, and his army will be wiped out. 27 Then the two kings will sit down to eat at the same table, but their motives will be evil, and they will lie to each other. They will not get what they want, because the time for it has not yet come. 28 The king of Syria will return home with all the loot he has captured, determined to de-

against the holy covenant. And he shall work his will, and return to his own land.

29 "At the time appointed he shall return and come into the south; but it shall not be this time as it was before. 30 For ships of Kittim shall come against him, and he shall be afraid and withdraw, and shall turn back and be enraged and take action against the holy covenant. He shall turn back and give heed to those who forsake the holy covenant. 31 Forces from him shall appear and profane the temple and fortress, and shall take away the continual burnt offering. And they shall set up the abomination that makes desolate. 32 He shall seduce with flattery those who violate the covenant; but the people who know their God shall stand firm and take action. 33 And those among the people who are wise shall make many understand, though they shall fall by sword and flame, by captivity and plunder, for some days. 34 When they fall, they shall receive a little help. And many shall join themselves to them with flattery; 35 and some of those who are wise shall fall, to refine and to cleanse them and to make them white, until the time of the end, for it is yet for the time appointed.

36 "And the king shall do according to his will; he shall exalt himself and magnify himself above every god, and shall speak astonishing things against the God of gods. He shall prosper till the indignation is accomplished; for what is determined shall be done. 37 He shall give no heed to the gods of his fathers, or to the one beloved by women; he shall not give heed to any other god, for he shall magnify himself above all. 38 He shall honor the god of fortresses instead of these; a god whom his fathers did not know he shall honor with gold and silver, with precious stones and costly gifts. 39 He shall deal with the strongest fortresses by the help of a foreign god; those who acknowledge him he shall magnify with honor. He shall make them rulers over many and shall divide the land for a price.

40 "At the time of the end the king of the south shall attack him; but the king of the north shall rush upon him like a whirlwind, with chariots and horsemen, and with many ships; and he shall come into countries and shall overflow and pass through. 41 He shall come into the glorious land. And tens of thousands shall fall, but these shall be delivered out of his hand: Edom and Moab and the main part of the Ammonites. 42 He shall stretch out

stroy the religion of God's people. He will do as he pleases and then return to his own land.

29 "Later on he will invade Egypt again, but this time things will turn out differently. 30 The Romans will come in ships and oppose him, and he will be frightened.

"Then he will turn back in a rage and try to destroy the religion of God's people. He will follow the advice of those who have abandoned that religion. 31 Some of his soldiers will make the Temple ritually unclean. They will stop the daily sacrifices and set up The Awful Horror. 32 By deceit the king will win the support of those who have already abandoned their religion, but those who follow God will fight back. 33 Wise leaders of the people will share their wisdom with many others. But for a while some of them will be killed in battle or be burned to death, and some will be robbed and made prisoners. 34 While the killing is going on, God's people will receive a little help, even though many who join them will do so for selfish reasons. 35 Some of those wise leaders will be killed, but as a result of this the people will be purified. This will continue until the end comes, the time that God has set.

36 "The king of Syria will do as he pleases. He will boast that he is greater than any god, superior even to the Supreme God. He will be able to do this until the time when God punishes him. God will do exactly what he has planned. 37 The king will ignore the god his ancestors served, and also the god that women love. In fact, he will ignore every god, because he will think he is greater than any of them. 38 Instead, he will honor the god who protects fortresses. He will offer gold, silver, jewels, and other rich gifts to a god his ancestors never worshiped. 39 To defend his fortresses, he will use people who worship a foreign god. He will give great honor to those who accept him as ruler, put them into high offices, and give them land as a reward.

40 "When the king of Syria's final hour has almost come, the king of Egypt will attack him, and the king of Syria will fight back with all his power, using chariots, horses, and many ships. He will invade many countries, like the waters of a flood. 41 He will even invade the Promised Land and kill tens of thousands, but the countries of Edom, Moab, and what is left of Ammon will escape. 42 When he invades all those countries, even Egypt will not be spared. 43 He will take away Egypt's hidden treasures of gold and silver and its other prized posses-

his hand against the countries, and the land of Egypt shall not escape. 43 He shall become ruler of the treasures of gold and of silver, and all the precious things of Egypt; and the Libyans and the Ethiopians shall follow in his train. 44 But tidings from the east and the north shall alarm him, and he shall go forth with great fury to exterminate and utterly destroy many. 45 And he shall pitch his palatial tents between the sea and the glorious holy mountain; yet he shall come to his end, with none to help him.

sions. He will conquer Libya and Ethiopia. 44 Then news that comes from the east and the north will frighten him, and he will fight furiously, killing many people. 45 He will even set up his huge royal tents between the sea and the mountain on which the Temple stands. But he will die, with no one there to help him."

TEV Section Heading: The evil king of Syria

NJB uses a straightforward historical reference as a section heading here, "Antiochus Epiphanes." However, it is recommended that this kind of information be left to the footnotes.

11.21   RSV   TEV

In his place shall arise a contemptible person to whom royal majesty has not been given; he shall come in without warning and obtain the kingdom by flatteries.

The angel went on to explain: "The next king of Syria will be an evil man who has no right to be king, but he will come unexpectedly and seize power by trickery.

Since this is the beginning of a new section in TEV, the translators decided to remind the reader who the speaker is, by adding "The angel went on to explain: . . . ." This renews the information originally given in 10.11 and repeated (by TEV) at verse 2 of this chapter. This will be a helpful model for many other languages.

In his place shall arise: this expression is exactly the same as the beginning of verse 20. It again speaks of the successor to the throne of Syria.

A contemptible person: literally "a despised one." The word "person" does not appear in the original. Some models may be "a wretch" (NJB), "a vile creature" (Knox), "despicable creature" (Mft and REB).

To whom royal majesty has not been given: literally "to whom they (indefinite) did not give royal honor." The passive form of RSV will have to be avoided by some translators. This idea is simply that the person in question had no legitimate claim to the throne. Translators may say "people did not show him the honor due to a king."

Come in: the verb used here may be better translated "invade" or "attack" in certain languages.

Without warning: this has been understood by some as meaning "in time of peace" (FRCL), but the meaning "when least expected" conveyed by RSV and TEV is to be preferred. Compare 8.25.

Obtain the kingdom by flatteries: the word translated **flatteries** comes from a root meaning "to be smooth." REB renders it "smooth dissimulation." In this context it clearly refers to "trickery" (NJV) or "intrigue" (NRSV, NJB, NIV, and NEB). NAB has "stealth and fraud." Many languages have idiomatic ways of expressing the sense of this term: "smooth talk," "sweet talk," "greasing people up," "pulling people's thinking," and so on.

Seleucus IV had a son named Demetrius who should have succeeded him, but Antiochus IV, the brother of Seleucus IV, seized the royal power when his brother was assassinated. Later Antiochus IV took the name of Epiphanes.

11.22 RSV	TEV
Armies shall be utterly swept away before him and broken, and the prince of the covenant also.	Anyone who opposes him, even God's High Priest, will be swept away and wiped out.

The wording of this verse is unusual, but its meaning is relatively clear. It literally reads "The arms of the overflowing will overflow before him and will be broken, and also the leader of the covenant." But RSV and several other English versions change the text slightly to read "utterly" in place of "overflowing."

Armies: literally "The arms," but used here in the sense of "the armed forces" or any opposition forces. See comments on "forces" in verse 15. On the verb "overflow" compare "flood" in 9.26 and comments on "overflow" in verse 10 of this chapter.

Be . . . swept away before him and broken: the two passive ideas may easily be rendered actively as "he (the king of the north) will sweep over and destroy" or something similar. REB reads "As he advances, he will sweep away all forces of opposition."

The prince of the covenant: or "covenant leader" (NJV), "the head of the priests," or to be quite precise, "God's High Priest" (Mft as well as TEV). See 9.25. This refers most probably to Onias III, the Jewish High Priest who was assassinated in 171 B.C. by order of Antiochus IV.

11.23 RSV	TEV
And from the time that an alliance is made with him he shall act deceitfully; and he shall become strong with a small people.	By making treaties, he will deceive other nations, and he will grow stronger and stronger, even though he rules only a small nation.

The structure of the beginning of this verse is very different in RSV and TEV. A more literal rendering of this is "And after coming together with him . . . ." But the idea of coming together is in the sense of a military alliance. This explains the rendering of RSV as well as "treaties" in TEV. But TEV gives the impression that it is by means of the treaties that he deceives other nations, while RSV seems closer to the meaning of the original. It is after agreements are reached with other nations that this ruler proves to be cunning and dishonest.

An alliance is made with him: the passive formulation can easily be rendered actively by saying "he will make treaties with other nations." The idea of treaties or alliances found here comes from the same root as in verse 6.

He shall act deceitfully: on the idea of "deceit" see 8.25 and comments.

With a small people: it is much better to read this "with few people," to avoid giving the impression that the physical size of the individual people is in view. Translators may consider saying "in spite of the fact that he rules over few people," or negatively, "although he does not rule over many people." The Syrian kingdom was significantly reduced at the end of the reign of Antiochus III, but it is difficult to speak of it as having "few people." It is perhaps better, with FRCL, to say something like "he had few followers (among the people of Israel)." Compare REB "although only a few people are behind him," and NRSV "with a small party."

The possible historical references of this verse are too vague to be able to identify them with any degree of certainty. The interpretation of GECL, which speaks here of "the holy city" falling into his power, is too specific and should be avoided.

11.24	RSV	TEV
	Without warning he shall come into the richest parts^e of the province; and he shall do what neither his fathers nor his fathers' fathers have done, scattering among them plunder, spoil, and goods. He shall devise plans against strongholds, but only for a time.	He will invade a wealthy province without warning and will do things that none of his ancestors ever did. Then he will divide among his followers the goods and property he has captured in war. He will make plans to attack fortresses, but his time will soon run out.

^e Or *among the richest men*

As in verse 21, the verb translated **come into** may be rendered "invade" or "attack" in this context.

Without warning: or if the other interpretation was followed in verse 21, "in time of peace." But the idea "suddenly" or "unexpectedly" is preferable.

The richest parts of the province: literally "in the fatness of the province." Compare the "fatness of the earth" in Gen 27.28, 39, where the same Hebrew word is used with essentially the same meaning. The term is used to make people think of the idea of richness and fertility of the land.

Neither his fathers nor his fathers' fathers: this refers to the ancestors and should probably be so translated, but the form is rather emphatic, since the word **fathers** alone is often used for ancestors. Perhaps this emphasis can be conveyed by saying something like "not a single one of his ancestors." REB attempts to convey this emphasis with "succeed where all his ancestors failed." In some languages the word for "grandfathers" must be used to translate the idea of "ancestors."

Scattering among them plunder, spoil, and goods: the first noun in this list may refer to either the act of pillage or the result of such action, but it is the second possibility that is appropriate here, and it has almost the same meaning as the second term. On the third term, see the comment on "supplies" in verse 13. The pronoun **them** refers not to the noun **fathers** or ancestors (which comes immediately before it) but to the "people" at the end of verse 23. This is made clear in TEV when it speaks of dividing "among his followers." The word rendered **scattering** may mean "distributing" or "lavishing on."

Devise plans against strongholds: or "he will plot to overthrow fortresses" (NIV). The idea is that of making military plans in order to defeat opposing forces protected in fortified positions. Some other ways of saying this are "conspire to take over fortified cities" or "plot the downfall of strong places." Mft makes it clear where the fortresses are located: "make plans . . . against the fortresses of Egypt."

But only for a time: literally "until a time." The most probable meaning of this expression involves the notion of time restriction. It may be expressed in a variety of ways: "but all that will not go on indefinitely" (FRCL), "though only for a limited time," or "the time will come when it is finished."

As in verse 18, the possible historical references of this verse are too general to be identifiable with any degree of certainty.

11.25	RSV	TEV
	And he shall stir up his power and his courage against the king of the south with a great army; and the king of the south shall wage war with an exceedingly great and mighty army; but he shall not stand, for plots shall be devised against him.	"He will boldly raise a large army to attack the king of Egypt, who will prepare to fight back with a huge and powerful army. But the king of Egypt will be deceived and will not be successful.

Note that a new paragraph is begun at this point in TEV, NJV, REB, and NJB. This is probably a good idea also for translations in other languages.

He shall stir up his power and his courage: on the verb translated **stir up**, see verse 2. The word rendered **courage** in RSV is one of the Hebrew words used for "heart." Many other languages represent the idea of courage with an expression containing the word "heart."

Wage war with . . .: translators should be aware that the king of the south (Egypt) is not fighting against **an exceedingly great and mighty army** but that he is using such an army in his war effort. The latter is, in fact, a kind of comparison with the **great army** of the king of Syria that was attacking him. The Egyptian ruler's army will be even greater and more powerful. It will be noted also that TEV and REB correctly use the verbal expression "fight back," indicating the defensive posture of the king of Egypt in response to the attack against his country.

He shall not stand: compare verses 15 and 16.

Plots shall be devised against him: the RSV passive reflects a Hebrew original that may be rendered "they (indefinite) devise plots against him." This construction, using an impersonal third person plural subject, may be a good model for other languages where the passive presents problems. There is no clear indication as to exactly who is the author of these plots.

Verses 25 and 26 are probably a reference to the conflict that pitted Antiochus IV against his nephew, Ptolemy VI (son of his sister Cleopatra; compare verse 17). In the course of the conflict Ptolemy VI was betrayed by certain of his generals.

11.26 RSV	TEV
Even those who eat his rich food shall be his undoing; his army shall be swept away, and many shall fall down slain.	His closest advisers will ruin him. Many of his soldiers will be killed, and his army will be wiped out.

Those who eat his rich food: the focus of this expression is not so much on the fact of eating at the king's table as on the intimacy that the sharing of food represents. On the word for **rich food**, see 1.5. AB has rendered the expression "members of his court," which is very similar in meaning to TEV.

Shall be his undoing: the idiomatic English of RSV does not reflect the original. The rendering of NAB is much more literal: "shall seek to destroy him."

Shall be swept away: literally "his army shall overflow," as in KJV and NASB. (The same verb is seen in 9.26 as well as verses 10 and 22 in this chapter.) Such an expression in its active form normally conveys the idea of a victorious army. But this does not fit the literary context here, which speaks of treason and the death of many soldiers, neither does it fit what we know of the historical context. HOTTP/CTAT propose that the traditional Hebrew text with the active verb form be retained; but the majority of modern translations and commentators follow the text of the ancient Syriac and Latin versions, which have the verb in the passive form, "will be overflowed." The passive idea of "being defeated" may be rendered by an impersonal third person plural subject "they" or by some other passive-avoiding construction.

Many shall fall down slain: in this context this can only mean "many soldiers will die." But an idiomatic way of saying "die" is appropriate here if one can be found.

And as for the two kings, their minds shall be bent on mischief; they shall speak lies at the same table, but to no avail; for the end is yet to be at the time appointed.	**Then the two kings will sit down to eat at the same table, but their motives will be evil, and they will lie to each other. They will not get what they want, because the time for it has not yet come.**

The first part of this verse is very difficult to follow. Literally it reads "Those two, the kings, their heart toward evil, at one table, will speak a lie." This has given rise to considerable restructuring and filling in of detail in TEV.

During the course of his military campaign, Antiochus IV took his nephew (Ptolemy VI) prisoner but apparently treated him well (receiving him at his own table) in order to scheme and seek ways of seizing political power in Egypt.

Minds: literally "hearts." In Hebrew the "heart" is the center of feelings, emotions, and passions, but it is also the source of intellectual activity. In this context both aspects may be in focus. There was intellectual activity based on a desire to do evil. Translators should use the term in their language that most naturally refers to such mental and emotional activity.

Mischief: this English translation is probably too weak. The corresponding word indicates something more profoundly evil than "dirty tricks" or **mischief**. Most versions prefer the term "evil."

Lies: as indicated in the literal rendering above, this noun is singular in Hebrew, but it is collective in meaning and may therefore legitimately be translated as a plural. In some languages it will be essential to indicate to whom they lied. The meaning is clearly ". . . to each other," as in TEV.

At the same table: this clearly suggests the idea of eating. Some languages speak of "having hands in the same bowl," "eating the same food," or something similar.

To no avail: in many languages this may be better translated as a separate sentence: "Their conspiring will be of no use," "Their plans will come to nothing," or "They will not succeed in their schemes."

For the end is yet to be at the time appointed: this is a rather free quotation of Hab 2.3, and its meaning is not altogether clear. It is generally thought that it indicates that human beings are incapable of putting an end to all their problems by themselves—God alone can do so, and that at the time he has fixed. Some possible models are "for the time fixed (by God) has still not yet come" or "because the end will still come at the time (which God has) appointed."

A possible model for translating the whole verse is:

> Those two kings will want to harm each other. They will sit down to eat together at the same table, but they will lie to each other. And no matter what they decide, it will not help

either one of them, because God is the one who has set the time for their end.

11.28   RSV   TEV

And he shall return to his land with great substance, but his heart shall be set against the holy covenant. And he shall work his will, and return to his own land.	The king of Syria will return home with all the loot he has captured, determined to destroy the religion of God's people. He will do as he pleases and then return to his own land.

He: in most languages it will probably be better to translate the pronoun by a full noun phrase, either "the king of Syria" or "the king of the north," depending on the decision made earlier. See verse 5.

Return to his land: since this king stopped for some time in Jerusalem on his way home, it has been suggested that this be translated "he will leave for his country" (FRCL) or "he will start back home." Essentially the same phrase is used again at the end of the verse, where he continues and completes his journey back to his own country.

Great substance: compare verses 13 and 24. But here the same term is applied to booty or loot captured in war.

His heart shall be set against: the heart is here seen as the seat of intelligence and will (see 1.8, "resolved," and 2.30, "mind") and therefore symbolizes his plans against the people of God.

The holy covenant: in verse 22 the "prince of the covenant" referred to the leader of the Jewish religion, the High Priest. The expression used here refers to the religion itself or the people who adhere to that religion. It involves the agreement between God and his people about their relationship. In many languages the concept of religion is difficult to translate directly. If this is the case, translators may consider "the proper worship of God" as a valid translation.

He shall work his will: literally "he will do (act)." According to some interpreters the Hebrew translator of the supposed Aramaic original misread it or had a faulty copy. The original is presumed to have meant "as he passes through," which fits the context and the known historical facts much better (see AB, page 270). But most versions accept the text as it stands and translate something like "he will take action" (NJB) or "he will do as he pleases" (TEV). The latter takes it to have the same meaning as "do according to his own will" in verses 3, 16, 36.

Return to his own land: this is essentially the same expression as earlier in the verse. FRCL avoids the repetition by translating the first occurrence as indicated above. Another possibility is to translate this second occurrence as "then he will complete the journey back home" or something similar.

At the end of his Egyptian campaign, Antiochus IV returned with a large amount of captured loot. On his way home he carried out an attack on Jerusalem and the Jewish religion in particular.

11.29   RSV   TEV

"At the time appointed he shall return and come into the south; but it shall not be this time as it was before.

"Later on he will invade Egypt again, but this time things will turn out differently.

At the time appointed: compare 8.19 and verse 27 above. The whole of chapter 11 is presented as a prediction of future events. These events are considered fixed in advance by a divine master plan. This explains why this expression is used. It avoids any precise time reference. In translation it is possible to use a very vague statement like "Some time later," but it is also possible to maintain the notion of a divinely fixed time by saying "In God's time" or "When (God decided that) the time was right."

He: in some languages it will be prudent to say clearly here "the king of the north" or "the king of Syria."

Return and come into the south: the comings and goings of the Syrian king may be made clearer by translating here "travel again to the kingdom in the south" or "go back to the land of Egypt."

It shall not be this time as it was before: the word **before** refers to the first incursion into Egypt (verses 25-28), while **this time** speaks of the second campaign. The expression as a whole indicates a fundamental difference in the two expeditions. The first was a success and the second ended in failure. It is legitimate to translate "but this time he will not be victorious as before," or "but he will not do as well as he did the first time," or "but the result will not be the same as his other campaign." REB translates "but he will have less success than he had before." Further details are given in the following verse.

The second campaign of Antiochus IV against Egypt took place in 168 B.C. It did not go well for him, because the Romans intervened and forced him to leave the country (see verse 30).

11.30   RSV   TEV

For ships of Kittim shall come against him, and he shall be afraid and withdraw, and shall turn back and be enraged and take action against the holy covenant. He shall turn back and give heed to those who forsake the holy covenant.

The Romans will come in ships and oppose him, and he will be frightened.
"Then he will turn back in a rage and try to destroy the religion of God's people. He will follow the advice of those who have abandoned that religion.

Ships of Kittim: the word **ships** is used figuratively to represent the people who used them as a means of transport. And this should be made clear in many languages. The word **Kittim** originally referred to people from the island of Cyprus, but in Jer 2.10 it probably refers to Mediterranean peoples in general. These peoples were "westerners" to those living in Judea. Although this word may have served as a general term for people from the west in Daniel (compare NIV "ships of the western coastlands" and NEB "ships from the west"), it is more likely that this was intended as a reference to the Romans. The Qumran writers used the term **Kittim** consistently to refer to the Romans. And the ancient Greek translation of Daniel renders it thus. This is followed by GECL, AT, and Mft, as well as TEV, and is also recommended to modern translators. Those versions that transliterate the Hebrew term are forced to add a footnote to help the reader understand the meaning.

Withdraw . . . turn back . . . turn back: the text pictures the Syrian king as retreating in fear when first attacked by the Romans. But what is meant by "turning back" and why does it occur twice in this verse? Evidently it does not mean that he turned back to attack the Romans after first retreating, but rather that he went back toward Jerusalem, where he expressed his anger against an easier enemy. In most languages it is unnecessary and probably unwise to translate both occurrences of the verb **turn back**.

Take action: as in verse 28 (and 39), AB proposes "as he passes through." But most other scholars retain the idea of taking action.

The holy covenant: see verse 28.

Give heed to those who forsake the holy covenant: the text speaks of giving attention to those who have abandoned the Jewish religion to follow the pagan practices of Antiochus IV. But what kind of attention is meant? It may indicate that he "will follow their advice" (TEV) or that he will "favour" them (NJB), that is, give them preferential treatment. The same verb is used with the negative in verse 37. Commentators give very little help on this question, and most translations leave it neutral, "pay attention to" or "have regard for."

11.31	RSV	TEV
	Forces from him shall appear and profane the temple and fortress, and shall take away the continual burnt offering. And they shall set up the abomination that makes desolate.	Some of his soldiers will make the Temple ritually unclean. They will stop the daily sacrifices and set up The Awful Horror.[a]

[a] THE AWFUL HORROR: *See 9.27.*

Forces from him: as in verses 15 and 22, this is literally "arms" but refers to "armed forces" or military personnel. Translators may say "soldiers in his command" (REB) or "armed forces dispatched by him" (NEB).

Appear: literally "stand up," this verb in military language indicates the taking of a position with the aim of attacking or besieging an enemy.

Profane: this verb has to do with "destroying the sacred character" of something previously considered especially for God. The entry of foreigners (enemy soldiers) into the Temple of Jerusalem deprived the building of its character as a building reserved exclusively for the service of God. In some languages the verb **profane** is best rendered "make corrupt (or contaminate) (by entering)" or something similar.

The temple and fortress: literally "the sanctuary, the fortress." There is no conjunction in the Hebrew, and the two terms are probably intended to refer to a single structure, that is, to the Temple at Jerusalem. NJB translates "the Citadel-Sanctuary" (compare "the fortress of the Temple" in Neh 2.8). NAB has "the sanctuary stronghold," and NIV reads "the temple fortress." In other languages it may be necessary to say "our fortress which is the Temple" or "the stronghold, the Temple itself."

Take away the continual burnt offering: see 8.11-12 and comments.

Set up: in some languages it will be necessary to include what the original readers would have known: "on the altar itself."

The abomination that makes desolate: see 9.27 and comments. In place of a general formulation like this or the one in TEV, some translators may be forced to say more precisely what this was: "they will make people do a very awful thing: worship foreign gods in our holy place." But if possible, the more general formulation is preferred. Compare the rendering of the corresponding New Testament expression in Matt 24.15 and Mark 13.14.

In December 168 B.C. King Antiochus IV (who gave himself the blasphemous name "Epiphanes," meaning "manifestation of God") gave orders to his troops to penetrate the Temple in Jerusalem. He prohibited the celebration of Jewish worship and placed on top of the altar of the Temple another altar dedicated to the Olympian god Zeus. This meant that in that place which was so sacred to the Jews, people offered animals that were considered unclean (such as pigs). This practice was particularly abhorrent to all faithful Jews. On the idea of abomination in general, compare Lev 11, where the term is used several times.

11.32 RSV TEV

He shall seduce with flattery those who violate the covenant; but the people who know their God shall stand firm and take action.

By deceit the king will win the support of those who have already abandoned their religion, but those who follow God will fight back.

He: it will be better in many languages to translate the pronoun as "The king" or "The king himself," making the subject of the verb clear.

Seduce: this verb may be translated literally "make hypocrites of" (see NJB footnote). The idea is one of winning them over to the evil side. Some other renderings are "pervert" (Mft), "corrupt" (AT), "make . . . apostatize" (NAB).

With flattery: literally "with smoothness (slipperiness)." Compare verse 21.

Those who violate the covenant: this expression represents a Hebrew participle used to describe people who act with treachery, and the noun for **covenant** or agreement. It has to do with those who do not honor their own word and do not respect agreements. In this case it refers to Jewish people who no longer honored the agreement of their people with God.

The people who know their God: this is in contrast with the previously mentioned group, who have abandoned their relationship with God. The verb **know** emphasizes not merely an intellectual knowledge of a subject, but an intimate personal and positive relationship. In some languages translators may wish to say "those who are close to their God," "those who remain loyal to their God" (NAB), or "the people devoted to their God" (NJV).

Stand firm and take action: the first verb speaks of someone maintaining a position, while the second focuses on active resistance. The **action** is taken by NEB and TEV to mean "fighting back." NIV translates the two verbs together: "will firmly resist him."

Antiochus IV knew how to use promises and threats at the same time. He mercilessly persecuted those who remained faithful to the religion of their ancestors, and he promised rewards to those who would renounce it.

11.33 RSV	TEV
And those among the people who are wise shall make many understand, though they shall fall by sword and flame, by captivity and plunder, for some days.	Wise leaders of the people will share their wisdom with many others. But for a while some of them will be killed in battle or be burned to death, and some will be robbed and made prisoners.

Those who are wise among the people: by the very nature of the phrase, and also in light of the immediate context, this is to be understood as referring to "leaders" who are wise. It is so translated in NEB/REB and NJB, as well as TEV. NAB has "the nation's wise men."

Shall make many understand: the idea here is not one of forcing people to understand, but rather of helping others to understand. In some languages the most natural way to say this will be by the use of the causative form of the verb. As in verses 14, 18, and 26, the noun translated **many** is a term often used in the Qumran writings for the ordinary members of the community as distinct from the leaders. This is added reason to translate "leaders" in the first part of the verse.

They shall fall: the pronoun subject probably refers to the "wise leaders" rather than to the people in general. They would certainly not have been excluded from the persecutions. Verse 35 expresses this more clearly.

Fall by sword and flame, by captivity and plunder: the four misfortunes that will happen to the wise leaders may be described in a variety of ways according to what is natural in the translator's language. The verb "to fall" indicates death and goes with the first two nouns, and the word **sword**, as often in Scripture, is symbolic of warfare in general. So the meaning is that some will die while engaged in war, and others will be burned to death. The other two nouns speak of exile (or imprisonment) and theft as two other ways in which the wise leaders will suffer.

For some days: the word **days** is not to be taken literally in this context. This whole expression refers to a relatively short period of time, but not necessarily one that is most naturally measured in days. Compare verse 20.

11.34   RSV   TEV

When they fall, they shall receive a   While the killing is going on, God's
little help. And many shall join   people will receive a little help, even
themselves to them with flattery;   though many who join them will do
                                             so for selfish reasons.

When they fall: the pronoun reference may need to be made clearer in some cases. **They** stands for "the people who know their God" in verse 32. The verb **fall** very probably does not refer to mere stumbling but to falling in battle, and therefore refers to death. Another possible way to word this may be "during the course of the persecutions" (FRCL), or possibly "while they (indefinite) were killing God's people."

They shall receive a little help: literally "they will be helped with little help," or "they will not receive much help," or "the help they receive will be small."

Join themselves to them: in all probability this refers to the joining of insincere people to "those who are faithful to their God" (verse 32).

With flattery: literally "in slipperiness," or perhaps more accurately, "by trickery" (compare verses 21 and 32). Some other possible renderings are "insincerely" (AB) or "with hypocrisy" (AT).

The persecution by Antiochus IV provoked the passive resistance of the *Chasidim* (the Pious Ones, or the Righteous Ones), who expected help only by the direct intervention of God (an attitude praised by the author of Daniel in verse 14), and the active resistance of the Hasmoneans, who distinguished themselves in the armed struggle of the Maccabees (a method criticized in the Book of Daniel). The writer thinks that the successes of the active resistance do not constitute anything more than negligible **help** toward the final victory of Judaism. And in the eyes of the author, the efforts to unite the two kinds of resistance represented "hypocrisy." The two forms of resistance were, in fact, impossible to reconcile as far as he was concerned, because the secret intention of the **men of violence** (verse 14) was to take control of the entire resistance movement.

Some commentators interpret the last part of this verse differently. Some people hypocritically joined the armed resistance rather than the passive resistance, due to the violent pressure put on them by Judas Maccabeus (for example, the forced circumcision of children and the burning alive of adversaries). This interpretation seems less convincing, because it requires

312

that the pronoun **them** (in the expression **they joined themselves to them**) must take an antecedent different from the subject of the main statement.

11.35 RSV	TEV
and some of those who are wise shall fall, to refine and to cleanse them[f] and to make them white, until the time of the end, for it is yet for the time appointed.	Some of those wise leaders will be killed, but as a result of this the people will be purified. This will continue until the end comes, the time that God has set.

[f] Gk: Heb *among them*

Some of those who are wise: referring to a part of the group of "wise leaders" introduced in verse 33.

Fall: taken by TEV as in the two previous verses to refer to death. Note, however, that NJB and NIV seem to take it in another sense, translating "stumble." Similarly AB takes it to mean "will be tested." Given the immediate context, probably the idea of being killed is intended.

To refine and to cleanse them and to make them white: the structure of the Hebrew indicates that the result of the death of the wise leaders is described by these verbal infinitives. The three terms have almost the same meaning and convey the idea of the purification of metals and the cleaning of articles of clothing. The function of the object pronoun **them** (repeated in RSV, but occurring only once in Hebrew) is unclear. But the pronoun should almost certainly be taken to refer to "the people (of God)," that is, those who were left. The people as a whole seem to be referred to. The three verbs in Hebrew may be reduced to one or two in many languages.

For it is yet for the time appointed: this is yet another reference to the fact that, in the mind of the writer, God has a definite foreordained plan into which all historical events must fit. Here it is specifically the end that is seen as being a set time.

11.36 RSV	TEV
"And the king shall do according to his will; he shall exalt himself and magnify himself above every god, and shall speak astonishing things against the God of gods. He shall prosper till the indignation is accomplished; for what is determined shall be done.	"The king of Syria will do as he pleases. He will boast that he is greater than any god, superior even to the Supreme God. He will be able to do this until the time when God punishes him. God will do exactly what he has planned.

The king: in some cases it will be clearer to indicate which of the two kings is intended here. Note that TEV has "the king of Syria."

Shall do according to his will: see verses 3 and 16.

Exalt himself and magnify himself: see 8.4, 8, 11 on **magnify**; the two verbs are used here as synonyms.

Astonishing things: elsewhere the expression **astonishing things** may be understood to refer to wonderful and extraordinary events and may have quite positive connotations. In Exo 34.10, for example, the same root word is used to speak of miracles in a very positive sense, as "marvels." It may, however, also be used in a very negative sense of "abnormal things" that may even be scandalous (see 8.24, "fearful destruction"). The RSV translation, and even NIV "unheard of things" (which is not necessarily negative), are too weak. NAB captures the idea with "dreadful blasphemies." And the same idea is conveyed in more common language by "awful things" (NJV). NRSV revises RSV with "horrendous things."

The God of gods: this certainly refers to the God of Israel, who is considered superior to all other possible gods. The expression does not indicate that the Jews admitted the actual existence of gods other than their own, but they did recognize (on the linguistic level) that other peoples worshiped what they called "gods." As far as religions can be compared, the Jews affirmed that their God was superior to anything that any other people might consider their "god." If in the translator's language the use of the expression "God of gods" will carry the sense of polytheism (the existence of several gods placed in hierarchical order), then a different kind of expression should be used such as "the Supreme God" (TEV) or "the Most High God" (GECL). Also, since it is not a good idea to say "the God of idols," translators may consider a longer expression like "the God over all those (beings, things) that others consider to be gods."

Until the indignation is accomplished: the word translated **indignation** in RSV is better understood as "divine wrath" (REB) or "God's anger." This should be made clear in the translation. And because of the passive form, it will have to be restructured in some languages to say something like the TEV rendering, or possibly "until God pours out his anger on him," or "until the time when God shows his wrath."

What is determined shall be done: the passive verb should probably be made active, even in many languages where the passive is grammatically possible. It is clearly God who will bring about what he has planned.

This verse begins to paint a striking portrait (in veiled terms) of Antiochus IV. The statement that **he shall exalt and magnify himself above every god** is probably a reference to the title "Epiphanes" (see verse 31), which the king bestowed on himself. On the idea of speaking **astonishing things against the God of gods**, see 7.8, 20, "speaking great things."

11.37 RSV TEV

He shall give no heed to the gods of his fathers, or to the one beloved by women; he shall not give heed to any other god, for he shall magnify himself above all.

The king will ignore the god his ancestors served, and also the god that women love. In fact, he will ignore every god, because he will think he is greater than any of them.

He: once again it may be necessary to make the subject of the sentence clear by using a noun or noun phrase such as "the king."

Give no heed to the gods of his fathers: the same verb is used in verse 30 in a positive sense. But here it has the sense of intentional neglect. The word rendered **gods** by RSV may be understood as either a singular or a plural. A few modern versions take it as a singular (NIV and NJV as well as TEV). NIV even has it with a capital letter, making it refer to the one true God, but this is not recommended in this context. As in 2.23; 9.6; 11.24, the word translated **fathers** means "ancestors" here. It may be wise in some languages to say more directly "the gods that his ancestors worshiped."

The one beloved by women: the passive idea can easily be transformed into an active expression like "the god women love" or "the god that women worship," but what does it mean? The reference is most likely to the god called Tammuz in Hebrew (or Adonis in Greek), who was thought to make women fertile (compare Ezek 8.14). This information, however, should not be placed in the text but in a footnote.

Any other god: or "anything else that other people consider to be a god." See the comments on "God of gods" in verse 36.

Magnify himself: see the previous verse.

11.38 RSV TEV

He shall honor the god of fortresses instead of these; a god whom his fathers did not know he shall honor with gold and silver, with precious stones and costly gifts.

Instead, he will honor the god who protects fortresses. He will offer gold, silver, jewels, and other rich gifts to a god his ancestors never worshiped.

The structure of this verse will probably have to be altered in many languages. In the first sentence the words **instead of these** may have to be shifted forward, as in TEV. And the second sentence in RSV has the direct object before the subject and verb, but this will be awkward for many translators.

The god of fortresses: it is probably a good idea to make clear the relationship between the god and the fortresses by saying something like "the god who protects the strongholds" or "the god who defends fortified cities." This probably refers to Jupiter Capitolinus, the supreme god of the Romans and the equivalent of the Olympian Zeus, for whom Antiochus IV built a richly ornamented temple in Antioch.

Instead of these: that is, instead of the gods mentioned in the previous verse ("the gods of his fathers," "the one [god] beloved by women," and "any other god"). The meaning given to the Hebrew in some versions ("on its pedestal," compare NJV) is not impossible but is unlikely if the use of the same expression in verses 20 and 21 is taken into account, where RSV translates "in his place."

A god whom his fathers did not know: the word **fathers** refers, of course, to ancestors. And the idea of knowing a god may be difficult to understand if translated literally. The intention of the writer was almost certainly "a god not honored by his ancestors" (compare TEV).

Honor with gold: the same verb is repeated in Hebrew, but in the second case it may be better to translate it "offer," as in TEV. Or translators may prefer to say more clearly "he will show honor by giving gold."

11.39   RSV   TEV

He shall deal with the strongest fortresses by the help of a foreign god; those who acknowledge him he shall magnify with honor. He shall make them rulers over many and shall divide the land for a price.

To defend his fortresses, he will use people who worship a foreign god. He will give great honor to those who accept him as ruler, put them into high offices, and give them land as a reward.

Deal with the strongest fortresses: taken at its face value, this seems to mean "He will come against the strongest (enemy) fortresses." But a minor change in the Hebrew vowels makes it mean "He will defend (his own) fortresses," as in TEV (as well as NJB, NAB, NEB, AT, and Mft). This is probably the best solution.

By the help of a foreign god: the text is extremely difficult, and many guesses have been made as to its real meaning. But a change in the vowel of the Hebrew word that RSV translates **by the help of** makes it mean "people." This gives the text a much better sense and is followed by NAB, NJB, NEB/REB, and others, as well as TEV. It is probably best to adopt this meaning in the translation, even though this is contrary to the recommendation of HOTTP.

Those who acknowledge him: this can mean either that they acknowledge the "god of fortresses" mentioned in verse 38 (FRCL and TOB), or that they accept this king as the legitimate ruler of the country (TEV). Still other versions take it to mean "those whom he (the king) acknowledges" (NJB) or "those whom he favours" (NEB/REB). Many English versions leave it rather vague but seem to suggest the interpretation that is expressed clearly in TEV. It is probably best to follow TEV's interpretation and make the meaning clear in the translation.

Make them rulers over many: the word here rendered **many** refers to common people or the "multitude" and is the same as used in verse 34.

Divide the land for a price: the last word usually referred to a sum of money that served either as payment for a purchase or as a reward to a person for something done. By extension the word came to mean the value of an article or a reward given to a person, even if the transaction did not involve money. In the present context either interpretation is possible. On the one hand it may mean the sale of conquered lands (at a bargain price) to the favorites of the king (NEB, NIV, NJB and NJV). But on the other hand it may refer to the distribution of the conquered territory to them as a reward for their services (AT, NAB, REB, FRCL, TOB, and AB, as well as TEV). The latter interpretation is probably to be preferred.

This verse seems to be a reference to the installation of the troops of Antiochus IV in Jerusalem, where they set themselves up even in the vicinity of the Temple itself. According to some, this is what was meant by **the strongest fortresses**.

In view of the numerous problems regarding the text and its interpretation in this verse, it is perhaps wise to summarize the recommended translation:

> He will use foreigners who worship a different god, to protect his fortresses. And he will give great honors to those who acknowledge him as the true ruler of the country; he will give them positions of importance in his government, and he will distribute conquered lands to them as a reward for their loyalty to him.

In addition it may be a good idea to add a footnote indicating that the word **fortresses** may refer particularly to Jerusalem, where the Jews especially resented the presence of non-Jewish troops.

11.40   RSV   TEV

"At the time of the end the king of the south shall attack[g] him; but the king of the north shall rush upon him like a whirlwind, with chariots and horsemen, and with many ships; and he shall come into countries and shall overflow and pass through.

"When the king of Syria's final hour has almost come, the king of Egypt will attack him, and the king of Syria will fight back with all his power, using chariots, horses, and many ships. He will invade many countries, like the waters of a flood.

[g] Heb *thrust at*

At the time of the end: this may be taken to refer either to the end of the world or to the end of the tyrannical rule of the king of the north. TEV follows the latter, and this also seems to be behind the rendering of NAB, "at the appointed time." But most versions leave the time reference ambiguous. Compare verse 35 and 8.17.

Shall attack him: the verb used here actually means "push, thrust, gore" and is often used of a butting animal. The writer again takes up the metaphor of the verb used in 8.4, "I saw the ram charging." Some English versions attempt to capture something of the figure of speech by translating "shall lock horns with him" (NJV) or "shall butt at him" (Mft). This may be done in other languages by saying something like "thrust at him like a goat." The pronoun **him** stands for the "king of the North," Antiochus IV of Syria. In many languages it will be better to use the full noun phrase here, and the pronoun in the sentence that follows.

Rush on him like a whirlwind: literally "he shall whirl away." The counterattack of the Syrian king is described with a different figure of speech. In this case the quickness and devastation of a sudden storm is envisaged. The metaphorical use of the verb is changed into a simile by RSV and several other English versions.

With chariots and horsemen: the word for "chariot" is singular here but undoubtedly has a collective meaning and should therefore be translated as a plural in most languages. It will be noted that, instead of **horsemen**, TEV has "horses." The Hebrew can be understood either way, but in view of the context of military equipment, it seems more likely that the meaning "horses" is intended.

Come . . . overflow and pass through: see verse 10. This is in keeping with the image of the storm or whirlwind presented earlier in this verse.

Historical sources provide no evidence for an attack on Egypt by Antiochus IV at such a late date in his reign.

11.41	RSV	TEV
	He shall come into the glorious land. And tens of thousands shall fall, but these shall be delivered out of his hand: Edom and Moab and the main part of the Ammonites.	He will even invade the Promised Land and kill tens of thousands, but the countries of Edom, Moab, and what is left of Ammon will escape.

Come into: in most languages the context will require a less neutral verb indicating a military invasion. NJV and Mft as well as TEV use "invade."

The glorious land: that is, the land of Israel as in verse 16. See also the comments on 8.9.

Tens of thousands: the traditional Hebrew text has "many (people)" (as in NJB, NAB, NJV, TOB). But the form of the text is unusual, and a minor change in the vowels (recommended by HOTTP/CTAT) yields the text of RSV, which is also followed by TEV, NEB/REB, NRSV, and others. See verse 12 and 7.10.

Fall: indicating death, as in verses 33-35.

These: the structure of RSV, using this demonstrative pronoun at the beginning of the sentence and then defining it later (**Edom and Moab**), will be awkward in many languages and should probably be transformed with the geographical names at the beginning of the sentence.

Shall be delivered out of his hand: as in 1.2 and elsewhere, the **hand** stands for the "power" of the king and his army. And it should probably be so translated in many languages.

The main part of the Ammonites: in addition to the rendering of RSV (as well as NJV and NAB), the traditional Hebrew text may also be understood to mean "the beginnings of the Ammonites" or "the chiefs of the Ammonites" (followed by NIV). But by proposing a correction in the Hebrew, some scholars have arrived at a text that corresponds to what is found in the Syriac, and that may be rendered "what remains of the Ammonites." This is the basis of the TEV rendering, which is also followed by AB, NEB, and AT. This emended reading seems to fit the context best.

11.42   RSV   TEV

He shall stretch out his hand   When he invades all those coun-
against the countries, and the land   tries, even Egypt will not be spared.
of Egypt shall not escape.

Stretch out his hand against: or "use his power against," or "extend his domination over."

The countries: the reference here may be to Edom, Moab, and Ammon mentioned in the previous verse (TEV), or possibly to "other countries" in addition to them (FRCL and NEB/REB). NIV has "many countries." This interpretation seems more likely than that of TEV. But if the interpretation of TEV is followed, it will probably not be necessary to repeat the proper names. It is quite likely that a more definite reference such as "those countries" will be appropriate.

The land of Egypt: this is another clearly-stated geographical reference to Egypt, confirming the translation of "king of the south" as "king of Egypt" (see the discussion under verse 5).

Shall not escape: or "will also be captured."

11.43   RSV   TEV

He shall become ruler of the trea-   He will take away Egypt's hidden
sures of gold and of silver, and all   treasures of gold and silver and its
the precious things of Egypt; and   other prized possessions. He will
the Libyans and the Ethiopians shall   conquer Libya and Ethiopia.[b]
follow in his train.

[b] *Hebrew* Cush: *Cush is the ancient
name of the extensive territory south
of the First Cataract of the Nile River. This region was called Ethiopia in
Graeco-Roman times, and included
within its borders most of modern*

Sudan and some of present-day Ethiopia (Abyssinia).

Become ruler of: literally "He will dominate." Compare "will gain control of (over)" (NEB, NIV, and NJV) and "treasure . . . will lie in his power" (NJB). In other languages translators may say ". . . will be under his power" or "he will conquer."

All the precious things of Egypt: in this context, following the mention of **gold** and **silver**, it will be appropriate in many languages to add the word "other" and say something like "all the other valuable things of Egypt." Or the whole thing may be restructured to say something like "he will seize all the treasures of Egypt, including its silver and gold."

The Ethiopians: literally "the Cushites." The term "Cush" refers to the region situated to the south of Egypt and identified with the ancient Nubia (NIV, TOB) or with "Sudan" in earlier editions of TEV. Since the term "Cush" undoubtedly referred to an area much larger than the present day state of Sudan, the use of "Sudan" is not recommended. The ancient Greek version rendered the term "Cush" as "Ethiopia," and this has been followed by a great many modern English versions (including RSV/NRSV, AT, Mft). Others simply transliterate the Hebrew here, using "Cushites" (NEB/REB, NJB, NJV). In those languages where all the geographic terms are equally unknown, the latter solution is preferable.

Shall follow in his train: literally "(are) at his steps." This expression indicates submission to a higher authority. Some versions have translated it by "follow in his footsteps" (Segond and *Bible de la Pléiade* in French), but this is unfortunate, since that expression carries with it the idea of "following the example of," which is not found in the Hebrew. NJV has "follow at his heel," and NJB renders the same expression "will be at his feet," both of which give the idea of submissive adherents. Libya (to the west) and Cush (to the south) were a part of the kingdom of the Ptolemies. So the conquest of the "king of the north" is not limited to Egypt as such but extends throughout the "kingdom of the south."

11.44 RSV	TEV
But tidings from the east and the north shall alarm him, and he shall go forth with great fury to exterminate and utterly destroy many.	Then news that comes from the east and the north will frighten him, and he will fight furiously, killing many people.

But: TEV considers "Then" a better transition word in this context (similarly AT and Mft). But the majority of English versions retain that contrastive conjunction, since there is a contrast between victory in verse 43 and alarm in this verse. Note, however, that REB leaves the conjunction untranslated.

Tidings: the same Hebrew word is translated elsewhere as "report" (Isa 53.1). It comes from the same root as the verb "to hear" and so carries the idea of "things heard." In this case it has been rendered "rumours" (NEB/REB and Mft), "reports" (NJB, NRSV, and NJV), or simply "news" (TEV).

Go forth with great fury: compare verse 11, "moved with anger, shall come out . . . ."

Exterminate and utterly destroy: the two verbs in Hebrew mean more or less the same thing and have been rendered by a single verb in FRCL, GECL and TEV.

Many: in a number of languages it will be required to make this more precise: "many people."

The Parthians (in the eastern part of the Seleucid Kingdom) and the Armenians (to the north) proved to be somewhat turbulent. So Antiochus IV had to go to these regions to reestablish order.

11.45   RSV   TEV

And he shall pitch his palatial tents between the sea and the glorious holy mountain; yet he shall come to his end, with none to help him.

He will even set up his huge royal tents between the sea and the mountain on which the Temple stands. But he will die, with no one there to help him."

Pitch his palatial tents: the word translated **palatial** occurs nowhere else in the Hebrew Old Testament, but its meaning is undisputed. It comes into Hebrew through Aramaic and is ultimately from Old Persian. The reference is to the lavish tents that served as the living quarters of the king during his military campaigns. Some possible models are "set up the large tents made for the king and his family" or "raise up the fine tents which the king would live in."

The sea: the word here is plural in the original, and standing alone it can possibly designate the Dead Sea and the Mediterranean together. But in that case the second object, **the glorious holy mountain**, will be very difficult to explain. Commentators think that the use of the plural without the definite article here is merely in accordance with ancient poetic usage (thus Judges 5.17; Deut 33.19). The reference is almost certainly to the Mediterranean, which is seen as being composed of more than one "sea."

The glorious holy mountain: this expression is used to designate the hill in Jerusalem on which the Temple was built. See, for example, Isa 56.7; Obadiah 16; Psa 2.6; 15.1. This has been rendered in a more direct manner by TEV as "the mountain on which the Temple stands" and in GECL as "Mount Zion." But others object that this makes very precise the expression in the text that is intentionally vague. Some other possible renderings are "the hill of the sanctuary," or "the holy mountain in the most beautiful land" (FRCL), or "the holy hill, the fairest of all hills" (REB).

Come to his end: this is yet another veiled allusion to the death of the tyrant, Antiochus. See 8.25. In many languages it will be more natural to use the verb "to die." Some other ways of saying the same thing are "he will meet his doom" (NJV) or "death will surprise him" (FRCL).

With no one to help him: this phrase expresses the idea of loneliness as well as helplessness.

In fact Antiochus IV Epiphanes died at Tabae in Persia toward the end of the year 164 B.C., during his campaign against the troublesome Parthians (see verse 44).

The time of trouble: 12.1-4

RSV

TEV
The Time of the End

1 "At that time shall arise Michael, the great prince who has charge of your people. And there shall be a time of trouble, such as never has been since there was a nation till that time; but at that time your people shall be delivered, every one whose name shall be found written in the book. 2 And many of those who sleep in the dust of the earth shall awake, some to everlasting life, and some to shame and everlasting contempt. 3 And those who are wise shall shine like the brightness of the firmament; and those who turn many to righteousness, like the stars for ever and ever. 4 But you, Daniel, shut up the words, and seal the book, until the time of the end. Many shall run to and fro, and knowledge shall increase."

1 The angel wearing linen clothes said, "At that time the great angel Michael, who guards your people, will appear. Then there will be a time of troubles, the worst since nations first came into existence. When that time comes, all the people of your nation whose names are written in God's book will be saved. 2 Many of those who have already died will live again: some will enjoy eternal life, and some will suffer eternal disgrace. 3 The wise leaders will shine with all the brightness of the sky. And those who have taught many people to do what is right will shine like the stars forever."

4 He said to me, "And now, Daniel, close the book and put a seal on it until the end of the world. Meanwhile, many people will waste their efforts trying to understand what is happening."

TEV Section Heading: The time of the end

Some other possible models are "The end of history" (REB), "A time of anguish and a promise of reward," or "Hope in time of despair."

Note that verses 1 to 3 are set off as poetry in NAB and NEB/REB. But this is not recommended to other translators.

12.1   RSV   TEV

"At that time shall arise Mi-chael, the great prince who has charge of your people. And there shall be a time of trouble, such as never has been since there was a nation till that time; but at that time your people shall be delivered, ev-

The angel wearing linen clothes said, "At that time the great angel Michael, who guards your people, will appear. Then there will be a time of troubles, the worst since nations first came into exis-tence. When that time comes, all the

ery one whose name shall be found
written in the book.

people of your nation whose names
are written in God's book will be
saved.

At the beginning of this chapter and new section, it may be important to identify the speaker again, as has been done in TEV: "The angel wearing linen clothes said." This is not in the original text, but it is information from the wider context, and this information may need to be supplied again here for readers, in view of the extremely long monologue of the angel (10.20–11.45). It may also serve to mark the transition from the historical part of the angel's discourse to his final words.

Michael: see 10.13, 21. The Hebrew for **shall arise** carries the idea of assuming a position, or taking a stand, and it is repeated here in the Hebrew for **who has charge**, showing that he has taken a position of responsibility for the people of Israel.

Great prince: REB has "great captain." However, in order to avoid giving the impression that Michael was an earthly prince or captain, it may be desirable in some cases to state clearly that he was a "great angel" (TEV) or "mighty angel." Several terms describing Michael as **prince** here are used also in 10.21, where he is also shown to be guardian angel of the people of Israel.

Who has charge of your people: literally "the one standing over the sons of your people." On expressions beginning with "sons of . . . ," see comments on 1.6.

There shall be a time of trouble: this affirmation seems to reflect the text of Jer 30.7 (see also Joel 1.15-18 and Zeph 1.14-18). In the thought of the people of Israel, the time of the end is closely related to the theme of judgment and the resulting punishment of those who have not been faithful to God.

Since there was a nation: this may be understood to refer to the beginning of nationhood in general (NRSV has "since nations first came into existence"). However, it is also possible that it refers to the beginning of the nation of Israel. But since the people of Israel almost certainly thought of themselves as being the first nation to come into existence, the two may be thought of as being identical. NJV translates "since the nation came into being," making it refer clearly to the existence of the nation of Israel in particular. This understanding seems also to be behind the rendering of REB ("since they became a nation"). Probably this is the best kind of model to follow in other languages at this point. Another possible model is "ever since our nation began" or "since our people became a nation."

At that time: the repetition of these words (found also at the beginning of this verse) may be repeated if it is natural to do so in the receptor language. But such repetition will have to be avoided in some languages, possibly by using a transition word like "Then" (FRCL as well as TEV). Others may wish to render it "But when that time comes."

Your people shall be delivered: this passive formulation may be rendered actively as "God will deliver your people," making the subject clear. But the following phrase, **every one whose name shall be found written in the book**, places an important limitation on the number of those who will be delivered. The **book** referred to may have to be more clearly identified, using an expression like "the book of God" (GECL and TEV) or "the book of life" (FRCL), as in Exo 32.32-33; Psa 69.28; Rev 3.5.

12.2   RSV   TEV

And many of those who sleep in the   Many of those who have already
dust of the earth shall awake, some   died will live again: some will enjoy
to everlasting life, and some to   eternal life, and some will suffer
shame and everlasting contempt.   eternal disgrace.

Many of those: more accurately, "the many." Compare 11.14, 33, 39.

Who sleep . . . shall awake: the images of sleep for death and awakening for resurrection are common in the New Testament and possibly have their origin in Daniel. this is, in fact, the only passage where virtually all Old Testament scholars agree that there is a reference to a resurrection from the individual from death to life. If these images are likely taken literally and thereby misunderstood by readers, then their meaning should be translated more clearly. The verb **sleep** will be rendered "have died," and **awake** may legitimately become "will live again," "will be revived," or "will return to life."

In the dust of the earth: literally "in the earth (land) of dust." This is an expression used to refer to the world of the dead, the *sheol* of the ancients (compare Isa 26.19, "land of the shades"; Psa 22.15, "the dust of death"; 30.9, "the Pit . . . the dust"). The idea of burial is understood in this expression and may be made clear. FRCL renders it "in the bottom of the tomb," and NJB translates rather literally "the Land of Dust." In many languages the most natural way to convey this idea will be to say straightforwardly "who (have died and) have been buried."

Some . . . and some . . . : according to the view described here, the resurrected persons were made up of two distinct groups: (a) the faithful, who were destined to **everlasting life** in communion with God; and (b) the others, destined for **shame and everlasting contempt** in the absence of communion with God. According to certain commentators, a second interpretation is possible, namely that the resurrection really concerned only the faithful, who would receive eternal life. The others would not be raised but would remain in a state of shame and rejection forever in the world of the dead. This second interpretation allows the establishment of a good parallel with the previous verse, and this parallel form may be outlined as follows:

verse 1   those living at the time of the end
           the faithful will remain alive
           (UNSTATED: the others will die);
verse 2   those who lived in previous generations
           the faithful will be raised to life
           the others will awake to permanent shame.

The choice between the two interpretations is difficult to make, but it is important to try not to be influenced by later theological developments (for example, John 5.28 and Rev 20.4-5). However, the first interpretation is the most commonly held and probably correct.

The Hebrew word rendered **contempt** is rare and is found elsewhere only in Isa 66.24 ("abhorrence"). The root meaning has the idea "repel," and so it seems to express the thought that other people will not want to be near anyone to whom this word applies. It follows another word that is better known, **shame**, and this provides some meaning to this term. If two such words are not easily found, it is acceptable to render them by a single noun in the translation, as in TEV.

12.3 RSV	TEV
And those who are wise shall shine like the brightness of the firmament; and those who turn many to righteousness, like the stars for ever and ever.	**The wise leaders will shine with all the brightness of the sky. And those who have taught many people to do what is right will shine like the stars forever."**

Among the faithful something special is reserved to those who are particularly wise or have the gift of discernment and have shared their wisdom with their fellow Jews: in the life eternal they will participate in the very light of God. In contrast with the notion that might be communicated by a literal translation of the text, there is absolutely no question of two different groups, one of which is **wise**, and another group **who turn many to righteousness**. Rather, the parallelism of this verse in Hebrew shows that the second part provides additional information that complements the first. It is possible to restructure the verse as in GECL and say something like "The people who have maintained the wisdom of God and have shown the way (of life) to many others, they will shine brightly forever like the stars in the sky." Another possible model is "those wise people who teach others to do what God requires will continue to glow (or sparkle) always like the sky in the day or the stars at night." On the idea of shining, translators may wish to refer to their rendering of the passage about Moses' face shining after being in the presence of God (Exo 34.29).

Those who are wise: TEV makes it clear that this refers to the "wise leaders" mentioned in the previous chapter (11.33, 35).

Those who turn many to righteousness: literally "those who make many righteous" or "those who justify many." This is not to be understood in terms of Christian theology (whereby believers are made righteous by the grace of Jesus Christ, see Titus 3.6-7). Rather, it is a question of wise teachers who instruct fellow Jews how to live in a right relationship with God. REB translates "those who have guided the people in the true path."

Like the stars: the verb to "shine" used earlier in the verse is also to be understood here. If a more formal translation is adopted (rather than the

restructuring suggested above), then it may be necessary to repeat the verb
here or find another verb of similar meaning.

For ever and ever: literally "for always and continually." The two Hebrew
words may legitimately be translated by a single term in other languages.

12.4	RSV	TEV

RSV	TEV
But you, Daniel, shut up the words, and seal the book, until the time of the end. Many shall run to and fro, and knowledge shall increase."	He said to me, "And now, Daniel, close the book and put a seal on it until the end of the world. Meanwhile, many people will waste their efforts trying to understand what is happening."

For reasons of English style, TEV closes the direct quotation at the end
of verse 3 and introduces the continuation with the words "He said to me . . . ."
This will be unnecessary and even considered awkward in many languages
where it will be quite possible to continue the direct quotation without such a
break.

But: this is probably not the best transition word to use here since it
usually marks contrast, and, although the action required of Daniel is different
from the above, it is still a positive thing and not in sharp contrast with what
comes before. It is important to start a new paragraph at this point, in spite
of the fact that several English versions fail to do so. Both NAB and AB begin
this verse with "As for you, Daniel."

Shut up the words, and seal the book: this does not refer to two
different actions but rather to a single procedure: "keep the words secret by
sealing up the book." This temporary sealing of the book is necessary because
the end of time is thought to be some distance away. The order given here
contrasts with Rev 22.10, where the book is *not* to be sealed because the end
was thought to be within sight. On the term **seal** see comments on 8.26 and
9.24. Here some translators may have to use a more general expression "put
your mark on it."

Until the time of the end: some other ways this has been rendered are
"until the time of the final phase" (AB) and "till the crisis at the end" (Mft). In
some languages the best translation may be "until the last days," although this
has special theological connotations in English.

Many: see 11.14, 33, 39, as well as verse 2 above.

Run to and fro: based on a slight change in the Hebrew text, the
corresponding verb is taken by AB to mean "will apostatize." Mft seems to
follow this understanding when he translates "will give way." Likewise AT has
"many shall prove disloyal." Other commentators seem to feel that this has
something to do with being perplexed about the book that is sealed up. FRCL
has "many will consult it (the book)." (This is presumably after it is reopened.)
Still others translate more generally but probably understanding a wandering
in search of truth: "many will be at their wits' end" (NEB); "go here and there"

(NIV); "be running back and forth" (NRSV). The verb in question is used elsewhere of rowing a boat in Jonah 1.13, of swimming in Isa 25.11, and of wandering (in search of a word from the Lord) in Amos 8.12. It is perhaps this latter meaning that is most appropriate in the present context.

And knowledge shall increase: this is the clear literal translation of the traditional Hebrew text, and it is also followed by NIV and NJV, as well as RSV. But the meaning of this text is uncertain and the ancient versions present a wide variety of possibilities. A slight change in the text yields the reading "evil shall increase" (NAB). This is also adopted by NJB, AT, NRSV, and Mft. NEB follows the same text but translates "punishment will be heavy." REB, however, reverts to a rendering of the more traditional text with ". . . trying to gain such knowledge." It will be better to preserve the meaning of the traditional Hebrew text at this point. Certain modern versions may be useful: "many will go here and there to increase knowledge" (NIV) and "many will range far and wide and knowledge will increase" (NJV). The following models may also be helpful: "people will learn more and more" or "learning will expand (or become greater and greater)."

The Final Vision:
The Time of the End

Daniel 12.5-13

Vision: The two angels by the river: 12.5-7

RSV

TEV

5 Then I Daniel looked, and behold, two others stood, one on this bank of the stream and one on that bank of the stream. 6 And I said to the man clothed in linen, who was above the waters of the stream, "How long shall it be till the end of these wonders?" 7 The man clothed in linen, who was above the waters of the stream, raised his right hand and his left hand toward heaven; and I heard him swear by him who lives for ever that it would be for a time, two times, and half a time; and that when the shattering of the power of the holy people comes to an end all these things would be accomplished.

5 Then I saw two men standing by a river, one on each bank. 6 One of them asked the angel who was standing further upstream, "How long will it be until these amazing events come to an end?"
7 The angel raised both hands toward the sky and made a solemn promise in the name of the Eternal God. I heard him say, "It will be three and a half years. When the persecution of God's people ends, all these things will have happened."

Section Heading: The vision of two angels by the river.

While there is no section heading in TEV at this point, the outline at the beginning of this Handbook suggests that one be included here. If translators are following this outline, another way of saying this is "Daniel sees two angels beside a river." Translators who distinguish major section headings and subheadings may wish to express "The final vision" as "Daniel's last vision" or "The last vision Daniel saw was about the end (or, the things that would happen at the end)."

12.5

RSV

TEV

Then I Daniel looked, and behold, two others stood, one on this bank of the stream and one on that bank of the stream.

Then I saw two men standing by a river, one on each bank.

The structure of the account requires another new paragraph at this point. This makes the previous paragraph consist of only one verse, but translators should not be worried about this.

Then I Daniel looked: on the use of **I Daniel**, see comments on 7.15; 8.15, 27. The verb here should not be translated in such a way as to give the impression that Daniel looked for the first time. Rather, as he kept on looking he "saw" or "noticed (two men)."

Behold: see comments on the Aramaic equivalent at 2.31, and on the Hebrew in 8.3.

Two others: if the translator's language requires that the nature of the two **others** be clearly stated, then it will probably be best to say "two other angels" (see AB), since this is the clear meaning in the context. Some translations, however, have "people" (NJB) or "men" (TEV). If there exists a more neutral term, like "beings," this will also be appropriate. But if the translator is forced to say something more, the word "angels" is probably best.

The long and awkward description of the location of the other two angels at the end of this verse may be rendered much more naturally in many languages as "on opposite sides of the water" or "one on each bank" (TEV).

The stream: this does not represent the same word as translated "canal" or "river" in chapter 8, and so it very likely does not refer to the Ulai. Nor is it the same word as the great river in 10.4. However, the use of the definite article makes readers think that it refers to something already mentioned. It may be, however, that it does refer back to chapter 10. But since this is a vision, the precise river referred to is unimportant. It may therefore be legitimately translated "a river," as in TEV.

12.6 RSV	TEV
And I[h] said to the man clothed in linen, who was above the waters of the stream, "How long shall it be till the end of these wonders?"	One of them asked the angel who was standing further upstream, "How long will it be until these amazing events come to an end?"

[h] Gk Vg: Heb *he*

I said: the HOTTP/CTAT recommended text actually says "he said," and this would seem to refer to one of the two beings introduced in the previous verse. CTAT, however, takes the third person pronoun as indefinite and proposes the translation "someone said." The rendering of RSV is based on the ancient Greek version, and it assumes a different underlying Hebrew text. As in 8.13-14, 16, here also Daniel listens in on a conversation between two angels, but he does not participate in it. Instead of **said** it will be better to use the verb "ask" in many languages, since it is a question that follows. Note that in the Hebrew the question does not follow immediately, so in some languages it will be necessary to restructure the sentence.

The man clothed in linen: we know from earlier references such as 10.5 that this is not an ordinary human being but an angel. So this should be made clear in most languages. In some cases it will be important to distinguish this, the original angel of the vision, from the two angels ("two others") introduced in verse 5. But this may be done by retaining the detail **clothed in linen** found in the text.

Above the waters of the stream: chapter 10 does not mention the exact position of this angel, and the wording here is the subject of some debate. Some interpreters maintain that the vision pictures the angel as floating above the surface of the stream or possibly large figure with one foot on either side of the stream. But others take this expression to mean "further upstream" from Daniel's position described in 10.4. This would mean that the other two angels were downstream on opposite sides of the river. This is the solution adopted by NAB, NJB, and NRSV, as well as TEV. Other scholars, however, see this interpretation as being based on modern reasoning which is absent from the original text.

How long . . . ? Compare 8.13 and comments.

Wonders: see 8.24 ("fearful") and 11.36 ("astonishing things"), where another word from the same root is used with practically the same meaning. Here the term has been rendered "portents" (REB), "astonishing things" (NIV), and "marvels" (Mft).

12.7   RSV   TEV

The man clothed in linen, who was above the waters of the stream, raised his right hand and his left hand toward heaven; and I heard him swear by him who lives for ever that it would be for a time, two times, and half a time; and that when the shattering of the power of the holy people comes to an end all these things would be accomplished.	The angel raised both hands toward the sky and made a solemn promise in the name of the Eternal God. I heard him say, "It will be three and a half years. When the persecution of God's people ends, all these things will have happened."

The man clothed in linen: that is, the angel. See verse 6.

Who was above the waters: see verse 6. NRSV has "who was upstream." In some languages it may be considered unnecessarily redundant to repeat the position of the angel again at this point.

Raised his right hand and his left hand toward heaven: this may be clumsy in a number of languages. It may be more natural to say simply "raised both hands," or simply "lifted up his hands," using the plural noun. Also the words **toward heaven** may be redundant, depending on the particular verb used in the receptor language. In some languages the same word is used for "up" and "sky," or "heaven." Normally a person lifted up only one hand to swear. Here the writer seems to want to emphasize the exceptionally solemn nature of the oath.

Swear: this may be better translated "make a promise" in some languages. And in some cases it will be more natural to make the verb a part of the direct quotation: "I heard him swear that . . . ," or "I heard him promise that . . . ."

By him who lives for ever: this clearly refers to God, and in many languages this should be made clear in the translation: "God who lives forever." The expression used here is reminiscent of the "Ancient of Days" in chapter 7 but is not similar in form.

A time, two times and half a time: this is the response to the question "How long . . . ?" in verse 6 and repeats the Aramaic expression found in 7.25. Here, as in the previous case, it will be necessary to make the meaning clear so that the modern reader can understand the meaning of this curious expression. As in TEV it is possible to say "three and a half years."

The shattering of the power of the holy people: the remainder of the verse is extremely obscure. The word translated **power** is literally "hand," but this is not the source of the difficulties. The probable meaning is that the persecution (**all these things**) will only end with the final crushing (**shattering**) of the armed resistance in Israel (**the power of the holy people**). There can also be here an expression of the writer's disapproval of the policy of armed resistance to Antiochus IV (compare 11.14, 34 and comments). If the above interpretation is accepted, a possible model for this last sentence is "all this persecution will not end until the opposition (fighting) of God's people is completely crushed."

Explanation not to worry: 12.8-13

RSV

TEV

8 I heard, but I did not understand. Then I said, "O my lord, what shall be the issue of these things?" 9 He said, "Go your way, Daniel, for the words are shut up and sealed until the time of the end. 10 Many shall purify themselves, and make themselves white, and be refined; but the wicked shall do wickedly; and none of the wicked shall understand; but those who are wise shall understand. 11 And from the time that the continual burnt offering is taken away, and the abomination that makes desolate is set up, there shall be a thousand two hundred and ninety days. 12 Blessed is he who waits and comes to the thousand three hundred and thirty-five days. 13 But go your way till the end; and you shall rest, and shall stand in your allotted place at the end of the days."

8 I heard what he said, but I did not understand it. So I asked, "But, sir, how will it all end?"

9 He answered, "You must go now, Daniel, because these words are to be kept secret and hidden until the end comes. 10 Many people will be purified. Those who are wicked will not understand but will go on being wicked; only those who are wise will understand.

11 "From the time the daily sacrifices are stopped, that is, from the time of The Awful Horror, 1,290 days will pass. 12 Happy are those who remain faithful until 1,335 days are over!

13 "And you, Daniel, be faithful to the end. Then you will die, but you will rise to receive your reward at the end of time."

Section Heading: The Explanation of the Vision of the Angels.

As at verse 5, there is no section heading in TEV here. But the outline in the introduction suggests that one be included. Some other possibilities are "The vision of the two angels is explained" or "Daniel is told not to worry."

12.8   RSV   TEV

I heard, but I did not understand. Then I said, "O my lord, what shall be the issue of these things?"	I heard what he said, but I did not understand it. So I asked, "But, sir, how will it all end?"

I heard: in many languages it will be essential to state what was heard. TEV does this by adding "what he said." Others may prefer to say "I heard what the angel said" or "I heard the answer." If the person referred to by the pronoun **I** is not understood in the translator's language, it would be possible to add the name of Daniel, as in FRCL.

In some languages the words **I did not understand** will be better rendered "I did not know the meaning of the words," or "I did not catch the meaning of this message," or "the answer was like a riddle to me."

Then: as a result of Daniel's lack of understanding he is forced to ask another question. In some languages the relationship between the two sentences may be made clearer with a word like "Therefore" or "So" (NAB, NIV, NJV, NRSV, and NEB/REB, as well as TEV).

O my lord: this is the same form, *'adonai,* which is sometimes used of God and sometimes of other respected persons. (See the discussion at 9.3.) Here it is used as a form of address to a respected being, but not to the deity. It should therefore probably be rendered by the equivalent of "sir" in the translator's language. The same term is also used in 10.16-19, when Daniel addressed the angel.

What shall be the issue of these things?: the question is no longer "how long?" or "when?" but "what result?" or, perhaps better, "what is to be the (final) outcome?" (NJB and many other versions). Mft has "what is to be the last phase before the end?"

12.9   RSV   TEV

He said, "Go your way, Daniel, for the words are shut up and sealed until the time of the end.	He answered, "You must go now, Daniel, because these words are to be kept secret and hidden until the end comes.

Said: in view of the context, this verb may be better translated "answered," as in TEV.

Go your way: this imperative does not constitute a refusal to respond to Daniel or the chasing away of a troublesome person asking difficult questions. But a literal rendering of RSV or TEV may be understood so in some languages. It is rather a word of encouragement and therefore may legitimately be rendered something like "Don't worry, Daniel" (FRCL) or "You may go in peace." Mft renders it "Ask no more," giving the reason in the following phrase. In some languages it may be better to translate "Leave the matter, because . . . ."

Shut up and sealed: on the word **sealed**, see 6.17 and comments. Compare also verse 4, where Daniel is instructed to "shut up the words, and seal the book." The two verbs may be translated as one in some languages.

12.10 RSV	TEV
Many shall purify themselves, and make themselves white, and be refined; but the wicked shall do wickedly; and none of the wicked shall understand; but those who are wise shall understand.	Many people will be purified. Those who are wicked will not understand but will go on being wicked; only those who are wise will understand.

Scholars see this verse as being intentionally structured in a chiastic or "crossed" form (see discussion at the end of 9.4). The elements are in A-B-B'-A' order but may be better translated as A-A'-B-B' or B-B'-A-A'. The elements are as follows:

> A. Many (wise) will be purified
> B. The wicked will act wickedly
> B' The wicked will not understand
> A' The wise will understand.

Purify themselves, and make themselves white and be refined: these three terms of similar meaning are used in a slightly different form and order in 11.35. While it may be necessary to reduce them to one or two verbs in the language of translation, the cumulative effect is important and should be retained where possible. The first two verbs, **purify themselves** and **make themselves white**, are translated reflexively in RSV, but the underlying Hebrew forms may be understood as passives, "be purified" and "be made white" (as in NRSV, NIV, NJV, NJB, NAB, and TOB). Since there is a significant difference in meaning between the reflexive (in which the subject of the verb does something for himself or herself) and the passive (where someone else does something for the subject), translators must decide which of these two meanings to adopt. The passive meaning is recommended, but in those languages where the passive is unnatural or does not exist at all, they may be forced to make the verbs active and state clearly who performs the action. In this case it is, of course, God who does it. So translators may have to say something like "God will make many people pure and clean . . . ."

The wicked shall do wickedly: the idea is one of continual or habitual action. NJB has "will persist in doing wrong," while REB has "will continue in wickedness." Some languages have special verb forms to express habitual actions. Such forms may be appropriate here.

Some languages may require that the object of the verb **understand** in the last part of this verse be stated specifically. NCV makes the object "these things," referring back to verses 7 and 8. Mft, however, has simply "things."

But given the context, even the rendering of Mft may be understood to refer to the events talked about in the preceding verses. Knox has an interesting translation of the last part of this verse that may prove helpful to some languages: "the riddle, for these others, must remain, but wise counsellors there be that will find the clue to it."

12.11 RSV	TEV
And from the time that the continual burnt offering is taken away, and the abomination that makes desolate is set up, there shall be a thousand two hundred and ninety days.	"From the time the daily sacrifices are stopped, that is, from the time of The Awful Horror,[c] 1,290 days will pass.

[c] THE AWFUL HORROR: *See 9.27.*

This verse is contained in parentheses in NJV. This is perhaps because many commentators consider this verse a later addition to the book of Daniel. But translators are not advised to follow this as a model.

The continual burnt offering is taken away: that is, "halted" or "stopped." See 8.11-13; 11.31, and comments.

And: in order to avoid giving the impression that the termination of the sacrifices and the setting up of the Awful Horror are two distinct and unrelated events, this transition word is translated "that is" in TEV.

The abomination that makes desolate: see 9.27; 11.31, and comments.

There shall be: in many languages a verb appropriate to the passing of time will be required in this context. Translators may consider "(. . . days) will go by" or "shall pass" (Mft).

A thousand two hundred and ninety days: this corresponds to the "three and a half years" in 7.25 and in verse 7 above. But here it is probably better to retain the numbering in days, in keeping with the apocalyptic nature of the book.

12.12 RSV	TEV
Blessed is he who waits and comes to the thousand three hundred and thirty-five days.	Happy are those who remain faithful until 1,335 days are over!

Blessed: this word corresponds to the one that begins each of the Beatitudes in Matt 5. In some languages the most natural equivalent will be an idiomatic expression containing the idea "to have a sweet liver (or stomach) . . ." or something similar.

He who waits: this expression is singular in form but clearly does not refer to just one male individual. For this reason it should probably be made plural in the translation: "those who" (NRSV, REB, as well as TEV). The verb

waits should not be understood in the sense of waiting passively in desperation. The idea is rather that of waiting confidently. It is for this reason that TEV translates "remain faithful." In AB the verb is rendered "has patience."

Comes to: the idea seems to be that of surviving or arriving (alive) at the conclusion of the time period given. REB translates the two verbs "who wait and live to see." Another way of rendering this is "remains firm (or steadfast)."

The thousand three hundred and thirty-five days: this corresponds to three and half years (or the 1290 days mentioned in the previous verse) plus an additional 45 days. It should not be converted into weeks or months in the translation.

12.13	RSV	TEV

But go your way till the end; and you shall rest, and shall stand in your allotted place at the end of the days."	"And you, Daniel, be faithful to the end. Then you will die, but you will rise to receive your reward at the end of time."

The vocabulary of this verse is intentionally different (metaphorical) and takes its inspiration from the theme in Isa 26.19, although some maintain that the reference in Isaiah relates better to verses 1-4 above.

But: in some languages a different transition word must be sought to introduce this concluding verse of the Book of Daniel. Mft leaves it untranslated, and TEV prefers "and." Naturalness in the receptor language will have to be the determining factor.

Go your way till the end: the initial imperative is the same admonition as in verse 9, but the context here is slightly different. Translators should, however, still avoid using an imperative with negative connotations. Here it is possible to translate "be at peace until the end," "hold fast to the end," or something similar. The **end** referred to here is probably that of Daniel, that is, his earthly existence, in which case the best translation may be "till the end of your days" or "to the end of your life." But given the rest of the verse, it is quite possible to translate in more general terms here: "to the end." The words **till the end** at this point in the verse are .omitted in certain manuscript evidence and are therefore dropped by some English versions (NAB, NJB, and NRSV), but translators are advised to retain these words.

You shall rest: this is a reference to Daniel's death. Depending on the translator's language, it may or may not be acceptable to make a clear reference to death here. Where possible it is probably a good idea to use a clearly understood euphemism rather than a direct statement about death.

And shall stand in your allotted place: the Hebrew word corresponding to **allotted place** in the ancient texts is the name of the objects (stones or dice) used in drawing lots. By extension it refers to whatever is gained by the drawing of the lot (see for example, the stories of the dividing up of the Promised Land in Num 26.55-56 and Josh 15.1). Here the idea of drawing lots is not in focus, and the word simply means "that which is set aside (by God) for a person." Some renderings are "your share" (Mft), "your allotted inherit-ance" (NIV), "your reward" (NJB, NRSV, and AB), and "your destiny" (NJV and REB).

The verb **stand** is a figure of speech for the final resurrection, as is indicated by the addition of the words **at the end of the days** (compare verse 2). Many English versions render the verb "rise" or "arise" and one translation even has "rise from the dead" (NCV). The last expression may be rendered in some languages as "at the end of the world," "at the end of the age" (REB), or "at the end of time" (TEV and NJB).

Textual Problems
in
The Book of Daniel

This is a listing of most of the sixty textual problems in the Book of Daniel that are dealt with by the *Preliminary and Interim Report on the Hebrew Old Testament Text Project* (Vol. 5). It should be noted, however, that not all textual problems in Daniel are listed in HOTTP. For example, in 5.25 Theodotion omits one of the occurrences of *mene*, and this is followed by NAB. And in 7.2 both the Septuagint and Theodotion omit "and Daniel spoke and said." Both TEV and NAB follow this reading rather than the Masoretic Text.

In this list the column headed DOC indicates the "degree of certainty" of the HOTTP reading, with {A} being the most certain and {D} least certain. Eight modern versions that have appeared since the discovery of the Dead Sea Scrolls are compared with the HOTTP recommendation. **A plus (+) symbol under a given version indicates that it has followed the reading recommended by HOTTP.** A minus sign (-) shows that it has followed a different reading. Since it is not always possible to determine which text a given translation has tried to follow, there will be some blanks in the chart. This is especially true of more dynamic translations that may leave out the object pronoun altogether in some cases. For example, in Dan 8.14 the textual problem hinges on whether to say "answered him" or "answered me." But a translation may say simply "the answer came" (REB). Although it is not always absolutely clear which reading a version has followed, in most cases translators should be able to see at a glance what the consensus of modern scholarship is on any given textual problem. In certain cases more details are given in the text of the Handbook that do not always follow the recommendation of HOTTP. It should be noted that several of the problems treated in HOTTP and listed here for the sake of completeness are really inconsequential for modern translators.

Ref	HOTTP Recommended Reading	DOC	Other Reading(s)	RSV	TEV	NIV	NAB	NJB	NJV	NRSV	REB
1.2	to the house of his god(s)	B	0	+	+	+	·	·	+	·	+
1.21	D. was/lived/continued	A	D. was/lived there	+	·	·	·	·	+	·	·
2.34	a stone	B	a stone [hewn] from a mountain	+	·	·	+	+	+	+	+
2.40a	and like iron which shatters everything	B	0	+	+	+	+	+	+	+	+
2.40b	all these	B	the whole earth	+	+	+	+	·	+	+	+
2.41	and the toes	C	0	+	+	+	+	·	+	+	·
3.7	harp	B	harp and bagpipes	·	·	·	·	·	+	+	+
3.28	yielded their bodies	C	yielded their bodies to the fire	+	+	+	+	+	+	+	+
4.9 (6)	for you, the visions	B	for you, listen to the visions	·	·	·	+	+	·	·	·
4.33 (30)	eagles . . . and birds	B	birds . . . and eagles	+	·	+	+	·	+	+	+
5.3	of gold	B	of gold and silver	·	·	·	·	·	·	·	·
5.11	your father, the king	B	0	+	+	+	+	+	+	+	+
5.14	of god(s)	A	of the holy god(s)	+	·	·	·	·	+	·	·
5.28	peres	B	parsin OR upharsin	+	·	+	+	·	+	+	+
7.7	huge [teeth]	A	huge [teeth] and claws of bronze	+	·	+	·	·	+	+	·
7.17	kings	C	kingdoms	+	·	·	·	·	·	·	·
8.2	and I saw in a vision (2x)	B	and I saw in a vision (1x)	+	+	+	+	+	+	+	+
8.3	and both horns (2x)	B	and both horns (1x)	+	·	+	+	+	+	+	+
8.8	prominent ones [horns]	B	other ones [horns]	+	·	·	·	·	·	·	·
8.11a	[horn] was lifted	C	he [Ant.?] lifted [himself]	+	+	+	+	·	·	·	+
8.11b	and was thrown down	C	and even threw down	+	+	+	+	+	+	+	+
8.12a	and the army/host	B	0	+	·	+	+	+	+	+	+
8.12b	and she [host] is given up	C	and she gave up	+	·	+	+	+	+	+	+
8.12c	it [horn] threw [truth] down	C	[truth] is thrown/cast down	·	·	·	·	+	·	·	·
8.13a	of the continual burnt offering	B	of the continual burnt offering which is suppressed	+	+	+	+	+	·	+	+
8.13b	and of the army/host	B	0	+	+	+	+	+	+	+	·
8.14	answered to me	C	answered to him	·	·	+	+	+	+	+	·
8.21	the he-goat	B	the he-goat of the goats	+	+	+	+	·	·	+	+
8.24	and/but not with his power	B	0	·	+	·	·	·	·	·	·
9.17	because of the Lord	B	because of you, O Lord	·	·	·	·	·	+	·	·

Ref	HOTTP Recommended Reading	DOC	Other Reading(s)	RSV	TEV	NIV	NAB	NJB	NJV	NRSV	REB
9.22	he made understand	C	he made me understand OR he came	-	+	+	+	-	+	-	-
9.23	to announce/declare	B	to announce to you	+	-	-	+	-	+	-	+
10.1	and he understood the word	B	to him, to understand the word	+	-	+	+	+	+	+	-
10.5	of Uphaz	B	of Ophir	+		t	r	a	n	s	l a t e d
10.13a	and I was left/remained	B	and I left him	-	+	+	+	+	-	+	+
10.13b	with the kings [of Persia]	B	with the prince of the kingdoms	+	+	+	-	+	+	-	-
10.19	be strong and be strong	C	be strong and powerful	+	-	+	-	-	+	-	-
11.1a	and I, in the first year of Darius the Mede	B	0	+	-	+	-	-	+	+	-
11.1b	my standing up was	B	with me/ on my side	+	-	+	-	-	+	+	+
11.1c	for him	B	for me	+	-	+	-	-	+	+	+
11.5	his dominion [is a] great [dominion]	B	greater than his dominion	+	+	-	+	-	+	-	-
11.6a	and his arm [=power]	C	and his offspring	-	+	+	+	-	+	-	-
11.6b	and he who has begotten her	C	and the maiden/ [her] child	+	+	+	+	-	+	+	-
11.7	towards the army	B	towards the fortifications	+	+	+	+	-	+	+	-
11.16	and destruction	B	and everything/ all of it	-	-	+	+	-	+	-	-
11.22a	and the arms [=powers] of the flood will be swept away	B	and the arms [=powers] will be utterly swept away	+	-	+	-	-	+	-	-
11.22b	and they will be broken and also the prince of a covenant	B	and even the prince of a covenant will be broken	+	-	+	+	-	+	-	+
11.26	and he will sweep away	B	and [army] will be swept away	-	-	-	-	-	-	-	-
11.35a	in/among them	B	them	-	-	-	-	-	-	-	-
11.35b	until the time of the end	B	until the time, for there is yet an end	-	-	-	-	-	-	-	-
11.39	with [a foreign god]	A	the people [of a foreign god]	+	+	+	-	-	+	-	-
11.41a	and ten thousands	C	and many	+	+	-	-	-	+	+	+
11.41b	the main/best part of	C	the remnant of	+	-	+	+	-	+	+	+
12.4	the knowledge	B	the evil	-	+	+	-	-	+	+	+
12.6	and he/someone said	B	and I said	+	+	+	+	+	+	+	-
12.13	go your way to the end	B	go your way	+	+	+	-	-	+	-	+

Selected Bibliography

Ancient Texts

Biblia Hebraica Stuttgartensia. 1966/77, 1983. Edited by K. Elliger and W. Rudolph. Stuttgart: Deutsche Bibelgesellschaft.

Septuaginta: Id est Vetus Testamentum graece iuxta LXX interpretes. 1935; combined one-volume edition, 1979. Edited by Alfred Rahlfs. Stuttgart: Deutsche Bibelgesellschaft. (Cited as Septuagint.)

Biblia Sacra: Iuxta Vulgatam Versionem. 1983. Edited by Robert Weber. Stuttgart: Deutsche Bibelgesellschaft. (Cited as Vulgate.)

Lexicons

Brown, Francis; Samuel R. Driver; and Charles A. Briggs. 1968. *A Hebrew and English Lexicon of the Old Testament.* London: Oxford University Press.

Koehler, Ludwig, and Walter Baumgartner, editors. *Lexicon in Veteris Testamenti Libros.* Two volumes. Leiden: E.J. Brill; and Grand Rapids, Michigan: Eerdmans.

Versions

Die Bibel in heutigem Deutsch: Die Gute Nachricht des Alten und Neuen Testaments. 1982. Stuttgart: Deutsche Bibelgesellschaft. (Cited as GECL, German common language version.)

The Bible: A New Translation. 1926. James Moffatt, translator. London: Hodder & Stoughton. (Cited as Mft.)

La Bible: L'Ancien Testament. 1956, 1959. Two volumes. Translation and notes by Édouard Dhorme, Jean Kœnig Frank Michaéli, Jean Hadot, and Antoine Guillaumont. Paris: Gallimard. (Cited as *Bible de la Pléiade.*)

La Bible: Traduction œcuménique: édition intégrale. 1988 [édition révisée]. Paris: Éditions du Cerf; Pierrefitte: Société biblique française. (Cited as TOB.)

La Bible en français courant. 1982. Paris: Société biblique française. (Cited as FRCL, French common language version.)

The Complete Bible: An American Translation. 1923. J.M. Powis Smith and Edgar Goodspeed, translators. Chicago: University of Chicago Press. (Cited as AT.)

Good News Bible: The Bible in Today's English Version. 1976, 1979. New York: American Bible Society. (Cited as TEV.)

Hartman, Louis F. 1968. "Daniel." In *Jerome Biblical Commentary,* pages 446-460. Englewood Cliffs, New Jersey: Prentice-Hall.

————, and Alexander A. Di Lella. 1978. *The Book of Daniel* (Anchor Bible, Volume 23). Garden City: Doubleday. (Cited as AB.)

The Holy Bible (Authorized or King James Version). 1611. (Cited as KJV.)

Holy Bible: New Century Version. 1991. Dallas, Texas: Word Publishing. (Cited as NCV.)

The Holy Bible: New Revised Standard Version. 1989. New York: Division of Christian Education of the National Council of the Churches of Christ in the United States of America. (Cited as NRSV.)

The Holy Bible: Revised Standard Version. 1952, 1971, 1973. New York: Division of Christian Education of the National Council of the Churches of Christ in the United States of America. (Cited as RSV.)

The Living Bible. 1971. Translated by Kenneth Taylor. Wheaton, Illinois: Tyndale House. (Cited as LB.)

The New American Bible. 1970. New York: P.J. Kenedy & Sons. (Cited as NAB.)

The New American Standard Bible. 1960, 1973. Chicago: Moody Press. (Cited as NASB.)

The New English Bible. 1961, 1970. London: Oxford University Press; and Cambridge: Cambridge University Press. (Cited as NEB.)

The New International Version. 1978. Grand Rapids, Michigan: Zondervan. (Cited as NIV.)

The New Jerusalem Bible. 1985. Garden City, New York: Doubleday. (Cited as NJB.)

The Revised English Bible. 1989. London: Oxford University Press; and Cambridge: Cambridge University Press. (Cited as REB.)

La Sainte Bible. 1910. Traduite par Louis Segond. Nouvelle édition revue. Paris: [British and Foreign Bible Society]. (Cited as Segond.)

La Sainte Bible: Nouvelle version Segond révisée. 1978. Paris: Alliance biblique universelle. (Cited as NVSR.)

TANAKH: A New Translation of the Holy Scriptures According to the Traditional Hebrew Text. 1985. Philadelphia: Jewish Publication Society. (Cited as NJV, New Jewish Version.)

Commentaries

Anderson, Robert A. 1984. *Signs and Wonders: A Commentary on the Book of Daniel.* Grand Rapids, Michigan: Eerdmans.

Baldwin, Joyce G. 1978. *Daniel: An Introduction and Commentary* (Tyndale Old Testament Commentaries). Downers Grove, Illinois: Inter-Varsity Press.

Hammer, R. 1976. *The Book of Daniel* (The Cambridge Bible Commentary). Cambridge: Cambridge University Press.

Keil, C.F. 1949. *Biblical Commentary on the Book of Daniel,* Grand Rapids, Michigan: Eerdmans.

Lacocque, André. 1979. *The Book of Daniel.* Atlanta: John Knox.

Montgomery, J.A. 1950. *A Critical and Exegetical Commentary of the Book of Daniel* (The International Critical Commentary). Edinburgh: T. & T. Clark.

Porteous, N.W. 1979. *Daniel: A Commentary* (Old Testament Library). Second revised edition. London: SCM Press.

Towner, W. Sibley. 1984. *Daniel* (Interpretation Series). Atlanta: John Knox.

Special Studies

Bruce, F.F. 1969. "The Book of Daniel and the Qumran Community," *Neotestamentica et Semitica: Studies in Honour of Matthew Black,* pages 221-235. Edited by E.E. Elles and M. Wilcox. Edinburgh: T. & T. Clark.

————. 1965. "Josephus and Daniel," *Annual of the Swedish Theological Institute* 4:148-152.

Buth, Randall. 1987. "Word Order in the Aramaic of Daniel from the Perspective of Functional Grammar and Discourse Analysis," *Occasional Papers in Translation and Textlinguistics* 1:3-12.

Coxon, Peter W. 1986. "The 'List' Genre and Narrative Style in the Court Tales of Daniel," *Journal for the Study of the Old Testament* 35:95-121.

Jones, Ivor H. 1986. "Musical Instruments in the Bible, Part I," *The Bible Translator* 37:101-116.

—————. 1987. "Musical Instruments in the Bible, Part II," *The Bible Translator* 38:129-143.

Peacock, Heber F. 1980. "Translating 'mercy,' 'steadfast love,' in the book of Genesis." *The Bible Translator* 31:201-207.

Rebera, Basil A. 1985. "Yahweh or Boaz? Ruth 2.20 reconsidered," *The Bible Translator* 36:317-327.

Shea, William H. 1980. "Poetic Relations of the Time Periods in Dan 9.25," *Andrews University Seminary Studies* 18:59-63.

Soesilo, Daud, 1990. "Poetic Sections of Daniel," *The Bible Translator* 41:432-435.

"Daniel Stage II Notes July 12, 1971," unpublished notes of the TEV translators.

Other Works

Achtemeier, Paul J. 1985. *Harper's Bible Dictionary.* New York: Harper and Row.

Barthélemy, Dominique. 1992. *Critique Textuelle de L'Ancien Testament.* Tome 3. *Ézéchiel, Daniel et les 12 Prophètes* (Orbis biblicus et orientalis 50/3). Fribourg, Suisse: Éditions universitaires; Göttingen: Vandenhoeck & Ruprecht.

—————; A.R. Hulst; Norbert Lohfink; W.D. McHardy; H.P. Rüger; and James A. Sanders. 1980. *Preliminary and Interim Report on the Hebrew Old Testament Text Project,* Volume 5, *Prophetical Books II.* New York: United Bible Societies. (Cited as HOTTP.)

Fauna and Flora of the Bible. 1972, 1980. New York: United Bible Societies.

Glossary

This Glossary contains terms that are technical from an exegetical or a linguistic viewpoint. Other terms not defined here may be found in a Bible dictionary.

ABSTRACT NOUN is one that refers to a quality or characteristic, such as "beauty" or "darkness."

ACTIVE. See **VOICE.**

ADJECTIVE is a word that limits, describes, or qualifies a noun. In English, "red," "tall," "beautiful," and "important" are adjectives.

ADVERB is a word that limits, describes, or qualifies a verb, an adjective, or another adverb. In English, "quickly," "soon," "primarily," and "very" are adverbs.

ADVERBIAL refers to adverbs. An **ADVERBIAL PHRASE** is a phrase that functions as an adverb. See **PHRASE.**

AGENT is one who accomplishes the action in a sentence or clause, regardless of whether the grammatical construction is active or passive. In "John struck Bill" (active) and "Bill was struck by John" (passive), the agent in either case is "John."

ALLUSION in discourse is an implicit reference to another object or event.

AMBIGUOUS (AMBIGUITY) describes a word or phrase that in a specific context may have two or more different meanings. For example, "Bill did not leave because John came" could mean either (1) "the coming of John prevented Bill from leaving" or (2) "the coming of John was not the cause of Bill's leaving." It is often the case that what is ambiguous in written form is not ambiguous when actually spoken, since features of intonation and slight pauses usually make clear which of two or more meanings is intended. Furthermore, even in written discourse, the entire context normally serves to indicate which meaning is intended by the writer.

ANCIENT VERSIONS. See **VERSIONS.**

ANTECEDENT describes a person or thing that precedes or exists prior to something or someone else. In grammar an antecedent is the word, phrase, or clause to which a pronoun refers.

APPOSITION is the placing of two expressions together so that they both refer to the same object, event, or concept; for example, "my friend, Mr. Smith." The one expression is said to be the **APPOSITIVE** of the other.

ARAMAIC is a language that was widely used in lands east of the Mediterranean Sea before and during the time of Christ. It became the common language of the Jewish people in Palestine in place of Hebrew, to which it is related.

ARTICLE is a grammatical class of words, often obligatory, which indicate whether the following word is definite or indefinite. In English the **DEFINITE ARTICLE** is "the," and the **INDEFINITE ARTICLE** is "a" or "an."

BENEFACTIVE refers to goals for whom or which something is done. The pronoun "him" is the benefactive goal in each of the following constructions: "they showed him kindness," "they did the work for him," and "they found him an apartment."

BORROWING is the process of using a foreign word in another language. For example, "matador" is a Spanish word that has been **BORROWED** by English speakers for "bullfighter."

CAUSATIVE relates to events and indicates that someone or something caused something to happen, rather than that the person or thing did it directly. In "John ran the horse," the verb "ran" is a causative, since it was not John who ran, but rather it was John who caused the horse to run.

CHIASMUS (CHIASTIC) is a reversal of words or phrases in the second part of an otherwise parallel construction. For example:

A.	I	
B.	was shapen	
	C.	in iniquity
	C′	in sin
B′	did my mother conceive	
A′	me.	

CLASSIFIER is a term used with another term (often a proper noun) to indicate to what category the latter belongs. "Town" may serve as a classifier in the phrase "town of Bethlehem," and "river" as a classifier in "river Jordan."

CLAUSE is a grammatical construction, normally consisting of a subject and a predicate. An **INDEPENDENT CLAUSE** may stand alone. The **MAIN CLAUSE** is that clause in a sentence that can stand alone as a complete sentence, but which has one or more dependent or subordinate clauses related to it. A **SUBORDINATE CLAUSE** is dependent on the main clause, but it does not form a complete sentence.

CLIMAX is the point in a discourse, such as a story or speech, which is the most important, or the turning point, or the point of decision.

COLLECTIVE refers to a number of things (or persons) considered as a whole. In English, a collective noun is considered to be singular or plural, more or less on the basis of traditional usage; for example, "The crowd is (the people are) becoming angry."

COMMAND. See **IMPERATIVE**.

COMPARATIVE refers to the form of an adjective or adverb that indicates that the object or event described possesses a certain quality to a greater or lesser degree than does another object or event. "Richer" and "smaller" are adjectives in the comparative degree, while "sooner" and "more quickly" are adverbs in the comparative degree. See also **SUPERLATIVE**.

COMPONENTS are the parts or elements that go together to form the whole of an object. For example, the components of bread are flour, salt, shortening, yeast, and water. The components of the meaning (semantic components) of a term are the elements of meaning that it contains. For example, some of the components of "boy" are "human," "male," and "immature."

CONJECTURE. See **TEXTUAL**.

CONJUNCTIONS are words that serve as connectors between words, phrases, clauses, and sentences. "And," "but," "if," and "because" are typical conjunctions in English.

CONSONANTS are symbols representing those speech sounds that are produced by obstructing, blocking, or restricting the free passage of air from the lungs through the mouth. They were originally the only spoken sounds recorded in the Hebrew system of writing; **VOWELS** were added later as marks associated with the **CONSONANTS**. See also **VOWELS**.

CONSTRUCTION. See **STRUCTURE**.

CONTEXT (**CONTEXTUAL**) is that which precedes or follows any part of a discourse. For example, the context of a word or phrase in Scripture would be the other words and phrases associated with it in the sentence, paragraph, section, and even the entire book in which it occurs. The context of a term often affects its meaning, so that a word does not mean exactly the same thing in one context that it does in another context.

CONTRASTIVE expresses something opposed to or in contrast to something already stated. "But" and "however" are **CONTRASTIVE CONJUNCTIONS**.

CULTURE (CULTURAL) is the sum total of the beliefs, patterns of behavior, and sets of interpersonal relations of any group of people. A culture is passed on from one generation to another but undergoes development or gradual change.

DECLARATIVE refers to forms of a verb or verb phrase that indicate statements assumed to be certain; for example, "prepared" in "She prepared a meal." Such a statement is, for example, declarative rather than imperative or interrogative.

DEFINITE ARTICLE. See **ARTICLE**.

DEMONSTRATIVE PRONOUN refers to one or more specific persons, things, events, or objects by indicating or singling out what is referred to. "That," "this," and "those" are demonstrative pronouns in English.

DEPENDENT CLAUSE is a grammatical construction consisting normally of a subject and predicate, which is dependent upon or embedded within some other construction. For example, "if he comes" is a dependent clause in the sentence "If he comes, we'll have to leave." See **CLAUSE**.

DEUTEROCANONICAL BOOKS is another term for the apocryphal books (Apocrypha), writings included in the Septuagint and Vulgate but excluded from the Jewish and Protestant books of the Old Testament.

DIRECT ADDRESS, DIRECT DISCOURSE, DIRECT QUOTATION, DIRECT SPEECH. See **DISCOURSE**.

DIRECT OBJECT is the goal of an event or action specified by a verb. In "John hit the ball," the direct object of "hit" is "ball."

DISCOURSE is the connected and continuous communication of thought by means of language, whether spoken or written. The way in which the elements of a discourse are arranged is called **DISCOURSE STRUCTURE**. **DIRECT DISCOURSE** (or, **DIRECT ADDRESS, DIRECT QUOTATION, DIRECT SPEECH**) is the reproduction of the actual words of one person quoted and included in the discourse of another person; for example, "He declared 'I will have nothing to do with this man.'" **INDIRECT DISCOURSE** (or, **INDIRECT QUOTATION, INDIRECT SPEECH**) is the reporting of the words of one person within the discourse of another person, but in an altered grammatical form rather than as an exact quotation; for example, "He said he would have nothing to do with that man."

DOXOLOGY is a hymn or other expression of praise to God, typically in a heightened or poetic literary form.

EMOTIVE refers to one or more of the emotions (anger, joy, fear, gratitude, etc.). The emotive impact of a discourse is its effect on the emotions of the person(s) to whom it is addressed.

EMPHASIS (EMPHATIC) is the special importance given to an element in a discourse, sometimes indicated by the choice of words or by position in the sentence. For example, in "Never will I eat pork again," "Never" is given emphasis by placing it at the beginning of the sentence.

EQUIVALENT: describes an expression with very close similarity to another in meaning, as opposed to similarity in form. See also **FORMAL EQUIVALENT**, which refers, by contrast, to close similarity in form..

EUPHEMISM is a mild or indirect term used in the place of another term that is felt to be impolite, distasteful, or vulgar; for example, "to pass away" is a euphemism for "to die."

EVENT is a semantic category of meanings referring to actions, processes, etc., in which objects can participate. In English, most events are grammatically classified as verbs ("run," "grow" "think," etc.), but many nouns may also refer to events, as for example, "baptism," "song," "game," and "prayer."

EXAGGERATION is a figure of speech that states more than the speaker or writer intends to be understood. For example, "Everyone is doing it" may simply mean "Many people are doing it."

EXCLUSIVE first person plural excludes the person(s) addressed. That is, a speaker may use "we" to refer to himself and his companions, while specifically excluding the person(s) to whom he is speaking. See **INCLUSIVE**.

EXCLUSIVE AND INCLUSIVE LANGUAGE are terms that apply to certain uses in languages such as English, where a term that includes only a portion of a group is used to refer to the entire group. For example, "brothers" is appropriate as an **EXCLUSIVE** term if indeed the intended meaning of the text does exclude sisters; however, when "brothers" designates, for example, fellow believers among whom both male and female are included, it is far better to use an **INCLUSIVE** expression such as "fellow Christians" or "believers." Of course, in languages where the term for "brother" already includes both male and female, there will be no such problem.

EXEGESIS is the process of determining the meaning of a text (or the result of this process), normally in terms of "who said what to whom under what circumstances and with what intent." A correct exegesis is indispensable before a passage can be translated correctly.

EXPLICIT refers to information that is expressed in the words of a discourse. This is in contrast to implicit information. See **IMPLICIT**.

FEMININE is one of the genders in Hebrew and in many other languages. See **GENDER**.

FIGURE, FIGURE OF SPEECH, or **FIGURATIVE EXPRESSION** involves the use of words in other than their literal or ordinary sense, in order to bring out some aspect of meaning by means of comparison or association. For example, "raindrops dancing on the street," or "his speech was like thunder." **METAPHORS** and **SIMILES** are figures of speech.

FIRST PERSON. See **PERSON. FIRST PERSON PLURAL** includes the speaker and at least one other person: "we," "us," "our," "ours." **FIRST PERSON SINGULAR** is the speaker: "I," "me," "my," "mine."

FOCUS is the center of attention in a discourse or in any part of a discourse.

FORMAL EQUIVALENT is a type of translation in which the features of form in the source text have been more or less mechanically reproduced in the receptor language.

FULL STOP is a marker indicating the end of a sentence; the marker is usually a period.

FUTURE TENSE. See **TENSE**.

GENDER is any of the grammatical subclasses in Hebrew and many other languages of nouns and pronouns (called **MASCULINE, FEMININE,** and in some languages **NEUTER**), which determine agreement with and selection of other words or grammatical forms. In most languages the classification of nouns is not related to the identity of male or female sex.

GENERAL. See **GENERIC**.

GENERIC has reference to a general class or kind of objects, events, or abstracts; it is the opposite of **SPECIFIC**. For example, the term "animal" is generic in relation to "dog," which is a specific kind of animal. However, "dog" is generic in relation to the more specific term "poodle."

GENRE refers to a class or group of writings that has its own style, content, or form, marking it as different from other writings. For example, the Book of Psalms belongs to the genre of poetry, while the four Gospels contain much that belongs to the genre of narrative writing. Other examples of genre include prophetic oracle, short story, parable, proverb, legal document, and many more.

GRAMMATICAL refers to **GRAMMAR**, which includes the selection and arrangement of words in phrases, clauses, and sentences.

GREEK is the language in which the New Testament was written. It belongs to the Indo-European family of languages and was the language spoken in Achaia, which is Greece in modern times. By the time of Christ Greek was used by many of the people living in the eastern part of the Roman empire, so that early Christians could speak and write to one another in Greek, even though they were born in different countries. By that time the entire Hebrew Old Testament had been translated into Greek, a version referred to as the **SEPTUAGINT**.

GREEKS, strictly speaking, were the inhabitants of Greece, corresponding to the Roman province of Achaia in New Testament times. In the New Testament, the term is used in a wider sense as referring to all those in the Roman Empire who spoke the Greek language and were strongly influenced by Greek culture. Frequently the term Greeks is used as synonymous with Gentiles.

HEBREW is the language in which the Old Testament was written. It belongs to the Semitic family of languages. By the time of Christ many Jewish people no longer used Hebrew as their common language. The **HEBREWS** originally included people who did not belong to the twelve tribes of Israel, but after the Israelites settled in Canaan, the term generally was used to refer to the people of the twelve tribes, who had their own Hebrew language and culture.

IDIOM, or **IDIOMATIC EXPRESSION**, is a combination of terms whose meanings cannot be understood by adding up the meanings of the parts. "To hang one's head," "to have a green thumb," and "behind the eightball" are American English idioms. Idioms almost always lose their meaning or convey a wrong meaning when translated literally from one language to another.

IMMEDIATE CONTEXT is that context which immediately precedes or follows a discourse or segment of discourse, with no intervening context. For example, John 3.17 is a passage in the immediate context of John 3.16. (See also **CONTEXT**.)

IMPERATIVE refers to forms of a verb that indicate commands or requests. In "Go and do likewise," the verbs "Go" and "do" are imperatives. In many languages imperatives are confined to the grammatical second person; but some languages have corresponding forms for the first and third persons. These are usually expressed in English by the use of "must" or "let"; for example, "We must not swim here!" or "They must work harder!" or "Let them eat cake!"

IMPERSONAL VERB is a usage of the verb that denotes an action by an unspecified agent. It may involve the use of the third person singular, as in "It is raining" or "One normally prefers cake," or in some languages the use of the third person plural, as in "They say . . . ," or in still other languages the use of the first person plural, as in "We cook this way," meaning "People cook this way." Such use of a pronoun is sometimes referred to as the **INDEFINITE PRONOUN**.

IMPLICIT (IMPLY, IMPLIED) refers to information that is not formally represented in a discourse, since it is assumed that it is already known to the receptor, or evident from the meaning of the words in question. For example, the phrase "the other son" carries with it the implicit information that there is a son in addition to the one mentioned. This is in contrast to **EXPLICIT** information, which is expressly stated in a discourse. See **EXPLICIT**.

INCLUSIVE first person plural includes both the speaker and the one(s) to whom that person is speaking. See **EXCLUSIVE**.

INCLUSIVE LANGUAGE. See **EXCLUSIVE AND INCLUSIVE LANGUAGE**.

INDEFINITE ARTICLE. See **ARTICLE**.

INDEFINITE PRONOUN. See **IMPERSONAL VERB**.

INDEPENDENT CLAUSE. See **CLAUSE**.

INDIRECT ADDRESS, INDIRECT DISCOURSE, INDIRECT QUOTATION, INDIRECT SPEECH. See **DISCOURSE**.

INDIRECT OBJECT is the benefactive goal of the event or action specified by a verb. In "John threw Henry the ball," the direct object or goal of "threw" is "ball," and the indirect object is "Henry." See **DIRECT OBJECT**.

INFINITIVE is a verb form that indicates an action or state without specifying such factors as agent or time; for example, "to mark," "to sing," or "to go." It is in contrast to the finite verb form, which often distinguishes person, number, tense, mode, or aspect; for example "marked," "sung," or "will go."

INTERJECTIONS are exclamatory words or phrases, invariable in form, usually used to express emotion. "Hey!" or "Oh!" and "Indeed!" are examples of interjections.

INTERPRETATION of a text is the exegesis of it. See **EXEGESIS**.

INTERROGATIVE pertains to asking a question.

LEVEL refers to the degree of difficulty characteristic of language usage by different constituencies or in different settings. A translation may, for example, be prepared for the level of elementary school children, for university students, for teenagers, or for rural rather than urban people. Differences of level also are involved as to whether a particular discourse is formal, informal, casual, or intimate in nature.

LINGUISTIC refers to language, especially the formal structure of language.

LITERAL means the ordinary or primary meaning of a term or expression, in contrast with a figurative meaning. A **LITERAL TRANSLATION** is one that represents the exact words and word order of the source language; such a translation is frequently unnatural or awkward in the receptor language.

LITURGICAL refers to liturgy, that is, public worship; more particularly to the prayers, responses, and so forth, that are often expressed in traditional or archaic language forms.

LOAN WORD is a foreign word that is used in another language. See **BORROWING**.

MAIN CLAUSE. See **CLAUSE**.

MANUSCRIPTS are books, documents, or letters written or copied by hand. A **SCRIBE** is one who copies a manuscript. Thousands of manuscript copies of various Old and New Testament books still exist, but none of the original manuscripts. See **TEXT, TEXTUAL**.

MANUSCRIPT EVIDENCE is also called **TEXTUAL EVIDENCE**. See **TEXT, TEXTUAL**.

MARKERS (MARK, MARKING) are features of words or of a discourse that signal some special meaning or some particular structure. For example, words for speaking may mark the onset of direct discourse, a phrase such as "once upon a time" may mark the beginning of a fairy story, and certain features of parallelism are the dominant markers of poetry. The word "body" may require a marker to clarify whether a person, a group, or a corpse is meant.

MASCULINE is one of the genders in Hebrew and other languages. See **GENDER**.

METAPHOR is likening one object, event, or state to another by speaking of it as if it were the other; for example, "flowers dancing in the breeze" compares the movement of flowers with dancing. Metaphors are the most commonly used figures of speech and are often so subtle that a speaker or writer is not conscious of the fact that he or she is using figurative language. See **SIMILE**.

METER, in Hebrew poetry, refers to the measured number of accented words in a line. In most Hebrew poetry, a regular pattern is formed.

MODIFY is to affect the meaning of another part of the sentence, as when an adjective modifies a noun or an adverb modifies a verb.

NONFIGURATIVE. See **FIGURE, FIGURATIVE**.

NOUN is a word that names a person, place, thing, or idea, and often serves to specify a subject or topic of discussion.

NOUN PHRASE. See **PHRASE**.

OBJECT of a verb is the goal of an event or action specified by the verb. In "John hit the ball," the object of "hit" is "ball." See **DIRECT OBJECT, INDIRECT OBJECT**.

PARAGRAPH is a distinct segment of discourse dealing with a particular idea, and usually marked with an indentation on a new line.

PARALLEL, PARALLELISM, generally refers to some similarity in the content and/or form of two parts of a construction; for example, "The man was blind, and he could not see." The structures that correspond to each other in the two statements are said to be parallel.

PARTICIPIAL indicates that the phrase, clause, construction, or other expression described is governed by a **PARTICIPLE**.

PARTICIPLE is a verbal adjective, that is, a word that retains some of the characteristics of a verb while functioning as an adjective. In "singing children" and "painted house," "singing" and "painted" are participles.

PARTICLE is a small word whose grammatical form does not change. In English the most common particles are prepositions and conjunctions.

PARTICULAR is the opposite of **GENERAL**. See **GENERIC**.

PASSAGE is the text of Scripture in a specific location. It is usually thought of as comprising more than one verse, but it can be a single verse or part of a verse.

PASSIVE. See **VOICE.**

PAST TENSE. See **TENSE.**

PERFECT is a form of a Hebrew or Aramaic verb that expresses the action as a unit, or as a complete, total action, regardless of the time of the action in relation to the time of speaking or writing. See also **TENSE.**

PERSON, as a grammatical term, refers to the speaker, the person spoken to, or the person or thing spoken about. **FIRST PERSON** is the person(s) speaking (such as "I," "me," "my," "mine," "we," "us," "our," or "ours"). **SECOND PERSON** is the person(s) or thing(s) spoken to (such as "thou," "thee," "thy," "thine," "ye," "you," "your," or "yours"). **THIRD PERSON** is the person(s) or thing(s) spoken about (such as "he," "she," "it," "his," "her," "them," or "their"). The examples here given are all pronouns, but in many languages the verb forms have affixes that indicate first, second, or third person and also indicate whether they are **SINGULAR** or **PLURAL.**

PERSONAL PRONOUN is one that indicates first, second, or third person. See **PERSON** and **PRONOUN.**

PHRASE is a grammatical construction of two or more words, but less than a complete clause or a sentence. A phrase is usually given a name according to its function in a sentence, such as "noun phrase," "verb phrase," or "prepositional phrase."

PLAY ON WORDS. See **WORDPLAY.**

PLURAL refers to the form of a word that indicates more than one. See **SINGULAR.**

POSSESSIVE PRONOUNS are pronouns such as "my," "our," "your," or "his," which indicate possession. See also **PRONOUN.**

PREPOSITION is a word (usually a particle) whose function is to indicate the relation of a noun or pronoun to another noun, pronoun, verb, or adjective. Some English prepositions are "for," "from," "in," "to," and "with."

PRESENT TENSE. See **TENSE.**

PROGRESSIVE is an aspect of an event referring to its continuation or duration. For example, "the bird is singing" is the progressive aspect of "the bird sings."

PRONOMINAL refers to **PRONOUNS.**

PRONOUNS are words that are used in place of nouns, such as "he," "him," "his," "she," "we," "them," "who," "which," "this," or "these." See also **PERSON**.

PROPER NAME or **PROPER NOUN** is the name of a unique object, as "Jerusalem," "Joshua," "Jordan." However, the same name may be applied to more than one object; for example, "John" (the Baptist or the Apostle) and "Antioch" (of Syria or Pisidia).

PROSE is the ordinary form of spoken or written language, without the special forms and structure of meter and rhythm that are characteristic of poetry.

PURPOSE CLAUSE designates a construction that states the purpose involved in some other action; for example, "John came in order to help him," or "John mentioned the problem to his colleagues, so that they would know how to help out."

QUALIFY is to limit the meaning of a term by means of another term. For example, in "old man," the term "old" qualifies the term "man."

QUOTATION. See **DISCOURSE**.

READ, READING, frequently refers to the interpretation of the written form of a text, especially under the following conditions: if the available text appears to be defective; or if differing versions of the same text are available; or if several alternative sets of vowels may be understood as correct in languages such as biblical Hebrew, in which only the consonants were written. See also **TEXT, TEXTUAL**.

RECEPTOR LANGUAGE is the language into which a translation is made. For example, in a translation from Hebrew into German, Hebrew is the source language and German is the receptor language.

REDUNDANT describes anything that is entirely predictable from the context. For example, in "John, he did it," the pronoun "he" is redundant. A feature may be redundant and yet may be important to retain in certain languages, perhaps for stylistic or for grammatical reasons.

REFLEXIVE has to do with verbs where the agent and goal are the same person. Sometimes the goal is explicit (as in "He dresses himself"); at other times it is implicit (as in "He dresses").

RELATIVE CLAUSE is a dependent clause that describes the object to which it refers. In "the man whom you saw," the clause "whom you saw" is relative because it relates to and describes "man."

RELATIVE PRONOUN is a pronoun that refers to a noun in another clause, and that serves to mark the subordination of its own clause to that noun; for example, in "This is the man who came to dinner," "who" is the relative pronoun referring to "the man" in the previous clause. The subordinated clause "who came to dinner" is also called a **RELATIVE CLAUSE**.

RENDER means to translate or express in a language different from the original. **RENDERING** is the manner in which a specific passage is translated from one language to another.

RESTRUCTURE. See **STRUCTURE.**

RHETORICAL refers to forms of speech that are employed to highlight or make more attractive some aspect of a discourse. A **RHETORICAL QUESTION**, for example, is not a request for information but is a way of making an emphatic statement.

ROOT is the minimal base of a derived or inflected word. For example, "friend" is the root of "friendliness."

SCRIBE, SCRIBAL. See **MANUSCRIPT.**

SECOND PERSON. See **PERSON.**

SEMITIC refers to a family of languages that includes Hebrew, Aramaic, and Arabic. Greek belongs to quite another language family, with a distinct cultural background.

SENTENCE is a grammatical construction composed of one or more clauses and capable of standing alone.

SEPTUAGINT is a translation of the Hebrew Old Testament into Greek, begun some two hundred years before Christ. It is often abbreviated as LXX.

SIMILE (pronounced SIM-i-lee) is a **FIGURE OF SPEECH** that describes one event or object by comparing it to another, using "like," "as," or some other word to mark or signal the comparison. For example, "She runs like a deer," "He is as straight as an arrow." Similes are less subtle than metaphors in that metaphors do not mark the comparison with words such as "like" or "as." See **METAPHOR.**

SINGULAR refers to the form of a word that indicates one thing or person, in contrast to **PLURAL**, which indicates more than one. See **PLURAL.**

STRUCTURE is the systematic arrangement of the elements of language, including the ways in which words combine into phrases, phrases into clauses, clauses into sentences, and sentences into larger units of discourse. Because this process may be compared to the building of a house or bridge, such words as **STRUCTURE** and **CONSTRUCTION** are used in reference to it. To separate and rearrange the various components of a sentence or other unit of discourse in the translation process is to **RESTRUCTURE** it.

STYLE is a particular or a characteristic manner in discourse. Each language has certain distinctive **STYLISTIC** features that cannot be reproduced literally in another language. Within any language, certain groups of speakers may have their characteristic discourse styles, and among individual speakers and writers, each has his or her own style. Various stylistic devices are used for the purpose of achieving a more pleasing style. For example, synonyms are sometimes used to avoid the monotonous repetition of the same words, or the normal order of clauses and phrases may be altered for the sake of emphasis.

SUBJECT is one of the major divisions of a clause, the other being the predicate. In "The small boy walked to school," "The small boy" is the subject. Typically the subject is a noun phrase. It should not be confused with the semantic **AGENT**.

SUBORDINATE CLAUSE. See **CLAUSE**.

SUPERLATIVE refers to the form of an adjective or adverb that indicates that the object or event described possesses a certain quality to a greater degree than does any other object or event implicitly or explicitly specified by the content. "Most happy" and "finest" are adjectives in the superlative degree. See also **COMPARATIVE**.

SYMBOL is a form, whether linguistic or nonlinguistic, which is arbitrarily and conventionally associated with a particular meaning. For example, the word "cross" is a linguistic symbol, referring to a particular object. Similarly, within the Christian tradition, the cross as an object is a symbol for the death of Jesus.

SYNONYMS are words that are different in form but similar in meaning, such as "boy" and "lad." Expressions that have essentially the same meaning are said to be **SYNONYMOUS**. No two words are completely synonymous.

SYRIAC is the name of a Semitic language, a part of the Aramaic family, used in Western Asia, into which the Bible was translated at a very early date (the **SYRIAC VERSION**).

TENSE is usually a form of a verb that indicates time relative to a discourse or some event in a discourse. The most common forms of tense are past, present, and future.

TEXT, TEXTUAL refers to the various Hebrew, Aramaic, and Greek manuscripts of the Old and New Testaments. **TEXTUAL EVIDENCE** is the cumulative evidence for a particular **READING**. **TEXTUAL PROBLEMS** arise when it is difficult to reconcile or to account for conflicting readings. See also **MANUSCRIPTS**.

THEME is the subject of a discourse.

THIRD PERSON. See **PERSON**.

TRANSITION in discourse involves passing from one thought-section or group of related thought-sections to another. **TRANSITIONAL** expressions are words or phrases that mark the connections between related events. Some typical transitionals are "next," "then," "later," "after this," "when he arrived."

TRANSLATION is the reproduction in a receptor language of a message in the source language. This is best done when it is the closest natural equivalent, first, in terms of meaning, and second, in terms of style. **TRANSLATIONAL** refers to translation. A translator may seem to be following an inferior textual reading (see **TEXTUAL**) when he is simply adjusting the rendering to the requirements of the receptor language, that is, for a **TRANSLATIONAL** reason.

TRANSLITERATE (**TRANSLITERATION**) is to represent in the receptor language the approximate sounds or letters of words occurring in the source language, rather than translating their meaning; for example, "Amen" from the Hebrew, or the title "Christ" from the Greek.

VERBS are a grammatical class of words that express existence, action, or occurrence, such as "be," "become," "run," or "think."

VERBAL has two meanings. (1) It may refer to expressions consisting of words, sometimes in distinction to forms of communication that do not employ words ("sign language," for example). (2) It may refer to word forms that are derived from verbs. For example, "coming" and "engaged" may be called verbals, and participles are called verbal adjectives.

VERSIONS are translations. The ancient, or early, versions are translations of the Bible, or of portions of the Bible, made in early times; for example, the Greek Septuagint, the ancient Syriac, or the Ethiopic versions.

VOCATIVE indicates that a word or phrase is used for referring to a person or persons spoken to. In "Brother, please come here," the word "Brother" is a vocative.

VOICE in grammar is the relation of the action expressed by a verb to the participants in the action. In English and many other languages, the **ACTIVE VOICE** indicates that the subject performs the action ("John hit the man"), while the **PASSIVE VOICE** indicates that the subject is being acted upon ("The man was hit").

VOWELS are symbols representing the sound of the vocal cords, produced by unobstructed air passing from the lungs though the mouth. They were not originally included in the Hebrew system of writing; they were added later as marks associated with the consonants. See also **CONSONANTS**.

VULGATE is the Latin version of the Bible translated and/or edited originally by Saint Jerome. It has been traditionally the official version of the Roman Catholic Church.

WORDPLAY (**PLAY ON WORDS**) in a discourse is the use of the similarity in the sounds of different words to produce a special effect.

Index

This index includes concepts, key words, and terms for which the Handbook contains a discussion useful for translators. Hebrew and Aramaic terms have been transliterated and are found in English alphabetical order.

Heart 18, 166
    heart . . . lifted up 146
Heaven 107, 109, 119, 190
    a voice from heaven 122
    four winds of heaven 282
    host of heaven 212
    King of heaven 127
    Lord of heaven 149
    under the whole heaven
        201, 242
Herald 74
Hiddekel 264
Holy 105
    a holy one 215
    a watcher, a holy one 109
    holy covenant 307
    holy hill 245
    most holy place 253
Homage
    did homage 67
Honor 36
Horn 75
    animal horns 206
Host 126, 213, 216
    host of heaven 212
    host of the stars 212
House 102, 149
    house of God 12

I

Image 55, 71
Incense 67
Interdict 161
Iron 56

J

Javan 281
Justices 73

K

King 10
    King of heaven 127
    king of kings 59
    king of the north 283
    king of the south 283
Kittim 309
Knowledge 14

L

Latter days 53
Learning 14, 25
Leopard 182
Letters 15, 25
Light 138
Linen 264
Lion 181
Live forever 34
Lo 182
Loins 264
Lord 11, 231, 234
    'adonai 11, 232, 234, 332
    lord 20, 127, 234, 273, 332
    Lord of heaven 149
    Yahweh 232, 234
Love
    steadfast love 235
Lyre 76

M

Magicians 27, 31
Magistrates 73
Majesty 122, 127
Man 37, 218
    son of man 190, 220
    the sons of men 272
Mantles 88
mekashef 31
Mercy 239
Messiah 254
Michael 270
Mighty 56
Mind 111, 166
Miry clay 62, 64
Moat 255
Most High 112, 195
    Most High God 93
Mourning 262
Multitude 288
muphaz 265
Mysterious 47
Mystery 43

T

Temple 12, 132
Ten 27
Terrible 183, 234
Thanks
    gave thanks 164
Thousand
    a thousand thousands 187
    ten thousand times ten thou-
      sand 187
Threshing floor 58
Thrones 186
Tidings 321
Tigris 264
Time, times 46, 111, 189
    appointed time 221
Transgression
    transgression that makes
      desolate 215
Treachery 239
Treasurers 73
Trigon 76
Truth 243
Tunics 88

U

Understanding 14, 138
Uphaz 264

V

Vegetables 22
Vessels 12, 132

W

Vision, visions 25, 53, 179, 251,
    266
    vision of the night 44
Voice 240
    a voice from heaven 122

W

Walk 128
Watcher
    a watcher, a holy one 109
Ways 149
Weeks 252, 254
Whirlwind 318
Wickedly
    acted wickedly 236
Wine 16
Wisdom 14, 25, 138
Wise 325
Wise men 39
Wives 132
Wonders 101
Wool 187
Word 123, 261
Wrong
    done wrong 236

Y

Yahweh 232, 234
Youths 14

PRINTED IN THE UNITED STATES OF AMERICA